RAILROADS, RECONSTRUCTION, AND THE GOSPEL OF PROSPERITY

RAILROADS, RECONSTRUCTION, AND THE GOSPEL OF PROSPERITY

Aid under the Radical Republicans, 1865–1877

MARK W. SUMMERS

Princeton University Press
Princeton, New Jersey

Copyright © 1984 by Princeton University Press
Published by Princeton University Press,
41 William Street, Princeton, New Jersey 08540
In the United Kingdom: Princeton University Press,
Guildford, Surrey

Publication of this book has been aided by a grant from
The Whitney Darrow Fund of Princeton University Press

This book has been composed in Linotron Baskerville
with Bodoni display
Clothbound editions of Princeton University Press books are
printed on acid-free paper, and binding materials are
chosen for strength and durability.
Paperbacks, while satisfactory for personal collections,
are not usually suitable for library rebinding.
Printed in the United States of America by
Princeton University Press, Princeton, New Jersey

To my parents,
Clyde and Evelyn Summers,
this book is dedicated.

CONTENTS

vii

Contents

PART FIVE.
THERE IS NO SALVATION:
THE FALL OF THE RAILROADS

PREFACE

"THERE is statesmanship in a Railroad, and a statesman is the builder," an Alabama editor announced in 1870. His words offer a glimpse into a fresh aspect of Radical Reconstruction: the attempt to build a new South and a biracial Republican majority on the railroad aid issue.

Economic interpretations of Reconstruction politics are nothing new. Scholars once depicted Southern Republicanism as wild-eyed agrarianism mixed with racial amalgamation, with appeals for confiscation side by side with exhortations for the freedmen to strike back at the planter class. This view has long been discredited. Also discredited is the view of Reconstruction as a Northern invasion of the South to make a financial killing in patronage, acreage, stocks, and bonds. Recent historians have emphasized the political ideology of the Reconstruction party. They have stressed the significance of appeals to loyalty, liberty, disfranchisement of former Rebels, and civil rights for former slaves.

Race and Unionism *did* have crucial importance, for no new party could have come into being without both Negro and white loyalist support. But as scholars have noted, there were men in the South whose support Republicans needed and could not obtain by appeals to racial equality or the flag. Additional issues had to be found to win the ex-Confederates, issues that appealed as well to the freedman and the Unionist. These selling points turned out to be economic ones, and among these the most significant was that of railroad aid.

No one thus far has done a definitive and coherent study of the railroad aid question across the postwar South. This is, to me, astonishing, for so momentous, scandalous, and, in the end, so tragic a program as Republicans put through cries out for a chronicler. Some state studies have detailed the workings of railroad construction after the Civil War. For thoroughness and insight, Charles Lewis Price's dissertation on North Carolina lines has no peer. In their studies of Florida, Mississippi, Arkansas, and Louisiana Reconstruction, Jerrell Shofner, William Harris, George H. Thompson, and Joe Gray Taylor devote chapters to railroad building and, in connection with it, aid policies; but naturally, they cannot concentrate on patterns common to the whole South, and for other states little has been written. At the other extreme, many historians evaluating the Reconstruction experiment have referred to railroad aid, but have not studied the program on its own merits. The aid policies are used to shed light on the intentions and deficiencies of Republicans in power. Scholars ask the same questions, though they come to different conclusions: Were the Republicans as corrupt as the Conservatives claimed? Was Republican rule and taxation as odious as has been charged? Do Reconstruction governments deserve full blame for the state debts, high taxes, and waste that characterized the postwar South? Did the corruption really matter?

These are proper questions, inescapable ones, that must be answered. Yet I hope to carry the discussion beyond them by posing new questions: Did the aid program work? If not, where were its greatest shortcomings? What defects in the laws and legislative process made the policies so disappointing? If there was corruption, why was it needed? How did railroad aid actually work and how did it aggravate sectional, local, economic, and political rivalries? Why did Southerners turn against the policies they had supported under Conservatives and Republicans alike? Is it possible that the South's economic problems were too great for railroad construction to solve?

Undoubtedly, political questions—in particular, equal rights—mattered more to the history of Reconstruction than the questions I raise. Historians have been wise to concentrate their attentions there. We would, however, be wrong to underrate the political as well as the economic importance of the aid program. The promise of a South reborn had great impact on the Republican appeal; and in office, far more of the legislature's time was spent trying to revive the section through railroad legislation than in penalizing former Confederates or increasing the civil rights of black constituents. Had the aid program succeeded entirely, the Republican party might not have been able to maintain itself against the white-liners. Yet I would suggest that no other program would have done more to efface the race issue and woo Conservatives. If failure of Republican railway programs did not wreck them politically, it certainly contributed to their ruin, gave respectable Conservatives a powerful issue complementing that of race, and aggravated the divisions already present in the Republican ranks. Railroad aid, then neither gave birth to Republicanism nor wrecked it, but made its passage into power easier, its factionalism more bitter, and its downfall more devastating than it might otherwise have been.

If I am not so bold as to proclaim aid *the* issue of Reconstruction, I will not be so brazen as to declare this the definitive history of Southern Republican ideas and economic policies. It pretends to be neither. There is more to Republican ideology than I can say, and the economic program included many other concerns to which I have too little space to do justice: levee construction, river and harbor improvements, debtor relief, and redistribution of lands. I bring them in only to show the breadth of Republican economic appeals and to illustrate the side effects of the "railroad mania." It is my hope that some future historian will give these concerns and Southern Republican political thought the treatment they merit. Till then, this work should serve notice that there is a world out there waiting for scholarly mining as much as the South awaited the promoters' exploitation in the years just after the Civil War.

Whether the mania was tragedy masked as farce or farce parading as high tragedy, I leave to readers to decide for themselves.

ACKNOWLEDGMENTS

THE number of people to whom I am indebted is immense, and many of their names I do not know: librarians and archivists who did their best to find what I hardly could describe. In particular, the staff of the Alabama State Department of Archives and History deserves my gratitude. In spite of my protests, they spent a full afternoon trying to ferret out a report that I had mentioned in passing, a document which I suspected had never existed. All day long as I scribbled notes, I could hear assistants making furtive calls to retired members of the staff in order to locate an elusive document. Elsewhere I found librarians eager to help and full of useful admonitions. I can hardly express my gratitude.

More important is my debt to Professor Kenneth M. Stampp, my adviser, who corrected me more gently than I feared I would deserve, and whose direction of my study helped limit it; any reader can understand the value of this when he realizes that the present draft is narrower in scope and terser in style than the work I had originally planned, perhaps by five hundred pages.

To Professors Thomas Barnes, Richard Sutch, and Terry Seip for their advice, I am also deeply in debt. Then there are the debts to my friends inside and outside of history for help given. In history, there are two: David Bailey and Robert A. Holtermann. Many hours we spent thrashing through what I had found and what I thought it meant, and what else it might mean. Bob spurred my imagination on, and Dave reined it in; and both were quite right.

Outside of history, there are five, and all were indispensable: Stephen Siegelman, Steven Franaszek, Lawrence Schwartz, Susan Liddle, and David Walline. They forced me to make my thoughts clear so that even those outside of our often arcane discipline could tell what was going on. When I spoke of my work, they listened patiently, but they did still more. By turning my attention to other things, from music of the 1920s to British folklore, they kept my interest from turning into a monomania, and kept the topic from becoming stale. If my writing is comprehensible to people outside of Civil War history, then that result I owe to them.

Finally, I owe a debt to my mother and father—my mother for having originally typed this vast text over many months with good humor and better sense, and my father for having read the chapters and given powerful criticisms of their logic and organization. They are both trumps.

PART ONE

The Gospel of Prosperity

CHAPTER 1

"Our Poor Distressed Country"

It betokens us not degenerated, nor drooping to a fatal decay,
but casting off the old and wrincled skin of corruption, to
outlive these pangs and wax young again, entering the glorious
ways of truth and prosperous virtue, destined to become great
and honourable in these latter ages. Methinks I see in my mind
a noble and puissant nation rousing herself like a strong man
after sleep and shaking her invincible locks.

John Milton, Areopagitica

THE South that travelers saw at the close of the Rebellion was far different from the proud land that four years earlier had bade defiance to national authority. The war had left scars everywhere, even in towns miles from the front lines, and although the old leaders tried to rebuild Southern society, they lacked the material with which to achieve its economic reconstruction.

The first thing that observers noted was the physical devastation of the South, and they saw the most severe damage in the states along the Atlantic coast and in the border regions, where the fighting had been heaviest. While passing through South Carolina and Georgia, Union armies had inflicted heavy damage on major towns, partly out of military necessity and partly from spite. Retreating Confederate troops were just as destructive. But even if the towns had survived the war intact, they could never have thrived with so much hardship in the surrounding countryside. Southern merchants were pathetically dependent on a few cash crops which, because of the hazards of war and the effects of emancipation, the hinterlands found impossible to produce and transport. Four years of neglect had not left all plantations as badly off as those along the Mississippi, some of which had reverted to marsh and others to brush, but none were fit to produce as much as they had before the war. At best the Southern economy would remain unsettled for a time, and if pessimists were right, the hard times would last for generations.[1]

Neither planter nor merchant could thrive without a dependable transportation system, but the war had wrecked that, too. Most roads were no more than ruts, and railroads were nearly inoperable. From Virginia to Georgia and in many areas north of the Alabama black belt, soldiers had torn up the rails, burned boxcars, dismantled engines. In some places rolling stock had vanished without a trace, but it would not be missed, since the stations had disappeared as well. If a train did manage to run, it would have to stop at a river's brink and ferry passengers across; both armies had burned bridges. If it took on freight, it might find delivery complicated by the lack of warehouses along the way: soldiers had burned these, too. The directors might wish to repair damaged engines, but often they had no repair shops left to do the work. After both armies had done their worst, the Mississippi Central had one locomotive left.[2] Here, too, the necessities of war inflicted more harm on the railroads than did the armies themselves. The tracks needed repairs constantly, but for four years the companies had lacked sufficient manpower for such work. Rails were worn out, but the Confederacy could not spare iron for anything not related to ordnance. Even if the companies had been able to find supplies and manpower to keep the roads in shape, they could not have paid for them. Confederate money had inflated tremendously, and by the end of the war it had become worthless. In fact, the lack of a valid currency was one of the most serious shortages that the South suffered. Businessmen had little hope of obtaining credit. Farmers needed advances with which to buy seed and supplies to carry them through the harvests; railroads needed loans to renew their operations. Planters needed funding to rebuild the dikes and levees that would help them reclaim their lands. Although some found capital, many did not.

To survive the postwar years, Southerners needed hard work, good crops, and luck. Many simply gave up trying. All over the South, plantations were for sale, some for a pittance. One estate worth $24,000 went for the $80 in taxes that its owner could not afford to pay. In Florida, the entire town of Fernandina sold for $10,608.[3] The federal government had established the Freedmen's Bureau to help destitute blacks, but its agents found thousands of whites equally desperate. By June 1865, one brigadier general was estimating that it would take eight hundred bushels of corn and thirty thousand pounds of meat a day to prevent starvation in just ten Georgia counties.[4] In some places, the war seemed to have broken the Southern spirit to rebuild, a spirit which Northerners doubted had ever been very strong.

In this they were mistaken, just as they were wrong in their predictions that the South was ruined beyond recovery. Atlanta had hardly finished burying its dead before the rebuilding began, and by the end of 1865, as one visitor noted, a new city was rising from the ashes of the old.[5] Other commercial centers also made rapid, impressive revivals. There are at least four partial explanations for what seemed an incredible recovery.

First, neither the wartime damage nor the economic recovery occurred in equal measure throughout the South. Despite outward signs of sectional revival, the immediate economic effects of the conflict could and would be felt for a decade in some areas. Second, for all the damage it had suffered, the South had advantages that assured it at least a partial recovery: the North's need for cotton, the large Negro labor force still dependent on the cotton grower for its livelihood, the social ties and sectional allegiance that made Southerners prefer to do business with each other than with Yankee interlopers. Third, the North proved a powerful friend; that is, it sent help, both public and private, though never as much as was needed. Northern philanthropists raised money to nourish the destitute, while Northern investors came south to get rich in business or planting. The federal government provided the railroads with materials they needed to resume operations. Under a presidential order of August 1865, companies were allowed to buy engines and cars that the government had brought down from Northern railroads. In fact, most of the $7 million in rolling stock thus transferred was never paid for. By 1866, as a result, most railroads were providing at least rudimentary service. A few had made remarkable gains. With one-fourth of its cars remaining at the end of the war, and with only fragments of track for them to run on, the Mobile & Ohio might have been expected to have done poorly. Instead, it turned a small profit in the last half of 1865; the government's aid helped it survive.[6]

A fourth factor remains: the will of the Southern people and their vision of the South. Battered and beaten the former Rebels may have been, but they never lost their vision of sectional greatness, only of their political prospects. Indeed, they overestimated their advantages and their potential. They had great faith in their ability to regenerate the South, and even more faith in the riches the soil would yield, both mineral and agricultural. Nevertheless, the astonishing thing is how much Southerners seemed ready to give up of what they had cherished for so long. "I am tired of South Carolina as she was," said Governor James Orr. "I covet for her the material prosperity of New England. I would have her

5

acres teem with life and vigor and industry and intelligence, as do those of Massachusetts."[7]

Something had happened to the vision of the Old South. Even before the war, the vision was less a reality than an ideal; it had now become an ideal that even some old established figures found outmoded. They would not often use the term "New South" to describe what they hoped to replace it with, but in some ways it was a new South they were seeking.

Whether that garden world where banker, merchant, factory maid, and railroad contractor were alien figures had ever existed in the pristine sense declaimed by Southerners makes scant difference. They all conceded that it would be impossible to recreate such a civilization in the future. Too much had been lost, and too much had changed. The labor system was in shambles, the cotton market in jeopardy, the commercial elite bankrupt or in exile, and the Northern financial interests in control of national economic policies. When Southerners returned to the Union, they found that the Republicans had enacted a protective tariff, federal subsidies for a transcontinental railroad, a national banking system, income and excise taxes, taxes on cotton and tobacco, and homestead legislation. This federal policy of industrial development could not be repealed. Consequently, the postwar South had to adjust itself to the new order of things.[8]

By "adjust," the proponents of a new South meant much more than the replacement of slavery with free labor. As one Arkansas correspondent remarked, the cry everywhere was "build! build!" No place had richer soil than the cotton states, polemicists argued, and the climate could allow anything to be grown from wheat to wine grapes to wool. A few writers even foresaw the subdivision of plantations into smaller farms which immigrants would cultivate. Rich veins of iron and coal simply waited for Southerners to exploit them. Little Rock, said one of its champions, could "smelt iron, run ingots, mould pigs, spin thread, weave cloth, make wooden ware—all but nutmegs."[9]

To bring about this new South, a dependable transportation system and Northern support were crucial. The section must have railroads. "Don't talk of old ties," a newspaper upriver from New Orleans berated city merchants. "The ties of commerce must be iron ties—not a watercourse that swells into lakes here or narrows to canal-width there."[10] But neither the railroads nor anything else could be built without the funds of Northerners, many of whom had profited immensely from the war. Financiers had funds to invest in less-developed areas, and no area needed development more than did the South.

The question was, How much would Southerners be willing to pay for Northern support? Postwar conditions gave the former Confederates little control over the financial conditions that outsiders might impose on borrowers. Even that limited discretion would be lost if Southerners did not act quickly to restore their own fortunes. If they did not rebuild and develop their own resources, Northern financiers and managers would do the job on their own and be in a position to dictate the economic future of the section. Therefore, only an effort on Southerners' part to make the former slave states economically self-reliant could preserve the South's sectional identity.

Self-reliance—that was the obverse side of the Southern appeal for renewal. The defeated people took on Northern desires for progress and industrialization for sharply different ends. Northerners may have hoped to create a second North, whereas Southerners saw in industrial improvement the means of reasserting their independence from the forces that had conquered them. They envisioned a self-sufficient South that would humble the arrogant millowners of New England and make them respectful of their fellow citizens in the South. No longer could planters dictate to the North, but someday, they hoped, they could keep the North from dictating to them. Self-sufficiency also made good sense as a means of keeping Southern self-esteem. It was galling to Southern pride to have to admit that out of eight million people left in the South after the war, not one was capable of reviving the section's prosperity, "or building a railroad, or a manufacturing establishment, without the money and personal presence of some man of the Northern Radical type."[11]*

* By "Radical," the editor of course meant Republican, for that was what every member of that party was called by its enemies. Like "carpetbagger" for Northern-born Republican and "scalawag" for white Southern Republican, the word had pejorative connotations. Time has erased some of the stigma, and I shall use all three. "Radical" is most troublesome, however. Conservatives made it apply to all Republicans, and so, when I present the Conservative slant on Southern affairs, I shall use their word in their way. But "Radical" also applied to the faction inside the Republican party most interested in wiping out every vestige of planter rule and in advancing the cause of civil rights. When referring to that faction, I shall use the uncapitalized "radical."

By "Conservative," I mean the political group that ran the South during the immediate postwar period and the party that during Radical Reconstruction ranged itself against Republican authorities. This is more convenient than accurate: in different states and at different times, the opposition took a host of names, from "Democratic" to "Democratic-Conservative." Recognizing that their party included old Whigs as well as antebellum Democrats, I have chosen to use all labels interchangeably.

Consequently, spokesmen for the New South were eager to obtain Northern money and economic principles, but they were not willing to give very much in return. The same ambivalences recurred in Southern responses to immigration. Although settlers were welcome, their social and political views were not. Even the *West Baton Rouge Sugar Planter*, which made appeals for emigrants from anywhere, described New Englanders as "those harpies who have fed and fattened upon our nation's woes"—a description not likely to inspire Yankees with a confidence that they would be welcome additions to Southern culture.[12]

Thus, dependent though they were on outsiders for support, Southerners felt compelled to do all they could to work their own recovery with as little Northern aid as possible. This task, however, required more capital than they possessed. Planters and commercial men could make only modest improvements. Desire railway construction though they might—indeed, a passion for railroads swept the South in the years just after the war—the task was far beyond what Southerners could accomplish. They had too little money to repair all the tracks destroyed in wartime, much less to expand their railroad system. Their farms could not even produce enough to sustain the lines in existence, and the price of cotton fell too low to make an increase in freight rates practicable. As long as a railroad was only in partial operation, it could hardly earn the revenue it had collected in its completed form. When it lacked the rolling stock and locomotive power needed to carry what trade it had, its efficiency declined still more. The Memphis & Little Rock, for example, had as bright a future as any road, as a possible link with the West Coast. Memphis financiers backed its operations, but even they could not keep it running for long. In April 1867, the Memphis & Little Rock suspended operations. So did many other roads which had gone into bankruptcy and been sold.[13] Others remained solvent only because the state governments helped them with interest payments on their bonded debts and eased the conditions under which they might sell their bonds.

If Southerners were to build and run the section's lines, they would need government assistance. This assistance was quickly provided by the Conservative authorities who ran the South between 1865 and 1867. Postwar legislatures passed general and special acts of railroad aid. For example, Alabama permitted any road which had completed 20 continuous miles of track to receive $12,000 a mile in government endorsements of its first-mortgage bonds. The actual rate was somewhat higher, since lawmakers made additional allowances for bridges and trestles. Georgia gave $10,000 a mile in endorsements to the Macon & Brunswick, and the Texas Constitution of 1866 gave legislators the right to make $15,000 a mile in guarantees. Other states gave various amounts.[14]

Such aid, however, was hardly a break with tradition. Congressional largess had given the antebellum governments money for such promotions by remitting to certain states the federal lands within their borders, on condition that the proceeds from their sale go to internal improvements. In keeping with this stipulation, various states set up special funds and boards: the "2 percent fund" and "3 percent fund" in Alabama, the "5 percent fund" in Arkansas, and similar resources in Florida and Louisiana. From these funds Florida loaned railroads $10,000 for every mile of track laid and gave $6,000 a mile outright. Even before the war, states and cities had become major stockholders in railroad corporations. South Carolina ran the Blue Ridge Railroad, which had promise of breaking through the mountains and making Charleston the rival of New York for the Midwest trade. Georgia owned a project completed for the same purpose, the Western & Atlantic, which ran from Atlanta to Chattanooga.[15] Conservatives simply built on the foundations their predecessors had laid. In doing so, they committed the governments to the advancement of railroad schemes more than ever before.

Legislators did more to help railroads than just finance their construction. They issued liberal charters by the dozen. In Texas, for example, an act of incorporation took a two-thirds vote in each house of the legislature, but the first postwar General Assembly had no trouble chartering sixteen roads. In Mississippi, lawmakers disbursed charters so freely that the *Vicksburg Herald* suggested that they "incorporate a road from every person's back yard to some point out of the State. Unless they do there is great danger of some point in the State growing to importance." Resenting a tax of one-half of 1 percent per mile on passenger rates, railroad presidents met in Jackson to seek its repeal. Since the chairman of the House Ways and Means Committee was Abram Murdock of the Mobile & Ohio, and another leading politician, William Yerger, was a railroad attorney, the appeals met a friendly response. Louisiana, too, gave tax advantages, and in Virginia, General William Mahone obtained generous rights of consolidation between companies under his control following a lavish disbursal of money to lobby his bill.[16] Such political haggling and corruption was typical of all efforts to foster internal improvements.

Charges of political profiteering and use of money to secure passage of the laws were common in almost every state. Nor was this surprising, for never had Southern governments intervened in so many economic matters. Alabama and Mississippi passed "stay laws," thereby delaying the introduction of suits for collection of debts. Other laws appropriated funds to feed the hungry and compensate widows and orphans for their losses in the war, repealed usury laws, opened public lands to white homesteaders, exempted certain acreage from public sale, gave new factories temporary tax exemptions, and spent money on bridges, roads, and public works.[17] Although these laws encouraged the economic restructuring of the South, that was not their intent. Lawmakers simply wanted to prevent Southern conditions from growing worse. Each law was passed for its own sake and in no case was it part of a unified program.

The Conservatives had excellent intentions, but from the first they found the problem of recovery more than they could handle. There were many reasons for this, but the most important ones were the financial obligations that earlier state governments had contracted and the postwar poverty of Southern property holders. Raising taxes to retire state debts was out of the question. Furthermore, citizens could not even pay the old rates. The governments had to resort to borrowing to continue the most rudimentary services. Increased debts were inevitable; in short, the South was simply overwhelmed. It encountered too much poverty, too few credit facilities, too many applicants for aid and too many projects needing support. What the South needed was a much larger infusion of capital than it had, and many more facilities for credit.

The Southern states thus could not bring about their own salvation, but at the same time Northern businessmen were unprepared to give the assistance required. As their plight became clear, Conservatives began to wonder whether the federal government might not solve their problems best. States along the Mississippi could not prosper until the levees were repaired, and this task required national legislation. With thousands of people lacking food and shelter, Louisiana landowners suggested that the military commander in their state employ the idle. Other Southerners proposed that Congress lend $40 million to farmers. Less ambitious Conservatives called for a remittance of the cotton tax and lobbied for a transcontinental line across Louisiana and Texas.[18]

None of these appeals had much effect, for Congress was in no mood to give economic support to an unregenerate South. The Conservative governments had not given the cooperation on political reconstruction that Northerners thought due from a defeated people. That Conservatives proclaimed their political independence with "manly" defiance made their laments or economic dependence sound ludicrous. The Republican paper in the capital, the *Washington Chronicle*, mocked the appeal for a loan as "cupboard love" and "pocket loyalty." In their present political mood, said the editor, Southerners would only waste the money or spend it on "powder and ball . . . and get us into another fight."[19]

More troubling to Southern business than any specific law was Congress's refusal to agree to the terms of Reconstruction that the seceded states had declared themselves willing to accept. By declining to admit Southern representatives to Congress, the Republican majority made clear its reluctance to recognize the postwar governments as legitimate. As long as the Southern civil authorities lacked federal recognition, they could not assure anyone that their bond issues would not be annulled or that the advantages they bestowed on corporations were valid.

That the Conservatives were unable to achieve the salvation of the South is not only obvious but crucial to any understanding of Radical Reconstruction. It is equally important to recognize the factors beyond their control, factors which left them helpless. There are two reasons why this is so important.

First, the Conservative experience shows how little the Republicans would break with the past when they came to power in the late 1860s. Almost every economic policy Republicans tried, the Conservatives had tried first, if on a more limited scale: railroad aid, levee construction, debtor relief, debt repudiation, encouragement to immigration, and the use of public revenues to serve private enterprise and political interests. The "New South" did not have to wait for Republicanism or Henry Grady of the *Atlanta Constitution* to give it voice. The Radicals made the appeal a partisan creed and gave it significantly different emphases, but they did not promise anything very different from the ideas that Conservatives had embraced just after the war.

Second, just as the Radicals had inherited policies from their predecessors, they would be burdened with the same problems—problems that marred the Radical experiment from the start. Advocates of "the bottom rail on top" might talk of a new era and a new beginning, but the problems of the old era remained, and a new beginning could not really be made. State treasuries needed immediate replenishment, heavy state debts awaited payment— nearly $5 million in Arkansas, over $15 million in North Carolina, and $23 million more in all the eleven former Confederate states than had been outstanding at the war's end—future revenues were pledged to corporations and bondholders, and credit had yet to be revived.[20] The same handicaps would persist under the Republican governments: a lack of credit facilities, shortage of circulating medium, small tax base and large immediate needs, and an unresponsive federal government. If the Conservatives with all their business skills and experience could not relieve the economic crisis, how could their successors, who were far less qualified and prepared for office, do much better?

By 1867, the initial postwar optimism of Southerners had vanished. Everywhere the press reported misery and deprivation. In the Mississippi River valley, spring floods added to the general ruin, as levees broke and rivers inundated thousands of acres of bottom land. "There never has been a people more entirely in distress than ours," mourned one citizen. The floods simply aggravated a bad situation. Throughout the South farmers complained that they were ruined. Although cotton prices had been expected to rise, they in fact had fallen since the war. One newspaper reported destitution equal "in ghastliness of features" to the Irish famine, and an Arkansas correspondent told of how thousands of jobless field hands, deprived of their wages, were preying on the community. "Hogs, sheep, cattle, poultry—and the like, are being swept away like shucks before a whirl wind," he wrote, "and an air of insecurity is added to the other calamities of the country." Hard times in the country meant stagnation in town, as construction ceased, workmen were idle, brickyards and sawmills did no business, lumber went without buyers. Rents rose, interest rates increased, and no one could afford to borrow. Consequently, moderate men declared that conditions were worse than at the close of the war. Property values were lower, resources were fewer.[21]

In 1865, Southerners had bewailed their misfortunes, but had been confident that they could rebuild their section. By 1867, they were less sure. "In the name of mercy, what is to become of our poor distressed country?" a Conservative asked. "It does seem that the Almighty in the 'fierceness of his anger' has left us to hopeless and irretrievable ruin. This morning my faith wavers."[22]

There were other men, in the North as well as the South, of a sterner faith. Just as the Southern people most felt their helplessness, Congress agreed on a plan to overturn the Conservative governments and reconstruct the South. With the Military Reconstruction Acts of 1867, a new political party took shape in the former

Confederacy and through its policies and leadership offered the Southerners a second chance. It promised more than political revolution; it promised the economic renewal and salvation of the South.

Temporarily disfranchising many white leaders and enfranchising blacks, the acts weakened the strength of the reigning political elite. In requiring elections for conventions to create new state constitutions, Congress made equally possible a completely new Southern society or one in which no change at all occurred. Conservative leaders kept control of the provisional governments, the press, and the courts. The acts did not introduce the secret ballot. Nor did they protect the freedom against economic intimidation. Any change must come through the usual political methods of party organization and free election, and special voting requirements in this process gave the Conservatives a good chance of defeating the whole congressional program just by staying home. The friends of Reconstruction had troops to protect their right to campaign. In the blacks and loyalists, they had substantial constituencies ready-made for exploitation, but these advantages were not enough to offset those of Conservatives.

Revolution would not come easily. Republicans hoped that the Negro voter would know his friends, but they were not sure that blacks could translate radical sentiments into political power. Reliant on the Conservatives for sustenance, the freedman might not vote Republican or for that matter, not at all, when confronted with a threat to his livelihood. After all, it was easy to bribe poor men and to gull ignorant ones. Terrorism could affect blacks more than it would white Southerners. Armed with a pistol, the white Southerner might fight back, but most blacks had no such means of protection. It was even possible that some freedmen would vote against Reconstruction out of principle or from loyalty to their former masters. In view of the efforts Conservatives made in 1867 to woo Negro voters, builders of a Republican party could not put too much faith in victory through the solidarity of the colored race.

Even with a full turnout of freedmen, Southern Republicans could not expect to win on racial issues. Blacks outnumbered whites in South Carolina, Louisiana, and Mississippi, but nowhere else. There were two whites to every black in Texas and North Carolina and three to one in Arkansas.[23] On every level of government, the party needed leaders with political experience, and this need meant a drive for white recruits, even in states with black majorities. Most unionists did not care for the Negro. The poor men among them hated the black as a competitor. Furthermore, the former slave owner found it hard to see him as an equal. There were exceptions, but for most white Southerners, racial equality was far from effective as a battle cry. Often Southern Republicans themselves put limits on how much equality civil rights should bestow. In their platforms they avoided issues of segregated schools and cemeteries and even debated whether blacks' right to vote entailed a right to hold office. Indeed, a few Republicans wondered whether a vote on race lines would be wise even where blacks held a majority. "Race conflicts are sure to ensue if party lines are based on race," Henry Clay Warmoth told a black audience. ". . . The more negroes becoming Democrats will bring whites into Republican party, and in that is the safety of the Republic and the prosperity of the people."[24]

The Union issue might draw whites, but it, too, had defects. The Southern Republicans could appeal to loyalist sympathies for some votes. Nationalism, however, did not have as great a following as some people assumed. Most Southerners of all persuasions had gone with their states and did not resist the Confederacy. After the war, the Southern governments gave satisfaction to many of the Unionists of 1861. Cooperationists and wartime dissidents who had given mere lip service to the Confederacy had become governors and legislators. Faced with the Negro suffrage issue, the Unionist minority would become even less significant.

Moreover, Republicans could not afford to stress the Unionist position. To have done so would have driven off the eleventh-hour patriots, including some of the most respectable recruits to the party. To succeed, Southern Republicans needed another issue to supplement the two that the Reconstruction Acts had guaranteed them. They needed one that would not only encourage Rebels to drop wartime sentiments and make common cause with the Unionists, but that would enable yeoman farmers to subdue their prejudices and stand beside blacks in a new coalition. Such an issue Republicans found in the South's economic condition.[25]

They could hardly have done otherwise. Republican rhetoric in the North had long connected slavery with the planter class and the cause of free labor with the industrial growth and economic reform that the South so badly needed. In adapting their appeal to the white Southerner, they built a myth of Progress as a redeemer of the Old South. No one called it "the Gospel of Prosperity"—that is this historian's conceit—but so charged was the rhetoric with religious and moral implications that the phrase seems to fit it better than any other.

The economic ruin that threatened everyone obscured every other concern. "Go to the Freedmen's Bureau," one Virginian cried. "You do not find all negroes there." White women by tens and fifties came there for rations. "Talk not . . . about political issues. We are talking now in behalf of humanity. Our people, black and white, hundreds and thousands of them, are at the very door of starvation."[26] Such misery made a particularly powerful issue because it appeared so unnecessary. In the South, Republicans saw a new West, an unexploited land of incredible wealth which could have rebuilt itself with no trouble even if every factory, farm, and cotton warehouse had been put to the torch, had its people only known the secret of rebuilding.

After the war, there should have been a resurgence, but none occurred. Consequently, Republicans blamed the spirit of the South. With the wrong attitude toward the North and toward productive labor, the section could not achieve the stable order essential for prosperity. Nor could the South relieve itself of the burden that a slave culture had placed on it. In religious terms, it could not work its own salvation without penitence and conversion.

As Republicans explained it, the South before the war had been government by the planters, for the planters. Because they lived off the labor of others, they had despised all labor as degrading and discouraged honest industry. They had paid lighter taxes and gerrymandered legislatures. Plantations prospered at the expense of industrial growth, small farmers, and the individual's dignity. Crowning all, to protect their privileges, the "aristocracy" had pushed the South into a war that brought death, debt, destruction, and the draft to the poor while rich men sat out the fight and sent substitutes to the front.[27] Republicans exaggerated the planters' power, but they needed to do so to make their point: that the race issue was a false one, created to gull the poorer whites into seeing the wrong enemies.

White and black had the same cause to promote; after all, labor made the man and color did not, or so Southern Republicans argued. The war was not won, Albion Tourgee wrote, until "master" was abolished as well as "slave." "The real issue," reasoned the *Vicksburg Republican*, "is not over a 'white-man's party,' but the *poor-man's party* and of equal rights to all." Republicans respected the poor white and accepted the black because both earned their keep by producing something. If they had little, they deserved every penny of it and more. The planter, in contrast, did not. Neither he nor that large part of the commercial elite that had profited without producing anything tangible deserved to succeed. Such men added nothing to the general wealth, for they had not followed the formula of hard work and a fair fight to all; they broke their competitors by manipulating the laws or by using cheap labor. Republicans did not object to wealth—only to the unsocial means by which wealth was gained and in which it was used. These unjust means must end, and the Civil War had given the South the opportunity to remove them. The conflict freed the slave, but it did more. It freed the white from custom and afforded him a chance to seek his economic salvation. The war having swept aside old leaders, old ideas, and old systems, "it is a good time to establish a new order of things," said the *Vicksburg Republican*.[28]

By "a new order of things," Southern Republicans meant progress—innovation—and a society in which all classes had a share in the governing. "Progress" was not just economic growth, but advancement in social ideas. It assumed a society that would evolve over time toward spiritual truth, and its supporters talked about "a higher order of growth, development and civilization." Nonetheless, "progress" seems to have revealed itself in the prosperity it brought and was to be measured in economic terms. No one imagined a "progress" of shanties, small towns, and middling farmers. Like the *Little Rock Republican*, Southern Republicans described as "progress" "thriving cities, smiling fields, blooming valleys and vineclad hills, and over all the glad sunshine of peace, happiness and prosperity."[29]

Pressed to describe "progress," Republicans pictured a North making the most of its meager resources. Some Southerners scoffed at "Yankee notions," but Judge Thomas Settle welcomed a people so "smart." "We want their capital to build factories, and work shops, and railroads. . . . We want their intelligence, their energy, and enterprise to operate these factories, and to teach us how to do it." Not that Southern Republicans wanted a South remade in the North's image or worked to Northerners' gain any more than Conservatives had. Indeed, they feared loss of Southern power to the burgeoning influence of the North. If the South waited outside the Union much longer, Republicans warned, the section would lose all chance of economic restoration and with it all political strength. Like Conservatives, Republicans opposed the cotton tax and wanted a transcontinental railroad for the Southwest. Unlike their foes, they did not interpret the present Northern advantages as proof of the corruption and despotism of Republican states. The fault lay with the Confederates who left the Union and abandoned policy-making and benefits to one part of the country. Nor did Republicans share the Conservative dream of manufacturing as a means of breaking the economic and political power of the North over the South, for they were not Southern nationalists, but nationalist Southerners. What they wanted was a South which would, in an economic sense, make a more perfect Union, one able to produce for itself so that neither Indiana farmers nor Massachusetts manufacturers could hold it in thrall. Instead, it would be able to enhance the industries of the rest of the country to the greater benefit of all.[30]

The Gospel of Prosperity necessarily meant a new South. The Southern press had supported factories to meet home demand and nothing more, but Republicans made manufacturing the critical part of the economy without which no society could prosper. Its development would pull thousands of laborers out of the fields and give them employment, and would also force the planter to raise wages to attract field hands. Nearby factories would also save the farmers the transportation costs that sending raw materials northward involved. A diverse economy called for a diverse people, and Republicans wanted thousands of immigrants. Unlike Conservatives, however, they were not seeking laborers to replace the Negro, but yeoman farmers and men with capital—with their Republican beliefs intact. By building up such an affluent class on the Republican side, the new party could break the power of the present commercial elite. To protect the small farm, Republicans promised exemptions under the bankruptcy laws from forfeiture and sale of a certain amount of land and personalty, as well as laws to stay the collection of any debts. To increase the landholding population, some orators promised confiscation of the large estates and state homestead laws; other promised much the same effect through stiffer tax rates on property.[31] All of these programs would protect and promote the interests of the producing classes. The Gospel of Prosperity itself was good for the economy and the soul.

The way in which Republicans expressed their faith in progress is as intriguing as the doctrine itself. Through all their rhetoric ran a religious motif.* States could redeem themselves from the sins

---

* No doubt, some of the religious analogy was rhetorical flourish. Orators loved to exaggerate, and audiences thrilled at hyperbole. Freedmen, too, could appreciate biblical allusions more easily than classical ones, for not many of them knew their classics and most of them cherished their Christian faith. Many ministers went into

of slavery by declaring faith in Republican institutions. Progress was divinely ordered, and the party stood committed "as a party of substantial and universal progress." Where Democrats sought classical images to identify themselves, Republicans took their allusions from the Bible. They were the "Hebrew host of old," said one paper, following Progress, that "Pillar of Fire." In such a cause as theirs, W. S. Furay told Republicans, the Lord would bring triumph, though the nation be tried in fire seven times hotter than the oven's. "The enemy and his legions must at last succumb, the sword of the Lord and of Gideon will at last prevail. . . . The world's earnest prayer shall not fail to call an answer from the skies."[32]

Judge H. K. McCay had a more elaborate vision when he appealed to Georgians in Cherokee County to build a railroad. The Lord was working toward the Millennium, but he needed man's help, the Judge reminded listeners, and could only get it if the world became one great city. "You and I, and they, all must do our part in this great work which is going to be done, and which will make the world throb with one heart, one thought and one religion." Build a railroad, and citizens took themselves one step nearer to "the great center of the world," and forged one more link "in the mighty chain of progress and advancement that is to bind the universe together and bring about the great moral millennium which God has ordained shall come into the world."[33]

The Gospel of Prosperity was no philosophy for doubters. Southern Republicans thought progress was inevitable. "We cannot go backward if we would," said the *Little Rock Republican* of its party's mission. " 'Forward' is . . . the very law of our being, from which there is no escape." This belief skirted some unpleasant questions. For example, was progress always good or necessary? Was there not something to be said for a town or state being a pleasant place to live instead of a continuously growing community? If they ceased to make progress, did that mean that Republicans had failed their mission and that it was time for another change? What of those Republicans who could not keep up with the forward pace? According to the *Little Rock Republican*, they must fall away, for the party would not wait for stragglers.[34]

The Gospel of Prosperity was messianic, relentless, but not par-

---

Republican politics, and their influence may have added an evangelical coloring to the rhetoric. But with all this said, it seems to me that the allusions said something about the different parties' different visions of political power. The sets of images conjured up were different: the one, bespeaking austere traditions and the preservation of ancient virtue, the other, a new world, new standards, and the leap of faith so necessary to those attached to the Old South.

ticularly radical. If anything, it had conservative implications and favored policies that Northerners would have thought conventional. Granted, Republican ideology attacked entrenched interests and denounced privilege. Granted, too, there was a vein of hostility to the corporate structure and a concentration on programs to benefit the agricultural worker at the expense of the commercial and agricultural elite—at least, in 1867. But occasional rhetorical excesses should not obscure the basic Republican message.* With

---

* If the Gospel of Prosperity was so moderate, how can one justify radical Republican rhetoric about confiscation? Conservatives insisted then, and later historians echoed the claim, that the Reconstruction coalition meant to force the large estates onto the market by taxation and invidious legislation. One North Carolina Conservative, for example, recorded in his diary that a certain preacher was reputed to have demanded "a division of the lands or something like that," and to have virtually proclaimed "the negro . . . entitled to the labor, *and would have it.*" In almost every case, Conservatives had heard "something like that" rather than the real thing. Put on the stand before congressional committees, they bolstered their claims only by hearsay. Conservative polemicists in 1867 and 1868 needed the horror stories to shake whites out of their lethargy and prove to them how monstrous Reconstruction could be. Perhaps their resort to such stories is a testimonial to how soothing an effect the Republican Gospel of Prosperity was having.

Certainly, many radical Republicans hoped for a redistribution of lands. No new society could be built unless the planters' power was broken. "Civil rights are good for nothing, the ballot is good for nothing, till you make some men of every class landholders," an Alabamian exclaimed. The federal government had made tentative and limited promises of homes for the freedmen, and though it had reneged, the dream persisted. Yet most Republican leaders believed too heartily in the rights of private property to accept outright confiscation. In every state party convention where confiscators made a fight on the issue, they lost badly. As Republicans cultivated white support and as Conservatives exploited the extremists' statements, even some early backers of confiscation retreated or claimed that they had been completely misunderstood. At the same time, Republicans did not want to stifle the expectations of the thousands of landless constituents; so they played a canny game on the issue. They denounced the tyranny of the large landholder and vowed to end it; they promised homesteads for all; they promised to put the brunt of taxation on the planters; and yet they drew a distinction between policies confiscatory in design and those confiscatory in effect. Best of all, they used fears of confiscation to keep Conservative voters home. Of course, the "new order of things" did not mean confiscation, they argued, at least *not yet.* The moderates in the Republican party could hold back their wild men, at least *for now.* But if whites turned out in full force against the conventions and defeated Reconstruction, things would change. Who knew what an angered Congress might do? Thaddeus Stevens and his friends were waiting for their chance: rejection of moderate Republicanism would give them the opportunity they craved. It was a stunningly powerful argument. *"Now* is the time to build up the Republican party," one North Carolinian wrote another. "Negro suffrage connected with the fear of confiscation has knocked secession out of traitors."

See Stephen M. Appell, "The Fight for a Constitutional Convention: The Development of Political Parties in North Carolina During 1867," M.A. thesis, University of North Carolina at Chapel Hill, 1969, pp. 52–55; Henry W. McVay to Thaddeus Stevens, March 1, 1867, Stevens Papers, LC; Jonathan B. Odom to Thomas Settle, May 18, 1867, Settle Papers, SHC; *Little Rock Republican,* September 23, 1867; *New Orleans Tribune,* July 24, 1867.

several vital distinctions, it mirrored economic ideas many Conservatives had been expressing for two years. By giving every man the opportunity to realize his potential, Republicans hoped that a reconstructed South could realize its own potential. By "revolution," the *Little Rock Republican* meant no more than the development of railroads, levees, and mines.[35] Yet no moderate doubted that this change would be enough of a revolution to transform the South and, by its example, perhaps the world.

Republicans parted company most sharply with Conservative thought in linking prosperity to the Congressional Reconstruction program. They made their slogan not just Radicalism and Prosperity, but Radicalism or Ruin. The South was rich, but its wealth could not be realized without outside help, both public and private. Neither would be forthcoming until the states had been readmitted to Congress. Republicans knew this, and they were aware that Conservative businessmen knew it as well. With federal aid so important, orators reminded voters that readmission would enable the South to be heard. Everyone agreed that Congress was prodigal, even criminally so. Thus Republicans from a reconstructed section *could* make their colleagues on Capitol Hill share the wealth with the South. "In the Union, her levees will be rebuilt," one editor promised, "her railroad grants restored, the mouths of the Mississippi opened, sandbars and snags removed, canals dug, marshes drained, taxes taken off cotton and sugar, emigration directed southward instead of westward, and all the material interests of the state spring into robust vigor and healthful activity."[36]

The Gospel of Prosperity was more than a Gospel of Pork Barrel, and appealed to the voters' logic more than to their greed. Republicans knew that private capital would provide most of the funding needed to regenerate the South. They did not pretend that the Northerner stayed out of Southern markets because he was a Republican. Instead, they stressed his good sense. As long as the Southern states were not restored to the Union along Republican lines, no Northerner, Unionist, or freedman would be safe. As long as the Southern states lacked Congressional recognition, their governments were not legitimate, nor were their securities, nor any private securities depending on state guarantees. Under such circumstances, a Northern investor would be a fool to invest his capital or come south.[37] Without restoration, so everyone admitted, there could be no economic salvation. Republicans went farther: without Republican governments, there would be no restoration.

Conservatives hoped that the suffering of the South would hurt

Northern financiers and force national leaders to accept the legality of the provisional and Conservative governments. Republicans did not think that the South could wait that long. They did not underestimate the tenacity of the North's resolve or the extent of damage already done to the Southern economy, and so their rhetoric took on a dire tone. To reconstruct was to avail the South of all it had ever hoped for. Not to reconstruct was to abandon the South to a ruin out of which it could never rise. It was as simple as that. It was the Politics of Hope and the Politics of Despair—Despair over all the section had stood for, and Hope in all it had for so long resisted.[38]

Developing variations on the themes of the promise of Progress and the prospects of ruin, Republicans used both to support specific panaceas. In Georgia, the issue of homestead exemption and debtor relief eclipsed almost every other. Texas Republicans called for free homesteads, and moderate party leaders backed "men who will vote money and lands to build railroads and appropriate at least a million of dollars to bring in a swarm of thrifty immigrants." South Carolina moderates promised to use public funds to aid the poor and destitute. Arkansas Republicans endorsed a general system of internal improvements as well as federal aid to levee construction and overflowed land reclamation. More than one Republican promised retrenchment, and most pledged to make land bear its share of taxes. Did Southerners want roads? polemicists asked. Did they want improvements, mines, and manufactories? All prosperity depended on the vote. "This is no ordinary election."[39]

Against this campaign the Conservatives could put up only modest resistance. They could not counter Republican economics effectively, in part, because they agreed with much of it and, in part, because they could not conceal their own failure to bring prosperity in their two years of power. For that matter, some Conservatives in the spring of 1867 had echoed the Radical argument that the South must accept Reconstruction to achieve prosperity and did not choose to go back on their words. More important, Conservatives simply did not recognize economics as the main issue. To them, no issue outweighed sectional degradation brought about by racial equality.[40] Although they tried to make the sole issue one of race, this attempt just did not work, and the Gospel of Prosperity deserves some of the credit for the election results. Whites could defy the color line and vote Republican because they had been convinced that they had as much to gain as did the Negro. Others could stay home because Republican ideology did not have very much radicalness in it—outside of its acceptance of impartial suffrage, which was inevitable in any reconstructing that Congress would sanction.

When the votes were counted, the Republicans found themselves triumphant in every Southern state. They would have their conventions, and the opponents of Reconstruction would be badly outnumbered in all of them. But if the figures gave excuse for pleasure, they gave equal cause for uneasiness. Blacks had voted for the conventions, and so had a majority of registered whites in some states. However, had all eligible whites bothered to register and vote, the results could have been changed. Even with the army to protect them and a disorganized opposition, blacks did not come out in full force. In nineteen Arkansas counties, over one in four stayed home, and in some Alabama senatorial districts over 40 percent of the freedmen did not vote.[41] Without white backing, the Republican party would be in sorry shape everywhere in the future.

The election was something of a mandate, but a mandate for what? The Republicans had promised so much that someone was doomed to disappointment. Certain promises were obviously irreconcilable with others. For example, retrenchment was promised, as well as relief for the poor and aid to internal improvements. Republicans assured incentives to capital, but the promise of "relief" meant the annulment of old debts and violation of contracts; such a course would not appeal to capitalists. Republicans promised to encourage manufacturing, but manufacturing required cheap labor, and the promise of homesteads for all seemed to militate against a landless class dependent on the mills and mines for a living. What, then, *would* the Radicals do with their power?

As it turned out, when the constitutional conventions met in late 1867 and early 1868, the Republican majority used its economic mandate cautiously, even conservatively. In part, it did so because the issues of race and Union occupied the delegates' attentions more. To refashion the Southern political system, Republicans had to reach a final settlement of the basic questions of the past decade, and in doing so, to make possible a party system based on economic and social issues in the future. In part, the delegates practiced moderation in economic matters because they needed white and upper class support so badly. Whatever the reasons, the conventions did not carry out the threats of confiscation and state debt repudiation that Republicans had occasionally spoken of in 1867. The slight agrarian flavor that the issues of debtor relief and planter domination had given Radical polemics faded further. In almost every contest over economic reform, the majority of each convention showed itself more radical in name than deed.

Before the conventions, a few orators had spoken of an *ab initio* Reconstruction, one rooting out every vestige of the Rebel governments. *Ab initio* would free debtors from judgments against them, release the states from financial obligations created since secession, and put in jeopardy the corporate privileges which made Conservatives masters of the South's commercial and political life. It would also alienate almost every white Southerner and moderate Republican congressman from the new governments. Annulment of seven years' legislation and jurisprudence would bring utter chaos by challenging every local municipal charter, sale of land, and act of incorporation. When the issue arose in Texas, Louisiana, and Arkansas, therefore, moderate counsels prevailed.[42] Supporters of drastic change had to content themselves with limited challenges to the provisional governments' authority: to special charters, public debts, judgments for private debts, and conferral of privileges.

Even in these attempts they were not particularly successful. Those Republicans who wanted to vacate Conservative incorporation laws could not muster enough support to pass such an ordinance in a single convention. The moderate delegates were content to mutter empty threats at the worst corporate offenders. In Louisiana and Alabama, delegates offered proposals to examine the books of railroads in which the state government held stock, or to encourage payment of their obligations to the state. However, these proposals never got beyond the committees to which they were referred. An Arkansas resolution to investigate the Little Rock & Fort Smith Railroad was made positively toothless when one member amended it to forbid the special committee to incur any expense.[43]

The Conservative state debts were more open to challenge. The *ab initio* faction feared that by assuming old liabilities, the Republican governments would cripple themselves from the start. To pay those debts, the new governments would need to exact increased taxes. Such a step would hardly contribute to the stability or popularity of any new administration. Every dollar of taxes that went to pay old debts was one less dollar for school systems, railroad aid, levee construction, or land reclamation. Without improvements such as these, and with high taxes, no state could attract the capital and immigrants necessary for its economic renewal. To such arguments, however, moderate Republicans replied that repudiation would alienate the major investors outside the state and leading commercial figures inside it. Since the railroads had received or expected to receive securities under Conservative aid laws, repudiation would hurt corporations that a new South so badly needed. The Republican party needed all the respect it could muster, and the best way to win respect was by upholding the state's fiscal integrity. At most, the conventions turned state debts to partisan advantage with the same investigations and recriminations that they had wasted on Conservative charters. Thus no convention repudiated past obligations.[44]

The *ab initio* faction had slightly more success with the issue of canceling private debts, if only because destitution was so widespread throughout the South and the demand in every class so great. Friends of relief reminded radicals that a constitution without a stay law attached could not pass. Accordingly, in almost every state, delegates supported laws staying judgments against debtors and setting up bankruptcy procedures that would allow the poor to exempt from sale some of their land and personal property. Even so, the conventions adopted surprisingly restricted relief measures with a few loopholes. Property was not exempt from forced sale for unpaid taxes, for the purchase price of the land, or for mechanics' or laborers' wages. In Arkansas, the homestead provisions applied only to debts contracted after adoption of the new constitution. Most conventions did not even consider the means of redistributing property to increase the number of small freeholders in the South. They changed the tax structure to shift the tax burden from personalty to real property, but only in South Carolina did delegates instruct the legislature to set up a land commission that might buy, subdivide, and resell plantations.[45]

Republicans did not quarrel about every economic issue. If moderates deplored measures that violated Southern legal traditions and disrupted the section's commercial system, they agreed with the radicals that hard times justified extraordinary measures. If radicals wanted the conventions to do more to weaken the Conservative elite and to elevate the masses, they, too, appreciated the need to encourage the South's commercial and industrial interests. On issues such as national aid or railroad construction, every faction thought alike. Together, they petitioned Congress to repeal the cotton tax, to continue the operations of the Freedmen's' Bureau, and to loan $30 million to thousands of destitute farmers. The conventions showed an equally strong interest in federal funding for internal improvements. The Georgia convention asked that the Federal Treasury lend $100,000 to the South Georgia & Florida Railroad and make a gift outright to another railway between Atlanta and Charlotte, North Carolina. Alabama's convention considered a memorial to extend for five years the time limit set on federal land grants to Southern railroads, and a Louisiana delegate offered a similar resolution for relieving the New Orleans, Opelousas & Great Western.[46]

The conventions did not mind spending state money for worthy projects. North Carolina delegates passed five ordinances giving financial assistance totaling $2,150,000 to railroads. The convention also endorsed the bonds of the Wilmington, Charlotte & Rutherford, and chartered another railroad through the Piedmont counties.[47]

What the Republicans did by direct act was less important than what they promised by implication. With two exceptions, every constitution allowed extensive state aid to internal improvements. In Mississippi, the new document forbade the pledge of credit to help a private corporation, and in Texas, the Republicans wrote in a prohibition of land grants over the strong protest of Conservatives and leading moderates. In other states west of the Appalachians, the government was forbidden to become the proprietor of internal improvements projects, but this restriction only encouraged aid to enterprises over which the state authorities had no control. In Arkansas, the delegates banned all special acts of aid and incorporation and opened the way to general aid laws. At the same time, Republicans did exercise caution in giving aid. North Carolina allowed railroad aid but made sure that until state bonds reached par the legislature would accompany any new debts contracted with special taxes. Alabama and Georgia forbade the state to lend its credit to any company without a two-thirds vote in both houses and the corporation's promise of a prior lien to the state. Although Alabama delegates defeated an attempt to require that any state loan of credit be submitted to referendum, Arkansas Republicans wrote this provision into their constitution.[48]

The necessary corollary to the legal sanctioning of state aid was a system of raising revenue that would afford the government a liberal outlay. The delegates established this as well, though perhaps less for internal improvements purposes than for a wide range of needs. Republicans wanted to shift the tax burden from the commercial classes to the landholders, and while they retained the right to levy poll taxes and license taxes, they demanded equal and uniform taxation on property according to its value.[49]

The delegates did what they could to encourage economic development. Because the South needed manpower, the Radicals established bureaus of immigration. Because it needed capital, a few constitutions removed restrictions on interest rates. Before a state could develop its natural resources, it would need a clear idea of what minerals it had, and to this end the conventions created bureaus of industrial resources.[50] Although different conventions chose different means of refashioning the Southern economy, they had the same purposes in mind: to broaden the opportunities for Southern industrial and commercial expansion and to win from men of capital trust in the new governments.

When the conventions finished their deliberations, members should have been as proud of the moderation in economic policies they had shown as they were of their devotion to reform. Democratic fears of "agrarianism" ascendant had proven groundless. Nevertheless, could the new party attract enough white support to gain political legitimacy? And could the economic issue be used to the Republicans' benefit?

It could be used, and was used, wherever there were white votes needed for victory. State and local conventions promised development of Southern mineral potential and backed schemes of internal improvement. Reconstruction in Georgia, one reporter concluded, "means the 'State Road.'" He was mistaken. It meant *many* roads. Rufus Bullock, Republican candidate for governor and former president of the Macon, Milledgeville & Augusta, openly supported an express railway from Atlanta to the northeast corner of the state and went on record in favor of the principle of railroad aid. Georgia Republicans turned relief into a major issue, as politicos played on debtors' fears for the future. The *Atlanta Daily New Era* only echoed what others were saying when it printed the following epigrams between its editorials:

> Bullock is a friend of the working man, and the working men are for Bullock.
> Ben. Hill is opposed to the Homestead Bill. Bullock is for it, and so are the people.
> Ben. Hill is down on the 'Poor Masses.'—Bullock is for them.
> Ben. Hill is opposed to relief.—Bullock is for it.
> Bullock is a railroad man, and Ben's crowd, like Pat are paying their way on foot.
> The mechanics and working men are all declaring for Bullock.
> Roast Beef, and good times ahead, boys. That's the talk.

At times, newspaper references to rebellion, race hatred, intolerance, and black codes vanished entirely. The Republicans wanted

Confederate veterans to vote for the constitutions, and they even wanted white supremacists to do the same. In a small way, the desire to broaden the party's base—like the selection of such moderate gubernatorial candidates as Harrison Reed in Florida and Powell Clayton in Arkansas—was a step away from the radical implications and the first principles of the Reconstruction coalition.[51]

The Democrats did not accept the Republicans' terms of combat, but made race, not restoration of prosperity, the prime issue and almost the only issue. As such, they exploited it shamelessly. Orators attacked political equality, denied its constitutionality, and vowed to overthrow it. After all, political equality meant black sheriffs and assessors, freedmen on the bench and in the jury box. It meant the destruction of every barrier that made white men in all classes feel a kinship for one another and also prevented horrible race warfare. Racial equality at the polls, Democrats warned, would foster equality of every other sort. Vote down the constitution, John M. Bradley admonished one Arkansas audience, "if you do not want to be compelled to send your children to school with niggers—if you vote for it, you invite the nigger into your parlour—you invite him to ride in your carriage—you offer him one of your daughters in marriage, socially and politically."[52] Such talk was nonsense, but very effective nonsense.

Because they saw Reconstruction in terms of black misrule, and because they saw the freedmen as landless savages, the Conservatives completely misunderstood the economic implications of a Republican triumph. To the *Iberville South*, Radical rule meant "the death of industry, ruin of commerce, extinction of civilization, return to Fetich worship and breach clouts, and ultimately . . . the proscription of white men, Southern and Yankee alike." Others foresaw the confiscation of large estates, continuation of the cotton tax, and an end to Northern immigration and investment. One Northern visitor to Mississippi came away convinced that no one would subscribe to railroads if the new party came to power. Perhaps most astonishing in light of later developments, was a Louisiana newspaper's suggestion that Radicals would not give levees and railroads the financial support they deserved.[53] Democrats clearly misread the conventions and the Reconstruction coalition, for wild-eyed agrarians were in charge of neither. Their economic policies were not much different from those of Conservatives. If anything, the Republican governments would fail to bring prosperity because they followed to their logical conclusions the assumptions of the Conservative leadership.

Believing as they did that the fate of their culture was at stake,

Conservatives sanctioned every means of winning the election, from proscription to murder. Black laborers were told that support for the Republicans would cost them their jobs, and whites were threatened with ostracism. Secret societies bullied, beat, and murdered radicals that they found offensive. Against this disorder the army could do very little and the state governments chose to do even less.[54]

Opposed with such force and such arguments, Republican appeals took on an element of revivalistic desperation. As Radicals described them, the constitutions were fundamental laws that most Southerners could not live without. They were the South's last chance to redeem itself. "The day of grace has almost expired," the *Little Rock Republican* pleaded. "Unrepentant sinners are now for the last time being asked to make their peace and to come within the fold of the Union. . . . Will you be saved, or do you prefer to be damned?"[55]

If the elections were any indication, the white South declared a preference for damnation. In every state but two, Republicans won victories, but only in a limited sense had they been able to establish the biracial party on which Reconstruction ultimately depended. Black, not white votes, had saved the party, and in no state had the color line broken down completely. Alabama Republicans cast a majority of the votes in the election, but they could not obtain a majority of all registered voters and thus failed to fulfill the congressional requirements for ratification. In Mississippi, the Conservatives defeated the Reconstruction constitution outright, while Georgia's constitution passed only after being explained in opposite ways in different parts of the state. That ratification would lead to political turmoil.[56]

Southern Republicans were troubled by their failure to attract a substantial white following. Social ostracism, threats, and violence made the future bleak. Black and white men were deserting the Republican cause, a carpetbagger wrote, and they hoped their recantation would "place them in a condition to be allowed to remain in the Country." Without unusual measures, the party would surely perish. Congress provided just such measures by changing the law to readmit Alabama, remanding a refractory Georgia to military rule, and leaving Mississippi unreconstructed until it voted correctly. All of these acts gave the Reconstruction coalition a respite but not the permanent stability it needed. Rather, the months after the elections only made the insecurity of the new governments more clear, and terrorism and factionalism threatened to bring the Republican authorities down.[57]

A majority of voters was not a sufficient base for Republicanism. As long as a substantial part of the public did not see the election process as legitimate or the officials elected as anything more than usurpers, the government could not endure longer than armed force would protect it; until "the better sort" in Southern society recognized the Republicans' *right* to govern, nothing but military might could keep the peace. Until Republicans themselves could keep the peace, they could not bring political stability and the accompanying prosperity.

One convert to the party, then, was not as valuable as another. The more important and affluent the convert, the more valuable he would be. Without bringing the "best men" in Southern society to their side, Republicans could not infuse men of a lower social position with the courage or desire to join them. Until they made "respectable" men into Republicans, they could not make Republican men "respectable" enough to protect them from intimidation and murder. Such a need required moderate men and moderate measures.

When the Republican legislatures opened in special session, they showed themselves temperate in everything. They did all that Congress required of them, but little more. Lawmakers legislated to protect their governments from overthrow by military and registration laws, but they neither passed bills opening public facilities to all nor stiffening restrictions on Conservatives' political rights. Republican circumspection showed most plainly in economic policy. The legislators passed a few weak statutes protecting the lien of the agricultural worker and mechanic on their employers' crop. Only South Carolina created a land agency. Furthermore, some states did not even establish school systems or bureaus of immigration. Those that did gave the immigration officer very limited powers.[58] One scans in vain for laws that could be called agrarian or economically radical—laws to repudiate or scale down the existing debt, to give additional relief to the homeowner or debtor, or to repudiate the franchises of Conservative corporations. Instead, the books are loaded with statutes of local import, corporation charters, and internal improvements laws.

The last two kinds of laws are the most interesting. From their rhetoric, one might have assumed the Republicans to be men suspicious of corporate privilege; yet their first legislatures gave sanction and revenue to a multitude of enterprises. They provided state endorsement for first-mortgage railroad bonds, renewed old land grants to established companies, gave liberal charters to new projects, and endowed other schemes with tax exemption and exclusive privileges. Aid many enterprises though they did, Republicans were most attentive to the needs of railroads.[59]

Legislation was only one sign of the political transformation. One can detect a slight change in Republican exhortations, too, as its press placed more emphasis on economic development than on economic reform, and stressed the need for peace and stability so that industry and commerce could thrive. "The one great need universally felt by all the people is prosperity," said the *Little Rock Republican*. "It is in our poverty and straightened circumstances that we . . . find the principal cause and fruitful source of all our harassing cares and perplexing anxieties." Railroads took on an added importance for polemicists, and not just because they fit the vision of a South reborn. As one North Carolinian wrote the governor, the internal improvements policy was so popular that the first party to complete the state's transportation system "[would] hold the reins of power for years to come." Small wonder that in 1868 the Arkansas Republicans urged voters to "vote for railroads and the Republican party."[60]

Reconstruction was not betrayed, but it had undergone a subtle change of emphasis. The constitutional conventions had made that transformation possible by settling some of the most serious problems of the time. Reunion had been achieved, treason rebuked; now the real reconstruction of society that would give it a new form and a different outlook remained to be done. The task, however, was a hard one, and one that most Republican leaders seemed ever more unwilling to undertake, except in ways appealing to the commercial and social elite of the South. It was also a task that had no practical political solution in any other terms.

If, that is, it had a practical political solution at all. But did it? Republicans had in fact found the perfect issue for winning office and the worst one for keeping it. The South had been unable to attain its old prosperity, and so Republicans had declared that their rule would restore sectional fortunes. They assumed that economic development was a good thing in itself, whatever the cost to social order, tradition, or local harmony. They damned Conservative rulers and methods for not having ended hard times, and they made material success the yardstick by which failure or success of a regime could be based. But they did more: they proclaimed that economic failure or success depended wholly on a government's policies.

That, as this prologue has suggested, was a simplistic view, for there were a thousand other factors beyond the range of a state government's powers that influenced a state's development: local resources, national monetary policy, London markets, natural disasters, even the competition of other Southern states for a limited amount of commerce. One can hardly blame Republican polemicists for their words. After all, oversimplification is the mother's milk of all politics, and the less learning a constituency has, the more necessary oversimplication becomes. It would be foolish to have expected a canvass full of complexity.

"The people want prosperity," the *Little Rock Republican* warned. "They are earnest in the matter. The dominant party must bring it about. That is its pledge, and it must not be broken." Here was the snare Republicans had set for themselves. What if the pledge could not be kept? The conventions had pledged relief, but the South remained in hard times, and the ills plaguing Conservatives now plagued their successors, who were about to adopt the same batches of economic panaceas. With some justice, Republicans could echo the words of one delegate about the constitution of Arkansas. He spoke of the freedmen as the children of Israel following their passage from bondage to deliverance. "I came here with extremely honest purposes," he said, "to effect some good for my country, and to get a constitution republican in form, and in the hopes that we might pass over Jordan. But it is a hard road to travel, to get into the Promised Land. Gentlemen, we are not yet over."[61]

CHAPTER 2

The Necessities of State Aid

Which of you, intending to build a tower, sitteth not down first
and counteth the cost, whether he have sufficient to finish it?
Luke, 14:28

No traveler in the postwar South could have missed the so-called
railroad mania. If he did not hear of railroad advancement in
conversations or see the ties being laid along his way, he might
have visited any number of mass meetings called to stir local enthusiasm. Villages with no railroads had to have one, and those
with one wanted two. As thriving trade centers, towns demanded
new lines, less out of need than as a right. The enthusiasm was
adaptable to any economic program or local condition. If a town
had a large population, it could certainly support a railroad, and
if it had a small population, it could not afford to pass up the only
means left for advancement. "Every paper we pick up has its col-
umns speaking on railroads," a Republican marveled. "You talk to
a fellow citizen as to the future, and the conversation drifts upon
railroads.—Every map that now comes to hand is a network of
railroads, and the lever power of the nineteenth century seems to
hinge upon railroads."[1]
   On examining the modest results of Southern promotion, the
passion seems difficult to understand. Yet understand it we must
or miss the meaning of the era. Southerners had not lost touch
with reality in putting such faith in railroads. Nor were Republican
governments misguided in giving support to this form of development over all the others on which they had laid such stress prior
to 1868. Stripping away the oratory, the historian discovers that
Southerners understood correctly their economic problem and recognized with equal precision that the railroad provided the easiest
and perhaps the wisest solution.
   Southerners realized that their poverty was not due to a lack of
resources but to a lack of development. They spoke of fatness,
fertility, limitless wealth, looms, forges, and mines. But looms could
not clank nor machinery hum until their owners had a system of
transport to bring the raw materials in and to carry the goods away

at prices competitive with those of Northern industry. Primeval forests could be turned to profit only when lumber could be carried to people willing to buy it. Furthermore, immigrants could not settle a wilderness they could not reach. Farmers could clear land only when their crops could be sent to markets and sold at fair prices. Until the railroad provided convenient transport and spurred industrial growth, Southerners could not expect "the glad advent of the pick and bar" that would tap the fabulous wealth that more than one Republican governor described.[2]

Although much of the lowland South was accessible by water, the planters could hardly depend on boats the way they could on trains. Steamers were uncertain, streams dried up in summer. A pilot could run afoul or a flatboat could be swamped in a torrent. The Arkansas River became so low in the postwar years, joked the *New Orleans Crescent*, that natives had to sprinkle the bed to keep stern-wheel boats from raising clouds of dust. Counties remote from streams had to rely on roads, many of which were little more than cow paths and crude trails. Ruts and mud were so deep that during much of the year carts could not travel them, and wagons would sink to the hubs. At best a farmer could carry his crop no further than the county seat, which rarely had rail communication. He was obliged to take the local trader's price or nothing, and often saw no reason to grow goods for sale at all. Such conditions forced North Carolina consumers to buy Illinois corn at three times the price they might have paid for the tens of thousands of bushels of corn that rotted for lack of a market "all along the fat valley of the Yadkin and the flanks of the Blue Ridge."[3]

Because railroads were the start of everything, they were not just economically imperative, but more politically attractive than programs to develop canals or factories could have been. They not only appealed to every class and every taste, but gave energy to the New South and promised revival to the Old. They assured local interests of all they could ask and did the same for the visionaries of national scope. Longing for a return to the flush times before the Rebellion, the planter looked to the railroad to double land values. Hoping to revive their antebellum prosperity, city merchants sought to expand their markets into the hinterland. Believers in a New South hoped that railroads would bring in thousands of new people and a new society as well, with Yankee notions and Yankee diligence. Indeed, only the poorer classes seemed to have doubted the usefulness of the steam engine—and they did not transform their disquiet into majorities when the issue was put to a popular vote. Why should they, when the railroads' friends assured them that a line would mean cheap prices on goods if the poor man bought them, high prices on goods if he sold them, cheap homesteads if he bought one, high land prices if he sold it, and jobs whenever he needed them?[4]*

The enthusiasm and expectation for railroads seemed unlimited. One of the leading citizens of La Grange, Georgia, who hoped to build a line through that city from Rome to Columbus, declared, "This, sir, is a world railway. . . . This is a railway which the God of Heaven seems to have marked out as the great line railroad between the Northern Lakes and the Gulf of Mexico, and it is only our good fortune that we have been permitted to have our residences along the line of such a magnificent enterprise as this will be." Perhaps fearful of having understated its benefits, he added, "Why, sir, it is one of the grandest projects that has ever been inaugurated." A rival Georgia line, the Western & Atlantic, was even more sanguine. In its advertisements, it announced itself the only Southern road selling through tickets to "Yokohama, Japan, Hioga, Japan, Hong Kong, China, Nagasaki, China," and reminded readers of the San Francisco steamer schedule to the Orient.[5] Although the promoters may have done badly at geography, one wonders how many Georgia farmers put that knowledge to the test by demanding a through ticket to Nagasaki.

If one listens to the oratory, one is struck not only by the confidence in the future it exuded, but also by the uncertainty, indeed,

---

* If the promises sound absurd today, sensible observers found them so then. Backing a city subscription to a road to the Gulf port of Indianola, the *San Antonio Express* filled its readers with bright visions until at last, it would seem, the editor could stand it no longer. He published a column lampooning the paper's promises. "We have heard of so many blessings that are coming, at the rate of sixty miles an hour, that we are afraid we are not ripe for them," he confessed. "We are sure we don't deserve half of them." Facts and figures showed that the president of the line was "a philanthropist of enlarged views, with two sets of bowels of compassion, and enough of the milk of human kindness to start a cheese factory; that there is a danger of the Indianola road running through our city and coming out the other side; that by accepting the proposition every head of a family will . . . save enough on the item of flour alone, to build himself a two-story house with a cupola on top and a pizarro all around . . . and have enough money over to go to New York in thirty-five minutes and buy a stock of goods, for the transportation of which, on the Indianola road, he will receive two dollars per hundred for every mile, without having to pay commissions and wharfage; that he will also be presented with a brass mounted statuette of the two railroad financiers three times daily." Of course, another gentleman had brought figures that proved beyond doubt exactly the reverse, the editor admitted. When a third visitor appeared in the editorial offices with his own incontrovertible statistics, the editor had resigned to preserve his sanity. *San Antonio Express*, November 11, 1871.

the fear, that underlay it. Small communities saw a chance for greatness in the building of a railroad, but more important, they saw it as their last chance. Large communities saw an opportunity to spread their commercial empires, but also saw that if they failed to get railroads they would lose what prominence they already had. An Alabama politician summed up the effect of a railroad bypassing a town—"it would dry it up like a dried apple, and presently there would be but little of it left." The dread was not just that a town would not obtain a railroad, but that someplace else would, and the fear infected every community, no matter how large or how many railroads it had. These fears were not always phantoms; that is, the danger was real. For every Atlanta, reviving postwar beyond anyone's expectations, there were a dozen Milledgevilles, where an unwillingness to pay for a railroad had robbed the town of economic and then of political importance.[6]

The railroads, then, had to be built immediately, men in both parties agreed, but how was this to be accomplished? The South had few banks and investors had little money to spare. Northern capital was at best chary. Furthermore, private parties could not raise large sums by borrowing because Southerners owed too much to ask for more. Nothing could be done without public funding.

That funding would have to be more generous than ever before, for in spite of state aid programs the South lagged behind the rest of the country in building lines. In 1866, 1,716 miles of track were laid nationwide, but only 209 of these were in the eleven Confederate states and Kentucky. This figure was all the more depressing to those who knew that Kansas alone had built 200 miles and Pennsylvania 369. The next year the gap between Southern and national construction was still wider. Arkansas, Louisiana, and Mississippi added not a mile between 1865 and 1868. Elsewhere the increase was pitiful.[7] Without massive public support, the railroads would remain alluring visions, and the South would take a generation to rebuild.

The value of a governmental subsidy greatly exceeded the amount the state could give in cash or lands. No corporation could expect to build on public aid alone. Men of commerce needed proof that a project was destined to succeed before they would invest private funds. By passing a special act granting aid to a railway, the legislature gave just such evidence that here was a plan to be trusted, one that would have sufficient funding to lay track and buy rolling stock. Competitors had neither the head start which aid provided nor the prospect of future government backing. Special aid in this way not only served one line but crippled its rivals, and as rivals failed, the aided railroad became the most likely choice for potential contributors or investors. On the same principle, a railroad general-aid law winnowed out the weaker companies by setting up guidelines for state support. The railroads that met the standards and received state bonds were doubly endowed, with cash and credibility.

Nevertheless, few projects had such national importance that Northern capitalists would invest in them without question; most corporations had to coax bankers outside the South to buy their bonds. The postwar prosperity had given rise to projects all over the country, and most of them more attractive, some of them more secured from loss, than Southern railroads. The capitalist needed a guarantee that the railroad he invested in was to be built, and the bonds that it sold were to be paid. To give this assurance and persuade the Northern investor that he was safe from loss, states either let the railroads sell state bonds or else guaranteed interest and principal on the bonds of the private company. Railroad companies might go bankrupt, but states did not. Several states had repudiated their bonds before the war, but few of them were Southern, and those few were Democratic. The Republican party now ran the South and would not countenance repudiation. Northern investors never had the same mania for buying Southern securities that Southern investors had for building railroads, but at least they bought, and without the moral support of state aid, Southerners could not even have expected that.

Railroad aid suited Republican purposes not simply because it was practical and essential, but because it was thoroughly conservative. Nothing fitted Southern tradition so well, or had less of the taint of intrusive Northern radicalism. So clear had it been to the antebellum South that roads could not be built with private means alone that such an alternative was hardly considered. Certainly, there would have been no 300 miles of railroad in Texas by 1861 or 800 in Missouri without public funds. Where state aid had come least or latest, such as to Arkansas, very little track was built and that which was needed official help.[8] A state might spend millions of dollars and not make real progress—Louisiana had proven that before the war and would again afterward—but there seemed to be a close connection between substantial aid and substantial construction. The Old South had been perfectly willing to give one to assure the other.

The promoters did not have to rummage through Southern history for precedents. States north of the Ohio River gave adequate examples. There, growth had been simply remarkable. Although Alabama and Illinois had entered the Union at the same time, Illinois had far outstripped Alabama in commercial prominence. State aid to the Illinois Central received the credit. At a Democratic barbecue, a speaker stressed similar contrasts. Look at Indiana, he exclaimed: because of its railroad aid, the state's wealth grew between 1850 and 1857 from $137 million to $317 million. Or Ohio—in the same period its wealth rose from $439 million to $849 million. Or Tennessee, which he claimed in 1860 was worth $159 million and a year later was worth $361 million!9 The speaker's figures were bizarre, and where he obtained them he did not say, but statistics always sound impressive. Perhaps he did not expect many listeners to remember the precise numbers anyway. Certainly, no one challenged them. The message was clear: aid provided meant potential realized.

And yet, could not another lesson be drawn from antebellum state policy in the North as well as the South? Just as governments' aid had a precedent, so did default by private companies and "safeguards" that had no value. Taxpayers gave $26 million to help Tennessee railways, or about 76 percent of the total invested. Missourians disbursed three dollars out of every four paid for construction up to 1860, with few lines completed to their termini and only one not in default on bonds and interest. A closer look at the Northern states' policy would have revealed many shortcomings: mounting debts, waste, mismanagement, popular frustration, and disgust in the period after railroad aid had been given and before affluence was produced. After enduring programs that had begun in incompetence and ended in private bankruptcies, eight states liquidated their disastrous public works policies and adopted constitutions making such ventures impossible in the future.10

Had the Republicans known more history, they might have shown more caution, but they were no less attentive and no more foolish than the most educated and respected men of the South. Not one figure in the commercial or political elite sounded a note of caution. He might pronounce the Republicans unqualified to run a program of public works, denounce the choice of beneficiaries, or suggest that the policies would mean heavy debts. But it was rare, almost unknown, for a man in public life to warn that railroads in general were losing propositions and that state aid under any party's auspices would bring great cost with little immediate profit.

That was precisely the warning that should have been sounded.

After all, not all areas had the trade to sustain a railroad once built. Even in good times, with an easy money supply, some companies laid tracks through the Midwest and then went bankrupt. Even the most able capitalists lost everything by overestimating the return from roads in the corn belt when money was tight. The South lacked a flexible money supply and also had few of the Midwest's advantages. Between the rich prairies and Alabama's red clay hills there was a world of difference. Unfortunately, the passion for improvements made any honest appraisal difficult.

The promoters would certainly not tell people in the counties from which they hoped to solicit subscriptions that the railroad projects would not pay, and the people would not have listened to such defeatism. Occasionally, someone said the unimaginable—that a road would take years before it turned a profit—but only about other people's railroad ambitions. No town's editor bothered to ask whether *it* needed more. That a town could use all the railroads it could get was gospel. "Whenever you find a railroad being built," Chief Justice Joseph Brown of Georgia cried, "you may be assured that it is a good and safe investment."[11] This was rash advice.

In their faith and desperation, communities would pay any price and not bargain for better conditions or safeguards. With the projected line from New Orleans to Mobile and Chattanooga before their eyes, the citizens of Carrollton knew that many towns would vie for the road's advantages and that haggling with the directors would be ruinous. The city council had rejected the terms set by the corporation for making Carrollton a depot along the road, and the *Republican Standard*, without knowing what the terms were, called for a mass meeting to force the council to reconsider. No price was too great for the people to pay, the editor insisted. The *San Antonio Express*, on being told that the city had no money to subscribe to railroads, replied that the money must be borrowed, and, it implied, on any terms the financiers would give. Furthermore, delay in subscribing "[would] be fatal to our existence as a *city*."[12] Fear fostered a seller's market, and meant three things: first, towns and states committed themselves without examining the consequences in detail, and discovered too late that they had paid too high a price; second, railroads could extort communities into giving more generously than they would otherwise, by playing the aspirations of one village against those of another; third, the generous terms fostered a system of railroads built to appeal to local desires and not to fit the practical needs of Southern commerce.

The same desperation made upright men willing to wink at the methods by which their dreams were made reality. No city was so foolish as to spurn tainted money when no other kind was available. In Mississippi, a general aid law caused some Conservative ire, but not much. To charges that a "ring" had put through the bill, the Conservative *Liberty Herald* responded that true or false the accusations made no difference. The bill was splendid, said the editor, and Radicals had put through "at least one wise and politic law. God knows they stand sorely in need of it."[13] A powerful desire, this railroad mania, when it could dissolve all scruples and make even rabid Democrats utter praise for Republicanism!

Given such fervor as they found in every Southern community, the Republicans would have been fools not to have turned it to their use, and lunatics to oppose it. They were neither fools nor lunatics, unless belief in progress was a sort of lunacy, for their faith in improvements was so great that they outdid the Conservatives in their optimism. They identified their party with railroad aid and did so joyously. "It will . . . benefit the party more than any other measure that could possibly be brought before (the legislature)," the *Jackson Pilot* boasted of the general aid bill, "and will prove to the thinking people that the great Republican party is one of progress, of energy, of principles founded upon good, sound common sense."[14] Republicans conceded the political motive behind their support of subsidies, but it was never the only reason. As should already be clear, railroads were more than a political ploy: they were intrinsic to the Republican program of economic restoration and patriotic regeneration.

Aid came in many forms and went to achieve many different ends. States east of the Appalachians worked to forge new links with the Midwest, and those west of the Mississippi strove to tie themselves to the Pacific and attract the Western trade. Alabama hoped to open its coal and iron lands to industrial exploitation, while Mississippi worked to open its remote lands to cotton culture and to renew the fortunes of the river cities, Natchez and Vicksburg. Arkansas needed basic railroad communications, while Georgia, with a substantial network, sought to distribute the benefits of railroads to the southern and western counties which had none. Florida did not just need railroads to make its land available to settlers; it needed an east-west line to keep the state from disintegrating. Yet, for all these differences, which later chapters will examine in detail, the Southern governments adopted policies which were largely the same.

Preliminary to all forms of state aid was the necessity of incor-

poration. The fact that most states had no general incorporation
law—Florida, Alabama, and Arkansas were exceptions—meant that
each company needed a legislative dispensation to build, but that
dispensation brought with it an exclusive right to build a particular
line. This encouraged jobbery and the award of incorporation based
on political instead of economic considerations, but it also eliminated competitors for certain trade routes and gave one company
a chance to thrive where two would have bankrupted the surrounding communities and each other. By incorporation, the state endowed privileges no company could do without. A charter could
fix the rate of interest a railroad would pay on its bonds and could
allow stockholders limited liability for all debts. Articles of incorporation could give privileges for ninety-nine years. A charter could
also grant rights-of-way over state lands and the use of materials
off of those lands to build its track. Most states did not declare their
own right to set fares, and by default, it could be argued, left the
right to the company. Arkansas decreed that no line should be
forced to charge less than would insure the company a 15 percent
profit on the capital paid in. Most states limited the capital stock,
but sometimes promised to let the directors increase it if they chose;
sometimes they put no limit on how much the increase might be.[15]
Certain charters proclaimed the state's right to tax, but others made
no mention of the right.

At the same time, the restrictions the charters set up gave the
railroads a semblance of trustworthiness, by making it seem that
the state was keeping close watch on their activities. Many charters
purportedly guaranteed swift construction by compelling the work
to begin within one year and be completed within five.[16] Others,
like the Arkansas law, demanded that maps, affidavits, and financial
statements be submitted to the state regularly. By demanding a
certain amount in cash subscription before the corporation could
obtain legal status, the state seemed to preclude mountebank promoters, and by setting a maximum on capital stock—no matter how
vaguely—the government appeared to put restrictions on the crud-
est forms of stock watering. Thus the laws demanded little that the
railroads could not give, and gave them much in return, but that
made the laws no less essential—for without government consent,
not even the wealthiest businessman could raise the funds to build
his road.

For most railroads incorporation was only the beginning. Given
legal status, they needed the financial status that public benevolence
alone could give. One major source was local government. Some

state constitutions restricted the communities' rights to tax, spend, and pledge their credit, but in most cases, a railroad could force a referendum on the subject, whether county officers favored aid or not, and a majority of those voting could decide the question in favor of aid. Should a majority vote against aid, the promoters needed only to call another election. Some state laws gave special rights for railroads to seek local aid. North Carolina allowed cities to subscribe to the Edenton & Norfolk line, but said nothing of counties. South Carolina allowed counties to pledge aid to the Charleston, Georgetown & Conwayboro Railroad, but did not mention cities and towns. Other charters, even in these two states, let any corporate body subscribe. Some laws specified subscription in bonds, others allowed it in labor, lands, or materials. Some laws set no limit on the amount counties could subscribe, others allowed subscriptions up to 1, 2, or even 5 percent of the assessed value of real and personal property in the township. Under most laws, a majority or two-thirds of those voting could make the decision, but other laws in the same states required two out of every three qualified voters to favor subscription, an almost impossible provision to meet. At least one state law specified how much preferred stock the county should receive in return for its loan. So freely did Alabama grant exceptions to its law restricting county tax rates that the provision lost all meaning. When railroads wanted special rights to city streets or access to waterfronts, legislators granted them or allowed local officials to do so.[17]

Thus encouraged, towns and counties gave and did not calculate the cost. The city council of Montgomery issued $500,000 in bonds to aid the South & North Railroad, but insisted that they be sold for 90 cents on the dollar or more. This demand was not unreasonable; the state had the same requirement. However, no one would buy city bonds at such a rate. To please promoters, the council adjusted the minimum to 75 cents. The "black belt" counties of Alabama paid heavily. For example, Mobile spent more than $1 million on two lines. Small towns like Moulton took up $10,000 of stock on railroads. Shreveport subscribed $500,000 to the Memphis & Shreveport Railroad, and six parishes in Louisiana promised $730,000 to another line. Of $898,500 in local bonds issued in four cities and four counties of northeastern Texas, $838,500 went to railroads.[18]

Valuable as local government could be in initiating construction, private capital and financial aid by the state were essential. First of all, local bond issues sold badly. Vicksburg gave the Memphis &

Vicksburg company $90,000 in bonds, which could not be sold. The railroad used them as collateral to borrow $50,000 in cash.[19] Furthermore, localities generally restricted the use of the funds they raised to construction within the town or county, and this demand made railroad building uneven. A line might have private financing enough to go through one county without county bonds, but weak financial support in the next county where population was sparse and taxpayers apathetic. Not many counties could risk a railroad bypassing them, but those counties blocking the way between trade centers, and confident that a line would have to be built across them, did not always rush to give money when they did not need to.

Because of limits on local funds, railroads sought a steadier supply, and for this they turned to the state legislature for funds. This supply Southern legislators were quick to provide, and some states made outright subsidies. Louisiana subscribed $2.5 million to the stock in one line and $1.122 million to another. To encourage a road to Texas, it gave the New Orleans, Mobile & Texas Railroad $3 million in bonds. Texas promised two roads to the Pacific $6 million in state bonds, and in Alabama state authorities delivered $2 million in bonds to the Alabama & Chattanooga over and above all other aid. Subsidies excited controversy, and the safeguards put on them were enough to narrow the risk to taxpayers. Texas never had to pay any of the enacted grants, and of the Louisiana $3 million allowance, the railroad could not qualify for more than one-fourth of the allotment.[20]

More commonly, states tried to finance construction by loaning the states' credit rather than by making a grant, either by endorsing the railroads' bonds or by exchanging state for corporate bonds. Under this system, the company would complete a certain number of miles of track, generally 20, and become eligible for endorsement of its bonds at a certain amount per mile, or the government would issue its own bonds in return for an equal number of first- or second-mortgage company bonds, and would continue to do so in increments of 5 or 10 miles until the track was completed.

Although the state was liable for interest and principal on state bonds sold by the company, the state nonetheless expected the company to pay both. Should the railroad default on its responsibility to either, the state could take advantage of its lien on the line. If it held a first mortgage, the government could take over the road, run it, and even sell it to pay off the debt. If it held a second mortgage, the state would receive the amount left over once holders of the prior lien had sold the road and settled their own claims from the proceeds. Since little or nothing was often left over after the first mortgage had been satisfied, most Southern legislatures demanded a prior lien. Only Arkansas took no lien at all, and there the law permitted authorities to sequester the earnings of a defaulting railroad.

The amount of endorsement varied, but in no case was it sufficient to build a road without private backing. Mississippi promised $4,000 a mile, Texas $10,000, Louisiana $12,500, Florida $14,000, Georgia $15,000, Alabama $16,000, North Carolina up to $20,000. In Arkansas, railroads with land grants received $10,000 a mile and those without received $15,000. Arkansas and Alabama laws allowed any railroad to qualify once it met certain conditions (although Alabama made one exception to this rule). Elsewhere each railroad received a dispensation. Arkansas law left the award of bonds to the governor's discretion. Alabama and Georgia law compelled the governors to deliver the securities when the required mileage had been completed.[21]

With close supervision, the process of advancing funds protected states against loss, since they paid for no more track than had been laid, and could protect their interests by seizure and sale. The law, however, did not usually establish means of keeping a close supervision. Subsequent legislation seriously undermined what guarantees there were. Alabama, for example, supplemented its general aid law with other grants. It raised the South & North's endorsement to $22,000 a mile, endorsed $2.5 million of bonds in the Mobile & Montgomery, which had already been built, and added $300,000 to the loan to the Montgomery & Eufaula Railroad. In no case did the state demand or receive increased security for the increased debt.[22]

In the long run, the Radicals learned, land grants and tax exemptions were more politic than endorsements, though not nearly as effective in attracting capital. Loss of revenues or public domain might ultimately cost the state as much as endorsement of bonds, but the loss was less visible and less immediate. It did not show up in the budget as a direct or contingent expense, and did not appear to add to tax burdens. The price state lands would fetch in the future was at best problematic. As a result, Conservatives would not object to either policy. Georgia legislation freed from taxation rolling stock in certain railroads until they had been completed. Mississippi collected taxes on all railroads, but reserved them to pay the companies' debts; the revenue collected would go to nothing else until the corporations paid an 8 percent dividend. Alabama gave a five-year exemption on company lands, and South Carolina made all new capital invested in railroads or manufactures tax-free for five years. These laws, however, were exceptional; for the most part legislatures retained the taxing power. They may have had no choice, for state constitutions insisted on equal and uniform taxation of property.[23]

The Republicans had less trouble granting lands. Only Texas' constitution forbade that, and in 1872, the voters removed the ban. A year before, the legislators had anticipated this decision by allowing one railroad to exchange its subsidy for twenty-four sections of land per mile should the fundamental law of the state be changed. As a reform governor, Elisha Baxter of Arkansas opposed subsidies, but happily signed into law a bill giving railroads more than a million acres of public lands and all property forfeited to the state for taxes in the next five years. "The donation costs the state nothing," explained the *Little Rock Gazette*, "—it costs the people nothing."[24] In fact, land grants could be worth a great deal. That was why railroads accepted them so readily. Excellent collateral for loans, land grants added an incentive to build the line, for with a railroad run across them, sale values would appreciate sharply. Time would only add to their worth, and this fact made them a much more reliable source than state or county bonds.

Once established, a railroad aid policy took on momentum not easily checked. On the one hand, generosity to one company encouraged all the others. Applicants for admission to the Treasury always outnumbered beneficiaries. On the other hand, aid gave the state a stake in a railroad's success and spurred new legislation to protect the public investment. In most cases, these laws tried to salvage companies by canceling out what few safeguards the government had against loss. By 1873, many legislatures were debating the issue of "relief" for struggling enterprises; in South Carolina, the issue troubled politics from the first. There, lawmakers gave up the first lien on the Greenville & Columbia and took a second, so that the directors could negotiate a new bond issue. If the company went bankrupt, the state would lose $1,426,545.80, but the alternative was to abandon hope in a line through the mountains to Tennessee. A year later, the legislature canceled its lien on the Blue Ridge Railroad for the same reasons and assumed responsibility for the state bonds the company had pledged to pay.[25]

Those two railroad projects have a larger significance, for, as with so many other aid schemes, they were inherited from antebellum governments. Both lines had been built during the 1850s with a friendly government encouraging them; the Blue Ridge had obtained stock subscriptions. Postwar Conservatives added to the companies' support, and Republicans at first insisted that they were simply keeping faith with the promoters. What was true in South Carolina was true elsewhere: if the antebellum governments had made promises, the Reconstruction coalition would fulfill the promises—and go beyond them. Thus the Montgomery & Eufaula owed $30,000 to the Alabama internal improvements fund. Republicans waived payment and let it borrow more. The Tennessee & Coosa owed money to two different state funds. Alabama released it from responsibility for both on condition that it take no more state aid—a condition that the company evaded by turning some of its mileage into a new road, which became eligible for endorsements. By not building enough mileage before deadlines set in the land grant laws, railroads forfeited their right to public domain, but legislatures revived the grants and extended the time limits.[26]

Most of the states had taken stock in railroads or taken over defaulting lines by 1868, but the Republicans preferred to lose a state investment long since given rather than to leave the lines incomplete or inoperative. Between 1868 and 1872, they arranged the sale of almost every railroad property in their custody. In selling the New Orleans, Opelousas & Great Western in 1869, Louisiana, New Orleans, and the parishes lost nearly $2.6 million. A year later, Colonel Henry S. McComb paid $461,000 for some 114,000 shares of public stock in the New Orleans, Jackson & Great Northern. That was less than a quarter its par value, and perhaps half its market value. Florida sold two roads under execution for $1,415,000, and in payment accepted at par bonds worth 35 cents on the dollar. Even then the purchasers did not have enough, and in defiance of the law gave a check for a third of the amount. The check proved worthless. To buy the two major lines of South Carolina, the governor and his cronies induced the legislature to set up a sinking fund commission with power to sell the state's interest in any corporation. The day after the bill passed, the commission sold the shares of the Greenville & Columbia to themselves at $2.75 a share; the market price was around $4.00 a share, and this purchase gave them a majority of the stock. In 1871, carpetbagger John J. Patterson bought the state's controlling interest in the Blue Ridge Railroad for a dollar a share, or one-tenth of 1 percent of the state's original investment.[27] Public aid, clearly, went hand in hand with the states' retreat from mixed enterprise.

A vast new program based on Southern traditions, a dramatic increase in government action even as the same lawmakers tried to disengage themselves from responsibility for administering the roads, a program to make an entirely new South and to appeal to those who longed for the cotton economy and prosperity of the old South—the "railroad mania" must seem bewildering to later generations. It is easy to dismiss the laws that came from it as irresponsible. Certainly, the liberality appears misguided, in retrospect. Yet, there does not seem to have been much else for Southerners to do. They needed economic regeneration, and needed it as quickly as possible. They trusted in railroads to achieve that end. Had they known how little their faith in such means would be justified, they might have been a little more cautious, but only a little. Great as the risks from railroad aid were, the risks from any other policy of comparable effect were greater. Disastrous as government programs to foster construction might be, they could not compare with the disaster Southerners felt they faced by doing nothing at all.

CHAPTER 3

An Imaginative Reinterpretation of the Law

That clause was inserted not so much to encourage State aid as to restrict State aid.

H. K. McCay

WHEN the Hale county court met early in 1870, N. B. Forrest of the Selma, Marion & Memphis could not have helped feeling elated. Six months before, local citizens had voted his railroad a $60,000 grant for construction. The court's issuance of the necessary bonds should have been a mere formality, but it did not turn out that way. With his endorsement essential to the bonds' validation, Probate Judge W. T. Blackford withheld his signature. At a formal hearing, Forrest's attorney produced many legal arguments. "Sir," the jurist burst out, "I don't care a damn about your nunc pro tuncs, your nolens volens or your amicus curis: I am not going to sign them bonds." So angry was the attorney that he threw himself at the judge, who waved a revolver at him. In the tumult that followed, Forrest managed to wrest the gun from Blackford and take a grip on his arm. "Wal, Judge," he drawled, "I don't care a damn whether you sign them bonds nunc pro tunc, nolens volens or amicus curis; you are going to sign 'em." They went into a back room, and when they came out a short time later, both men were in excellent humor. The judge's view of what the law expected of him had changed dramatically, too. Without a qualm, he now put his name to the securities.[1]

The judge's willingness to temper his interpretation of the laws to suit the corporations' needs was typical of his time. Excellent laws had been passed, but many set conditions which protected the state's interest and restrained promoters. In the enthusiasm for construction that characterized the postwar South, few citizens had patience with restrictions. Politicians worked to undo limits written into the states' fundamental law, promoters accepted the benefits of state aid more dutifully than the obligations, and officials with a duty to enforce the statutes let them be thwarted instead, thus hastening railroad expansion.² It is hard to say whether railroad construction was advanced more by the acts Republicans placed on the books or by their persistent evasion and violation of them.

Wherever else blame for this laxity may be placed, it should not fall on the authors of the Republican constitutions. The provisions they wrote subjected applicants for railroad aid to stiffer requirements than did the prewar statutes. In Georgia, Judge H. K. McCay pointed to the section allowing the pledge of state credit as his handiwork and boasted, "That clause was inserted not so much to encourage State aid as to restrict State aid." It forbade the government's subscription to company stock and put three conditions on any railroad seeking support. First, the enterprise "shall be an enterprise not merely local," said McCay; second, it must be one in which private parties had invested twice the sum they wanted from the government; third, the company had to complete 20 miles of track before it could become eligible for a subsidy. The same wariness shaped constitutions in other states as well.³ Undoubtedly, the delegates wanted to develop the South, but they insisted that it be done with circumspection.

The same could not be said for their successors. Republicanism fed the growing mania for railroad construction, and the interpretations that the first Reconstruction governments put on the constitutions differed sharply from Judge McCay's interpretation. As every precaution was obscured or flouted, it seemed that the constitutions had been written solely to release all the popular energy for development that antebellum leaders had kept on a tight rein. The fact that Mississippi could not lend its credit did not keep lawmakers from promising railroads $4,000 a mile, a promise conditional on there being money in the Treasury. If there were no money, the lines could take treasurers' warrants and return with them later when money *was* available or else use the notes to settle old debts with the state. Neither Mississippi nor Alabama could give state lands, but they could and did sell them for a pittance. Alabama's constitution restricted bank powers, but legislators voted to give the Mobile & Ohio banking rights without the usual restrictions placed on other financial institutions.⁴ Such ingenuity did not show that the lawmakers misunderstood the fundamental laws of the state. They understood them all too well, well enough to see that strict constitutional obedience would block railroad development. Every legal ambiguity had to be exploited, if constituent needs were to be satisfied.

Constitutional provisions could have been more specific, but no matter how clear these provisions were, railroad spokesmen could twist the words to suit corporate ends. Alabama could not lend its credit except on "undoubted security," but what made security "undoubted"? To State Senator G. T. McAfee, the only safeguard would be a lien on the road and evidence that the line would sell for more than the state had advanced. His colleagues settled for a corporate promise to set up a sinking fund someday—a "mere promise without security for its performance, which . . . may or may not be performed, and therefore amounts to nothing," said McAfee in disgust.[5]

Georgia's restrictions on lending state credit were evaded in one case with the argument that the state was not giving the Brunswick & Albany her credit, but *selling* it "for a fair, valuable and adequate consideration." The aid was meant, they claimed, as repayment for iron taken from the road in wartime. Opponents replied that the Confederate government already had paid for much of the iron and that the company had invested the money in cotton from which it had turned a handsome profit.

The constitutional restrictions were meant to protect the state from loss, but whether any aid law met this condition depended on to whom one spoke. Opponents of the Brunswick & Albany claimed that the railroad could not be sold for the amount Georgia had granted it. Proponents declared it "well known . . . that no road in the State can be purchased or built for any such amount."[6] Whether a railroad could ever be sold for as much as it had cost to build was a question friends of railroads in the lower South did not often address. Nevertheless, it was crucial to the meaning of the phrase "undoubted security."

Still, all such legal interpretation left room for debate. One *could* read constitutional provisions to give railroads the benefit of the doubt. Adherence to the letter of the law might have been just as much a misreading of Republican intentions, and would have prevented the enactment of any sort of financial aid. But there were other times when politicians did not gloss the meaning of the law; they broke it outright. Perhaps they were unfamiliar with the constitutions on which their authority rested, or they simply did not care. Possibly they desired credit for liberal measures, which the courts could take the blame for invalidating. In view of the states' immediate needs and the public clamor for action, the lawmakers must have considered their lawbreaking as a sin committed to promote a much greater public good.

In 1870, Louisiana voters amended their constitution to hold the state debt to $25 million, but the next legislature continued to aid railroads and commit the state credit as if no barrier existed. North Carolina's fundamental law required that a pledge of credit be put to a popular vote and be paid for with special taxes. In several cases, Republicans ignored these conditions. The Eastern & Western company's grant was never submitted to a popular vote. Pretending to be an unfinished road instead of a new one, the Chatham Railroad evaded a referendum, though it got $2 million in additional state aid without the legislature imposing a special tax. Since the Chatham was actually complete and was laying a track in a new direction, it stirred controversy. In December 1868, the New York Stock Exchange threw company securities off the boards. To remedy its oversight and save other railroad securities from a like fate, the legislature hastily levied special taxes to redeem the bonds of the Williamston & Tarboro, the Western North Carolina, and the Northwestern North Carolina, exchanged the Chatham's bond issue for a stock subscription, and recalled the bonds already issued to railroads. Even with these reforms, the state fell short of satisfying constitutional niceties. In early 1869, the state supreme court ruled the Chatham Railroad charter unconstitutional.[7]

In some cases, backers of railroad aid were guilty less of sophistry than of slovenliness. Arkansas' railroad aid law put the state guarantee on endorsed bonds, but did not specifically declare the obvious: that should the companies fail to pay the interest on those securities, the government would assume responsibility for it. Alabama's general aid law had the same defect. In Forida, critics later insisted that while the state might have the right to give aid, nothing in the constitution established the right to trade government bonds for company first-mortgage bonds; yet without that provision the subsidy program was undone.[8]

Certain oversights were serious enough to undermine the validity of the whole policy. In Arkansas, legal blundering went to the heart of railroad aid. Under the state constitution, no act could take effect until ninety days after the adjournment of the legislative session during which the act had passed, unless the law itself said otherwise. The 1868 aid act made no such provision when it set up a referendum on the subsidy issue. The referendum took place six months before legislative adjournment. The November vote endorsing aid by nearly 5 to 1 lacked legal basis; that is, was nine months too soon.[9]

Legislators were not solely responsible. In Georgia, they invited the collusion of local governments by passing laws allowing county subscription, when the constitution gave no such right. A Mississippi law provided for a referendum on subscription to the Nashville & Vicksburg, but applied it to only part of the county—an unconstitutional maneuver. It was almost as an aside that the governor's veto noted that the line benefiting did not even exist. In more than one case, federal courts annulled a city bond issue because its charter had no specific provision justifying internal improvements subscriptions.[10]

The willingness to sacrifice legal forms to the cause of railroad expansion affected those who administered the laws as much as it did those enacting them. Weak in some ways, the aid laws had been strong in others, with provisions requiring good construction, responsible private financing, and sale of state securities at a fair price. For every loophole or giveaway in a statute, there were a dozen specifics that the railroad had to meet to obtain all the benefits it desired. Without enforcement, however, the regulations could lose all meaning and often did.

Frequently, before a company could apply for aid, the laws demanded that private parties build a certain mileage, usually 20, and that the track be completed and equipped. Invariably, the governor had a moral if not legal responsibility to see that the work was done, but not all executives took time to investigate. When the Democrats looked into Georgia railroad endorsements, they found that the Brunswick & Albany had received aid before its first section had been completed, that the governor had endorsed 240 bonds of the Bainbridge, Cuthbert & Columbus before 1 mile of track was finished, and that he had put his signature on $100,000 in Cartersville & Van Wert bonds when less than 2 miles were completed and another $100,000 when 3 miles were ready for traffic. When Alabama Democrats found similar maladministration, they blamed their governor almost as much as his Republican predecessor. Most Alabama roads swore falsely that they had met the state's requirements for private funding. In fact, the East Alabama & Cincinnati never even opened books of subscription, and much construction had been done on credit and was never paid for. Clearly, respected businessmen and promoters bore a heavy responsibility for the delusion of the state.[11]

The laws might require that railroad aid bonds be sold for a minimum figure set by the state, but these provisions were hard to enforce and became harder as securities changed hands. The original purchaser might not have paid the legal minimum, but a later owner might have paid face value. The state could not check these facts thoroughly, and indeed to have done so would have revealed enough mismanagement to have sent bond prices still lower and the doubtful future of many roads in which the state had a commitment more bleak than ever. J. C. Stanton insisted that the Alabama & Chattanooga had complied with the law that forbade sale at less than 90 cents on the dollar. He proved incorrect, but perhaps he was a bit more truthful when he added, "I do not suppose there is another company in Alabama that can say as much. It's well known in financial circles that companies have been hypothecating their endorsed bonds at rates far below the minimum price fixed by law for their sale. Perhaps it would be safe to say that bonds have been pledged at forty, fifty and sixty cents on the dollar."[12]

Where the revenues from bond sales went was another problem that interested the governments less than it should have. In Georgia, H. I. Kimball used bond proceeds to erect an opera house in Atlanta. Bond revenues also helped companies win friends in the legislature through bribery or legitimate lobbying. In its imaginative use of funds, the Western & Atlantic outdid every contender. Officials provided one agent with a silver tea set, cutlery, and a shotgun, and listed the expenses as "assorted iron" and "block tin."[13]

States established guidelines for the quality of construction, but these, too, depended on government enforcement or corporate scruples. Under Alabama law, the railroad was to use rails weighing at least 50 pounds to the yard and bring embankments and excavations to "a proper slope." Culverts were to be of "substantial masonry," and bridges and trestles were to be "substantial, and of the most improved plan." On the East Alabama & Cincinnati, investigators found iron below the legal minimum weight as well as many other flaws. The contractors had not fastened rails by the "approved pattern." Their culverts were partly wood. Some trestles were temporary. The Selma & Gulf, Alabama & Chattanooga, and South & North had like deficiencies. Had other states set up procedures for investigation before they made endorsements, they might have found the same situation, but most governments did not look into the quality of work.[14]

Where laws existed, authorities showed little interest in their enforcement. Railroad presidents might file statements under oath about the lines' conditions, but administrators treated these as mere clerical formalities. They did not look for perjury. Endorsement was automatic. The Chatham Railroad filed a mortgage with North Carolina that included lands the company did not own; the mortgage was not filed with the secretary of state, as the statute of incorporation mandated. Nevertheless, the governor issued the bonds without debate. One might have expected that authorities would keep careful accounts of their bond transactions, but the governors of Alabama and Georgia did not even do that. Alabama officials could only hazard a guess as to how many bonds had been issued and to whom. At one point, Governor William Smith's private secretary asked railroad presidents and New York bankers for some record of how many bonds the governor had endorsed for them and for a list of their serial numbers. The records remained incomplete and unreliable, indicating the governor's lack of interest in a rigid accounting. His successor decried the disorder, but did not disentangle the state's finances. By custom, once paid for, bonds and interest coupons were returned to the state and canceled, but between 1870 and 1872 there was no record of such transactions. Late in 1871, the State Treasury received $4,500 in bonds, with every coupon still attached. So bad were the records that the interest due on these bonds had been sent to New York every six months and their coupons not taken as receipts for payment; where the extra money had gone no one knew.[15]

Government officials would have insisted that the laws may have been administered incorrectly but not fraudulently. Some acts with no legal sanction were committed to protect the state's interest. Called to testify before an investigating committee, Alabama State Treasurer Arthur Bingham conceded that he had once issued more bonds than a railroad deserved, but made clear that the irregularity was as prudent as it was trifling. Alabama had not lost a penny by it. Governor Robert B. Lindsay of Alabama acted outside the law when he induced the state's financial agents to advance the Selma, Marion & Memphis $16,000 in bonds. Had he not done so, Lindsay protested, the road would have defaulted on its interest and become a costly ward of the state. Lindsay had broken the law and would do so again, but he had saved the taxpayer expense and enhanced the value of the state's lien. Had he done the same for the Alabama & Chattanooga, when its directors appealed for a similar abrogation of the statutes in return for additional security, Alabama might have been saved the substantial cost that the government's enforcement of its rights eventually brought about. By standing too firmly on his legal right to negotiate bonds, Florida's comptroller prevented the governor from making a sale. On other occasions, states would have gained more by a looser interpretation of the law.[16]

There was often little that governors could do about lawbreaking.

They were not experts in railroad construction or financial detail, and at times the law was as puzzling to them as to the taxpayers. Given any excuse to do nothing, they seized on it gratefully, and the legislatures gave them such an excuse by limiting executive power. Governors were never very strong, and in North Carolina, they lacked even a veto power. They confronted legislatures eager to lead and prepared to impeach officers who stood in their way. To challenge the railroads in the early years of Reconstruction was a splendid way to shatter a governor's popularity and to wreck the financial stability of projects that were developing the state. Statesmanship and self-interest both seemed to advise timidity, and some governors excelled in diffidence. Alabama railroads collected aid for mileage already laid down by other companies and obtained through consolidation. They also had built some track before the aid laws' passage. Did either portion of track count in that first 20 mile stretch to be ready before the state could give support? The governor's secretary voiced confidence that whatever interpretation the promoters favored, the executive would have to accept. The law gave him no discretionary power in bond endorsement.[17] Rather than stir up controversy, Georgia and Florida executives preferred to trust the companies' professions, dubious though these may have been.

Not all governors were like those in Alabama and Georgia. Some took a steady interest in enforcing the law to the letter. Edmund Davis of Texas even tried to apply the constitutional ban on land grants to acreage given under antebellum laws. His arguments, however, found no favor in federal courts, where one judge ruled his attempts an unconstitutional impairment of the right of contract. Governor W. W. Holden had no right to withhold bonds, but he did so when the state supreme court ruled against the Chatham Railroad. His obstinacy brought the case into court and led to more bonds being ruled illegal. James L. Alcorn of Mississippi tried to persuade the General Assembly to erect a board of public works that would inspect railroads and have the right to condemn their construction. Lax when their own friends were concerned in a swindle, Robert Scott of South Carolina, Henry C. Warmoth of Louisiana, and Rufus B. Bullock of Georgia could also exercise the veto freely when their allies were not involved, and their messages included some of the most ringing indictments of badly made law and corrupt motivation. Even Governor Smith, slovenly though his record-keeping was, complained that he had not been given powers sufficient to look into railroads' failure to meet legal standards, and begged for reform in the aid laws.[18]

If the governors deserve extenuation, how much more the legislators merit explanation, even defense! The lawmakers were not usually trying to defraud the state. They simply did not care whether the state was cheated or not—as long as the road was built. Probably more than a few knew that the state would lose money on the roads, but it was a small price to pay for the long-range benefits that the company would bring the state and the Republican party. True, legislative errors showed carelessness and haste. Lawmakers had not given the technical aspects of the law enough consideration because they lacked the experience that would allow them to spot the defects in their own statutes. Furthermore, they were not inclined to learn better. Some of them had invested in lines, but few understood the intricacies of construction or the complexities of bond issues. For these facts they relied on the promoters, many of whom knew less about constructing lines than they imagined. In some cases, they deliberately left constitutional scruples to the governor. When Warmoth vetoed one railroad bill, the Louisiana General Assembly that had overwhelmingly passed it just as decisively sustained the veto.[19]

The fault lay not with the laws as much as with the way they were carried out. Governor Smith, for example, was mistaken when he blamed a general aid law for the abuse of the state's generosity. It allowed any road to share in the benefits once certain conditions were met, he noted, regardless of the road's importance to the commonwealth. Smith suggested that Alabama replace general aid with special acts for individual corporations. Unfortunately, Smith misunderstood the problem as well as the solution. The danger was that the state might lose its investment if the road could not pay its own way. Special aid laws would not protect Alabama from this risk because the laws would not pass on the basis of which railroad most merited aid, but which had the best lobby. The real solution, therefore, was a general aid law placing specific conditions on the railroads aided in terms of material used for construction, time allowed to complete the main line, number of miles to be completed each year, amount of private funds required before the road could apply for state aid, and guarantees given the government. All these conditions and more the Republican legislature of 1870 put on Alabama railroads. That they were poorly enforced was not only the legislature's fault; and the violation of general aid laws is hardly an argument against passing such laws in the first place.

The railroads had abused the law, but again there were mitigating circumstances. With some notorious exceptions, the lawbreakers did not act out of criminal intent. They simply wanted to finish work as quickly as possible and to begin collecting the revenue from freight and passengers that would assure the company of the funds needed to meet its obligations. At times, the law set deadlines for completion that made construction all the more hasty. A company might begin with confidence in its ability to finish 20 miles in time to obtain matching funds, but would encounter delays. Perhaps backers would retract earlier promises, or local and state bonds would sell for less than expected. A dry summer might delay shipments by river, and workers would be idle for weeks. Whatever the circumstances, directors would find themselves further behind schedule and more in debt than anticipated. They would need state aid sooner and in larger amounts than they had thought possible. If there were no deadline, they might still rush to complete 20 miles and collect the money desperately needed. A time limit on eligibility for state revenues added to their panic. Failure to meet the time limit might mean loss of aid or forfeit of land already granted and perhaps sold, or even annulment of the act of incorporation. Many railroads found themselves in such a predicament, and it makes their recklessness easier to understand.

In desperation, the promoters would abandon all care in doing what the state expected of them. They built rude trestles to support trains for a few months and made grades steeper than were safe. Until new iron could be paid for out of public funds, they might use iron from other tracks or iron rusted from exposure. Contractors would make a roadbed fit for track and not much else, and would leave repairs until the company had made revenue from hauling freight. This was what the commissioners appointed to examine the Alabama & Chattanooga meant when they described portions as "good and well-built as any new road of the same material," and added that the road would need filling and draining for two or three years to come. This was also why J. C. Stanton could defend his line as "in first-class condition for a new road," and then could admit that 7 miles had been put down only temporarily, 40 miles needed ballasting, and the road would cost $225,000 to become fit for regular service.[20]

It is also important to note how trifling most infractions were. The iron that the Alabama commissioners had cited for less than minimum weight had come within two ounces of meeting state requirements: a fifth of 1 percent of total weight. The company had bought the rails on the assumption that they met standards. The error, therefore, was the foundry's. One railroad had indeed built culverts only partly of stone, but the commissioners added that all were of a "substantial character."[21] The Arkansas referendum was fraudulent only in a pettifogger's sense. Six months more would not have reversed so overwhelming a public sentiment as the vote revealed. The letter of the law had been broken, but the spirit remained intact.

Finally, what constitutes a fraudulent use of bonds depends on what definition of fraud one cares to adopt. In the popular mind, every railroad that did not complete its line was guilty of fraud because it had failed to keep its promises. Men more versed in law would have limited the charge to companies deliberately failing to comply with their agreements, with intent to deceive. The former definition included most roads that accepted state aid, the latter exonerated most lines of anything worse than bad judgment. Although companies might use money realized from endorsed bonds for something besides construction, did that constitute fraud? In 1885, Alabama officials took I. T. Burr and his former associates to court for just such a criminal diversion of securities. The Supreme Court was unimpressed, for the real issue, Chief Justice Morison Waite decided, was whether the company had spent as much on actual construction as it received in state aid. Plaintiff and defendant agreed that it had. "There is no pretence that the road cost less than the value of the bonds," said Waite. "Consequently, if the bonds were not used to build the road, other funds belonging to the company must have been, and it was proper to treat the bonds as a substitute for other funds in the treasury of the company."[22] The state could not show that a fraud had been committed.

Even where fraud and violation of law could be shown, the state's proper response seemed unclear. One might argue that the government should react in proportion to the enormity of the offense. To requests for total repudiation of Alabama railroad securities, Democratic Governor Robert Lindsay made the logical reply that the law did not punish unlawful acts with a release of the state from all liability, but only from its duty to endorse the road's bonds in the future or to legitimate the illegalities. Otherwise, innocent bondholders would suffer. But bonds illegally endorsed must not be recognized. If the road was entitled to 4,720 bonds and had issued 5,200, the excess "represents a fiction, not a road, and the holder could by investigation have ascertained that fact."[23]

Subsequent court decisions did not go as far as Lindsay in renouncing state liability. In *Mason Young et al.* v. *the Montgomery and Eufaula Railroad*, a federal judge ruled that bonds were not void just because they had been endorsed too soon or endorsed for more than the maximum amount per mile. The state aid law might say that the bonds should yield no more than 8 percent interest per year, while the bonds themselves promised 8 percent in gold, a larger sum with gold over par, but that did not allow the state to escape all liability. In the eastern division of Arkansas, Circuit Judge Dillon made a similar decision. The law allowed roads to issue 6 percent bonds, but the Arkansas Central had assured 10 percent interest; this difference did not invalidate a city's obligation to honor its subscription to the road, since the law set up no penalties for the railroad's violation of its charter provisions. At best the city could force the road to pay no more than 6 percent interest on its securities.[24]

The legal implications of the railroads' legal violations are less important than their political implications. Right as the corporations might be judged by the courts, valid as their bonds might remain, most Southerners felt betrayed by these violations. They were not lawyers and did not think like them, and they had a strong distaste for paying for more than they had received. As long as the corporations built roads that ran efficiently and the state seemed safe from loss, taxpayers might wink at violations of the law and subordinate everything to the practical result of railroad construction. When the companies did not deliver all they promised, citizens were quick to begrudge the debts they had contracted and to highlight every flaw in legislation and administration to escape expense.

Clarendon, Arkansas was one such aggrieved party. In 1871, its officers subscribed $15,000 to the Arkansas Central Railway. When progress on the line halted, the city sued to have the subscription invalidated. Lawyers argued that the corporation had never had a legal existence, since it was formed from the consolidation of two companies, one of which they pronounced fictitious. The 1868 law allowing railroads to merge applied to "connecting railroads," and the two that consolidated in this case were parallel with the same termini. One of the original lines had been created under an act permitting all towns and cities to subscribe, but lawyers pleaded that this act could not apply to Clarendon, which had not come in existence until four years later. The district court dismissed these arguments almost scornfully, but its decision is less significant than the fact that such arguments got to court at all. What Clarendon could do, any town that felt betrayed would dare do.[25]

Under such conditions, the carelessness with which the railroad aid programs were fashioned and the contempt with which they were administered became more serious. The law could be interpreted creatively to further construction, but when the interest of the taxpayers outweighed that of the promoters in the politicians' minds, it suddenly became clear that the statutes could be read just as creatively in the interest of strict construction. Then the benefit of the doubt went to the public rather than the corporations. It became not only difficult to adopt the liberal view of the laws, but nearly impossible to understand how any lawmaker honestly could have embraced the looser interpretation. Surely, the weak safeguards and lax enforcement must have had a sinister explanation: local self-interest, corporate and legislative venality, and a deliberate scheme to milk the Treasury for personal gain. There was just enough truth to each of these charges to make them seem applicable to the entire railroad aid program.

The most cautious administration of the law could not have prevented legal challenge, but it would have made one more difficult. As long as any excuse was available, it was not necessary to have a reason for objecting to the law, but Radicals gave plenty of excuses and reasons. Even so, Southerners would not have had recourse to either had they been satisfied with the results of railroad aid. The real reason that the laws were overthrown was not the carelessness with which they were enforced, but the inability of the railroads, within the terms of the laws, to fulfill the promises they had made to the Southern people.

PART TWO

A Covenant of Public Works: Legislating for the Railroads

CHAPTER 4

"Railroad Fevers" and the Party Line at the Capitols

Now I take it that this is a very queer bill where both parties
crack the whip for the same purpose and to the same end.
                    Charles Lowell to the Louisiana House

STATE legislatures in the nineteenth century were a proving ground
for mediocre men who, by obtaining prominence there, might be
allowed to exercise their limited talents in more responsible positions. Reconstruction General Assemblies were no different. Without respect to race or party, they were usually conclaves of bickering,
disorderly representatives who enjoyed levity at the public expense
and, according to one Republican, often knew no more of their
duties than "a hog does of theology."[1] "The fact is, sir, this House
has done nothing but play for the last month," one representative
cried; "we have done nothing for the interest of the people; we
have wasted their money, . . . and I will tell you, . . . if they could
be here . . . not one of these Representatives would ever be elected
again." When the House Military Committee chairman interrupted
discussion of a revenue bill to toot on a 25 cent trumpet, or Democrats began chewing and hurling spitballs at other members, or,
as occurred in Texas, a member was allowed to ride a jackass onto
the floor of the House, the possibility for calm deliberation became
remote. When so many members did not understand the rules and
attended the sessions in a boisterous and drunken condition, or
drew revolvers to prevent their expulsion by the sergeant at arms,
business came to a standstill.[2]

Of course, no legislature was as bad as its worst members and
worst moments might indicate. No one looking at the legislative
journals or the bound statutes for the postwar years can fail to be
impressed by the diligence and occasional statesmanship of the
Republicans. But alongside statesmanlike acts, the documents show
laws badly drawn or in violation of Reconstruction constitutions.
Both the journals and the public press display legislative frivolity
and disorder.

63

Democrats blamed the excesses on Negro voting and Radical officeholding. However, this was only partly correct. Ignorant and inexperienced men from both parties *had* been elevated; but the problem was as severe in Conservative assemblies, all-white gatherings, and Northern legislatures. A better explanation might be the rapid turnover in elected officials.

Americans did not favor a seniority system among elected officials, but the tendency to allow public servants short tenure was especially pronounced in the postwar South. There, wartime casualties, the disqualification for office of much of the white political elite, and the enfranchisement of blacks brought in a new set of leaders on the local level. Before the war, a legislator might serve three terms in either house; afterward, the customary tenure was one. Not only did Republicans introduce new men to power, they replaced them every two years with more new men. Thus every time a lawmaker gained enough experience to understand the legislative process, he was forced to give way to another. Only three of one hundred Arkansas representatives were returned in 1870, and only four of the members elected that year were reelected in 1872. Not one survived all three elections. Only in South Carolina did the regular turnover fall below 80 percent. General inexperience made the standing committees all the more important to the efficiency of legislative business. There, a few members might become experts at some limited field of public policy; consequently, their opinions in that field would carry special weight. Yet the same lack of incumbents that hindered the House ensured that untried men would fill the committees. When the new Mississippi House met in 1872, every member of the fifteen committees was newly assigned. Nor did past legislative experience automatically entitle the legislator of any state to his former position. Incumbents had no special right to chairmanships, not even on the committees to which they had been previously assigned. Of seventeen incumbents in the 1873 Louisiana legislature, only two received chairmanships. In some states, a committee member could not depend on keeping his assignment until the final adjournment. Republicans would reconstitute committees at the session's end, and in Louisiana, the House made and unmade its committees three times in little over a year.[3]

Giving every aspirant a chance at political tenure may have been a praiseworthy philosophy; rotation in office had long been a democratic ideal, and Republicans were proud of a system that took officeholding out of the hands of a political elite and gave laborers and field hands a chance to serve as well as lawyers, merchants, and small farmers; but it wrought cataclysmic effects on the subsidy policy. In some areas, legislative naïveté might not have been a serious drawback. When state revenues were at stake, however, the government needed skilled lawmakers who knew how to draft a bill as well as spot a defect in proposed legislation. The South needed officials well acquainted with corporate law to protect the states' interest. Men were needed who knew how much a railroad would cost to build and who could also tell from company books how much chance there was of a line being constructed without ending up in receivership or bankruptcy. The public interest was too important to leave to lobbyists and promoters to define. For define it they did.

Unable to master the intricacies of railroad bills, members needed outside advice, which corporate officials were delighted to provide. Thus, in Texas, the two major subsidy laws were written by railroad executives. Marshall O. Roberts, executive of the Texas Pacific, wrote the bill granting his company large amounts of cash and land. It passed just as he submitted it. The vice-president of the International & Great Northern Railroad prepared the measure endowing his line with $10,000 a mile.[4]

Legislative inexperience had other ugly effects; namely, it undermined the legal basis for railroad aid. Many of the laws passed were of uncertain constitutionality. Others had provisions so impracticable that they were quickly repealed. As already noted, some of this lawmaking was deliberate. Other oversights, however, were mistakes of inexperience, a slovenliness in writing statutes that only time and tenure would remove.

Inexperience also may have had serious psychological effects on the Republican majorities. Legislators may have been all the more irresponsible because they had nothing to lose by it. Whether they served the public well or ill, they might not be renominated and probably would not be reelected. If they voted special privileges to railway companies or outlandish perquisites to themselves, who would call them to account? Such irresponsibility may even have encouraged bribery and freebooty. As long as lawmakers could not expect to turn public service into a career, and as long as Democrats refused employment to active Republicans, the transient lawmaker might as well make as much out of his office as he could: he would need it in the lean years to come. A corporation given special aid would prove grateful. Then again, for those men prepared to beat the odds and seek reelection, the knowledge of how poor their chances of success were may have persuaded them to use every inducement at their disposal. For example, corporation given aid might repay the debt at election time, or a county given not just one railroad project but several might drop considerations of faction and party to return its benefactor. Insecurity of tenure made it more difficult for the ambitious legislator to resist the railroad mania. Needing leadership also, the novitiate representatives may have put added faith in the party line. When the Republican majority made aid a part of their program, the new men may have followed out of blind obedience.

Finally, large turnover in office destroyed all sense of continuity in policy from session to session. The House might favor railroad aid enthusiastically one year and repudiate it the next, even though the same party held control of the chamber in both cases. Such repentance characterized South Carolina's passage of the Revenue Bond Scrip Bill in 1872, and its abrogation of that law the following year. Thus the lack of veterans led to instability and inconsistency in railroad aid policies. This, in turn, had a serious effect on railroad financing.

In the bear-garden atmosphere of the General Assemblies, the committees—whatever their deficiencies—did most of the serious work on railroad bills, and, more often than not, they did their work well. Often reports for or against a bill gave substantial reasons for the committee's decision, while a minority report could give strong arguments for the other side. A committee report was not necessarily the last word on a bill. Sometimes the House and Senate would propose more amendments or modify those which the committee had suggested. Occasionally, legislators would reject the conclusions of the committee majority. Should the committee fail to take action on a bill, interested legislators could offer a challenge on the floor and bring the measure to a vote. But each of these courses was exceptional, except the amending. Usually the committee's recommendations became the will of the chamber. Legislators seldom had the temerity or votes to challenge the decision of the select few. Nor were they given much chance. A railroad committee rarely reported unfavorably on a bill; instead, it preferred to let the bill vanish.* When the committee offered amend-

---

* For example, note the South Carolina House session of 1870–1871. There were twenty-four bills dealing with railroad charters and/or aid. The committee reported on ten of them, all favorably. All but two were passed by the House and one of them was simply delayed until the following session. None of the other bills were reported from committee or put to a vote. The 1868–1869 House reported sev-

ments to a measure, the House or Senate usually accepted those amendments; they also usually passed the bill reported favorably.[5]

With his prestige and official powers, a committee chairman could destroy or save a bill on his own. When South Carolina House Railroad Committee Chairman Timothy Hurley took a dislike to a bill subscribing a million dollars to the Port Royal Railroad, he simply stuffed the measure in his pocket and declined to report it even to his committee. While Hurley was absent, the scheme's backers tried to induce another committee member to make what purported to be the committee's report in favor of a substitute for the bill. Procedural rules foiled the ruse; the member lacked the original bill, which was necessary if any substitute was to be offered. Hurley still had the measure, so the Speaker ruled the substitute out of order. The next time this bogus bill was offered, Hurley was in his seat. He objected and defied House members to break into his locked desk to get the original. No one tried. The bill expired with the session's close.[6]

So well did members trust their committees that they did not trouble to scan legislation once it was reported. Several incidents suggest that the members were not even furnished with copies of the amended bills. As the Louisiana Senate discussed a railroad law in 1870, how little its members knew about the bill's provisions became clear. A friend of the bill, F. N. Ogden, insisted that since its introduction all the "ugly features" had been stricken out. "You say they are stricken out?" T. V. Coupland asked. "It is the same as if they had been," Ogden replied. Coupland persisted: Had any provisions been cut from the proposal? "If you choose to split hairs, no," Ogden admitted, "but it is exactly the same as if they were."[7]

The committees could expedite a bill's passage, and the representatives could pass a measure without knowing what they had enacted. There were, however, enough checks in the legislative process to protect the public interest—if lawmakers knew what they had written into the statutes. The opposition could stop a bill through dilatory tactics or quorum calls or ridiculous amendments. In some states, any railroad bill involving state funds had to pass by two-thirds in either house. Many bills never reached a final vote. Some

---

enteen railroad bills into the House Railroad Committee. The committee reported favorably on eight of them; six passed and two were postponed until the December session. The committee made an unfavorable report on two others; a substitute bill passed for one, and the other never came to a vote. The remaining seven bills obtained no committee decision, and only one of these passed: that which the committee had reported to the floor without comment.

were proposed to satisfy constituents' demands, and the authors knew that they could not obtain a majority in both chambers. Some proposals passed one house and perished in the other. Thus the crucial factor in the success of an aid measure was not merely the committee's endorsement or the lobbyists' persuasiveness. It was the popularity of railroad aid as a policy and the uncritical bipartisan support for almost any scheme proposed.

At the mania's height, legislators had neither the time nor the inclination to study the merits of individual bills. They would shepherd measures past all three readings in one day. At times, their output was dazzling. On August 30, 1870, the Georgia House passed ten railroad bills pledging state support. A few weeks later, the Senate broke its own record for "railroad mania" by dealing with thirteen different bills. The North Carolina and Florida legislatures of 1868 and the Texas and Mississippi General Assemblies of 1873 were no less enthusiastic. Not every bill passed both houses, and Georgia and Texas governors vetoed some that did. Lacking the veto power, North Carolina's executive prevented some acts from being enforced.[8] Even so, the statute books contain so many laws that it is obvious not all of them received sufficient consideration.

In a few cases, bills passed quickly and over strong opposition. This was especially true after lobbyists had used unscrupulous tactics to gain their ends. The party leaders by applying all their power and the experienced legislators by trying every parliamentary trick they knew could hasten the process. A friendly Speaker who recognized the right man at the right time could end debate before the opposition could make its case.

Legislative process in the South only partly explains the way every railroad aid bill went through and why the laws gave more than may have been wise. Party politics, too, should be examined. It is important to do so because both sides did their best to obscure the place that railroad aid held in party disputes. When aid was popular, every party claimed paternity. When it became controversial, Democrats and Republicans fastened the blame on one another. Where, then, did the truth lie? Who supplied the votes that enacted the subsidy bills? How consistent was the opposition in confronting the threat of railroad giveaways? To answer these questions, separate state studies based on roll call analysis are essential, for the legislation and the party system varied from state to state.*

* At the outset I must strip the figures I have come to of any pretense of absolute accuracy. Many problems make the figures slightly suspect.
I have determined party affiliation through: (1) the legislative lists published after

South Carolina: Plunder and the Party Line

Of all Reconstructed states, South Carolina most closely fit the stereotype suggested by some later historians. A corrupt Republican majority passed ill-advised subsidy schemes over Conservative

the elections in major newspapers, declaring which representatives belonged to which parties; (2) votes on key party issues in each session and the alignments created; (3) election returns for each county in the nine Radically Reconstructed states. These criteria at times conflict. A newspaper may list a man as independent when in fact he votes as a moderate Republican. Sometimes an overzealous newspaper will claim a representative for one party when in fact he belongs to the other. Again, it is possible that a county with a strong Republican majority will choose an "independent" or Conservative under a different label, and yet vote the Republican ticket on everything else. Some men proved turncoats. Many key issues divided conservative Republicans from moderate and radical Republicans. Issues which in some states split the parties did not do so in others. Finally, clerks often made mistakes and listed legislators voting for one position when they actually voted for the reverse.

Indeed, the problem of error in calculation is an awful one. Votes are listed in legislative journals, but the final counts may be wrong. Again and again, I have counted by hand the number of legislators voting on either side of an issue and found that the clerk miscounted by as much as a fifth. Perhaps his count is right; perhaps the roll call simply omitted a few names or added in a few absentees. There is no way of knowing.

A few members have baffling voting records. One Texas senator elected as a Republican voted almost the perfect Conservative party line in the first legislative session and nearly as uniform a Radical line in the second session. On which side, then, does he properly belong?

Another defect encountered while trying to discern party positions on the railroad issue is the baffling incompleteness of many of the votes. The journals may inform us that a certain amendment to a bill was voted down; but no mention is made of whether the amendment was restrictive or expansive in its intentions. An opponent of railroad aid might—and, indeed, many did—vote to increase a subsidy or spread its effects to other roads so that the majority would find the final bill too extravagant to support. Sometimes a devoted friend of railroad development would oppose a measure because it did not do enough, or because he had a similar proposal that was in some way superior to the one on the floor. Finally, many of the more important votes on bills were never recorded. One might have a roll call on a motion to suspend the rules and put the bill on its third reading. Then, there would be nothing to show who voted for the final bill or by how much it passed. Even worse, the only vote related to the final measure might be a proposal to delay consideration of it until the following Tuesday. Would this motion be a plea of its friends to delay consideration until they could muster their forces? Or would it be a plea of its enemies to stall the bill for a few days, until they had the votes to kill it outright? Without any roll call on the final proposition, all procedural questions are meaningless.

The figures, therefore, are approximate. It is possible that a few that I have treated as Conservatives were actually Republicans; though I have used many methods to find the truth, some measures inducted midway through the session are difficult to categorize. It is possible that the votes not recorded would give a very different picture of railroad aid. This is very unlikely, however. On almost every essential piece of legislation, some roll calls exist. Furthermore, the margin for error is slight because the overwhelming majority of lawmakers were easy to identify and characterize.

opposition. The state lost money on its investment. Republicans shared in the spoils which a Republican legislature had been bribed to provide. Consequently, little was accomplished. Republicans deserve much of the blame, for it was their votes that put the proposals into law. Yet a close examination of votes produces extenuating circumstances and reveals complicated political alignments.

Railroad aid passed because it had overwhelming Republican support. Democratic membership in the General Assembly was negligible, and it could do nothing to prevent passage of laws financing construction of the Greenville & Columbia and the Blue Ridge Railroads. Conservatives protested and resisted, especially when the aid measures served Radical financial or political interests. On the other hand, though Republicans were paid for their votes, they were generally sincere, consistent advocates of public aid. The vast majority backed every aid measure that reached the floor.[9]

At the same time, one can make too much of the Democrats' resistance from a sense of principle. Conservative governments had initiated the subsidy program. Democrats voted to a man to reaffirm the legality of such statutes when the new government called the laws into question. On many measures the Conservatives declined to vote either way.* Furthermore, they could rarely enforce a party line. Usually they split their votes. Occasionally, a majority of Democrats voted for subsidies or relief measures.[10]

It was left to a handful of Republicans to fight the majority's program. They did so fearlessly and for many reasons. First, some of them worried over the state's credit and opposed tax increases. Second, low-country legislators objected to public funding for up-country lines. Others scented corruption and feared for the party's integrity. On every subsidy bill, Republican dissidents either cast their votes against the majority or issued protests. Among the most

---

What is needed, and beyond the scope of this chapter, is an examination of the economic conditions of Southern legislators. It is probable that the wealth of different representatives could have had a clear effect on how they reacted to the subsidy policy. It is also possible that their occupations would have biased their judgment. I also have no doubt that a study discerning the shade of radicalism of the Republican members would be revealing; that is, I am convinced that the more radical a partisan was, the more distrustful of the railroad interests he was likely to be.

* On a bill promoting the Blue Ridge Railroad in September 1868, the House passed the measure by 88 to 8. Six Democrats entered a written protest on the journal, but only three of them voted against the bill. Voting for the bill were four other Democrats. Had the absentees cared as deeply about the measure as their protest implied, they could have attended the session or arranged a pair with the bill's supporters. They did neither.

zealous critics were leading blacks: W. J. McKinlay, Alonzo Ransier, Robert DeLarge, Lawrence Cain, and Simeon Farr. Their counsel, however, did not sway the General Assembly until 1874. By then, as the *New York Herald* put it, all parties were parties of reform.[11]

MISSISSIPPI: AID WITHOUT COST, PARTY LINE WITHOUT DISSENT

Affected no less than party members in surrounding states by the railroad mania, Mississippi Republicans did all they could within the limits of their constitution. More than elsewhere, the aid issue separated the parties. Yet here, too, a general commitment to economic development and a bipartisan distrust of special privilege blurred the lines.

Republicans favored using tax revenues to sustain the roads; Democrats, with more solicitude for the taxpayers, protested any such measures. Thus, whenever the fight involved the subsidy bill of 1871, Republicans united against Democratic attempts to repeal it. On subsidy measures in general, almost every relentless opponent was a Democrat, and almost all of the strongest supporters of aid were Republicans.[12]

Democrats did not oppose aid—only that kind most closely identified with the Republican party and with a direct financial commitment by the state. Even on this aspect of the railroad issue, they showed ambivalence. While Conservative legislators damned the 1871 general aid law, Conservative editors sang its praises, and local Democrats expressed gratitude at the benefits its promised. The legislative minority simply had no intention of letting Republicans take credit for railroad construction. A state senator confessed to the *Jackson Pilot* that after the next election brought in a Democratic legislature, he would vote for a bill identical to the one he opposed now. Nor was it mere chance, the editor went on, that Democrats left Republicans to lead the fight against the bill: by remaining out of the public eye, the minority could more easily reverse its stand during the fall campaign and compromise Republicans' efforts to identify themselves with state aid.[13]

Still, one out of every five Republican lawmakers made common cause with the Democrats against the subsidy policy. They did all they could to defeat the measures from the start, to challenge their constitutionality later, and to urge repeal of obnoxious laws. It was small wonder, then, that railroad aid laws passed by a narrower margin than in other states: 51 to 37, 51 to 27, 39 to 35 in the House, 11 to 10, 14 to 12, 12 to 10 in the Senate.[14]*

When the aid bill did not involve state funds, party lines shattered entirely. Many Democrats touted land grants and tax benefits for the railroads. Some Republicans backed aid in any form. Other party members resisted any surrender of the public domain. Acres of land and special funds set aside for public education were sacred to them, and the bestowal of privileges to corporations struck them as a betrayal of the spirit of Republicanism. When the House petitioned Congress for a land grant to the Mobile & Northwestern, twenty-six Republicans and one Democrat voted against the appeal. When the Senate passed a bill that sold one company state lands at 2 cents an acre, four-fifths of the Conservatives supported it; Republicans divided evenly.[15]

As late as 1873, the passion for aid infected both parties, though Republicans had the best of it. By 1874, however, the rising outcry of the taxpayers had eroded public support for railroad aid. Members of both parties were unstinting in their zeal to repeal some of the most obnoxious statutes.[16]

NORTH CAROLINA: RAILROAD SCHEMES WITHOUT NUMBER

North Carolina had the rudiments of a railroad system at the war's end, but it had built the roads more to suit the planters of the east than the farmers of the western uplands and the commercial ports. The dream of the trans-Appalachian route remained unrealized. With the election of the Reconstruction coalition, promoters and the Piedmont came into their own. No other state gave such lavish subsidies, so hastily or so thoughtlessly. Nowhere did Republicans

---

* Here are some of the specific votes cited for closeness:

Senate, May 5, 1871: H. B. 335, giving land grant to the Mobile & Northwestern, passes 14 to 10.

Senate, May 9, 1871: S. B. 355, to aid railroads: motion to demand referendum on the measure is tabled 14 to 12; motion to strike out the $4,000-a-mile pledge of credit and insert "$1.25 per mile" fails by 11 to 17 on May 11; bill passes third reading, 14 to 12.

Senate, May 10, 1871: motion to give the Vicksburg & Ship Island Railroad the privileges of the Ship Island, Mississippi & Paducah fails 11 to 14.

Senate, January 26, 1872: attempt to repeal the general aid bill of 1871 fails 14 to 4.

House, July 19, 1870: S. B. 265, a general railroad bill, passes 39 to 35.

House, March 21, 1871: attempt to kill the memorial to Congress to endow the Mobile & Northwestern with lands is tabled 40 to 30.

House, April 1871: H. B. 335 passes 51 to 27.

House, May 13, 1871: S. B. 377, to aid internal improvements, passes 51 to 27.

repent their benevolence so soon, for they deserve most of the blame for the aid program's passage. However, no fair judgment can absolve the Conservatives of all guilt.

The "railroad mania" afflicted the first Reconstruction legislative sessions beyond all expectations. Without debate or resistance, bill after bill passed pledging the state's credit. Strife was needless. As far as lawmakers were concerned, there were public funds enough for all. During the special session of 1868, the majority passed four bills allowing the exchange of $3 million in state bonds for an equal number of corporation securities. The government also subscribed almost $7 million to different companies' stock. The regular session that winter authorized $17,350,000 in appropriations for nine companies. It further endorsed $1 million in railroad bonds. Most measures passed easily, with more than two-thirds of each house in favor. So great was the Republicans' zeal for aid that when one railroad bill was introduced without provisions appropriating state funds, a Conservative state senator predicted its failure. It was, he pointed out, "rather *unpopular* to present a bill which asked for nothing."[17]

Partly to develop the state, partly to make railroads their political instruments, an overwhelming majority of Republicans in both houses supported railroad aid policies. Conservatives, also mingling ideology and ambition, opposed state aid two-thirds of the time. They voiced objections that many of the bills were unconstitutional. More important, the program served their enemies' partisan ends.

A Conservative press might assail the subsidy policy and its spokesmen in the General Assembly protest the bills' passage, but neither carried the fight into the courts. Irate Republicans did, and Republican judges overturned much of what the legislators had done. Conservative antagonism varied from measure to measure. On some aid bills, a substantial minority of Conservatives sided with the Republican majority. Indeed, a few members of the minority party backed almost every subsidy measure dear to the Republicans. Conservatives such as Robert Cowan of the Wilmington, Charlotte & Rutherford introduced bills and supported them. On the other extreme, a coterie of Republicans waged relentless war on the subsidy measures.* With good reason they feared for the

---

* For example, the 1868 bill aiding the Western North Carolina Railroad passed by 25 to 9, the minority being five Democrats and four Republicans. Only one Democrat voted for the bill; a bill aiding the Williamston & Tarboro passed by 23 to 9 with the same division between parties; or note the act giving the Raleigh & Gaston $2 million in stock subscription, which passed the Senate by 26 to 9. Four of the nine opponents were Democrats, with five Democrats in favor of the bill.

state's credit rating and the fate of other parts of the party program. The faction led by Senators William Sweet and Curtis Brogden wanted the commonwealth developed, but they did not intend to let it be done for so great a price.[18]

Events proved their distress well-founded, and the growing outcry at corruption brought a majority of Republicans to reconsider their benevolence. By late 1869, political alignments had shifted drastically. Democratic hostility to aid had strengthened. While most Radicals wanted as little investigation of the abuse of state aid as possible and still did not favor repudiation, they were ready to vote for repeal of railroad legislation passed in previous sessions and recall of the subsidy bonds. It was a Republican who introduced the necessary legislation. By the end of the session, the Republican defenders of aid had become the impotent minority. Even they were ready for constitutional restrictions on the corporations.[19]

Arkansas: A Republican Program by Default

Through insight or accident, the Arkansas Republicans chose to keep the legislature as free from the aid question as possible. With the passage of the general aid and incorporation laws of 1868, the governor and his appointees became responsible for furnishing the subsidies necessary to create a railroad system in the state. Consequently, the General Assembly did not vote on railroad issues, and when it did, its votes were not very revealing.

Everyone in the 1868 Assembly supported railroad aid, and almost everyone supported the specific legislation that was finally passed. Although Republican unity can be proven, Democratic attitudes are less clear. There was only one Conservative member, and his vote for the aid bills is too small a sample from which to judge his party. By the time the Democrats did elect a substantial delegation, the Republican enthusiasm for aid had dwindled. Had the minority party taken a strong stand against subsidies, it might have put together a formidable coalition. Instead, Democrats, too, split over the railroad issue. Where money was not involved, however, the overwhelming majority of both parties proved friendly to railroad interests. A bill allowing one line additional time to complete its track had only six opponents—four of them Republicans—and sixty supporters in the House. The governor's railroad aid policy was working well enough to satisfy all sections of the state. On every issue, members voted in contradiction to others from their own district; as in the previous session, opposition to aid was sporadic and inconsistent.[20]

By 1873, however, party lines had hardened, for the railroad aid issue had become one of the prime causes of dispute between the "Minstrel" Republicans running the government and the opposition in both parties. Democrats had lost what enthusiasm they had had for subsidies, though they continued to back land grants to the corporations. Republicans, too, had begun to question their favors to railroads, especially the gift of the public domain. So perplexing did party lines become that in 1874 a renegade Republican who had inveighed against the railroad aid policy obtained the help of his former enemies, Radicals and railway promoters, to overthrow the Republican governor who, with Democrats supporting him, had challenged the railroad subsidy program.[21]

GEORGIA: A DEGENERATIVE FORM OF THE "MANIA"

More than elsewhere, the passion for subsidies was self-propelling in Georgia. There, each legislator who received a subsidy for his constituents increased the pressure on his colleagues to demand the same privileges. In the mad scramble, party lines broke down. So did the Republican program.

When the General Assembly convened in 1868, the large Conservative bloc in both houses kept a check on the majority program. Republicans backed railroad aid by a heavy margin. Democrats tended to object to bills pledging state funds to corporations and defended the taxpayers' interests. When the legislature expelled its black members and put the House in Democratic hands, it became nearly impossible to pass subsidy measures.[22]

From the beginning, however, party lines did not explain railroad aid votes. Perhaps one-fifth of the Republicans opposed subsidies, while many Democrats bolted from the ranks to support specific measures. Of seventy foes of the Fourteenth Amendment in the House, thirty-two supported aid legislation more often than not. Democratic officials introduced bills aiding the Central of Georgia, which had close ties to their party. Areas having railroads fought attempts to give similar advantages to other communities. With no rail connections, southeastern and south central counties supported railroad aid bills, even those benefiting the northwestern uplands.*

* Georgia party affiliations are particularly uncertain, as both sides claimed certain members for their own. Using the vote on ratification of the Fourteenth Amendment as a criterion for conservative sentiments (closer to party lines than elsewhere) we

With the reinstatement of Negro legislators and expulsion of many Conservatives in 1870, the Republicans gained full control of public policy. They began to give aid indiscriminately. As they did so, Democrats lost their own sense of caution, and the party line disappeared. Some Conservatives consistently voted against subsidies or proposed amendments reducing the state's grant by a fourth. They could not draw their own party behind such moves. Other Conservatives submitted aid bills of their own. At times, the quarrel over bestowing a subsidy became a colloquy between Democrats. So fervent did the advocates become that one disgusted representative moved to have the House resolve henceforth to "do nothing but act on railroad bills, and when through with that business . . . adjourn."[23] Some Republicans, troubled by the grab-bag approach to aid and preferring a statewide system that would meet the most necessary requirements of Georgia commerce, urged that all railroad bills be held in the legislature and sent to the governor at the same time. In this way, he could select from among competing projects. The majority in both parties rejected even this modest step to limit their generosity.[24]

Dissident Republicans decried the mania, but they never commanded real legislative influence. Even on the issue of taking the Western & Atlantic out of state hands and placing it under private directors—thus depriving Republicans of patronage and allowing Conservative businessmen to run the enterprise—the Republican minority could not sway a majority of their party to their side. They could not even keep Democratic opponents of aid behind them. A Democrat proposed the lease, and his party supported it overwhelmingly.[25]

---

find: among members who did not vote on the amendment, including more than twenty-five Democrats who replaced black representatives in September 1868, and those Conservatives who would not vote to keep their state out of the Union, but could not bear to vote for the Fourteenth Amendment, the division is pro-railroad aid: 10, anti-aid: 25, neutral: 2. Supporters of the amendment were pro-aid by 43 to 13, with 8 neutral; foes of the amendment voted against aid by 34 to 32, with four neutrals.

Of the worst foes of all railroad aid, with the largest number of anti-subsidy votes on their record, fifteen had voted against the Fourteenth Amendment, eleven had not voted on it, and seven had voted for the amendment. During the 1868 session, if we include the blacks *and* their replacements, we find 85 strong pro-aid votes, 73 anti-aid, 14 swing votes. Naturally, since the Democrats were more inclined to oppose aid than the Republicans, the replacement of colored legislators in September diminished the pro-aid block considerably.

In the State Senate, opponents of the Fourteenth Amendment favored railroad aid by 8 to 7, supporters of the amendment backed aid by 19 to 5. Among the five, too, were several senators who may have been Democrats. On at least two separate occasions, three of them voted to unseat black lawmakers.

Democrats would repent quickly. By 1872, they would control the legislature and be ready to repeal all of the Republican programs except the lease of the Western & Atlantic. Future historians would cite railroad aid abuses as the worst of Radical excesses. In fact, the legislative journals would show that no one party was to blame. The true instigator of the subsidy policy was a public mood, that is, the feverish zeal for railroad building at any price.

ALABAMA: THE QUAVERING PARTY LINE

In Alabama, both parties were committed to developing the mineral region in the northern uplands. Republicans only extended the subsidy law written by their predecessors. Out of partisanship and a mounting fear of taxpayer protest, the minority offered tentative opposition to railroad aid; at the end of Reconstruction, however, party lines remained fluid, as a coalition of Republicans and Democrats from the up-country made war on the commercial centers and on one another.

During the 1868–1870 session, at the mania's height, Republicans championed the subsidy policy proudly. That most of the strongest friends of public aid belonged to the majority party was only natural. Only one Democrat sat in the Senate and eighty-five of the hundred members of the House were Republicans. But many of the most vocal foes of aid, too, were Republicans. Of those legislators voting against railroads three-quarters of the time, Republicans outnumbered Democrats by four to three.* Many Democrats supported aid, though not as strongly as did the majority party.[26]

Conservatives had no reason to resent the general aid law, for it applied to every railroad equally. Conservatives controlled the boards of directors of most aspiring lines, and knew enough to take advantage of a good thing. Party affiliation could make a difference. So could regional gain. "Can some one tell us why the *Mail* does not attack the railroad scheme of Gen. Forrest in *West* Alabama as it does that of Col. Pennington in *East* Alabama?" asked the *Montgomery State Journal* of its Conservative rival. "Both are asking for

* Most hostile to railroad aid in the House were these sixteen, with the number of votes against and for railroad measures listed in parentheses:
Hurt (8:1), White (8:1), McCall (5:0), Murrah (4:0), Burton (6:2), Henderson (6:2), Richardson (6:2), Hubbard (4:1), McKinstry (5:2), Mastin (6:3), Newsom (5:2), Van Zandt (5:2), Ninninger (5:2), Masterson (5:3), Parker (4:2), Reeves (6:4).
Hurt, White, Burton, Richardson, Newsom, Van Zandt, Ninninger, and Masterson are Republicans. The rest are Conservatives, although McCall and Henderson voted for the Fifteenth Amendment.

'county subscriptions' and 'State aid.' "[27] One reason was that Pennington's line did not serve Montgomery and Forrest's did; another was that Forrest led the Democrats while Pennington was a powerful Republican.

One railroad issue did unite Conservatives in opposition, but it did not harden party lines. When the Republican-dominated Alabama & Chattanooga applied for a special $3 million grant, Democrats united in opposition to such favored treatment. But special grants outraged Republicans, too. Fifteen of the twenty-eight opponents on the final vote were Republicans. In later sessions, Democrats would denounce the Alabama & Chattanooga and Republicans would vote together in its defense, but by then the real issue was the preservation of the state's good credit rating. Harass the Alabama & Chattanooga though they might, nearly half the Democrats would not vote for repudiation of the bonds already given. As late as 1873, a bill granting railroads relief passed the House with overwhelming Republican support and Democrats opposed it by a slight margin.[28]*

Political and personal considerations, therefore, determined voting in Alabama more than did principle; counties with no railroads objected to paying for a line through those more fortunate. Supporters of the South & North had no love for the Alabama & Chattanooga. In such scuffles, Republicans behaved as cynically as did Conservatives. As long as it thought that a bill giving the Mobile & Ohio banking privileges would receive a Democratic governor's signature, the official Republican organ described the measure as pernicious and unconstitutional. Then the governor vetoed it. At once, the Republican editor used the deed to prove Democratic parochialism.[29] It was such politicking that brought the railroad program and the Republican party to ruin. It was also such internal dissension that made it impossible for Democrats to take a common position on the railroad aid issue until 1875.

FLORIDA: THE FALSE ISSUE OF STATE AID

Florida needed railways not just to bring prosperity, but to hold the affections of the counties in the Panhandle. With so pressing a need and a long tradition of supportive government, the Reconstruction coalition moved quickly to spur construction. Though

* The actual House count on concurrence with the Senate and final passage was: Democrats opposed by 19 to 16, Republicans in favor by 39 to 4.

passed by a Republican legislature and signed by a Republican governor, the legislation itself had a mixed paternity. As long as government funds were not plighted, Democrats and Republicans were in complete agreement. Charters passed the legislature unanimously and would continue to do so late in Reconstruction. No company had difficulty obtaining a right-of-way or the right to consolidate with other enterprises. Only on the question of the expediency of giving money and lands to railroads did lawmakers disagree, and then not seriously.[30]

Later, Democrats would pronounce the whole railroad aid program a Republican creation. Republicans replied that the measures had originated with Conservative businessmen, had benefited leading Conservatives, and had received bipartisan support. If anything, they insisted, Republicans had more solicitude for the public weal. "Who was anxious to pass the Railroad bill last winter," Republican F. A. Dockray asked in 1872, "which created an additional guarantee of $4,000 a mile, and *which was defeated by Republican votes?*" Both disclaimers were misleading. The doughtiest defenders of railroad interests were Republicans, while the most aggressive foes of corporate advantage were Democrats. Both factions were minute. Nearly every member of either party stood somewhere in the middle. Republicans tended to be slightly more sympathetic to subsidy policies than Democrats, but only slightly. Most of them would vote against too great a bestowal of corporate powers. The subsidy bills of 1869–1870 had widespread Conservative support.* The bill promising the Jacksonville, Pensacola & Mobile $4 million passed the Senate without dissent and the House with only 3 votes against it, all Democratic.[31]

Both parties were flexible enough to change their views to match public opinion. Supporters of railroad aid voiced indignation at the predatory interests they themselves had supported, when denunciation served factional advantage. Even as the Democrats became more openly critical of railroad aid, the Republican majority moved to meet the challenge. After 1872, the Republicans led the way in undoing their own handiwork and increasing the safeguards

---

* For example, in six aid measures brought to a recorded vote in the Florida Senate, three pass unanimously, including the act giving $12,000 a mile in aid to the Jacksonville, Pensacola & Mobile; a bill authorizing the Pensacola & Louisville to acquire lands passes by 18 to 2, with Democrats 5 to 2 in its favor; an act to extend the time for completion of the St. John's Railway and to give it exclusive construction rights for 20 miles on either side of its track passes 17 to 3, with Democrats 6 to 2 in favor; and an act to enable counties to make internal improvements and give aid passes by 13 to 6, with Democrats against it by 4 to 1.

for the public interest. With only two Republicans dissenting, the State Senate voted for a constitutional amendment subjecting all corporations to taxation. In the next session, the vote for such a reform was unanimous. By 21 to 0, the Senate amended the fundamental law to forbid the government to lend its credit to or hold stock in any corporation. In the House, such a measure passed with only seven Radicals dissenting. When Democrats legislated privileges for the Atlantic & Gulf, Republicans became the outraged opponents.[32]

Florida party divisions on the railroad issue were thus ones of shadow rather than substance. A few Republicans on one extreme or a few Democrats on the other might protest the majority's will, but they could not drive one party from the other. The need for railroads was too acute for Democrats to unite against state aid.

LOUISIANA: "ATTACKED OF LATE WITH RAILROAD FEVERS"

The very commercial advantages that the Mississippi River brought to Louisiana retarded railroad development up to Reconstruction. Although promoters talked of the need for aid, little was done. With the inauguration of the Republicans the situation changed. The government did much to aid the railroads; yet, after six years of subsidy, river traffic still defined the state's commerce and few new roads had been built. Here more than anywhere railroad aid accomplished nothing. It should have become a major issue for the Democrats, but it never did. From the first, both parties agreed on the need for railroad aid, and in just the form that Republicans offered it. When repudiation was arranged, it was a Republican legislature that would take the lead.

In most cases, Louisiana promised aid and delivered none, but that promise had the support of both parties. Measures passed easily: by more than 2 to 1 in the Senate and by a larger margin in the House. Democrats did not support aid as readily as Republicans, but the distinction between parties was a fine one. An overwhelming majority in each party supported almost every railroad bill pledging aid. When the bill did not incur state expense—providing instead tax-exemption or a modest state appropriation for immediate repairs—Democrats voted for it even more solidly than did Republicans. At times, the Conservative press would oppose a bill while its spokesmen in either house would vote for it.[33]

In some states, Democrats broke the official party line to favor

subsidies. In Louisiana, railroad aid *was* the Democratic party line.*
When the grant for the New Orleans, Mobile & Texas was offered
in the House, a Radical leader noted that prominent members of
the minority party were exerting pressure on the rank and file in
favor of the measure. "Now I take it that this is a very queer bill
where both parties crack the whip for the same purpose and to the
same end," he commented. Had the Democrats made a staunch
fight against aid, the bill could not have passed the House the first
time with only 1 Democratic vote against it, and the last time with
Democrats 8 to 1 in its favor. In contrast, Republicans supported
aid bills out of pragmatism, and many did not favor extensive
appropriations at all. A small group of white Republicans consistently voted against every piece of supportive legislation. Others
did not conceal their contempt for the program they lent their
votes to.[34]

The real divisions over the subsidy program were regional. River
counties did not need all rail connections as badly as parishes in
the hinterlands. Their commercial advantages weakened their interest in aid policies. New Orleans representatives of both parties
united in seeking funds for every project that might benefit them
or anyone else. Democratic parishes northeast of the capital had
connections with the North, but wanted a road leading to Mobile
and then west to Texas. They, too, backed aid policies.[35]

Time dampened public enthusiasm for public funding, but Re-

---

* Among the examples of Senate divisions are the following:

S. B. 218, aiding the Louisiana Central Railroad, passes 21 to 6 on March 1, 1869:
Democrats 9 to 1 in favor, Republicans 12 to 5 in favor.

H. B. 10, aiding the New Orleans, Mobile & Chattanooga with a $3 million subsidy,
final passage, February 17, 1870: passes 22 to 10, with Democrats against it by 6 to
5, and Republicans for it by 17 to 4.

S. B. 87, aiding the Grosse Tete, Baton Rouge & Opelousas; passes by 15 to 10
on February 25, 1869: Democrats support it by 6 to 0, Republicans oppose it by 10
to 9.

Vote to override the governor's veto of bill aiding the Monroe, Homer & Fulton,
March 3, 1870: 21 to 7, with Democrats 7 to 3 for overriding, Republicans 14 to 4
for overriding.

Vote to override the governor's veto of the Arkansas & Red River Railroad aid
bill, March 3, 1870: veto sustained by 17 to 10: Democrats vote 9 to 2 for sustaining
the veto, Republicans split 8 to 8.

S. B. 164, to aid the Vidalia, Alexandria & Texas, February 9, 1872: 20 to 3 in
favor, Democrats split 1 to 1, Republicans 19 to 2 in favor.

H. B. 279, exchanging aid bonds to the New Orleans, Mobile & Chattanooga for
stock subscription, February 28, 1871: 27 to 8 in favor, with Democrats 4 to 2
against, Republicans 25 to 4 in favor.

S. B. 392, giving a stock subscription to the North Louisiana & Texas, February
28, 1872, passes 26 to 5, with Democrats 4 to 2 in favor, Republicans 22 to 3 in
favor.

publicans met the threat by recalling some of the subsidy bonds, repealing some of their laws, and scaling the state debt. Democrats did not do much more on assuming power. Having captured the lower house in 1875, they mounted no challenge to the railroad aid debt. Rather, they continued to bestow privileges on lines.

TEXAS: DEMOCRATIC VANGUARD, RADICAL RESISTANCE

Texas offered the most curious variation on the Southern fever for development. As usual, Republicans professed themselves the true friends of railroad aid; but Democrats did more to further construction, while a radical governor and his followers prevented members of their own party from implementing the subsidy policy.

Every legislator claimed to favor economic development. Texas had more miles of track than most Southern states, but it needed more. Commercial centers clamored for connections with one another and with the Pacific states. The General Assembly passed acts of incorporation with little dissent. Most members in both houses supported measures relieving lines from penalties for failure to carry out their original charters. There was strong bipartisan backing for bills giving lands or money to the corporations. Yet, during the first three years of Republican rule, the companies had to fight for every acre and dollar of state aid that they obtained.[36]

Party lines only partly explain this paradox. In theory, Democrats should have opposed subsidies and sought a change in the state constitution to allow land grants. This was the official party position, voiced by Conservative editors across the state. But legislators did not make the fine distinction. They supported government bond issues to railroads on every vote. With nearly a majority of seats in either house, Democrats could have stopped the aid program entirely, but that would have been bad politics and worse economics.[37]

A majority of Republicans took a similar position. They favored any form of aid and voted to pass the proposed amendment, as well as subsidies to various lines. The real opposition came from a minority of Republicans who were concerned for the state's credit and fearful of the power of monopoly.* With support in the coun-

---

* For example, see Senate votes on S. B. 2, 90, 191, H. B. 317, 327, 338 (incorporation bills) in 1870 session, which passed with three or fewer votes against them; H. B. 91 (endorsing bonds of the East Line & Red River Railroad), which passed in 1870 with only 3 votes—all Republican—against it; attempt on August 13, 1870 to override the bill relieving the Houston & Central, passing by 21 to 4 with three of the dissidents Republicans; vote on July 26, 1870 to override veto of act relieving Eastern Texas Railroad, which passes by 15 to 7, with six of the sustainers Repub-

tryside, particularly in the western counties around San Antonio, and with leading party papers cheering them on, the opponents of aid had only a paltry following in the General Assembly.[38] They could amend bills to protect the interest of the state and of homesteaders—that is, if they were lucky, if the land grant was unusually large, and if the railroad's location and political links made it enough of a party concern for Democrats to oppose—but they could not beat the measures altogether. They had to rely on the governor's veto power. Often there were votes enough to sustain him, though his friends dwindled as the "railroad mania" grew.

Texas politics carried the bipartisan coalition to its extreme, but everywhere in some form the same conditions apply. Each state had traits, but from them all, a general pattern emerges.

First, both parties cast votes for railroad aid, though in varying degrees. Democrats furthered and benefited from the aid policy. Though their representatives tended to oppose the aid bills, many bolted from the party to stand with the Republican majority on the issue. Republicans, too, had defectors. In each state a corporal's guard stood consistently against the subsidy policy. With each session their ranks increased. Still, that some Democrats outdid certain Republicans in defending railroad interests cannot obscure one vital fact: the railroad aid bills were proposed in Republican legislatures, modified in Republican committees, proclaimed Republican measures, and received the enthusiastic support of Republican majorities. The Conservative case against Reconstruction exaggerated the differences between parties, but it was a distortion, not a fabrication. If Democrats would later ignore the factors other than party that explained how legislators voted on railroad aid, they grasped the essential fact, that party lines were the primary basis for a lawmaker's stand on aid policies. It was a fact that dissident Republicans understood from the first, and their protests took on a defensive note as they tried to show how a representative could be a good Radical and a foe of aid at the same time. As the subsidies lost their popular support, the fact that the Republican party was

---

lican, and Democrats 7 to 1 for overriding; the July 25, 1870 vote to override veto of a bill aiding the Southern Pacific Railroad: 19 to 9 in favor, with seven Republicans for sustaining and nine for overriding; the vote on May 24, 1871 to override the governor's veto of an aid bill for the Southern Pacific, by 23 to 4, with three Republicans voting to sustain, and Democrats 10 to 1 for overriding.

For further railroad aid votes, readers are invited to consult my dissertation, "Radical Reconstruction and the Gospel of Prosperity," Ph.D., University of California at Berkeley, 1980.

so closely connected to them explains the bitterness of the factionalism that the railroad issue engendered inside the organization. Party considerations had made the public aid policy expedient. Party considerations would help unmake that same policy.

Second, different kinds of aid prompted different responses from either party. With a few exceptions, the Republicans identified themselves with subsidies above all other aid measures. Consequently, they paid dearly for their commitment. Democrats favored less expensive expedients, except on occasion. They would offer land grants more readily than would Republicans, and with equal fervor would provide broad rights of incorporation and other privileges.

Third, everywhere the railroad aid faction outnumbered its foes by a wide margin. Aid was popular, and yet legislative inexperience and parliamentary procedure augmented the promoters' advantages dangerously. The lack of veteran legislators assured that most important work on a bill would be done in committee, and that the committees would be filled with inexperienced men: two conditions that would surely enhance the lobbyists' influence on final legislation. Deference to the committee ensured a friendly reception to railroad measures and stifled opposition to the various bills. This is why support for railroads turned into a mania; furthermore, when the committees fell into the hands of critics of railroad aid, this is also why the laws were repealed with an equal amount of haste and lack of consideration.

Fourth, and as important as anything else, every railroad bill was shaped by special circumstances, localism, fear of outsiders, avarice, influence, factional disputes. All these factors undercut the party line and marred the railroad system.

The Gospel of Prosperity would not fail for the reasons Conservatives had suggested in their indictment of Radical legislators. Railroad aid was not a failure because ignorant lawmakers had no idea of what the state needed, but because too many Southerners had all too clear an idea of just what they wanted.

CHAPTER 5

The Enemy Within: Parochialism Run Amok

> We have no special desire to buy a club, nicely polish the handle, and then put it in her hand with an invitation to knock out our brains.
>
> Galveston Tri-Weekly News
> on Houston's civic ambitions

DREAMS of unlimited grandeur infected every town in the South. Pine Bluff had faith that it would direct the commerce of the whole trans-Mississippi South, even as Dallas claimed the same prospect for itself. Yet each community's vision countered that of another. The *Jackson Pilot* criticized Memphis for stealing commerce "which naturally belonged to Mississippi," and the *New Orleans Republican* abused every rival. Arkansas, Louisiana, and Texas were "ours beyond question," it proclaimed—a boast that a few businessmen in Little Rock and Galveston might have challenged. Indeed, Galvestonians showed such ill grace that they were accused of using yellow fever quarantines as a ruse to keep local merchants from traveling to nearby states for supplies lest they be unable to reenter the city. No one had the whimsy to suggest a quarantine on ambition.[1]

Citizens treasured their sectional identity, but took more pride in their own state, and still more did they stand by their communities against every rival. This led to bickering, jealousies, and competition all around. Small towns felt their prospects for growth undermined by the success of larger neighbors. As much from self-esteem as economic desire, they resented their own dependence. Between rail centers with a chance of outshining one another, the stakes were higher and the caviling much more lusty. Savannah spokesmen chafed at the rivalry of Atlanta, Helena and Memphis fought bitterly to control Little Rock's trade, and Montgomery felt resentment at the sudden rise of Birmingham. This pretentious hamlet, the *Montgomery Alabama State Journal* raged, consisted of three hotels, two planing mills, a national bank, and the "accidental

crossing of two trunk lines." Its officials were charlatans, its promotional literature a gull on the public, its very existence an example of corporate treachery.[2]

Inattention to community feelings could imperil a director's control over a corporation, particularly because local governments and
rural stockholders held so many shares. When John Screven sought
reelection as president of the Atlantic & Gulf, an ally wrote him
that local jealousies would cost him dearly: "Your rival is just the
dog to use this against you to the utmost." As mayor of Savannah,
Screven protected his position by wielding the proxy vote on city
stock, but other railroad officers were more vulnerable.[3] By catering
to local ambitions, the executive stood a better chance of keeping
his place, no matter how poor his general management of the line
might be. Fighting to keep control of the Pensacola & Georgia,
E. Houstoun pleaded with J. P. Sanderson, a prominent Jacksonville lawyer, to sustain him. He had always run the enterprise to
discriminate in Jacksonville's favor, the president argued. Surely,
the city would come to his aid now, in his struggle with "a set of
adventurers."[4] The question never discussed was whether it was in
the company's best interest that Jacksonville should have got special
treatment.

With such localism running wild, every railroad bill was weighed
in terms of community advantage. The *Jackson Pilot* thought construction of a trunk line from Mobile to Arkansas "THE project
of all railroad enterprises now proposed in the State," and favored
public aid. The *Vicksburg Times and Republican* considered the charter
one of the three worst mistakes in Mississippi history. Small wonder—for the project would pass through Jackson and miss Vicksburg. Not all newspapers were as frank in their motives as the
Galveston Tri-Weekly News. It protested that it did not hate the city
of Houston, "yet we have no special desire to buy a club, nicely
polish the handle, and then put it in her hand with an invitation
to knock out our brains."[5] But there is no question that every
community saw railroads in just such terms.

Competing lines provided a second form of rivalry, some of
which were simply uncooperative. The Houston & Texas Central
connected with the Galveston, Houston & Henderson. Some mu-
tually satisfactory timetable would have benefited both. Instead, the
two roads chose to go it alone. Other enterprises became enemies
because they vied for the same territory. And why not? Railroad
companies had a hard enough time surviving in the postwar South
without sharing their markets with intruders. While people in most

counties would gladly donate to the construction of one line, they could not afford to sustain two or more. In many places, friends of one railroad had to be enemies of another. Inevitably, this rivalry spilled over into politics. Established lines not only feared competitors, but objected to paying taxes which might be used to promote newcomers. New companies felt a special urgency to obtain aid, for without it, they could hardly mount a challenge to the economic interests entrenched since the 1850s. Those interests had grown on public aid. It seemed right, therefore, that public aid challenge their monopoly. Yet the interloper of one minute could act like the entrenched interest of the next. The Atlanta & Savannah, which had pleaded for a charter to challenge existing monopolies, also did its best to block a competing charter that would have run from Covington to Savannah.[6]

This complex of rivalries was so strong that Republicans could defy it only at their peril. If the location of a line was a matter of life and death for a town, local considerations could make that location a matter of life and death for the Reconstruction coalition there. A governor might have a duty to protect the state by vetoing a costly subsidy, but he would do so with more financial than political wisdom, for the people would not forget the man who had dashed their hopes for greatness. "There are 13,000 votes between Muscogee and Rome," one Georgian warned his Republican allies during discussion of a charter, "and these voters . . . desire that the bill should become a law, and that the road should be constructed."[7]

It would have been hard enough to use railroad policy for party gain if every section wanted connections, but in fact their every demand for recognition was based on a desire to take something away from someone else. This meant that the best—indeed, the only—means of making friends for the party through railroad legislation was by giving affront to the people of some other town or county, or else by giving aid so indiscriminately that everyone felt that his community had received the best of the bargain.

For obvious reasons, Republicans preferred the latter policy. In particular, Georgia and North Carolina aid programs looked like exercises in commercial profit sharing. North Carolina's General Assembly even chartered a series of state-owned lines, devised with more regard for constituent demands than for constitutional dictates. None of them went beyond the organizational stage. Even so, the legislators' intent to distribute advantages among as many areas as possible was obvious.[8]

There was something to be said for reciprocity as an act of fairness, and legislators made a habit of saying it—at least, when they were seeking the advantages some other places already had. If everyone paid taxes to support development, all should share in the rewards. Selectivity became synonymous with inconsistency, selfishness, and hostility.[9] But it was not reciprocity but sectionalism that showed up in legislative voting. Representatives were more likely to vote for a railroad bill that helped their district than for one making no such provision. When the South Carolina Senate passed a bill relieving the Savannah & Charleston, most support came from the downstate counties affected. Up-country senators either did not vote or opposed the bill.[10]

The extent of sectional division on railroad legislation should not be exaggerated. Compared with the issue of party, it had secondary importance. Men did not always vote their sectional interests, nor was it always clear what a section's best interests were. Furthermore, all the crosscurrents cannot be traced. The reporters did not discuss them and the legislators rarely confessed their pragmatism. Still, once the historian knows the constituency of a legislator, he can make some reasonably safe guesses about how the legislator would vote on a given piece of railroad legislation. Localism made even the most upright men inconsistent. A stalwart foe of railroad aid might denounce it on principle as a deplorable policy and back up his words with a discourse on right and wrong, but when his own county stood to gain, he overcame his scruples easily. Louisiana State Senator John Ray was no better than other critics when a bill funding the North Louisiana Railroad came up. "He is opposed to the principle," jeered John Lynch. "The principle is wrong, he says, but still he is willing to do violence to it in order to make the State of Louisiana pay $2,000 to test the sincerity of Senators on this floor." Plato Durham led North Carolina Conservatives against the aid bills and even promised to vote against one act aiding a road through his part of the state. That was one promise he did not keep.[11]

Railroad legislation was not just shaped by competing ambitions. It fostered them and embittered them. South Carolina's wrangling showed that. Port Royal had visions of supplanting Charleston as the state's first port. It strove for connections with Augusta and over the Appalachians and mocked its rival as "the City of the Dead." Small wonder that representatives of Port Royal wanted $2 million in aid for a railroad exploiting the city's advantages; small wonder that Charleston wanted the state to assume the city's antebellum debt, which was contracted for railroad construction; small wonder, too, that the two communities fought each other's demands to the death. "The Port Royal Railroad Ring" was one of the "rotten railroad schemes which clamor for assistance," said the *Charleston Republican*, which had rotten schemes of its own. Charleston, in fact, supported no major railroad bill not directly benefiting Charleston, and rivals repaid it in equally clipped coin. The state comptroller general could denounce the Blue Ridge Railroad aid bill as deadly to state credit, but his warning—correct though it was—was discounted as the spite of a Spartanburg resident. The Blue Ridge line had refused to deflect its line through Spartanburg.[12]

In at least two states the animosity went beyond rhetoric and roll calls and took on a tone of unreality. The secession from the Union had been suppressed, but the impulse of counties or sections to secede from their states had quickened. Railroad schemes did not initiate the pressure for partition of existing states, but they became a major irritant. To Southern dissidents, they were symbols for a host of grievances. No partition scheme came to fruition. Perhaps they were not meant to succeed. Still, this does not diminish their symbolic importance, for they showed how deeply economic antagonisms went.

As the largest state, Texas seemed the most unmanageable for any one deliberative body. The eastern counties had cotton plantations and a large black population, the western ones had grazing and desert lands with few Negroes and many German immigrants. While the east looked toward New Orleans for a market, the west looked toward Galveston, Corpus Christi, or Indianola as outlets. The east paid most of the taxes and got most of the benefits. The west and north needed development, but lacked either the funds to act or the political power to bend the legislature to their will. Naturally, there was no love lost between the sections.

The real slight that irritated sectionalists was the apparent selfishness of railroad aid policies established since the 1850s. San Antonio found its enemy in the Houston & Texas Central, which western tax revenues had helped build. Ungrateful, avaricious, the Central "ring" had descended on successive legislatures to grasp new advantages for itself and to kill any bill financing rivals for western markets. The west gave up its lands so that the state government could make grants to support eastern railroads. After the war, it wanted to share in the returns. For years, northern Texas had been left out of railroad programs. Though the Memphis, El Paso & Pacific had been given a land grant, the Reconstruction constitution had put the grant in doubt by forbidding future allotments; most of the acreage had not yet been handed over.[13]

The first Reconstruction legislature added to regional disgruntlement. For Galveston, the Galveston & Denver Air-Line road would prove a godsend, but for ports to the south such as Indianola, on which San Antonio and the southwest depended, it was one more slight on a section already underrepresented and overtaxed. By late 1870, with the first session adjourned, the north and northwest had received nothing. For this they blamed bitterly the Gulf ports and the established companies.[14]

Some Texans urged that the capital be moved. Most critics had a better alternative: divide the commonwealth into three states of roughly equal size. San Antonio Republicans saw the chance to become the new capital, with railroads exclusively to their advantage. A road from Indianola to El Paso would cut through their town and would make them a serious contender for the Pacific trade. Yet the very localism that inspired such a movement also ensured that the one plan offered in 1871 must fail. Dallas Democrats saw in the division a plot to keep coastal politicians in control and let them keep building their lines with grants from northern counties. Editors elsewhere claimed that the plan would enhance the northern counties, but slight Austin. Galveston residents feared that a new state in western Texas might establish competing port facilities. Republicans described Democrats as favoring it; Democrats labeled the plan a Radical contrivance. With no consensus on where the borders should fall, the House passed a bill which a Senate select committee refashioned. It never came to a direct vote. After the government subsidized trunk lines through the western and northern counties, the division question vanished, but not before it had shown a powerful vein of dissidence in the state.[15] For this, railroad aid bills were more responsible than anything else.

Florida proved more serious than Texas, but here conditions were strikingly different. In Texas, railroad aid fostered a spirit of division. In Florida, the spirit of division fostered railroad aid.

For the Panhandle counties, Florida's government had been little more than a political abstraction. They paid their taxes to it and sent representatives to Tallahassee, but they were shut out of the commonwealth's development. To reach the capital by train, Pensacola citizens had to spend a week traveling through two other states, a distance of 600 miles. Railroads across the Panhandle had been chartered and had come to nothing. With an excellent channel and good facilities for trade, Pensacola attracted most of its business from the north. It expected still more once Alabama developed its coal and iron deposits. State pride made Alabamians ship their goods through Mobile rather than the superior harbor of some other state. By seceding and joining Alabama, the eight Florida counties west of the Apalachicola River would remove this barrier to West Florida's prosperity. By 1869, sentiment was strong for just such a solution. Montgomery businessmen found the idea equally attractive, in part, because it would spite Mobile. To some extent, Mobile's success was a sign of Montgomery's failure to dominate the state's economy. Gulf merchants meant to lord it over the state in politics the same way, and this made them even less popular. In 1873, they proposed that the capital be moved to Mobile. Up-country representatives were aghast at the prospect of having to travel further than ever, and accused the port of deliberately fomenting a secession movement in the northeastern counties by their arrogance. It was a Montgomery state senator who delivered the ultimate insult. He introduced a resolution to raise the money to buy West Florida by selling Mobile to Mississippi.[16] The capital and the state's boundaries stayed just as they were, but the rivalries were clear to see, and whenever a railroad aid bill reached the floor, they broke out anew.

Citizens of Mobile paid the upstate in kind. They saw Florida annexation as an insult and toyed with a partition of their own, even as they resisted Montgomery's schemes. Mobile editors openly flirted with Mississippi and suggested that it need no longer be the only Gulf state without a good port. The movement involved more than spite. By courting Mississippians, businessmen made themselves eligible for favors from both states, as each tried to win the commercial center's allegiance. Mississippi legislators chartered and aided a railroad from Mobile northwest to Helena, Arkansas, the Mobile & Northwestern. Alabama lawmakers responded with bills to give the Mobile & Ohio bank privileges, and to entitle the Mobile & Northwestern to generous land grants.[17]

As Mobile plotted, the Republicans moved ahead with their plans. The three commissioners who had been sent to Tallahassee in early 1869 did not really want much beyond Pensacola city limits, but they were prepared to take more, and at first Floridians gave them a surprisingly friendly reception. A joint commission agreed to an intricate bargain. Among the other provisions was a promise that the Savannah & Gulf Railroad, a Georgia rival of eastern Florida promoters, should not be allowed to cross West Florida for three years after the date of transfer and that the Alabama general aid law should cover two lines radiating from Pensacola toward Tallahassee and Pollard, Alabama: a privilege for which no other roads should be eligible for three years after the date of cession.[18]

This annexation fever was pure pipe dream. If the eight counties were worth so much to Alabama that their possession at almost any price would be a bargain, what could motivate the people of central Florida to give them up? To the *Tallahassee Sentinel*, the negotiation made Esau's sale of his birthright look like "the acme of financial shrewdness." For once the *Sentinel*'s Democratic counterpart was in perfect accord. Indeed, a partition could presage the death of the commonwealth. For the *Savannah News*, West Florida's loss seemed destined to induce the middle counties to petition Georgia for annexation. "Let West Florida be annexed to Alabama," replied a Montgomery newspaper, "and we shall not make objection to middle Florida tacking on to Georgia."[19]

Annexation had little chance, but the people of Florida took the threat seriously. Something must be done to allay western discontent. As Conservative an organ as the *Tallahassee Floridan* urged that Pensacola be wooed with the one thing it so desperately wanted, railroad communications. Whatever Alabama promised, it declared, Florida should more than match in its offers. The legislature did just that. Governor Harrison Reed had long dreamed of a railway system that would tie together Tampa, Tallahassee, Key West, Jacksonville, and Pensacola. Now, in 1869, the governor built up the secession threat by treating the Alabama commissioners seriously and urging a summer session of the General Assembly that would give special attention to the Panhandle's railroad needs. George Swepson and Franklin Dibble had bought the old Pensacola & Georgia and Tallahassee Railroads at public sale. They hoped to merge the two and obtain bonds to extend track from Quincy to Pensacola. Reed backed them, and so did members of both parties. Nevertheless, the railroad bills ran into the usual difficulties. Savannah and Fernandina, fearful that Jacksonville might take their trade, mustered enough representatives to block action. Only the threats of Senator William Purman of Jackson that he would work for cession, the bribes of the promoters, and parliamentary juggling ended the stalemate and brought the bills to a vote.[20]

There were two major pieces of legislation. The first merged two incomplete roads into one, the Tallahassee Railroad. The second established the Jacksonville, Pensacola & Mobile and gave it the right to consolidate with Swepson's new road. This combination had the exclusive right to build westward and received $14,000 a mile in state bonds to further its work. In return, the corporation would give the State Treasury an equal amount of first-mortgage bonds. Early in 1870, Swepson and Littlefield sent their minions back to the legislature and had aid increased by another $2,000 a mile, with the same endorsement extended to the hundred miles of road already built east from Quincy. The road would not reach Pensacola until 1883.[21]

Still, the promise of aid was what counted, and western Floridians seemed content with it. In 1873, Governor David Lewis of Alabama sent another commission to Florida. The commissioners were not even given the common courtesies to which their rank entitled them. They returned in frustration. Florida's executive did suggest that a statewide referendum might be taken, but this was the same as condemning the plan to death. The General Assembly would not even do that much.[22]

Florida's experience was unusual in pitting interstate rivalries against intrastate ones, but the state pride that made one commonwealth desire an additional Gulf port while another polity resisted any move that would deprive it of its own territory manifested itself all over the South. The jealousy each Southern state showed to its neighbors permeated railroad policy. A charter for a 6-mile railroad from a lumber mill to a landing wharf ran into opposition among South Carolina lawmakers because it was charged that the line would ship its timber to Savannah instead of Charleston. Disapproving of land grants on principle, the *Alabama State Journal* put its argument against one railroad bill on grounds that any state patriot could appreciate. The beneficiary was from Mississippi, it pleaded. If Alabama must be robbed, let the looters be natives instead. The same state pride also encouraged countermoves to whatever a rival commonwealth was doing. To crush the threat which commercial interests beyond state borders were posing, Southerners agitated for roads of their own with termini of their own. The scheme of one commercial center fostered rival lines into the same territory just to keep present advantage. Fearing the loss of eastern Alabama trade to Columbus, Georgia, the Montgomery press urged a road in that direction. To fight Atlanta interlopers, Alabamians raised money to stretch a line into the northeast, though they won local referenda over a sea of fraudulent votes.[23]

Such railroad projects did not restore the autonomy that each state desired. If anything, they increased each commonwealth's dependence on its neighbors. For all its prosperity, Mississippi lacked commercial prominence because all of its trade flowed to New

Orleans, Memphis, and Mobile. North Carolina's trade tended to move toward Richmond and Charleston. Goods in Arkansas and Alabama tended to flow to Tennessee cities. The railroads were blamed for having created some cities and having failed to enhance the importance of others.

In fact, it was the other way around. No promoter with his eye on the main chance would consider building a road from nowhere to nowhere, in the hope that his selected terminus would experience a miraculous growth. He would start at a commercial depot and lay his track into the hinterland to take in the trade it offered, or in the vicinity of some other railroad which promised him a choice of markets for the goods he intended to ship. Railroads did not create new cities as much as they built up those already important as ports or railway termini. In this way, railroads became dependent on each other, and state borders became a nuisance for railway promoters rather than the barrier that editors smouldering with state pride had hoped they would be.

What the competitiveness did accomplish was the undermining of the financial basis for railroad projects. Rivalries added to the tendency to build more lines into an area than the trade would then permit and to restore local hegemony at the price of county indebtedness and corporate bankruptcy. In Florida, for example, the Jacksonville, Pensacola & Mobile vied with the Atlantic & Gulf for markets. Neither road had completed a route to Mobile by 1873, nor could either negotiate its bonds to raise funds for that purpose as long as it had a rival. Their only hope was merger. But out of fear that such a union would turn Florida into "the Peninsula of Georgia, or *Georgia's Horn*," Floridians resisted such a move and made the downfall of both lines inevitable.[24]

Many railroads were not what the South needed. It needed a *system*, one best fitting the needs of the entire section. There were only two ways to implement plans on a large scale. First, the states might leave construction to Northern capitalists with funds sufficient to realize such designs. Second, they might coordinate their railroad construction programs and their endowments to serve common needs. Either option would have meant the sacrifice of local interests and benefits for certain states at the expense of others. State pride and community interest made either alternative unthinkable, and while the Southern governments acted the only way one could have expected them to, their actions were doubly unfortunate. The economic effect of a lack of system was the creation of roads unable to support themselves. The political effect was the ultimate failure of the railroad aid policy, and with it the Republican party.

This was accomplished in several ways. First, parochialism polluted the legislative process. Corporate officials soon realized that only diligent lobbying could overcome local ties. Yet each side had its lobbyists. As corporate hirelings fought it out, legislation foundered. Logrolling became standard practice. So did corrupt inducements.

Local zeal protected improper influences from the public gaze at times. Only a rare editor would flay rascals whose bribery had brought his community a road it did not possess before. Yet localism also made corruption seem more prevalent than it was. Railway lobbyists did not tarnish the image of the subsidy programs as much as did parochial pundits who bandied words like "swindle" and "steal" whenever roads failed to help their particular communities. Beneficiaries make poor watchdogs, but malcontents scarcely make better ones. For these reasons, talk of corruption must be winnowed for evidence, and that is not as easy to find.

Corruption, it seems, meant any influence aside from verbal argument that a corporation might exercise in furthering a goal that the editor found distasteful. If the newspaper favored the project, a band of paid agents was useful and even necessary to acquaint the provincial minds in the capitol with their duty. Agitators for a less appealing line were called lobbyists, and to the polemicist of the 1870s, a lobby was a subversion of the democratic process by its very nature: it made legislators act not on the merits of a measure, but for personal and selfish motives.[25] If lobbyists took a legislator to dinner, that was corruption; if they gave a state senator a free pass on a railway line, that was a payoff. To the bill's enemies, the supporter's favor and the senator's favorable vote proved collusion. It was a broad definition. Yet no one publicly questioned it, and the press played the theme for all it was worth. In doing so, they undermined the basis for railroad aid laws. If such bills were passed by illegitimate means, they were open to legal question—and so was the validity of the bonds issued under the law.

The mudslinging did not stop at the capitol's doors. One town was perfectly willing to bring into disrepute every aspect of a rival's schemes, if that would discourage stock subscriptions and bond sales. The litany of abuse did not vary: a rival line had its way by stuffing ballot boxes for subscription, its bond issues were forgeries, its chances of completion were small, its chances of prospering were nil. Behind every calumny was little more than self-interest. Still, such talk could not help but weaken the chances any railroad had of prospering. A shrewd investor might recognize the bias in the source of criticism, but would still pause before putting his money into a road with enemies so well prepared to drive down the value of the company's stock and bonds.

Worse still, the distrust of outsiders foreshadowed the collapse of political support for the railroad aid policy. Without local control, the companies could not command local support as easily, and with that command gone, the rationale for aid was shattered. Outsider domination could mean that the taxpayers were raising money without visible reward. The company might fix rates that the towns-folk considered unfair, or proclaim rules that discriminated against the small towns that had founded the line. Then the railroad could become a scapegoat rather than a Golden Calf. Thus the *Tuskegee News* was enraged at freight rates on the short haul on the Montgomery & West Point, rates which built up Montgomery business interests. Montgomery had the same complaints about the South & North, while the president of the Mobile Board of Trade was sure that all companies had plotted to divert produce away from his city. "The whole railway interest requires revision," he announced. "It does not fulfill its duties to the people."[26] That no bondholder was entitled to respect unless his road served the aim for which the bonds were issued was a dangerous maxim. It was also a common belief, and if the impact a corporation had on the community became the standard on which an area based its judgment of railroads and their aid, if unpleasant local effects required "revision" of "the whole railway interest," then a railroad that could not please everybody—and no railroad could do that—was destined to create enemies of supportive legislation.

In the same way, localism and state pride undermined the support for a general aid policy. Because each community felt that it had a stake only in those roads directly beneficial to it, the rationale for a system of lines brought about through a general aid law was shaky from the start. In the first blush of railroad aid, when every project had an equal chance of success, one community would not begrudge another's sharing in the benefits of the progam. However, as time passed certain railway schemes proved disappointing, while others seemed to prosper solely because of state aid. Suddenly, railroad subsidies took on an outrageous character to the unhappy community. They would mean contributions to build up unworthy rival towns. They would ruin the community at its taxpayers' expense. Each year added to the disquiet over the aid policy because people could not see it in terms of a system intended to enrich the whole state, much less the whole South; and they were right, for localism had made any such system a mere abstraction.

For all Republican talk of one nation, for all Conservative reverence for the South as a unit, it was parochialism, not sectionalism or nationalism, that left the most serious marks on railroad policy. This should not be surprising. It was not the Republicans' fault. Yet it was unfortunate, for it helped destroy the consensus on which railroad aid had been based, and with it the Reconstruction coalition.

CHAPTER 6

Winning Friends and Influencing Legislation

We thought that railroad and bank directors would no
longer have it all their own way, and fill all the chairs in our
Legislatures. But money is ahead of us yet.

A Louisiana legislator

PARTISANSHIP, local and state ambitions, vested interests, and circumstances of the moment—the complexity of decision-making on
railroad matters confuses us; it should not surprise us. Whenever
an enterprise needs the support of many men holding different
views of the state's welfare, the law that results reflects the dissonance. Yet this interpretation of the aid policies was not the popular
one advanced during Reconstruction nor the one that later historians adopted. They saw another motive as paramount: "corruption."[1]

Contemporaries embraced a broad definition of "corruption."
They let the term cover any influence, from verbal argument to
the gift of a Havana cigar. However, so loose a definition would
force the historian to see all legislation in every era as corrupt.
Limiting the term "corruption" to those methods of persuasion
generally forbidden by law—the purchase of support through bribery and the sale of votes through extortion—one may better gauge
the extent to which illegal as well as *extra*legal practices determined
the fate of railroad legislation. In doing so, the scholar will discover
that the companies did indeed use improper means of getting what
they wanted, but he will also come upon a more intriguing fact:
the railroad lobbyist found "corruption" an invaluable tool because
nothing could be done without it.*

* I hope that I will not be seen as adopting the same amoral view of corruption
as did the lobbyists. In casting aside their ethics, it seems to me that directors based
their acceptance on fallacious assumptions:

1. If a program is in the public interest, then corruption to secure its passage is
not against the public interest.

2. When a program has popular support, then its passage is in the public interest,

The reason is paradoxical. The companies needed to exert pressure to obtain what they wanted *because* enthusiasm for railroad construction had become so intense. Every community wanted a line, but only for itself and along a route advantageous to local interests. Every company favored the subsidy policy, but only when applied to itself and not to rivals. With limited government funds and a limitless number of applicants for support, the underfinanced railroad did not just need to fight its way to the State Treasury. It had to fend off rival schemes. Later, having secured an endowment, the company needed to curb legislative enthusiasm for new projects that might draw off traffic and extend the public credit beyond the point of fiscal sensibility.

Corporations found the whims of individual legislators just as threatening to commercial ambitions as were the dreams of competing lines. Responsive as he was to constituent pressure and personal conscience, a politician might mar the best measures imaginable with what he considered improvements. He might propose that the line change its route to accommodate a major town in his district. He might amend the bill to compel the creation of branch lines to spread the benefits of future trade. Lawmakers could and did tamper with the boards of directors, tighten construction requirements, insert deadlines for completion of work, regulate passenger and freight rates, and seek increases in the state's protection against loss.

That public officials should participate in the making of public policies seemed an almost disgraceful intrusion to corporate directors. They recognized that democratic government is excellent when it expresses the popular will, but when that will is uncertain

---

and legislators who thwart the public will are serving their constitutents badly.

3. Railroads are in the public interest, and the government programs to aid their construction must therefore also be of benefit to the state.

I challenge these assumptions. It can be argued:

1. That the ends never justify the means. Even in the most righteous cause, corruption never serves the public interest because it subverts lawful processes. Each time good men undermine that process, others with less savory motives find it easier to do the same. When government integrity perishes, government decisions are based neither on the public will nor on the good of the state.

2. That popular support is no gauge of the public interest. People can err and often do, especially when their local advantage is at issue. A lawmaker owes his people more than a parroting of their opinions; he owes them his best judgment from all the facts available to him.

3. That any form of economic development is in the public interest does not mean that government support for that form is also justified. One could make a case for retrenchment as an equally good policy for Southern officials to have pursued.

on specific points of law or fragmented by local prejudice, they felt that men more knowledgeable and with more at stake than the average citizen should give guidance.

To give such guidance, the companies delegated their authority in two directions. Leading the fight in public, railroad executives went before legislative committees to enlighten the most important members. They published flattering accounts of the railroads' prospects and took to the stump to muster public opinion behind them. Respectable men did not consider their role disgraceful. Chief justices in Arkansas and Georgia worked hard to acquaint representatives with their corporations' point of view. One railroad president defended himself against charges of having gone onto the floor of the Arkansas legislature to lobby for a senatorial candidate by insisting that he had been there solely to press for legislation favorable to his company. The "real work," however, said the *San Antonio Express*, was done by the "*attorneys* and *agents*, who visit members while at home or buttonhole them around the corners of streets. Lobbying was perhaps never so scientifically performed." Sometimes the company employed professional lobbyists who worked for any client able to pay for services rendered. Whatever their experience, corporate hirelings thrived in the state capitols. Whenever an important bill came to a vote, such men appeared in large numbers and used every argument at their disposal.[2]

Not all the arguments were objectionable. Every enterprise tried to appeal to the lawmakers' sense of public good and logic by a recitation of the company's advantages. Indeed, that was the basic tactic each lobbyist employed because it was the least expensive. Men like Milton Littlefield of the Western North Carolina visited representatives at home to impress them with statistics showing the company's chances of becoming self-sufficient. Public opinion was mobilized to the same end. Promoters would circulate petitions among citizens along the projected route and bring the signatures back to the capitol to show that the company had popular backing. Newspapers were given evidence of the railroad's potential value. Should editors prove unenthusiastic, their support could be bought. A legislator employed by the Greenville & Columbia tried to buy the capital correspondent for the *Charleston Republican* and through him representatives of every paper in Charleston. He did not succeed, and the *Republican* expressed outrage at the attempt. However, other newspapermen saw no disgrace in letting their opinions be purchased. Approached by the president of the Cairo & Fulton with a similar proposition, the editor of the *Little Rock Republican* took umbrage only when the officer tried to pay him $12,000 in company stock. Declaring "that I would not give a picayune for his Cairo and Fulton stock; that I did not want it," he received a promise of $6,000 in cash.[3]

Since the party out of power often tried to make subsidy bills a political issue, and since political affiliations endangered any law in the long run, the corporations thought it wise to buy silence where they could not buy support among the most influential Conservative newspapers. Josiah Turner's *Raleigh Sentinel* waged a fierce fight against Radical railroad steals but said nothing about George Swepson, the ringleader of many of the worst schemes. Later, another Conservative paper revealed that Swepson had lent Turner $5,000 to afford the latter control over the newspaper; the loan was not repaid. The *Little Rock Gazette* led Conservative opinion in Arkansas. When the Republicans first put the state aid policy up to a popular vote in 1868, the editor called for its defeat. Then, suddenly, the *Gazette* reversed itself. Articles appeared extolling the "immense advantages to accrue" from the subsidy policy. Later, the *Gazette* would confess that "arguments" had changed its mind. Perhaps the arguments were more material than intellectual: the Cairo & Fulton had given the publishers a printing order for sixty-eight thousand ballots marked "For Railroads" and asked for five hundred copies of its 4-cent weekly issue at 20 cents apiece.[4]

The lobbyists did not just use arguments and statistics, purchased or given, to win converts. They could flatter and bully legislators into obedience. Before he began to push for a bill to give South Carolina's governor the power to sell the public railroad stock, one promoter sent the Northern press a glowing portrait of the General Assembly, and the *Charleston Republican* reprinted his paean. Everyone mentioned was either rich, able, intelligent—Patrick Henry reborn—or distinguished by excellent penmanship. On the other extreme, when one Mississippi state senator objected to a bill mulcting the school fund for the Mobile & Northwestern's benefit, his success in blocking the measure brought him into sharp disfavor. "For my action on this bill," he complained, "I was threatened with defeat in another election by the august Vice President of this road. He stated to me that he intended to see to it that my constituents held me responsible for the defeat of this pet scheme."[5]

Lobbyists knew that a legislator's readiness to accept the corporate viewpoint depended on his personal well-being, and they spent large sums to make public officials comfortable. Littlefield opened a bar at the west portico of the North Carolina capitol and treated men of both parties to the best of drinks and cigars, though later he refused to pick up the bill. Defending himself from charges of corrupt stock ownership, a Mississippi state senator insisted that he had been given "a box of cigars, perhaps, and a few other little things." All of these favors were small, but they cost a good deal to provide in the quantity that would satisfy a General Assembly—thirty-six baskets of champagne alone in one single session of the Texas legislature.[6] In no case, of course, did the lobbyists directly demand a favor in return for their feasts. The dinners were all part of a public relations effort.

So were the financial services that railroad men bestowed on impecunious politicians. North Carolina legislators received their salary in scrip worth far less than its face value and were so often unable to collect their *per diem* and mileage from the state treasurer that they were in danger of eviction from their lodgings. Railroad promoter George Swepson eased their distress by letting them redeem state warrants at par in his bank. When several lawmakers wanted to speculate in state bonds, Swepson put up their margin and protected at least one politician from loss. State Senator R. W. Lassiter had been trying to sell 165 acres of land for $2,600; Littlefield paid him $3,000 for it without even visiting the property in advance. Other legislators borrowed money from promoters. Sometimes they repaid the loans.[7]

Railroads also issued free passes to public officials to win their friendship. For legislators who needed regular contact with their constituents, such a gift saved great expense. It also allowed them to collect public revenue for mileage without having to spend anything. Some companies gave discount rates to delegates on their way to party conventions. Special fares encouraged large turnouts at political gatherings and increased railroad business, but no company was obligated to extend such courtesies. Lacking other means of travel, most delegates would have taken the train in any case. Perhaps railroad executives saw the political wisdom in their policy. Rank-and-file members would feel grateful for the bargain rates. Conversely, delegates would resent any change in established custom and might transmit their feelings of displeasure to their public officials.[8]

Without the good will of political figures in key positions, the railroad companies could accomplish nothing, and they knew it. Even before introducing a bill, promoters had to find friends on the committees that amended and reported all railroad measures. "Finding" friends usually meant putting them on the committees at the start of the session, and that is what the enemies of the Memphis, El Paso & Pacific "humbug" and other corporations accused them of doing, often to the perversion of the parliamentary process. Sometimes the charges were well-founded. During the 1870–1871 session of the South Carolina House, a member testified, one of the leading railroad manipulators, J. J. Patterson, reportedly paid the Speaker $25,000 to choose friendly committee members.[9]

The Speaker of the House could be vital to the enterprise's success even after committee selection. By recognizing the bill's friends, he could hasten its passage, while his rulings could also allow the railroad's enemies to keep any vote from taking place. When the bill consolidating the Greenville & Columbia with the Blue Ridge ran into difficulties in the South Carolina House—several black leaders tried every parliamentary motion they knew to stall action—Speaker Frank Moses encouraged them by refusing to recognize any of the measure's friends. Finally, one of the leading backers of consolidation lost all patience. "Go and ask that damned scoundrel how much he wants," he ordered. Moses wanted $10,000 "over and above everything already paid him." Consequently, as soon as he was promised the fee, he quashed the filibuster. In spite of almost unanimous passage through the Louisiana House of a bill favoring the New Orleans, Mobile & Texas, Speaker George Carter was said to have pocketed the bill and kept the law from being enrolled on the books until the company had made him its attorney at $10,000 a year.[10]

Faction leaders could summon their friends to beat a bill, and corporations often had to join intraparty feuds to win the support of a legislative majority. In Louisiana, Michael Hahn became Speaker of the House, and rumors persisted that he kept control of the chamber with money from the New Orleans, Mobile & Chattanooga. To oblige the faction led by Senator Thomas W. Osborne of Florida, Swepson and Littlefield trumped up a letter implicating their friend the governor in corruption and gave corporate funds to the movement that opposed his administration.[11]

Above all, lobbyists had to make friends with the chief executive in every state. Louisiana Democrats declared that Henry Clay Warmoth was powerful enough to make the legislature pass anything he wanted. When the House tried to investigate the sale of state stock in the New Orleans, Mobile & Jackson, Warmoth burst in on the inquisitors and cornered the chairman, whom he threatened with vengeance if a damaging report were published. It was not published, and the chairman himself was unseated.[12] Between War-moth and railroad promoter H. S. McComb there was such a close relationship that the businessman confessed, "My faith and confidence is more entirely reposed in you than in any other person in the entire South." In return for such courtesies the promoters had to provide political and financial favors. With the aid of one of Patterson's henchmen and $50,000 in public funds, Robert Scott managed to defeat an impeachment attempt. In another, and more tangled incident, he managed to secure South Carolina a $60,000 loan from some bankers who needed his help to extract their railway charter from the clutches of dilatory senators. "The Governor could not get along with less," a lobbyist wrote his employers "and I feel that it is good policy to go that extent." Other railroads provided State Treasuries with the same services.[13]

Scott's dealings show just how complicated the problems of illicit influence were. No doubt the company had been a victim of extortion, but that extortion was not committed for personal enrichment. Rather, it served the public interest. No doubt the transaction resulted in a measure different from the kind that the South Carolina General Assembly would have passed on its own, but did that make it any worse as legislation? If the company spokesmen were correct, the bill as it first seemed destined to pass would have been too impractical for stockholders to accept. By doing the people of South Carolina a service, the railroad had obtained a charter that would enable it to build a road that might enrich the two states through which it ran—yet, by the moral standards of the times, the promoters had given a bribe and Scott was guilty of extortion. The same pattern was repeated throughout the South. Railroads gave money to win their ends because they felt they had to. Furthermore, they believed that the public good achieved by their projects would outweigh all bad consequences.

As any sensible lobbyist knew, bribery must be the last resort. There were two reasons for feelings of reservation. First, the method was untrustworthy. One could hardly institute judicial proceedings against the man who promised the bribe and did not deliver or against the public official who accepted money and then acted according to his best judgment. Both parties to the agreement were known to have swindled each other. In South Carolina, for example, railroad men gave legislators a fraction of the amount originally promised.[14]

Second, with so little revenue available to complete their lines, most companies could scarcely afford the bribery that they felt was forced upon them. In most cases, the promoters had to use resources that the law had dedicated to construction purposes. Influential politicians were endowed with first-mortgage bonds and shares of preferred stock. Since the value of either security depended on the General Assembly's action, the transaction was more dependable than money itself in making statesmen reliable. When the Blue Ridge Railroad wanted legislative validation for a scrip issue, it paid public officials in those very warrants that the measure would make lawful. Swepson testified that eight railroads had agreed to pay one-tenth of their state-aid bonds to his ring for lobbying fees. In fact, some of these corporations had never so agreed, others failed to keep the agreement, and only one railroad complied with the arrangement. In one way or another, however, North Carolina's roads spent $254,731.31 to support their lobbyists; that does not even include the wide range of favors for which there is no accounting.[15]

Expensive and undependable as bribery might be, the promoters often found it the only means of eliminating attitudes that were, as far as the lobbyists were concerned, misguided and unreasonable. Under ordinary circumstances, it could be argued, a bill would have passed easily, but Reconstruction was an extraordinary time and the Reconstruction legislatures exceptionally willful. A bribe simply restored the smooth flow of legislative process by removing obstacles set up by arbitrary men: perhaps that is how company officials saw matters. Certainly, lobbyists claimed to have suborned politicians out of necessity rather than from choice. When a rival railroad had used money to have its way or the legislators made payment the condition of a bill's passage, one could see bribery as a means of assuring justice rather than an instrument for fastening a fraud on the people.

It was a means of assuring justice because so many members expected money for their votes. Furthermore, a scheme, no matter how practical, became the victim of legislative and judicial extortioners. The very financial weakness of a company made it more susceptible to such pressures. Directors could not get along without state aid and were ready to pay any price.[16]

More than anything else, railroad executives feared legislative investigation, and with good reason, for that was one of the most dangerous means of blackmail and defamation. Few enterprises were so above reproach that they could afford the scrutiny of men who would see their every act in the worst possible light. If hard facts did not exist, enemies of a line could use innuendo to make directors look like thieves and incompetents. When Charles Morgan tried to get state support for his railroad to Texas, Louisiana opponents asked for an investigation of the legality of his purchase of the state's stock in the Opelousas Railroad. When his own antagonists came to the legislature for help in 1873, they received the same inquisitorial treatment.[17]

If honest foes caused problems, dishonest ones could have a catastrophic effect. An Alabama Republican charged one Conservative legislative committee with trying to use its work to depreciate securities and make a killing in the market. In Louisiana, the Speaker was said to have stacked a committee to force the subject of the investigation to hire him at $5,000 a year. In return, he would suppress a damning report. "Do you suppose that if our Saviour would come here with a Bill ever so good . . . or it was thought best to get up a committee to investigate him," Governor Scott asked, "do you suppose he wouldn't be crucified again if he didn't pay something to prevent it?" Other committees had been established by members who publicly admitted that they had asked too little for passing the original railroad aid bill and wanted "to get something out of it now." Their wants were gratified.[18]

So the companies paid in anger, in resignation, but not in shame. How much in bribes it cost to pass any measure depended on circumstances: the importance of the measure, the financial advantage it promised the road, the company's ability to pay, the importance of rivals ready to pay money to block opposing plans, the venality of legislators, and the statewide popularity of the bill. According to an enemy of the Alabama & Chattanooga, its charter had cost it $200,000. The Spartanburg & Union was informed that a bill to extend the road would have to expend $20,000 to win the approval of the South Carolina Senate. One legislator estimated that the Bill consolidating the Greenville & Columbia with the Blue Ridge would cost $30,000 in the Senate and $80,000 in all.[19]

Individuals varied in price because they differed in value. A committee chairman might cost $25,000, though Timothy Hurley was said to have been offered $60,000 by the Port Royal Railroad and refused it because the Greenville & Columbia had offered him more. State senators as influential as P.B.S. Pinchback may have received $2,000. Governor Rufus Bullock of Georgia was reputed to have demanded $100,000 for his support of the Brunswick & Albany, though the sum seems incredibly high and Bullock himself denied the accusation. Most legislators received modest sums. The New Orleans, Mobile & Jackson was said to have spent $100 per legislator. The *Charleston Republican* proclaimed that "some sold themselves for gold watches; one poor member of the house sold himself for the paltry sum of $21; some sold the last remnant of their manhood when the judiciary committee's room was turned into a barroom, &c."[20] So little did some legislators get that one wonders whether they even knew they had been bribed and how the money could have affected their judgment.*

Indeed, the bribe-takers did their best to convince critics that the money had wrought no effect. North Carolina legislators claimed that the payments they had received were loans, though neither side anticipated repayment. In South Carolina, S. E. Gaillard conceded that he had been promised $5,000 to support the bill allowing the Blue Ridge to issue scrip but explained that he had already made up his mind to vote for the legislation. When he spurned a bribe for another bill, he had been assured that it would pass anyway and that since his vote made no difference, the payment was not an attempt to suborn him. Another representative admitted that he had been promised payment, and then voted as instructed, but tried to show that the $1000 he had accepted afterward was not really part of a formal understanding.[21]

Together, bribe-taker and bribe-giver tried to rob their transactions of moral stigma. The bribes were not always large, the legislators often needed the money, the bills were often good in their own right, and in some states bribery was not even against the law. Corruption is easy to explain, but it is impossible to excuse. Railroad promoters may have thought that they had no choice but to apply for state aid and pay the legislature to pass their bills, but they did have a moral alternative: to risk the failure of their plans by refusing to seek a government subsidy on dishonorable terms. The legislators had an equal responsibility to decline payment, whatever the circumstances under which it was offered. Their failure to resist corporate pressure showed moral insensitivity.

The lack of moral judgment became self-perpetuating. As more and more legislators succumbed to the allure of quick profit in return for aid, colleagues voting the same way found it harder and harder to stand aloof. Only a man of rare conviction could boast,

---

* How much did legislators receive? The price was not a fixed one. At times, a corporation would pay as much as $600 a head, at other times, $200 or less. In South Carolina, A. L. Singleton received $500, C. D. Hayne $200, Samuel J. Lee $3,000, Samuel Green $300 or more, Edward Mickey, S. J. Keith, and W. C. Glover received $200 each, while Sherman Smalls, Joseph Lloyd, W. E. Elliott, J. D. Boston, E. M. Sumpter, and Laurence Cain got $300 apiece.

as State Senator Alston Mygatt of Mississippi did, that he had taken
no monetary consideration "outside of my per diem . . . while thousands have been offered."[22] Many other public servants must have
learned through experience that if they demanded payment, they
could get it, and that they did not always have to ask. The lines
between a bribe, a pourboire, and a douceur were delicate ones in
any case.

Not surprisingly, then, once corruption began, it continued and
seemed to worsen. There was little talk of bribery during the first
sessions of the first Reconstruction legislatures, but within a year
the accusations of bribery touched every railroad bill of any consequence. Sometimes the change in attitude became apparent before the General Assembly's first adjournment. By 1870, some lobbyists in Alabama and Louisiana had become so indiscreet that they
ventured onto the legislative floor to thrust money into the hands
of their allies. Some representatives almost boasted about their
ability to command a high price, for so accepted was the bribery
that it had lost much of its pejorative connotation. Before one
congressional committee, a witness testified that Hurley of South
Carolina was not wholly corrupt. After all, he preferred to bribe
others rather than take the money himself, and he would not "go
back on his friends. If he contracts to put through a job, any one
else may offer him more money, but he will not forsake his first
man."[23]

Everyone knew that there was corruption, but men disagreed on
why the South suffered so much of it during Reconstruction. Conservatives argued that the enfranchisement of blacks had polluted
the political process. An ignorant electorate chose a venal government in which outsiders led former field hands into scandalous
habits. Only by overthrowing the Radical governments and the laws
that made them possible could the South free itself from corruption.

This explanation was totally unsatisfactory. First, black representatives were no more susceptible to bribery than whites of greater
education and political experience. Since position determined the
size of the bribe and since blacks held few major posts in the General
Assembly or the executive branch, they must have received far less
than white officials, even in states with a black electoral majority.
Indeed, blacks in several states voiced resentment at how often the
lobbyists neglected them. Certain whites had risen from beggary
to opulence, Beverly Nash told the South Carolina Senate. "The
poor niggers got nothing." Some black Florida legislators report-

edly met in caucus to find a remedy. Since the railroad could overlook an individual but not a bloc, said one account, they decided to sell their services *en masse*.[24]

Second, Conservatives were implicated in the corruption. With a few conspicuous exceptions, they gave the bribes, for they ran the railroads. The bribe-givers had risen to prominence in the days when white votes alone had run the South. They were men who commanded deep respect. Conservatives held few seats in the first Reconstruction legislatures, but as far as it possessed power the opposition party shared in the plunder. Its strength in most states increased with the elections of 1870, but general demoralization persisted. Democrats occasionally conceded that their own party backed every dishonest speculation. The *Augusta Weekly Chronicle* thought it a mortifying fact "that the extravagance of Bullock's administration—we say nothing as to the corruption—benefitted about as many Democrats as Republicans."[25]

Third, just as bribery affected both parties, so did hostility to its use. In every commonwealth, men of all factions denounced the venality of officials and tried to cleanse the government. Conservatives disliked Republicans as much for their principles as for their lack of scruples, but Republicans were even more indignant at their own membership. Reconstruction had begun with such fine intentions, and the party of human rights also thought itself the party of moral ideals. Republicans expected Conservatives to steal—that was their nature—but felt keenly the moral fall of their own colleagues. Black leaders became especially critical of the thieves. Several governors had the same "perfect horror of dishonesty" that was said to afflict Edmund Davis of Texas, a man so upright that his friends boasted he bent over backward. Elisha Baxter of Arkansas, Adelbert Ames of Mississippi, David P. Lewis of Alabama, Harrison Reed of Florida, and Daniel Chamberlain of South Carolina used all the power they had against the corruptionists. All of them lacked political skill and all brought disunity upon their party by their actions, but at least they had the courage to fight.[26]

Republicans with more political aptitude tried to keep the corruptionists at bay without sacrificing party unity. Pragmatists like Powell Clayton of Arkansas and William Pitt Kellogg of Louisiana made no effort to drive the money changers from the capitol, but they ran railroad aid policies honestly and competently. Louisiana Conservatives hated party boss Marshall Packard as a savage, cunning foe, but they conceded him "peculiarly honest." Finally, some chief executives who showed utter depravity in some matters made valiant attempts to slow corrupt influences in other concerns. Because of the corruption that railroad aid seemed to entail, William Smith of Alabama and W. W. Holden of North Carolina urged a reconsideration of the subsidy policy. Warmoth of Louisiana, Scott of South Carolina, and Bullock of Georgia all vetoed bills that they considered swindles. Their sporadic moral leadership, ineffective though it generally was, at least was better than none. Only one chief executive seemed wholly irresponsible and corrupt: Franklin J. Moses, Jr., of South Carolina.[27]

Fourth, corruption could not be blamed on political and economic carpetbaggers alone. "If we could tear the hands of the spoiler from her emaciated person," F. F. Warley commented of South Carolina, "methinks the rings upon the fingers of some would declare them members of our household." A *New York Herald* correspondent was more specific: natives had done most of the plundering. The Pettigrews, Meltons, Moseses, and Mackeys, once the *ton* of Charleston society, now "herd together upon no social standards for the sake of the luxurious husks of which the swine partake." Northerners did some bribing, but no more than Swepson, Rufus McAden, Samuel McDowell Tate, J. W. Harrison, A. M. West, and John Milner, Southerners all.[28]

Railroad influence in fact had infected politics across the nation. Wherever a railroad wanted favors, lobbies did not scruple in how they attained them. Virginia and Kentucky had Conservative governors and legislatures; yet railroad lobbyists' corruption flourished there. In the Northeast, the Pennsylvania Railroad and the New York Central used bribery against other companies even less scrupulous. Of one Illinois legislature the *Carthage Republican* concluded that it was "the most corrupt and imbecile . . . which ever disgraced the commonwealth." In the nation's capital, congressmen accepted stock in the Union Pacific Railroad while the directors were seeking federal support.[29] Corporations bought friends in both parties in all states. They could do so not because political figures were less educated, less affluent, and more dishonest than ever before, but because a little clandestine persuasion could do much more in a time when the government had much less to give.

The state's ability and willingness to subsidize railroad construction was the real cause of much Southern corruption. The subsidy laws were but one example of an increasing government role in economic life. As officials found more money at their disposal, they found more applicants for its use. As corporations discovered the potential value of state support, they increased their efforts to share the spoils. Any of the benefits a state could provide would produce a lobby: sale of public railroad stock, tax-exemption, land grants, exclusive rights of construction and scrip issue, banking privileges, and bond endorsement. The more state aid depended on individual whims, the more corruption permeated the political system. Arkansas had a general aid law and forbade the grant of privileges, while Mississippi did not allow the state to pledge its credit at all. Consequently, neither state suffered unduly from corruption. Most of the talk of corruption in Alabama did not concern the general aid bill, but the special statutes of 1870. The best way to have limited bribery would have been to prohibit all acts of special aid and to provide specific conditions which every corporation had to meet to qualify for support. Any other policy invited corruption and improper influence. Because Republicans did not realize this fact, they were partly to blame for the scandals that marred their administrations.

The amount of corruption varied from state to state. Governor Warmoth proclaimed it "all the fashion" in Louisiana. East of the Appalachians, legislators took money almost shamelessly for their support of railroad bills. Yet the difference between the best and worst states should not be exaggerated. Every government granted favors of some sort. Mississippi's constitutional restrictions could not eliminate the rascals. In 1870, James E. Richardson tried to induce the General Assembly to pass a railroad bill giving him exclusive rights for fifty years along a certain route. "He was undoubtedly the most corrupt man I ever saw," Governor James L. Alcorn recalled. "He was the only man that ever offered me a bribe; and when I refused it, threatened me." Alcorn vetoed the bill. And when he found that the veto might be overridden, he used the Secret Service fund to buy documents showing what influences had been at work. Apparently, Richardson had been giving legislators stock in return for support. Vowing to make the information public, Alcorn gave the bribe-takers the alternative of penitence or the penitentiary and forced them to sustain his veto. But even the governor had his weaknesses. He supported a bill selling the state's stock in the New Orleans, Jackson & Great Northern to private parties at a low figure. At the same time, he borrowed $30,000 from the purchasers. Perhaps Alcorn's support for the promoters and theirs for him were unconnected. Republicans pointed out that the loan had been promptly repaid.[31] Still the incident did not speak well for the governor's sense of ethics, for the closeness of the two favors looked suspicious.

All cases of corruption were reprehensible. They may have affected the legislators' judgment; but did they constitute *the* overwhelming reason that railroad bills passed? With a few exceptions, bribery was only one factor among many in a measure's passage. Most Republicans and some Democrats were friends of almost any railroad project of statewide importance and were particularly sympathetic to roads benefiting their own area. Even without outside pressure the railroad committees approved of legislation favoring corporate interests. The members may have been more strongly supportive of certain enterprises than their colleagues in general, but the difference was one of degree and not of substance.

Bribery, in fact, *was* a means of giving the legislative majority a chance to vote on a measure. It was needed on a large scale only when the enterprise seeking aid had such purely local importance that it could pass only after lobbyists had changed the minds of a large proportion of the membership, or when the proposal was so controversial that not even staunch friends of railroad aid would support it on its merits. The more a bill gave a company without demanding sufficient guarantees, the more the company had to rely on bribery to augment its other forms of influence. Thus measures to cancel state mortgages on lines or to add to the government's endorsement without adding to the strength of its lien encountered opposition that bribery could and must overcome. Less spurious concerns had stronger arguments, and could afford more ethical means of persuasion.

Finally, corruption had limits. No amount of bribery could pass a railroad bill that did not have at least some local support and a substantial legislative minority behind it from its origin. Nor could payments revive government sympathy for a road once the public had lost faith in its promises. Once the policy of state aid had fallen into disfavor, no amount of influence could pass a subsidy bill. Legislators dreaded their constituents' wrath more than they desired douceurs. As a result, most of the corruption took place during the early 1870s when "railroad mania" could excuse almost any legislative act it did not fully explain. Bribery lost significance as the governments began to reconsider their earlier generosity and to revoke the privileges they had bestowed.

Corruption, therefore, was one reason why railroad legislation passed, but not the only reason nor the most significant one. It was, however, a crucial factor in that policy's failure, for neither the subsidy laws nor the Republicans could afford to have their legitimacy put into question. Representing a race inexperienced in politics, the Reconstruction coalition had a special obligation to still white fears about the effects of universal suffrage. This *might* have been done by administering the South honestly and intelligently. Because the railroads relied so heavily on state aid, the promoters had to protect their securities from any imputation of fraud that would permit future officials to demand repudiation. Bribery undermined the credibility of the policy as well as of the party.

Charges of corrupt passage could obscure any bill's merits. Whether a bill passed because of bribery was less important than other questions going to the heart of the company's fitness for state aid: Did the government receive sufficient surety for its endowment? Could the state sell its bonds for enough to allow another extension of credit to one more private enterprise? Did the proposal have statewide importance? Even a bill that had become law through the most scrupulous means should have been scrutinized for its legal clarity and financial wisdom. This need seems elementary, and yet Southerners did not look far beyond the corruption issue. If the origin of a road was so improper, they wondered, did it not follow that the directors would operate the line in the same way? The two phases of railroad development, legislation and construction, should not have been confused, but they were. In the process, the means by which state revenues were obtained and the ways in which they were spent were confused and combined into one charge of fraud.

The commonness of corruption also made any gammon seem credible. The press published nonsense about dishonest dealings that went virtually unchallenged and was not always easy to disprove. Conservatives asserted that Alabama's treasurer had speculated in state bonds and pocketed funds earmarked for railroad construction. They asserted further that its governor had invested $50,000 in one of the lines to which he had extended aid.[32] Although untrue, such accusations found widespread belief.

More typically, critics of Reconstruction made vague allegations based on rumor and fabrication.* In one clause of the Liberty &

---

* It is essential for the historian to see how much of the talk was fustian. James Shepherd Pike, for example, recounted a visit to the South Carolina legislature:

There was a measure up for consideration the other day in the House, in which the negroes broke away and voted alone. It was a bill for a railroad very much needed, and to which there could be and was no honest objection. But some of the corrupt negro leaders thought the corporation could be forced to pay for the charter, and if members opposed it they could get pay for their votes. Accordingly, the great body of blacks combined, and the bill was refused a passage by a decisive majority, who chuckled over their achievement as they would have done if they had cornered a rabbit in a cotton field.

Woodville Railroad charter, the Mississippi legislature remitted taxes to every road in the state, and the *Pascagoula Star* blamed the law on two politicians, O. C. French and William H. Gibbs. Of Gibbs the *Star* said, "We *know* that he . . . did, in conjunction with French, . . . receive a bribe of ten thousand dollars in hand paid to 'put through' the bill." Unlike many other political worthies, French did not accept abuse as the price of fame. He demanded that a committee of his political foes make a full investigation. The basis for the *Star*'s assertions turned out to be a letter from N. B. Forrest, a prominent Democrat, who insisted that the two Radicals "and others did receive ten thousand dollars for certain bills passed through the Legislature of Mississippi." Just what bills had been bribed through, how much either man had received, how many others shared the fee, and where Forrest had found his facts the letter did not say. In vain the committee asked him to testify. Others had made like accusations and were invited to speak. Not one of them came forward to repeat their charges under oath. Furthermore, none of the witnesses called could utter a word of evidence against French, and the committee exonerated him.[33] Many other legislators never had the same chance to clear their names. As a result, Southerners continued to believe allegations, many of which were no more than the ravings of imaginative editors.

Popular suspicion was all the harder to remove because the public distrusted investigating committee reports. This distrust was fully justified. Any enterprise powerful enough to buy the kinds of laws it wanted was powerful enough to keep its misdeeds out of the public eye. Legislators were chary about implicating one another. Corporations feigned innocence of all charges, and even when proof of bribery was irrefutable they did not choose to blacken

---

Not one white voted with them, Pike added. Pike, *Prostrate State*, pp. 37–38.

The story sounds damning, but it must be noted: Pike did not say what railroad it was, nor who had told him that it was much needed and worthy of consideration, nor where he had heard word that the blacks opposed it from dishonest motives. Considering the scoundrelry of so many white Republican legislators, the idea that only blacks would hold out for payment on such a bill seems incredible. There are two alternative explanations for such a vote. First, the railroad might have been an upstate enterprise, and since most Negro legislators came from lowland counties, their sectional prejudices might have affected their vote. Second, the vote might have concerned the issue of equal accommodations on the railroad—quite a sore point and dividing line in several railroad charter votes at other times.

The final major objection to Pike's story is this: During his period in South Carolina, the legislative journals do not show any railroad bill defeated by such a vote as he describes. Indeed, except for the two scandalous railroads, the Blue Ridge and the Greenville & Columbia, almost no corporations sought charters or aid that winter at all.

themselves further by producing lists of everyone to whom they had given bribes. Since most lobbyists did not ask for receipts for their payments, the corrupt man could deny everything and make his accuser look like a liar as well as a self-convicted corrupter. After the Mobile & Ohio charter was amended, an Alabama committee reported that although the company had made improper inducements and at least indirectly offered bribes, no evidence incriminated anyone. Investigations of the Brunswick & Albany and the Western & Atlantic ended just as pitifully. In North Carolina, the House made itself into a committee of the whole to study the Swepson-Littlefield frauds and did its best to find nothing. After Littlefield testified to his own virtue, the committee dissolved itself. Then the Senate chose a three-man commission led by Thomas Bragg. Before testimony could be completed, Littlefield opened Raleigh's National Hotel to Republican legislators for an oyster supper. Leading politicians made after-dinner tirades against the Bragg committee, calling it a Conservative witch-hunt. Littlefield himself suggested that "if [the guests] knew as much about the Bragg Committee as he did, they would vote to repeal it the next day." His guests missed the deadline by only two days. The Bragg committee was abolished before it could make a final report.[34]

Worthless though the committees were as a way of proving the Republicans men of honor and the railroads enterprises worthy of respect, failure to appoint an investigative body became tantamount to a confession of guilt. Against baseless accusations, legislators felt helpless, even when the originators of the charges were known for their irresponsibility. Enemies of the Blue Ridge Railroad, for example, brought up a motion to have the South Carolina Senate investigate the company's actions. Republican leaders were furious, but had to give in lest they be accused of a whitewash.[35] Other legislative bodies faced the same dilemma.

Corruption blighted public faith in both the railroads and the Republicans. It also made Republicans lose faith in themselves. When they came to power, the Republicans had appeared to be friends of the workingman, but by 1870 some party followers were wondering about their leaders' true motives. The corruption was too blatant to allow true Republicans to take the political rhetoric at face value. After all, the poor neither did the corrupting nor seemed likely to benefit from it. The Republicans had been trusted to act as a purifying element in politics. As "Carolina" lamented, in 1868 the new government had seemed proof that "the day was passed when money could send Representatives to our Legislatures to vote money into the pockets of money. We thought that railroad and bank directors would no longer have it all their own way, and fill all the chairs in our Legislatures. But money is ahead of us yet."[36]

Corruption hurt more than a corporation's good name. It increased the actual financial cost to the railway promoters. A subsidy obtained by fraud invited legal attack, and investors became increasingly fearful of the risk they were taking in holding the bonds of a disreputable corporation. As bonds became a less reliable investment, they became harder to sell at any price. Other funds that might have gone for construction had gone to bribe legislators, towns reneged on subscriptions promised earlier, rival companies took the railroads to court and questioned their charters' validity. Promoters who thought that they could not build without state support found that they could not build with it. In losing their reputations, they had lost everything. Corruption thus took on its real significance only after the railroad seemed to have gained all it wanted.

Finally, the prevalence of corruption made the principle of railroad aid appear dubious. In theory, a government that bestowed favors could have escaped the scrambling between interests bidding for special consideration, but practice differed from theory. As long as the state had something to give, it seemed, there would be people ready to take, and by any means they could find. Railroad aid did not assure improper influences, but it certainly encouraged them. As the workings of the lobby became more visible, thoughtful men in both parties grew troubled. Perhaps political venality was too much to pay for a railroad system. As the grandiose visions of the late 1860s faded and more and more subsidized lines failed to keep their original promise, the number of people disturbed by the subsidy policy increased. When even Republican governors began to question the value of the programs they had championed, the whole railroad aid policy was in jeopardy.

Corruption through bribery and extortion had brought great damage to the railroads; yet this form of corruption was the least important kind. If the term is broadened to include other, more subtle betrayals of the public interest, "corruption" involved almost every man and measure of the Reconstruction period. Many corporations did not deserve aid. A systematic railroad policy could not endow all lines equally. Yet the legislature gave support to undeserving roads, not because the projects seemed good, but because the representatives, blinded by local prejudices and impractical visions, allowed themselves to place local gain above sectional and state good. State pride corrupted legislators. Directorial positions and personal involvement in projects corrupted politicians who put private advantage ahead of public good. Cities, towns, Radicals, Conservatives, promoters, directors, subscribers—all were corrupted by the prospect of railroad aid. They ravaged the Gospel of Prosperity by making impossible any railroad system beneficial to the whole South and protective of that section's commercial interests.

This shortsightedness might not have been enough in itself to ruin the railroads. Many lines under construction could not have succeeded under the most favorable circumstances; but selfishness, in all its forms, made the railroad aid programs a jumble of different subsidies and increased the financial burdens on taxpayers. Here was the real corruption that the Gospel of Prosperity fostered, not only a corruption of ethics, but a corruption of judgment. The latter was by far the more serious of the two.

PART THREE

"The Glory is Departed from Israel":
Using the Railroads

CHAPTER 7

"Let the Representatives . . .
Have a Hand in It."

If this is a great thing and a good thing, in the name of God, why not let the Representatives of the State of Louisiana have a hand in it?

A Louisiana legislator to his comrades

THE *New York Herald* prided itself on the best possible coverage of any topic, from the disappearance of Dr. Livingstone in Africa to the latest murder in Five Points. Responding to spreading rumors of Southern venality, the editors sent a reporter to South Carolina. What he found made fascinating reading. His main source was that outrageous carpetbagger, Timothy Hurley, chairman of the House Railroad Committee and a good-natured rogue. With cynical exuberance, Hurley described the way in which every public servant had as firm a hand in the till as on the tiller. "My God," he shouted, "it would turn your hair white if you were only to see what I see every day." In public, moral purists cursed the fraud and theft in bills aiding the Greenville & Columbia Railroad. That did not keep them from using their official position to obtain stock in the company for themselves. Brandishing a copy of the railroad contract, Hurley read off the names of respected public officials:

> Niles G. Parker, State Treasurer, $20,000; Comptroller General Neagle, $30,000; D. H. Chamberlain, $1,000 but he's sold out; John J. Patterson, $2,000; Timothy Hurley—that's me . . . $15,000; Reuben Tomlinson—he's pious, is Tomlinson, and has a fine voice—$10,000; George W. Waterman, that's the Governor's brother-in-law, $50,000; H. H. Kimpton, the Financial Agent of the State, . . . Joe Crews, the poker player. . . . R. J. Donaldson, $5,000 . . . Richard B. Carpenter, $10,000, but he's sold out. F. L. Cardozo, the negro Secretary of State, $5,000—he's pretty decent; John B. Hubbard, the State constable. . . . You see we are all in the same boat sure enough.[1]

What Hurley said sounded damning, and in this case it was; but, interested as he was in the sensational, the *Herald* reporter missed the larger story. The most dramatic kind of political profit-sharing might easily be seen as corruption. Other conflicts of interest were not seen that way, even though they all had a serious effect on the state aid program, the railroads, and politics. Republican officials in fact turned corporations to their advantage in many different ways.

That lawmakers sank money into the railroad enterprises that they had predicted would revive the Southern economy should surprise no one. For them not to have invested would have been more astonishing. Everyone else was doing so. Everyone knew that they would make good money. It was also good politics for a legislator to invest. A politician who attended mass meetings in favor of building lines through his home county, but did not offer to subscribe to any of the local schemes, would have seemed hypocritical, even hostile, to the welfare of his constituents. Still, the hunger for profit came first. As one lawmaker remarked in another context,* "If this is a great thing and a good thing, in the name of God, why not let the Representatives . . . have a hand in it."[2]

Railroads *were* a good thing, and Republican officials had a hand in them from the start. Railway incorporators in Mississippi included Senators James L. Alcorn and Adelbert Ames, the Speaker of the House, and two black leaders, one of whom would become lieutenant-governor and the other senator. In South Carolina, every important official from Senator "Honest John" Patterson to probate judge was involved. In Alabama, Governor W. H. Smith and State Senator J. L. Pennington took directorships on the Eufaula, Opelika & Guntersville Railroad, while leading upstate Louisiana Republicans, John Ray and Chief Justice J. T. Ludeling, controlled and mismanaged the North Louisiana & Texas. In the legislatures, most Republicans had comparatively little property and very uncertain tenure. They needed to find some means of income more desperately than did, for example, Governor Robert K. Scott of South Carolina, who came to power with widespread investments. It was therefore common to find a legislator among the incorporators of a line. Indeed, in Louisiana, South Carolina, Texas, and Arkansas, a corporation with no legislator involved seemed almost freakish.[3]

* It must be stressed that the comment *was* taken out of another context: the Louisiana legislator was referring to a proposal to make all House members incorporators in a slaughterhouse monopoly; there are even grounds to think that the lawmaker meant his words tongue in cheek, since after this defense, he opposed the bill, and fellow members treated the proposal as a joke. But the principle of public officials sharing in the railroads' benefits was not a joke, and for them the quotation holds good.

Democrats were just as deeply involved in railroad schemes, and had been since the 1850s. In Alabama, the party was led by Chairman James H. Clanton of the Montgomery & Eufaula Railroad, former Governor Robert Patton of the Alabama & Chattanooga, and Redeemer Governor George S. Houston of the South & North. North Carolina Conservatives Augustus Merrimon and Zebulon Vance went to the United States Senate: the two already had a long association on the board of the Western North Carolina Railroad. Lucius Q. C. Lamar of Mississippi, J. W. Throckmorton of Texas, Augustus Garland and Jesse Turner of Arkansas, James Orr and J. B. Kershaw of South Carolina, P. G. T. Beauregard and the Ogdens of New Orleans—all had railroad interests as well as public ones.[4]

Did railroads dominate the political process, then? Quite the reverse. First, most incorporators were dabblers: planters, farmers, merchants, and politicians. They found the companies they supported beneficial to their own narrow interests, and their interests so differed that on other issues, including railroad bills not affecting their immediate community, they had no common response. Second, Conservative and Republican involvement differed in a vital particular. Democratic leaders had invested heavily in railroad ventures long before Reconstruction. Most Republican leaders had scant political experience and modest financial status before 1866. They had started as politicians and then tried to break into the commercial circles which conservative men dominated. With political power, they could make the railroads bend to their will, and did so. In many cases, the battle between Republican and Democrat was the battle between new roads and old—or between new management and the entrenched directors.

Doubtless some legislators invested part of their salaries in railroads for political reasons or were invited into the corporations for the same end. Promoters tried to involve legislators as a way of adding prestige to the lines and as proof of the projects' local popularity. When a prominent politician took a directorship, he gave the company credibility: an unofficial declaration that the state backed the enterprise. With a legislator on the board, the line might expect a more sympathetic hearing from his colleagues, should it need their help.

At times, however, the legislators did not wait to be invited. When a charter came before them, they could and did add any names they pleased to those of the incorporators. That included their own. North Carolina representatives added six new incorporators to the

Southern Air-Line, four of them legislators. In the South Carolina Senate, the Railroad Committee reported the Anderson, Aiken, Port Royal & Charleston line's charter and listed among the incorporators the former House committee chairman, Timothy Hurley. At one senator's request, this was corrected. Hurley was replaced with the *Senate* Railroad Committee chairman. At times, the addition of names appeared to be a way of opening economic opportunities to black politicians, whom the white capitalists in charge of the project refused to list among shareholders.[5]

Such a mingling of public and private interest was not particularly unethical. To be listed among the incorporators did not entitle a lawmaker to any financial benefits, unless he bought capital stock. In some charters, the incorporators were proclaimed directors of the line, but this clause does not appear in any documents in which legislators' names appear. Perhaps lawmakers put their names into charters for the publicity back home; after all, every charter was published in the Republican local organ and was proof positive of the politician's concern for the prosperity of the voters.

In a few cases, however—and it must be stressed that these were very rare—political figures found that their power to wreck or rescue an existing line could be made profitable. In Arkansas, the "Brindletail" Republican faction found the Cairo & Fulton in desperate need of political friends. Unless 20 miles of track were laid by April 28, 1870, the federal government could revoke its land grant, and that would leave the company insolvent. With work uncompleted in early March, the road's president was becoming frantic. Friends in Congress might be able to extend the deadline, but such friends were hard to find: regular Republicans in Congress supported the governor's friends, and the governor's friends sat on the boards of lines whose success depended on the Cairo & Fulton's failure. In May, Senator B. F. Rice, of the dissident Brindletail wing, became the road's attorney. Almost at once he and a Brindletail congressman pushed through a bill extending the deadline until the end of the year. Before then, with little money of their own invested, Rice's faction took over the line. M. L. Rice became president, the senator became a director, and Joseph Brooks, a leading champion of the disaffected, joined still other Brindletails on the board. Threatening to repudiate the existing contract, they forced the construction company to make a new one, which made the senator's brother-in-law receiver in trust for nearly $3 million in stock paid to the railroad. Four months later, the politicians sold these shares and pocketed $440,000. They also collected huge fees for their services to the railroad. Such financial juggling may have been perfectly honorable. Brooks boasted of his profit, but insisted that he had violated no law. Perhaps Senator Rice needed no retainer to plead the railroad's cause. Perhaps the change in directors had nothing do do with the extension bill. Yet the facts seemed to fit the interpretation that regular Republicans gave: the Brindletails forced the company to give them control of the board and used this authority to seize one-fourth of the preferred and common stock of the road. Then they forced real capitalists to buy them out and took payment for something to which they had no title.[6]

Still, the possibility that Rice and his cohorts acted for political and not economic advantage is worth considering. It reveals another aspect of officeholder manipulation. Railroad corporations were among the largest private employers, and no political group could afford to overlook them. With public and private enterprise intertwined, politicians found it easy to see companies as adjuncts of the state and, therefore, of the political machine. When an enterprise looked to the government for favors, it was natural for those in power to expect patronage rights in return.

Transforming the companies into a source of patronage began long before Republicans took power. Before the war, North Carolina and Georgia governors filled railroad posts with their political friends. But for two reasons, the process became much more marked under the Republicans. First, the Conservatives had had a much larger pool of talent from which to choose employees than did the Republicans, and they filled positions with abler men. Second, the Reconstruction governments had a more desperate need to disburse jobs than did their predecessors. To a Conservative partisan, an appointment was useful, a sign that his good services had been recognized by party leaders. To a Republican, whose livelihood often depended on the planters or merchants who used their economic power as a weapon, a patronage job was a matter of survival. For his devotion to the party, a Republican might lose any employment he had and needed the state's assistance. One partisan favored parceling out places "even down to the section masters along the Railroads for if we ever get beat then we are gone and Trampled under foot."[7]

In most states, the governments held stock in railroads and with it a voice in whom the presidents of the lines would appoint. In North Carolina, the state could select the presidents in the major companies. Georgia owned the Western & Atlantic completely. Elsewhere, the government held first mortgages, allowing it to seize the line for default on payment of bond interest. This power gave the government a right to choose receivers and lawyers to represent the public interest in suits instituted by private bondholders. When the Laurens Railroad went bankrupt, for example, the governor's brother-in-law became receiver. The need for spoils made a businesslike management of the lines difficult, for political loyalty rather than ability tended to decide who got preferment. Consequently, some of the applicants thought that their lack of experience qualified them for almost anything, and with pathetic desperation asked for whatever they could get. "Solicit conductorship," wrote a defeated candidate for the State Senate. "Directorship or Agency of Depot or Baggage. Will work cheap."[8]

Under proper restraint, a patronage system need not have excluded talent. Some Republicans combined the true faith with capital and ability. Many businessmen eschewed politics, but could be won over to the party by a well-timed appointment. Governor Holden showed good judgment in his choice of presidents for the North Carolina Railroad, the Western North Carolina, and the Atlantic & North Carolina. William Smith of the North Carolina, in particular, found that he preferred a well-run road to a well-satisfied party. He was so successful that the governor was denounced for selling out to the Democrats. In public at least, the party propagandists proclaimed that competence was the first thing they looked for in any appointee and that the government found nothing but able men. When Edward Hulburt took over the Western & Atlantic's management, "Truth" wrote a paean to his past experience as supervisor on the Atlanta & West Point. "You might have placed a glass of water, three-fourths full, on the floor of a car and run it over the entire length of the road without throwing a drop . . . from it," he boasted.[9]

In fact, Hulburt was a perfect example of how the patronage system encouraged mediocre management. Company Treasurer Foster Blodgett later admitted utter ignorance about the job, but when Hulburt broke with the governor, he lost his place to Blodgett. Political skills were the essential trait. The Western & Atlantic employed at least twice as many men as were needed. According to one witness, the Republican administrators placated lawmakers by restricting conductors' job to the legislators' sons. Legislators themselves received still higher positions. Against Holden's good appointments one must set his atrocious ones. Three of the presidents he named swindled their stockholders and lost company bonds in speculation.[10]

Even in partisan terms, forcing the railroads to give patronage did harm. Because they had offices to give, the corporations created a focus for factional wrangling. Neglected Republicans were quick to accuse those more fortunate of party treason and to demand their ouster. North Carolina loyalists damned the president of the Western Railroad, and one of them boasted, "I get up at midnight to do it." The correspondents guessed that every employee above common laborer, with two exceptions, was a ferocious Democrat. "This Road has defeated the Republican party in this county." Communities insisted on more than their share of representation on the board and threatened to desert the party when they received less than they desired. Enemies of the incumbents hungered for patronage themselves and used promises of railroad posts to win defectors. Attempting to take the Western & Atlantic out of executive hands, Georgia Democrats were rumored to boast "that there are enough important places on the Road to buy up . . . the Senate, even over the Governor's veto."[11]

Patronage hurt the party because there were never enough places for everyone, but one way to ease the pressure of office seekers was to increase the number of railroads under government control. Partly for this reason Republicans tried to take over roads in which the state had only limited influence. In both Georgia and Louisiana, party leaders tried to elect friendly boards of directors by voting the states' stock in specific corporations, and Conservatives thwarted them only by voting the cities' holdings the other way. North Carolina Republicans made a more sustained effort to turn the companies into political instruments. The General Assembly offered to exchange aid for the state's right to appoint a majority of directors and to take election of company presidents out of the hands of private shareholders. In the most important roads under construction, the Republicans took full control. Forced to accept either division of the company or Republican control of the board, the directors of the Wilmington, Charlotte & Rutherford chose Republican control, while Conservatives on the Western North Carolina agreed to the division. It made no difference. What followed was a series of laws which gave the state mastery of both divisions and then rescinded it, as well as mastery of stockholders' meetings in which each party tried to catch the other napping. In the end, Republicans ended up in control of both divisions of the Western North Carolina and made the company an arm of the party.[12]

It was a very powerful arm. Where the government held a controlling interest in a road, the president turned his energies to keeping party hegemony. "I am ready sir with any means I may controll," J. L. Mott of the Western North Carolina Railroad wrote Governor Holden, "and with my own right arm to defend the administration of the state and those who vote the Republican ticket; and by the Eternal God I say deluge the state in blood from one end to the other rather than our people should suffer again the treatment of the last six months." By "any means" Mott meant the use of the line to ship political speakers free of charge, to carry voters to the polls, and to threaten with dismissal those employees failing to vote Republican. Railroad section masters used their power to force hands to vote right. That was the accepted practice. The only question was in which cause they would use their influence; and this was true at every level of employment. William A. Smith was said to have boasted that he could create ten thousand Republican votes as railroad president, and Conservatives gave him credit for making good on his word. Not only did he intimidate employees, but he ran freight trains ahead of schedule on election day so that their crews could reach the polls before closing time— the polls at which they would do the party the most good, Conservatives charged. Alabama Democrats insisted that the Alabama & Chattanooga brought 925 nonresident employees into the state and voted them for the Republicans. In Georgia, it was said that the state road imported Tennessee blacks to vote in the 1870 elections.[13]

Against the combined forces of personal gain and partisan advantage, no logical railroad policy could survive. The whole idea of a program rationally planned and efficiently carried out was thrown into doubt. Perhaps Hurley acted from solicitude for South Carolina taxpayers when he used his Railroad Committee chairmanship to smother a bill giving $2 million to the Port Royal Railroad, but he may just have acted from solicitude for his own pocket, since the road could have created a dangerous rival trunk line to his own Greenville & Columbia.[14] Possibly he would not have been able to tell which motive inspired him.

The motives behind any award of railroad aid became suspect. Arkansas showed how. Governor Powell Clayton molded almost every policy there to Republican advantage. It should not be surprising, then, that all of the railroads aided had party leaders among their directors. The Memphis & Little Rock received $1.2 million; Senator Alexander McDonald was one of the two Arkansans on the board. The Little Rock & Fort Smith was eligible for $1.5 million in aid; McDonald was vice-president of the line, as were Senator

Rice and State Senator Ozra Hadley. The Mississippi, Ouachita & Red River got $1,950,000; President Thomas A. Bowen was on the state supreme court, and two state senators and a candidate for Congress were directors. S. W. Dorsey's Arkansas Central road would receive $450,000 in aid, and Dorsey himself would go to the Senate. Two of the roads receiving aid consolidated, and Clayton, now senator, became their president. All of the roads received no more aid than they deserved under law, but the prominence of Republicans is striking in six roads aided out of eighty-six incorporated before 1872.[15] Elsewhere the pattern was no different. H. I. Kimball's roads took most of the aid actually issued in Georgia, where he served Republicanism faithfully. Texas gave aid to roads in which A. J. Hamilton, the Flanagans, and Edward Degener had money and friends. Governor Harrison Reed's close ally, Milton Littlefield, was the guiding spirit in the roads that Florida aided, while his associate George Swepson benefited greatly from a close friendship with Governor Holden of North Carolina, who either by coincidence or design managed to wreck every publicly owned road that Swepson could not take over.[16]

In no case were the projects aided strictly Republican concerns. Conservatives put their money and faith into them all, though they tended to have less influence there than in lines already built. West of Alabama, there were few accusations of the government using roads as naked political weapons. Republicans also participated in lines receiving no state aid. The companies aided may well have been the most deserving ones. Those in Alabama and Arkansas certainly were. Nevertheless, the close correlation between railroads aided and those in which the party in power had friends or followers put the aid policy into question.

The suspicion of favoritism was a serious one, for the contingent debt most Southern states assumed in aid of railroad projects was considerable and would later fuel complaints from taxpayers. The hint of conflict of interest would provide an excuse for declaring the whole debt invalid and casting off the tax burden it entailed.

Not only the means by which the laws were enacted but the constitutional validity of the laws were questioned. In Mississippi, J. S. Morris discovered that his duties as attorney general could reap him advantages as attorney-at-law. The state constitution forbade public loans of credit, but the 1871 subsidy bill was so cunningly worded that it seemed to evade the restriction. Early in 1872, the House Railroad Committee held hearings to consider the measure's repeal. At the advice of the vice-president of the Mobile &

Northwestern Railroad company, itself an interested party, the question of the law's constitutionality was submitted to Morris. On January 9, he declared the law binding until repealed. On January 10, the railroad paid him a $500 retainer to act as attorney for the line or, more accurately, as Morris later explained, to keep him from acting against it in a private capacity during the next year. In early September, the Ripley Railroad applied for its share of state aid bonds. Morris went to the state auditor's office and advised the deputy auditor of his duty to issue no warrants to the railroads. Then, on September 4, Morris reversed himself. The next day, Charles A. Brougher, partner in the private firm of Morris and Brougher, received a retainer from the Ripley Railroad. On October 2, the attorney general told the state treasurer that the subsidy was illegal and the warrants must not be honored. Later, he clarified his statement to mean that the railroad had a legal right to have warrants issued to it in aid, but not necessarily to have the warrants turned into cash or bonds; that would depend on whether there was money in the State Treasury or not. He had not explained this distinction to the treasurer, and certainly never told the railroad. Naturally, the contractors felt sold out, and none more so than Colonel W. C. Falkner of the Ripley Railroad, who had paid good money to Morris's law firm to buy a favorable decision.

The legislative investigation that followed was edifying and rather depressing. Morris insisted that he had never doubted the law's unconstitutionality, which contradicted one opinion he had put in writing and quite a few witnesses' testimony. He defended his acceptance of fees to defend in a private capacity companies that he had the power to crush in his public capacity. "That was entirely correct on my part," he said, "because, being Attorney General, I am still an attorney-at-law, and have a perfect right to practice law, and to be employed and paid to represent either side in any suit in which the duties of my office do not interfere." That his partner got twice the legal fees given a respected judge did not disturb him, but the judge reported that Colonel Falkner felt differently. "When he paid my fee he stated that it had cost him $4000 [to get the warrants issued], and mine was the only fee he regarded as a legitimate one in the whole transaction." Yes, the state engineer admitted, he *had* told Falkner that "money would put the thing through, and that he must not stand on five or ten thousand dollars," but of course he meant money for lawyers' fees. No one openly accused Morris of extortion, though Falkner came close, but the two payoffs were suspicious. Of the second, the investigating committee remarked archly, "It is another of those remarkable coincidences that is most unfortunate for the reputation of one who is the law officer of a sovereign State."[17] Whatever judgment Morris could make of the railroad aid law had lost credibility. The whole state subsidy policy suffered as a result.

What was true of Mississippi was true elsewhere. After all, what value was the decision of a South Carolina attorney general on the legal status of state aid when he owned bonds in the lines affected? When two members of the Arkansas Supreme Court were railroad directors, and the chief justice of the Louisiana Supreme Court was a railroad president, how much trust in their judgment on the bonds' validity could Conservatives have?

In financial terms, the politicking also extracted a staggering price. Charters were loaded with men with no capital to contribute; corporations were cluttered with men lacking all aptitude for railroad business, defended by lawyers of modest ability, protected by receivers with more political than financial experience. Because of their directors, railroads were dragged into political feuds and made the tools of scheming politicians. Without this meddling, the railroads might have operated more efficiently and profitably. The Ripley Railroad was sabotaged by ambitious politicians' desires; the North Louisiana & Texas was wrecked completely. Few railroads surpassed the Cairo & Fulton in resiliency, but even this company paid a fearful price for its involvement in time wasted and expenses created by delay. To break even, the company needed to reach Little Rock, but it found that the president of a rival line owned an exclusive right to build a bridge across the river into the city and would give no opponent the right-of-way. His privileges could not be revoked, for he was a leading Republican politician.[18] With so much against its progress, it is not surprising that the road could not pay workers and was taken over by the contractors.

State aid did not succeed for many reasons, but the mesh of public and private desires was one of the most damaging. Would Democrats have done much better in keeping the two interests apart? Their record before and after Reconstruction holds out little hope. But theirs was more a manipulation of politics for financial gain than use of private enterprise for political advantage. Republicans put the welfare of their party ahead of the welfare of the corporation—and many put their personal welfare ahead of either. They knew that the railroad could help them win votes as an issue, but they could not afford to rely on issues alone. They needed to create an organization. Thus they used the railroads because they had to, just as the Conservative businessmen used the Republicans because they had to.

Railroads suffered from party exploitation, and since prosperity was tied to railroad construction, the Southern economy suffered— a catastrophe for the party of prosperity. The "friends" of the Republicans would prove almost as dangerous as their open enemies, the Conservatives.

CHAPTER 8

Testing the Gospel of Prosperity, 1870–1871

Whenever the Republican party fails to be the party of
progress . . . I say to the people of the State, "vote the
Democratic ticket!"
             A Republican governor to his backers, 1870

A VISIT to Alabama in 1870 might have wrenched Charles Sumner's
egalitarian spirit. Something had happened to the Republican party
there since its formation as an organization dedicated to human
rights and the Union. In one public appeal, Republicans summoned
their friends to a mass meeting based on four ideals: "The Constitution as it is! Honesty, Economy, Prosperity!" Only once did the
appeal refer to Reconstruction, and then only to remark that the
old issues had been settled and done away with. Race was not
mentioned once.[1] Nor was the circular an aberration. In every
Southern state, the Republican press was shifting its political emphasis and trying to give new strength to issues favorable to a
biracial party. In this transition, the railroad aid question and the
Gospel of Prosperity were essential.

Success had transformed the South. By 1870, Republicans ran
every legislature south of Virginia and were writing party policies
into law. The first part of the 1870s brought the section into more
prosperous times than it had enjoyed for years. The ruling coalition
promised better times to come. Nevertheless, 1870–1871 was not
the morning of good times political and economic, but a false dawn.
No time, then, would be better for testing the Gospel of Prosperity.
It is time to probe for the weaknesses of the coalition in power.

The South had not entirely recovered from the effects of war
and emancipation, and the 1870 census showed how far it had to
go to return to the antebellum prosperity. Less cotton was grown,
and only two Southern states had more acres under cultivation
than a decade before. Some of the physical devastation remained
unrepaired. Every city still had business houses boarded up, wharves
decaying, or war-related problems of other kinds. Southern states

still had fewer miles of railroad than most Northern ones, a woeful lack of capital, and a much smaller greenback circulation per capita. In the best times, many farmers were unable to save their property from foreclosure, as tax sales showed.[2]

Even so, the South seemed well on the way to recovery. Signs of regeneration were everywhere. Montgomery businessmen boasted of the increase in trade, Little Rock merchants almost shouted of the city's immense growth. So quickly did industry grow in some towns that even optimists were thunderstruck. The revival affected cities as large as Charleston and villages as insignificant as West Point, Mississippi, where citizens prided themselves on having built "seven fine brick stores, six frame business houses, and many first class residences" in one year.[3]

The renascence of the South had many causes. First, prosperity may have been a state of mind as much as a phenomenon. The years just after the war had been so terrible that even moderate prosperity looked like "flush times" again. Showing the true community spirit, Southerners often forecast dazzling prospects even when there were no good reasons for such faith. Second, Southern farmers had reaped a splendid harvest in 1869 and 1870 and received good prices. They could also obtain advances more easily than before, as Northern economic conditions improved and financiers found it easier to lend to Southerners. Third, the railroads had done much of what Republicans had promised. Men sincerely believed that where the lines ran, commercial prosperity was flowing into the communities, as well as developing new communities to absorb the thriving commerce. They were often right. Railroad men built McComb, Mississippi and Birmingham, Alabama, while the Little Rock & Fort Smith made towns sprout up where corn and cotton had grown twelve months before.[4]

Railroads built more than towns. They provided jobs and enriched local commodity merchants. In eastern Louisiana, where drought had damaged the crops, hiring and buying by the New Orleans, Mobile & Chattanooga "literally clothed the naked and fed the hungry." Contractors hired at high wages every man who needed work. The company bought lumber at top prices, built dredge boats, and asked for supplies of every kind. "And if there be, in this community, a man who cannot say from the bottom of his heart, God bless this great enterprise, and all concerned with it," wrote a resident, "he must be a thankless fellow indeed!"[5] A railroad benefited the public no matter what it did—or so many seemed to think. If it paid cash for goods, the merchants gained.

If it paid in scrip, it added to circulation in the community. Later, when merchants tried to redeem the scrip or collect cash for goods given on credit, they might find that the railroads had been spending funds that they had no chance of obtaining, but the revelations of financial mismanagement did not appear until later. For now, everyone felt the railroad his best friend.

Southerners justly credited railroads with having added to the section's greatness. During the 1870s, the railroad construction had its full effect, an urban South dependent on rail connections rose everywhere. Committed more to water transport than rail, port towns such as Vicksburg, Mobile, and Natchez declined in size. By becoming a junction for two or more roads, other cities achieved prominence. Of the thirty-nine cities with over four thousand residents in 1880, all but one had rail connections, and the vast majority relied on them almost exclusively. Thanks to its link with the South Carolina lowlands, Greenville became the third largest town in the state. Montgomery increased its population from 10,588 to 16,713, Pensacola from 3,347 to 6,845. In Texas, where railroad fever was at its worst, towns grew all the faster: Galveston from 13,818 to 22,248, Austin from 4,428 to 11,013, San Antonio from 12,256 to 20,550.[6]

The Southern population increased everywhere, but it increased most where the tracks ran and least where they did not. The most dramatic growth occurred in the Alabama uplands, where rival trunk lines were built during the decade. In seven counties, population increased by less than one thousand. Only one of these had rail connections. Counties along Texas railway lines often doubled or tripled their population. Fourteen counties gained less than one thousand people there: only two had railways.[7]

In welcoming immigrants to the South, the companies had less success. In 1880, five Southern states had fewer foreign-born residents than ten years before. Land, not economic development, seems to have attracted the Europeans who came south.[8]

Promoters claimed that the lines would serve the cotton South well. Apparently, the promise was kept. Certainly climate and the quality of soil played a major role in determining how much cotton an area grew, but railroads furthered the process by making large crops marketable. The 1880 federal census maps are revealing: cotton was cultivated with diligence in those areas served by either river or rail communications. In Mississippi, every county with more than 15 percent of its land planted in cotton lay within 15 miles of a railroad or the Mississippi River. Those areas where less than 1 percent of the land went for cotton had no rail connections at all. Similar patterns held true in Arkansas, Florida, and Alabama: lands remote from major rivers and railroads produced less than those close to either.⁹

Yet even in the 1880 statistics, there were signs that the railroads had failed in their initial promise. Unlike river transportation, they were dependable in all seasons and offered a more convenient means of shipment than had been possible before. But they did not provide a cheaper form of transport. Mississippi counties often found that they could ship less expensively by river than by rail. In Jefferson County, for example, the few miles from Fayette to Natchez cost $3.10 per bale by train. The much longer river trip from Natchez to New Orleans cost only $.75. Upland counties were at the mercy of whichever company had the nearest track. Many northern Mississippi counties were closer to Memphis than Mobile, and could they have reached the trunk line to New Orleans, they would have paid $1.75 a bale. Instead, farmers had to rely on the Mobile & Ohio, which demanded up to $4.00 a bale.¹⁰

Yet the railroads were, for all their deficiencies, better than any other form of development the South could support. They were vital to the section's future, and Southerners knew it. By 1870, therefore, the section's mileage had increased tremendously. In 1865, the former Confederate states had 8,336 miles of railroad. Two years later, they had only 32 miles more, but by the end of 1868, they had 9,257 miles, and a year later, 9,821 miles. By the close of 1870, there were 11,015 miles completed. This growth rate exceeded that of New England or the Northeast, and was most noticeable under the Republican governments. Under Conservative rule, Virginia built 19 miles in three years. During that same period, North Carolina capitalists added 136 miles to their total, Georgians 358 miles, Texans 198, and Alabamians 545. Since the early 1860s, Arkansas had had only 38 miles of track, but in 1868, with the support of Republican lawmakers, it built another 48 miles, and another 42 the following year. In 1870, the state's mileage rose to 286 miles, in the second fastest growth rate in the country.¹¹

Southerners seemed to agree: the South was more prosperous than it had been, would be still more prosperous in the future, owed much of its revival to railroads, and could credit the aid laws with providing the impetus for so much construction.

Statistics seem to justify the prevailing view that there was a direct correlation between subsidies and construction, since the sharp rise in construction occurred just at the time that the legislatures passed subsidy legislation. Still, a close study of the figures for railroad construction nationwide may cast doubt on Southern assumptions. Following a period of sluggish development, an abrupt rise in track-laying took place everywhere. Wisconsin, for example, added 199 miles to its roads in 1868 and nearly 300 in 1869; yet Wisconsin's constitution forbade state railroad aid.[12] The real cause of railroad construction throughout the land was not government largess but a healthy economy and an expanding need for a better transportation network.

The impact of the aid law must not be dismissed. That an expanding web of railroads resulted from other causes in the rest of the country does not mean that the same causes existed in the South. As in so much else, that section was unique in its economic disadvantages. It had less personal wealth and fewer men of sufficient capital to finance a railroad. The cotton states were less attractive to outside financiers than the corn states. Without railroad aid, it is clear, many railroads would have been unable to attract Northern investors. Nonetheless, the national increase in mileage and the construction achieved by certain Southern roads without subsidies should have given Southerners cause to doubt that aid alone was responsible for the construction boom.

Because Republican governments had initiated the subsidy laws, they could take some of the credit for Southern prosperity, and their spokesmen leaped to take all of it. "If the management is good," said the *San Antonio Express*, "the country flourishes, commerce thrives and the people progress."[13] Such success was all the more astonishing in view of Conservative predictions three years before that Reconstruction would bring such disorder that farmers could not even grow cotton. From the industrial and commercial growth and the increased cotton harvests, Republicans drew a simple moral: the Reconstruction laws had not undermined business confidence. They had placed it on a firmer basis than ever. Republican programs were working and would continue to work, partisans insisted.[14]

Some Conservatives had warned that the subsidy policy would bankrupt the governments and that responsible Northern financiers would spurn a Negro government's securities. By 1870, the Republicans could laugh at such charges. Their securities—the basis for the railroad aid program—sold at a higher rate than Democrats had been able to obtain just after the war. In January 1870, Georgia 6-percent bonds sold at 80, while those of the Conservative states of Virginia and Tennessee sold for around 50. Alabama and South

Carolina party organs boasted that their securities, once scorned, now sold for more than almost any other state's.[15]

That a state's endorsement made a railroad bond appreciate in value showed that investors trusted the Republicans' financial practices. That trust was essential to railroad aid policies, for without it, the companies could raise no money except at ruinous discount. It was equally essential to the party's efforts to prove itself respectable.

The governments' reputation for financial stability, however, was wholly undeserved. Northern states usually sold their bonds for over par, Southern states did so rarely. The difference between face value and sale price might be slight, but it was an accumulating embarrassment. North Carolina's bonds had almost no value by mid-1870, and Louisiana and South Carolina issued securities so lavishly that within a year they, too, would find bond issues almost useless for raising money. The harm might not yet be visible in most Southern states, but in a generation, when the principal fell due, taxpayers might pay dearly. Virginians were doing so already. Forced then to cut back essential services or raise taxes, which Southerners already found too onerous, the Republicans' financial structure might then crash down. The problem of financiering deserved serious consideration, but it seemed so remote that Republicans chose to ignore it until the bonds had depreciated, the debts soared, and the Conservatives made the tax burden a campaign issue. For now, however, the bond issues seemed to do the states' credit no harm. They did not threaten the Republican argument.

It was an argument aimed at winning the conservative businessman, and that was only right. Republicans used the prosperity issue because it would obscure both class and racial divisions in Southern society. In 1868, the Reconstruction coalition had directed one note of its appeal to whites down on their luck. By 1870, the party's press was trying to usher in not just the poor but every man. If the party organs provide any indication, the articulate publicists were turning the party of progress into the party of consensus.

Republican polemicists hoped that successful men would favor the party whose policies had given Southerners the chance to accumulate wealth. Commercial men must see that Republicanism was their best protection. Putting their financial interests ahead of their outmoded attitudes on race and states' rights, such men would switch political allegiances because they were "entirely mercenary," said the *New Orleans Republican,* and invested "only in such ventures as pay or promise to pay."[16] Such a hope was based on very dubious assumptions: that the commercial classes did indeed put wealth ahead of white supremacy doctrine, that the man of means could see a connection between his prosperity and the Reconstruction governments, that such men had faith that the prosperity would last in spite of dramatic increases in state debts, taxes, and Republican misrule. Finally, the appeal skirted the prospect that Republican policies were as likely to alienate commercial men as to appease them.

That Republicans used economic appeals does not mean that they abandoned the blacks. On the contrary, editors insisted that they could stress other issues because the Reconstruction issues of human rights and Unionism had been settled and that most Southerners were resigned to that settlement. Speakers still reminded blacks that "Republicanism" and "freedmen's rights" were synonymous terms. Politicians evoked the image of the lash and manacles and printed in lurid detail every atrocity against blacks. There is not a scrap of evidence that black Republicans cared more about the prosperity issue than about the old issues, nor that the party as a whole meant to retreat from its past efforts for civil rights. But many prominent figures—including the governors of Arkansas, Louisiana, Mississippi, and Florida, as well as the official organs in every cotton state (and Kentucky, it might be added)—*were* making a concerted effort to persuade Conservatives that the old party lines no longer meant anything, and that they belonged in the party of railroad aid and flush times. Let there be one more victory at the polls, one editor pleaded, and the Conservative diehards would see that the old issues had lost their meaning. "A day of new issues will spring up." Then the majority party could go on to greater reforms, "because we shall be relieved from the great responsibility of contending for human rights."[17]

It was possible, but again Republicans made an assumption: that the economic issue would enhance their reputation. Would it? Already there were warning signs that the party was being corrupted and endangered by the programs it had set in motion. Republicans might argue that the party was the businessman's best friend, but no one was so bold as to proclaim that the businessman had become the party's firmest supporter. By 1871, most party papers admitted that Republican economic policies were in trouble, as taxes and debts rose to alarming levels. Republicans were already conceding that they had not yet delivered good government along with good times. At the height of their power, they were already looking for scapegoats for possible future failures, and they found the male-factors in their own ranks: unscrupulous men in office, traitors to the public interest, "trash and adventurers, . . . that set of leeches that have cut us loose from our neighbors, our friends, and . . . our people."[18]

The degeneration of public morals that the railroad aid programs had helped further was an issue ready-made for Conservatives. They could not make a very convincing case against economic conditions under the Republicans as of 1870. Evidence of prosperity was all over and incontestable. With so many Democrats tied to railroad projects and those projects having such vocal support, a direct attack on the aid programs would have been bad politics. But by concentrating on the methods by which the subsidy legislation had passed, the Conservatives could appeal both to those who thought the subsidy program a swindle and those who supported it without approving of the lawmakers who put it through. They could attack the enormities of governments chosen by Negro suffrage without making a headlong and politically risky assault on Negro suffrage itself.

"Through bribery, open and unblushing," one Democrat wrote, ". . . millions have been appropriated to railroad adventurers from abroad, representing bogus stocks . . . and the recipients, with brazen effrontery, 'stalk forth at noonday,' among the people whom they have robbed, and impudently threaten, with the money thus fraudulently obtained, to control the present election." Such vague charges were typical. Many Democratic accusations were so misty that they could not be proven or disproven. Others were more specific and unfounded. Conservatives took care not to object to aid in principle. Far from it, they insisted that the money, given for legitimate purposes, had been misused. "Millions for Plunder and not a dollar for Improvement" was the Radical motto, said a New Orleans editor. Naturally, Democrats held their tongues on bills subsidizing Conservative lines such as the Mobile & Montgomery or the South & North.[19]

The corruption argument was quite effective. Republicans had no satisfactory answer. They argued that corruption did not really exist, though this clashed with one editor's confession that "we cannot go much lower and live." Correctly, they pointed at Democrats around the public trough in every state. Finally, Republicans insisted that low moral tone in politics was an insignificant issue. After all, what mattered the Conservative catchword "fools and Thieves," when politicians could throw back the terms "general prosperity," "unparalleled growth," and "rapid progress"? Prosperity in general and railroad construction in particular became a defense against every accusation.

Democrats had less success in proposing alternatives to the Republican program. They upbraided their enemies for passing aid laws improperly, but took no firm stand for repeal. Yet every attack implied a conviction, sometimes spoken and sometimes not, that once in power the Conservatives would do something about Radical frauds. That "something," as investors feared and some party regulars hoped, would be repudiation of all endorsed bonds. Some polemicists said so openly. Others made veiled threats, still others frightened financiers by saying nothing. There was no way of knowing what Democrats would do.

Cautious men feared the unknown, and Republicans played shamelessly on this fear. In Alabama, the party press nearly turned the canvass into a referendum on railroad aid by highlighting the sentiments of Robert B. Lindsay, Conservative candidate for governor. "The election of Lindsay will cause the Destruction of all our Railroads," said the *Decatur Republican*, knowing that its readers cared about several lines that depended on public funds. Lindsay had not promised to repudiate the bonds given to existing railways, but he had called one special state loan unconstitutional and void. In doing so, he had called into question all loans of a like nature. Such a governor would oppose new grants, said the *Republican*, and might eventually repudiate all the bonds issued as "unconstitutional" loans.[21] Nor did Lindsay need to take formal action to wreck the railroads, other Republicans warned. Just by speaking out on the issue, he would depress the securities market and drive their prices below the minimum price negotiable under the state constitution. Deprived of funds, the companies would default on their interest payments and force government foreclosure. Then the contingent debt that Conservatives so often mistook for a real burden on the people would become the state's responsibility and fulfill the taxpayers' worst fears. The Republican bugaboo was a terrible one, all the worse for being so close to the realities of railroad finance. What Republicans did not recognize was that their own statements prophesying repudiation should Conservatives win might have the same serious effect on bond sales that Conservative rhetoric did.

Thoughtful men should have wondered whether a Republican triumph would promise anything better than that same uncertainty in railroad finance. Already, by the early 1870s, evidence was mounting that railroad aid was neither as beneficial to the companies nor as wise for the state as had been thought. Most newspapers informed their readers of the mounting debts in South Carolina and Louisiana, the damaging effect that North Carolina subsidies had had on the state's credit, and the sacrifice that Virginia was making to escape its debts. They might have applied these lessons to their own railroad legislation, for every state government had passed a roughly similar program. Conservative editors rarely made the comparison; Republican editors never did so. Indeed, in upholding railroad aid, propagandists showed an almost perverse disregard for the failures of other state programs. By June 1871, for example, Alabama's policy had brought the state close to economic ruin. Its credit gone, its debt more than doubled in three years, its governor taking illegal action to protect some railroads, its former governor admitting that the railroads had hoodwinked him, Alabama found the beneficiaries of the aid program near bankruptcy. Surely, this state should have served as a warning. Yet, when Mississippi Conservatives wanted an example of liberal aid proving a safe investment for the state and an unalloyed blessing to its people, some of them named Alabama.[22]

Indeed, Republican promises of stability used deliberate falsehood. Politicians told the people that the aid policy was working and the state's credit was sound when they knew otherwise. They touted precedents for subsidy programs that gave bond endorsements a conservative appearance, but they made up the precedents. Of Louisiana's railroad policy, Governor Henry Clay Warmoth boasted, "It is just the policy pursued in Illinois, in Indiana, and in Iowa. It is just the policy pursued in Missouri, where they have six or seven thousand miles of railroad, and are not a dollar in debt." As a former Illinois resident, the governor should have known that the state had repudiated its bonds. As a responsible public servant, he should have admitted that Iowa had never pursued an aid program even remotely similar to that of Louisiana. Missouri had a $15 million debt, and with 2,140 miles of track, it did not even approach Warmoth's figure for mileage.[23] Such fustian had wretched effects. If a public official, who was supposed to know what the state owed and what security it had for its loans, would not tell the truth, who would inform the people that their aid policy was fraught with risk? Republican leaders could have tried to cool the public fever for subsidies. Not many did. They exuded confidence where there was cause for concern and continued to make grand promises when they should have known better. By concealing the real situation, they encouraged indiscriminate support for railroad construction and made the eventual revelations of mismanagement and misappropriation all the more bitter. Had they told the truth, perhaps the state debts for internal improvements would not have grown so large, or the pressure to repudiate these obligations so strong; but had they told the truth, Republicans could not have sold themselves as the upholders of prosperity and stability and represented the Democrats as harbingers of chaos and uncertainty.

As the elections of 1870 and 1871 showed, the Reconstruction coalition needed all the political capital it could get. The governments could be manipulated by the coalition for partisan ends, and the party had gained from greater federal patronage and more efficient organization than in 1868. A strong case could be made for the Reconstruction administrations as well. Even so, the party in power did not improve on its 1868 showing. In Georgia, Alabama, and North Carolina, Conservatives won the legislature and governorship.[24] Florida Democrats elected a lieutenant governor, and Republicans lost ground in Mississippi and Texas. The defeated party insisted that the opposition won through fraud and terror and that the Republican organization would triumph two years hence. These arguments had some basis. The charges of terrorism were so well substantiated that Congress passed laws suppressing the Klan. Republicans would indeed revive in 1872. In no state, however, would their recovery be total. No excuse could obscure the fact that Republicans had failed to win the mandate they sought or even enough tolerance from Conservatives to protect their lives and property.

The election returns revealed several trends, most of which should have given the Reconstruction coalition distress. The party in power had done well, but Conservatives had done far better. In most places the Republican party had brought out as many voters as in 1868. Though the Republican vote declined in many counties across the South, especially where intimidation had been most severe, the party remained a vital force. It gained not only in the black counties where party workers ran the political machinery, but in counties that were hopelessly Conservative. Radical gains, however, were surpassed by Conservative ones, often in places where Republicans polled their heaviest vote. In Alabama, Conservatives increased their numbers most in central counties and the black belt, where the party in power needed a wide margin of victory to carry the state ticket. Texas Democrats more than doubled their numbers in many counties and in some added a thousand new men to their ranks.[25] In part, the gains showed that Conservatives were winning those men disfranchised under the Reconstruction Acts, but they also suggested that many citizens too apathetic or disgusted to take part in the elections were regaining an interest in politics, an interest possibly heightened by the knowledge that as taxpayers they might have to pay for the railroad subsidies passed during the past two years.

Because of modest Republican vote increases and large Conservative turnouts, the party in power lost most white counties, including those that had voted for the Reconstruction constitutions in 1868. North Carolina incumbents carried every black county but one, but they lost nineteen counties where blacks made up between a third and a half of the population and lost all but seven of the counties with an overwhelming white majority. Georgia Republicans had taken twenty-one white counties in 1868, but took only five in 1870, while Conservatives carried twenty-eight black counties—two of them by an almost unanimous vote. Clearly, the race issue still kept its power; clearly, many whites thought more about it than they did the Republican economic program—or, if they thought about that program, thought about costs more than the benefits.[26]

Apparently, railroad aid had won few friends where Republicans needed them most. Floridians in the Panhandle would have gained most from the public aid program, but of the twelve counties west of Tallahassee, eight were Democratic in 1870, half of them by more than a two-thirds margin. Admittedly, the area had gone Conservative two years before, but the Republicans could not even narrow their opponents' lead. Conservatives' margin widened in every county but one.[27]

In Texas, Conservatives proved irresistible. Galveston and Dallas had gained from the aid laws, but both voted for the white men's party. The counties along the projected routes of the two lines given a state subsidy did not express their gratitude at the polls. Only one switched to the Republican side, two stayed there, and at least four converted to Conservatism. The rest voted for the Democrats just as they had in 1869. Alabama Democrats augmented their vote most markedly in those counties along the two major trunk lines given state aid. North Carolina and Georgia showed no correlation between Republican votes and areas granted subsidies—though, since North Carolina lawmakers had gutted their own aid program months before, this was only natural. Only in Louisiana can one make a case for the political impact of internal improvements, and there the levees seemed to have more of an effect than railway lines. The parishes in which Republicans took more than two-thirds of the vote followed the path of the Mississippi River. Even there, however, the real reason for the heavy Republican vote was the large black majority in each of those counties.[28]

The Gospel of Prosperity was thus not a smashing success for the party. It may have been the best platform that a biracial party could have adopted. It had not won the governments a mandate, but for a few it had bought time for them to pursue their programs. The Reconstruction coalition had not prospered in the elections, but at least it had survived. It could not have done even that much had its spokesmen stressed only the race issue. Its white friends may have been decreasing, but many remained, and a few new white converts would be made in the next few years. The Republicans had every reason for concern, but they had some reason for hope as well.

"Whenever the Republican party fails to be the party of progress," Governor Warmoth told a Louisiana audience, "whenever it fails to do more than the Democratic party has done for the material interest of the State, I say to the people of the State, 'vote the Democratic ticket!' But while the Republican party continues to advance the prosperity of the State . . . and to bring order out of chaos, I say it is the duty of the people to stand up for that party."[29] Warmoth's appeal caught the mood of Republican publicists across the South. Yet his words foreshadowed the doom of the Republicans. By making prosperity the test of party success, the governor had made depression the proof of party failure. So far as politics and economics were concerned, 1870 was a fairly good year, but not good enough to enable the party to become a permanent institution in the South. Moreover, the Republicans would not have another year as good. The New South was not as successful as the Reconstruction coalition hoped. The state's credit was less secure than its spokesmen claimed. The railroad aid program would lead to cost and political dissension. Within a year, party factionalism would disrupt the Reconstruction governments. Within two years, the Southern railroad system would be on the verge of collapse. By 1874, the race issue would regain its old place as the central issue in Southern politics. In the coming upheaval, railroad policy would be both an irritant and a casualty. Inextricably linked to the Republican party, it was already headed for disaster.

CHAPTER 9

"They Must Stand Aside . . .":
The Republican Mission in Peril

> If there are any privileges to be given away, the money demon
> demands them for the rich. If laws are needed to protect the
> laborers, they must stand aside until railroads and banks are
> filled and satisfied.
>
> *Charleston Daily Republican, 1870*

RAILROADS were not enough. Taken by themselves they could not
fashion a new, industrial South, nor satisfy the wants of the Reconstruction coalition. These facts had been obvious from the start.
Republican platforms overflowed with worthy causes demanding
legislative action: federal aid for levee repair, equal and uniform
taxation, economical state and national administration, debtor relief, a generous, general system of public education, freedom of
expression, and civil and political equality.[1] Most party members
accepted the whole platform, but had they been asked which portion was most important, they might had disagreed fiercely.

Certainly, not all of them shared the same faith in railroad development. New Orleans merchants felt even more strongly about
river and harbor improvements. Alluvial farmers looked to levees
for their salvation. Blacks put emphasis on a government that would
protect their rights and help them obtain property. Political unity
depended on the Republicans maintaining a balance among all the
interests they represented. This balance was all the more necessary
because emphasis on one cause created problems for some other.
If Republicans really cared about a general system of internal improvements and a federal levee repair program, they would have
to abandon their promise of retrenchment. If the rank and file
considered a public school system of prime importance, officials
would have to limit spending for such needs as a comprehensive
railway network or debt retirement.

From the first, however, railroad aid assumed disproportionate
importance in the Republican program, and support for industrial
interests outweighed relief and protection for the poor. This was

true for at least three reasons: railroads were prerequisite to almost any other kind of program; many other policies were more controversial than railway construction; Republicans took the black vote for granted and concentrated, therefore, on winning the confidence and support of at least a respectable minority of the white commercial and political elite. Whatever the reasons, Republicans found that railroad aid intruded on every other consideration.

Without immigration, Southerners knew, all their plans for sectional development would fail. "We might make Alabama one network of railway," said the *Mobile Register*, "We might build mills . . . until their smokestacks touch the clouds;—but the ties of our roads would rot and our mill-gear would rust, unless we brought into our borders producers, who would give food to the one and freight to the other."[2] Radicals especially stressed immigration as a way to build a New South of efficient small farms. People must be found to open the swamps and forests to agriculture. Republicans knew that they would have to be outsiders.

Enthusiastic about outsiders in theory, Republicans failed to bring about the desired influx because they worried about the risks that any concrete policy had. The party in power wanted immigration to swell party ranks. Unfortunately, the people best fitted to develop the South were just the sort least likely to sympathize with Republicanism, and the groups most likely to back the Reconstruction experiment were not desirable immigrants. Republicans did not want just anyone; that is, they wanted men with capital enough to buy property and establish industries. They welcomed yeoman farmers. Instinctively radical in politics, it was thought, such farmers would counter the large planters' influence. Landless immigrants, by contrast, would compete for jobs already held by tenant farmers and sharecroppers. Since the latter were largely black Republicans, the party in power was unusually reponsive to fears that an increased labor supply would drive wages down to the advantage of the large landholders.[3] Black newcomers would have added to Republican ranks, but most men in both parties dreaded such an importation. If anything, moderates would have preferred that some of the Negroes already present move elsewhere.

Finally, immigration simply lacked the bipartisan consensus that made possible so much of the railroad legislation. Some Conservatives thought the whole policy of welcoming outsiders would compromise the section's character. Others called for very select immigration, though they disagreed in their selection. As to New Englanders, whose strong will and muscle appealed to Radicals, the *Hinds County Gazette* pronounced "*our first* class colored bucks ... vastly superior," and advised that the Yankee breed be improved by marrying women down East with fifty thousand Mississippi Negroes.[4] Southerners insisted that any Northerner who would identify with the interests of his new home was welcome, but all too often "identification" was confused with voting Conservative.

Railroads both eased the Republicans' dilemma and encouraged legislative inaction. Corporation presidents wanted Northerners to buy homesteads along the lines and did all they could to make outsiders feel welcome. Early in 1869, Southern railway presidents, superintendents, and other officers met to study Western railroads' methods of attracting foreigners. A committee urged widespread publicity of special excursion tickets for immigrants that would allow them to travel on any Southern line for 2 cents a mile and to stop wherever they wanted. The committee called on hotel-keepers to charge half their usual accommodation fee for excursion ticket holders. Companies were advised to establish immigration clubs and seek legislative sanction for their work. Some railroads adopted the committee's resolutions. Others did not.[5]

In Mississippi, H. S. McComb brought in fifteen hundred settlers within a few months and settled them along his road. To any man building a house and farm worth $1,000 along the New Orleans, Jackson & Great Northern, the company president promised a three-year free pass over the line.[6] The Florida Railroad tempted outsiders with gifts of up to eighty acres of land. All they had to do was live on the land for two years. "Colonies of ten families or more are promised additional favors," a newspaperman added.[7] These efforts made it easier for Republican officeholders to do nothing.

Many officials argued that no action on their part was needed. The development of the South that the railroads would bring would be the strongest incentive to immigration. This argument made some sense. Potential resources could not attract immigrants. Only the knowledge that the South had plenty of jobs at good wages would make them come south. Should railroads transform the South, outsiders' opportunities would expand. It could be argued, thus, that every penny spent now for railway construction was also a penny ultimately devoted to encouraging immigration.

The more a scheme for promoting immigration entailed expense and specific action, the less the Reconstruction legislatures were willing to do. They appointed commissioners of immigration, many of whom issued annual reports on the situation. Agents informed foreigners of the South's advantages and published brochures on the South's mineral wealth. Always, however, such programs were understaffed and underfunded. Furthermore, they were ineffective most of the time. When politicians wanted to satisfy demands for retrenchment, they restricted the bureaus of immigration still further, or consolidated them with other agencies.[8] It might have been good politics, but it certainly was bad economic policy.

Other programs suffered from the same neglect for the same kinds of reasons. River and harbor improvements would be as expensive as railroad construction, but they benefited only certain areas. Levees in Louisiana and Mississippi were essential to agricultural prosperity, and since most of the alluvial districts were heavily black and Republican, the majority party had an interest in levee repair; but if there was a natural constituency for such appropriations, there was also a natural opposition. Since upland legislators saw no reason why they should pay to protect the lowlands, they fastened the costs directly on the areas most in need of protection.[9] Representatives from the river parishes objected to a special tax of 10 cents an acre, and reminded colleagues that the levees added to the wealth of the whole state.[10] With such serious divisions over how to pay for levees and which parishes should benefit, good politicians preferred to stress other issues.

However necessary they were to prosperity, the levees were beyond Southerners' means, though Republicans worked hard and spent a great deal. For one thing, repair took a skill that most Southern contractors seemed to lack. For years, Louisiana legislators appropriated money to companies which built too little for too much cost.[11] For another thing, a truly efficient program against flooding needed federal coordination and funds greater than Southerners could command. Some Southerners, therefore, opposed state support for levee repair because it was of purely local concern, others because it was of national importance. Both groups agreed that it was not up to the state government, and while they could not block levee legislation, they could make its passage difficult and politically unpleasant.

In other areas, the government's failure to give adequate funding excited widespread criticism, and again the railroad aid program intruded. Republicans had promised free public education. Blacks felt the need for schools most keenly, but poor whites, too, clamored for facilities. Much *was* done, but not enough. Alabama did more for schools than any other Southern state, said one critic, and even there funding was too modest. Alabama spent $1.15 per child, a trifle compared with Nevada's $19.17 or Massachusetts' $16.45 per pupil. In many communities, schools remained open only three months a year.[12]

Railroads could have helped public education, but in many ways they proved a hindrance to it. Legislators were so interested in railroad bills that they neglected to establish school systems in some states. In others, their support, while greater than under any previous government, was still niggardly. "Our people are less inclined to start & support schools than I like to see them," David Hodgin wrote from the North Carolina House. "We are too apt just now to have rail-roads 'on the brain.' "[13]

Had Republicans wanted to, they could have applied corporate taxes to education or made subsidies conditional on some percentage of the projects' gross earnings being reserved for school construction. Mississippi showed how this could have been done. In return for a land grant, the General Assembly forced the Memphis & Vicksburg to build and maintain a schoolhouse for each 6 miles of track. Another law mandated that interest on money borrowed from the school fund be applied to subsidize the University of Mississippi—a meager sum, but at least a precedent for other governments to consider.[14] No other state did even that much for schools.

In Georgia, friends of public education sought to reserve the net earnings of the state-owned Western & Atlantic for schools, but met strong resistance. One legislator insisted that the $140,000 devoted already to education was four times as much as public instruction needed. His colleague declared that it could build three times as many schools as presently held session on the commonwealth.[15]

If Republican legislators did not exploit railroads to support public eduation, they did the reverse without compunction. Federal and state governments had reserved the proceeds from the sale of certain public lands in a special fund for school construction. Such a source of revenue was too enticing for promoters to ignore. Long before the war, they had petitioned the legislators to lend these funds for internal improvements schemes. Southern governments had lent the money, which in wartime had gone unpaid or else had been returned in worthless Confederate currency.[16] During Reconstruction, the companies sought three favors from the protectors of the school funds: release from obligation for debts never repaid in United States currency, new loans from the school funds, or grants of those lands themselves.

The supplicants insisted that such measures would in no way harm the school children's interests. The money would be lent, not lost, they argued, ignoring twenty years of experience.[17] The state need only invest the fund in the company's first-mortgage bonds and require that every penny granted be used for iron, fastening, and rolling stock. When the road had been built, the state could sell the first-mortgage bonds at par without difficulty, regain its original investment, and place the funds at another railroad's disposal. By enhancing the state's prosperity, every railroad added to property values and population. Since the state devoted poll taxes and property taxes to education, its grants to railroads would return in the form of increased tax revenues for schools. Finally, some Republicans argued that land grants would raise the value of those acres that the state kept and allow a higher sale price on them.[18]

The friends of free schools were unconvinced. A transfer of school fund lands would not enrich the entire community, shouted a Mississippi state senator. Rather, it would surrender valuable resources "to purse-proud aristocrats, to . . . advance their own pecuniary interests." One bill exchanging United States bonds in the agricultural college land scrip fund set up by the federal government for company bonds was on the face of it a deception. Federal law required that the bonds in which the fund was invested be secure. The railroad insisted that their securities were as reliable as the country's. If so, the *Vicksburg Times* asked, what would it profit the line to make the trade? And if not, what right had the state to countenance the arrangement?[19]

Republicans like Governor Edmund Davis of Texas could protest, but most party leaders were ready to give the railroads all they wanted. In Mississippi, the Chickasaw School fund had $815,715.52 in it. Legislators lent some of it to the Mississippi Valley & Ship Island Railroad Company. The Mobile & Northwestern demanded a gift of "every foot of the tax lands now forfeited to the State, and all the lands hereafter to be forfeited to it for taxes, from the Common School Fund," at 2 cents an acre. This bill was defeated, but others less sweeping passed easily. One aiding the Vicksburg & Nashville required the govenor to draw $8,000 per mile from the Agricultural Scrip fund to finance construction.[20] Texas railroads tried to obtain relief from their prewar obligations, but found the governor a doughty opponent. When the Houston & Texas Central tried to exchange its debt to the school fund for a surrender of depreciated company bonds at face value to the state, Davis sent in a veto. He could not keep the General Assembly from freeing railroads from the obligations imposed by antebellum statutes. An 1856 law lent any road completing 25 miles of track $6,000 a mile in state bonds from the school fund, and set the terms for gradual repayment. These terms many lines did not meet. Under the 1870 relief act, they were permitted to escape foreclosure by paying six months' interest on the amount due and by agreeing to pay the rest at 2 percent a year instead of the 8 percent originally stipulated.[21]

Schools and land were closely connected, but the problem of landownership merits attention in its own right. Most blacks were tenant farmers, unable to escape the tyranny of the crop lien and the need to concentrate their efforts on raising a cash crop. The freedmen desperately wanted to own land, and Republicans claimed to sympathize with that desire. However, they did not translate that sympathy into laws that would shift property ownership.

Republicans could have brought about real land redistribution in several ways. They could have encouraged homesteading and lent blacks money at little or no interest to make purchases. They could have used the taxing power to force large landowners to sell off every acre not devoted to farming. Laws could have made the tax per acre increase proportionate to the number of acres held or doubly heavy on land lying idle. Severe taxes could have placed every large estate on the market. The government did none of these things. Only South Carolina set up a public land commission to sell off confiscated property to homesteaders, and it was common practice in many states to pass laws staying forfeiture for nonpayment of taxes or even abjuring it altogether.[22]

Some state constitutions forbade the sale of tracts larger than forty acres, but these provisions were not enforced. No law kept large speculators from buying and keeping idle thousands of acres. Despite Louisiana's restrictions, speculators owned numerous acres of farmland, with effects that one Conservative paper pronounced more damaging to the state's economy than any act of the Radical government.[23]

To an outsider, tax rates might seem severe, but a lenient assessment could ease the law's effects. According to one Arkansas Republican, wealthy landholders would value acres worth $75 each at $.50; "by the use of a little champagne . . . thousands of acres in the rich bottoms . . . have never been assessed at all."[24] The right to pay taxes in depreciated scrip at face value made the provisions even more ludicrous. In Florida, for example, the property owner could determine his land's value. Many states corrected some or all of these legal defects before the end of Reconstruction, but by that time the postwar boom had ended and the poor themselves lacked the money to buy lands when they were put up for sale. Even when land values fell, most owners tried to keep their estates intact, said Charles Nordhoff, a Northern reporter. Owners "waited for better times. For my part, I do not much blame them. Nobody, except a land-speculator, likes to sell land; especially where it has been his home. And these people are not land-speculators."[25]

Nordhoff was only partly correct. Southerners *thought* like land speculators. Many of them clung to their estates because they were sure that the value would rise, no matter what the Reconstruction governments might do. Republicans fostered this confidence by promising eventual prosperity through railroad aid. Legislative support for railway enterprises itself must have encouraged Southern landowners to hope, for all agreed that the construction would increase the value of every estate.

For many reasons, Republicans dared not implement a confiscatory tax policy, whatever promises they had made before. First, they needed white support and acceptance by the commercial and "respectable" men of the South just to administer the law. Confiscatory taxes would have increased white Southerners' ire. After all, no state could build a prosperous economy on the ruin of a large number of its people, nor win legitimacy in the eyes of its foes by taking their estates. If property taxes injured the large landowner who had many employees supplying him with a steady income, as well as commercial connections permitting him to borrow money when necessary and to market his crop at lower cost, they would have done catastrophic harm to the small farmer. With a small crop and a few dozen acres, he had to pay the same tax rate and had less income with which to pay his taxes. His estates would have gone into the market all the more quickly, and he would have reverted to tenancy. Not surprisingly, lists of delinquent taxpayers included many whose lands were sold in small tracts for debts of a few dollars.[26] A graduated income tax—even a graduated property tax—might have achieved land redistribution; with the same rate per acre for the planter as for the subsistence farmer, a simple *ad valorem* tax only hurt the class for whom Republicans claimed to speak.

Second, the problem was not just that the large landowner would not sell, but that the tenant could not buy. Most Southern blacks and whites lacked the money for a purchase, even at $1.25 per acre. Once the land was bought, they could have kept title only with difficulty. More money was needed for seed and plows and implements, draft animals, and the construction of buildings on empty tracts.

A third argument against the encouragement of homesteading was much more cynical and not offered: it would work against the Republican vision of a new, industrial South. Industrialization could not be accomplished without a large pool of cheap labor, but if the Republicans encouraged tenants to become independent farmers, they would exhaust one of the largest potential sources. Factory owners could hardly encourage independent farmers to leave their plows for work in the mills and mines; nor could contractors hire them to lay track.

Again, railroads provided conspicuous examples of the Reconstruction governments' faltering purpose. Republicans could have tried to settle landless men on public preserves. Instead, they gave much of this land to lumber corporations, river improvements projects, and railway enterprises.[27] It seemed a more sensible application of the public wealth. Especially west of the Mississippi River, the real problem was not that all good lands had been put to use, but that much of the land could not be farmed until some means had been found to ship goods there and crops back. Land grants did not seem like much of a sacrifice, when so much public domain was marsh, sand, or clay, with pine woods to clear away. In practical terms, a lumber company could open up the lands to farmers. So could any railroad ready to sell the timber or use it for ties.

A land grant to a large corporation need not have made the acres unavailable for settlement. The companies needed funds at once to carry on construction. Promoters knew that only a rapid increase in population along their lines would bring the trade needed for corporate solvency. These exigencies forced the lands onto the market immediately at a price as low or lower than that offered by the state government. In time, as the railroad's progress made land values rise, the companies could set their own figures for acres still in their possession, but in the early 1870s, they were not so fortunate; and in one state, the law compelled immediate sale of at least one acre in every four.[28]

Republican governments thus had reasons for failing to do much for the landless, but the result was that little was done for those who most needed help. In 1871, Alabama blacks met and unanimously resolved that their race should be advised to emigrate to Kansas. "If we owned a considerable portion of the land in this State," said the chairman of the Resolutions Committee, "I would be the last man to say leave, or if I could see that we would be likely to get land, I would say stay. But it is not so; we are today where 1866 left us. Despite our energy the prospects grow less bright, and it can get no better until the laborers get more homes and wages are better." Only by emigration of a large part of the work force could either goal be achieved.[29]

Without broadening landownership, the Republicans could have done much to increase the economic and political security of the poor. They could have passed laws protecting the tenant from dismissal for his political involvement. Since the sharecropper lacked the money to prosecute the landlord for violations of his contract and often the ability to prevent the planter from imposing an unfair one, the state could have enacted measures to remedy these defects. Taking up the responsibilities that the Freedmen's Bureau had surrendered, the governments could have appointed local agents to examine and enforce labor contracts. Laws could have assured free legal services to tenants willing to prosecute their employers for negligence. All of these reforms were proposed at the time, but hardly any was put into law. The laborer was given a preferential lien on his crop in several states, though the Alabama Supreme Court ruled such a lien unconstitutional and South Carolina Republicans repealed their own handiwork. Some landowners paid their workers in scrip which could be redeemed at local stores at a substantial discount. South Carolina legislators outlawed payment in scrip, but added exceptions that made the statute worthless. If laborers' liens were weak, relief laws and homestead exemption statutes were even weaker.[30]

The tenant farmer and small farmer had reason to complain, for the tax structure worked to their disadvantage and to the benefit of the corporations. Most states judged landed property by one standard and industrial property by another, in spite of constitutional guarantees of equal taxation. The Republicans wanted industry, and they were quite willing to write the laws necessary to induce capital to come south. Under an 1873 act, South Carolina freed companies from state and local taxes on "the property or capital employed or invested in . . . manufactures or enterprises" until they were ten years old. The Arkansas Constitution forbade such discrimination, but friends of development evaded the document's spirit by suspending the *collection* of taxes on factories or mines. Railroads were especially privileged. Asked to submit a return of their property valuation, the South Carolina, the Northeastern, the Greenville & Columbia, and the Cheraw & Darlington protested that the tax laws did not apply to them though some of the lines owned much real estate not related to railroad purposes, and all had the state's generosity to thank for their construction.[31]

The laxity of the Reconstruction governments might have been understandable, but to many Republicans it was an infuriating example of how the party had betrayed its constituents. "If there are any privileges to be given away," one Radical complained, "the money demon demands them for the rich. If laws are needed to protect the laborers, they must stand aside until opulent railroads and banks are filled and satisfied." The discrimination hurt the poor doubly. On the one hand, fair taxation of the railroads would have increased the revenue of the governments and provided more funds for schools. It might even have allowed the railroads to help pay off the obligations that the South had contracted for railway construction. On the other hand, every dollar that commercial enterprise did not pay in taxes was just one more that the poor man would have to pay, directly or indirectly. As the *Charleston Daily Republican* noted, the South Carolina Railroad owned millions of dollars of property within city limits, but municipal authorities could not assess a penny on it. As a result, 25 cents was added to every dollar in taxes that merchants and mechanics paid.[32]

While these policies guaranteed that the railroads' needs were well taken care of, the basic Republican constituency did not share much in the Gospel of Prosperity as it went into law. Storekeepers took advantage of railroad developments to sell supplies. Some landowners saw railroads increase property values. Lumbermen and corporate officials, shippers and commercial men—all were served by the subsidy policy. Blacks found the Gospel of Prosperity illusory, for their poverty was not alleviated. Sharecropping did not decrease, nor did the tenants' share of the profits increase. Even James Shepherd Pike, with little sympathy for the freedman, was disturbed at the poverty he saw in the black laboring population of South Carolina. Sharecroppers there demanded nothing, he wrote, but they would respond warmly to fair treatment. Instead, they were forced to do much work for little return, "put up with the meanest habitations," and eat meager fare. More than half the state's population lived "in huts and hovels so poor that their total destruction . . . would not diminish the taxable values of the State one-tenth of one percent. They are worth no more than so many dog-kennels or pigsties."[33]

Pike caught the misery. He did not grasp the significance. As long as a large part of the population remained so poor, the Radical governments would lack the solid financial support they needed to further their plans. As long as the Republicans' constituency could not pay for the programs that served it best—such as government bounties for homesteaders and low-interest long-term loans—the governments would adopt programs oriented toward the taxpayers and mercantile interests, conservative though they were. Republican poverty thus may have been one of the restraints on a truly radical economic policy. Certainly, it weakened Conservative regard for the Reconstruction governments, which, in the opinion of property holders, taxed members of one party to enrich office-holders chosen by another.

But something else had been lost in the tangle of railroad bills and practical considerations that characterized the Reconstruction governments. The Republicans had lost their sense of mission. In 1867, Republicanism had not been merely a set of proposals, but a promise of spiritual cleansing, political purification, and a triumph over the forces of cynicism and mammon. Power, however, had forced the idealists to confront Southern realities; money still affected legislative chambers. Republicans shared in the general despoliation that they had decried. Even their rhetoric had lost its religious timbre for something more mundane, a recitation of acts and figures. Many of the strongest supporters of development did all they could to win former Rebels and to block legislation furthering racial equality: Alcorn, Warmoth, and Reed in particular. Republicans still spoke of "greater reforms" to follow a renewed mandate from the people, but they did not make clear what they meant by these reforms. If their legislative record is any indication, they probably meant nothing. It was no wonder that Republicans concerned with both hegemony and ideology began to reconsider the value of railroad aid in light of those who supported it. It was also not surprising that those who complained of "hermaphrodites" having crept into the party blamed the railroad aid issue for the perversion of Republicans' true goals.[34]

There was another aspect to the change in the Republican ideology and legislative program, however: its effect on the popular support for railroad aid. One can only speculate on how the developments already described affected Republican views toward railway development, but a conjecture is essential for any understanding of how enthusiastic supporters of aid could so quickly become its violent opponents. Railroads had been supported not only for themselves, but for their symbolic importance. They were opposed for precisely the same reason.

Railroads had been a means to an end. They stood for the sort of South that Republicans hoped to create. Party members did not want only to bring commerce to the cotton states, but a new economic order and different attitudes toward work and wealth. Without these changes, affluence could not last and would have little merit. The railroad epitomized the kind of South that would rely less on cotton and more on the foundry, mill, and mine than it had in the past. In such a society, the large landowners would have neither the political nor economic power that they had enjoyed before the war. Railroads would produce a society in which prosperity might alleviate race hatreds and free the black laborer from dependence on his former master. In short, the Gospel of Prosperity had meant equality, diversity, affluence, change, and reform. It had meant railroads inasmuch as the corporations worked to those same ends.

By concentrating on railroad aid at the expense of the rest of the program, the Reconstruction governments betrayed the ideals for which railroads had been a symbol. The lines had meant everything good in the Gospel; the first legislatures had shown that aid could also serve as a symbol of all the ways in which Republicanism had fallen away from its trust. Corruption, localism, sectional prejudice, selfishness, incompetence, extravagance, poor judgment—all these characterized the Reconstruction governments at their worst, and never more than in their railroad aid policy. From symbol for the deficiencies underlying the party's failures to scapegoat for those failures was only a small step, and many Republicans took it. No matter what the policy, when disappointed men scrutinized the reasons for its ineffectiveness, they could always find railroads to blame. The party fell apart, the program had been gutted, Conservatives had dictated policy, and it seemed that the railroads had furthered the process to serve their ends.

Such analysis is not entirely fair to the Reconstruction coalition and to the complexity of Southern issues. Although the governments had not done all they had promised, they had done more than any Southern government before them in legislating for the poor of every race. The Republicans built asylums and penitentiaries, passed relief laws and lien laws that offered at least a shred of protection to the worker and small landowner, and enabled more Southerners to attend school than ever before.

With or without railroad aid, the governments never could have found the money to do all that needed doing. The railroads did not need less money than they got; they always required more.

The industrial growth of the South did not call for fewer tax advantages; many more should have been given. The levees were underfunded. River and harbor improvements went undone. Even government salaries were at times too low to induce able men to serve.[35] All these needs were beyond the Reconstruction governments' power to satisfy. Their alternatives would have been to increase the tax rate far beyond that already imposed or to disburse railroad aid money for other purposes. Neither alternative was politically possible. Southern taxpayers already felt that they paid too much. They asked for tax relief even as Reconstruction began; by 1872, their cries had grown too loud for government to ignore. By 1873, the government that increased spending and tax rates assured its own defeat. Failure to support railroads would have angered members of both parties. Until 1871, at least, aid was popular with most Southerners. If it were not given as state bonds, it would have to be given out of the public domain, and even fewer acres would have been left for homesteaders.

The real problems with the Republican program had little to do with the railroads. Nor had railroads caused the disaffection and social conservatism of so many Republican officeholders, though fights over the subsidy issue may have helped make some of the rifts clearer. From the start of Reconstruction, Republicans had differed sharply about the party's purposes and had expressed conflicting opinions on how far human rights should be extended. A radical Reconstruction failed for many reasons unrelated to railroads. But perception is more important than reality in politics. Railroads could be *seen* as one cause of Republicans' inadequacies. That was how some Radicals did see it; consequently, they did the moderates a disservice.

The Reconstruction legislatures did the railroads an even worse one. In a stagnant economy, the corporations could not thrive. They needed growth and industrial development for a lasting prosperity. They needed larger receipts, which, in turn, depended on a larger producing population and a diversified economy. The railroads would have benefited most from a society in which there were fewer tenants living in penury and more yeoman farmers able to consume Northern goods. Had rivers and harbors been cleared, the Southern ports might have done more business. Instead of sending supplies to New York, South American merchants might have sent their goods to Mobile and New Orleans and shipped them across the nation by rail. Better levees would have assured a larger acreage for farming and increased production. This would have added to trunk lines' revenues. Every part of the Gospel of Prosperity would have been a boon to the railroad companies, but because the legislatures could not give every need the same care they gave to rail connections, these boons went unrealized. The railroads suffered for it. Their suffering made them less able to pay their bonded debts and brought about default or failure. This misfortune, in turn, resulted in the rescinding of railroad aid and later in the repudiation of the subsidy bonds. The Gospel of Prosperity, like the Republican party, thus wrought its own renunciation.

PART FOUR

Balm in Gilead?
Financing the Railroads

CHAPTER 10

Friends in Need on Capitol Hill

Passage to India!
Lo, soul, seest thou not God's
 purpose from the first?
The earth to be spann'd, connected
 by network,
The races, neighbors, to marry and
 be given in marriage,
The oceans to be cross'd, the distant
 brought near,
The lands to be welded together.
 Walt Whitman, "Passage to India"

WITHOUT federal support, the South could not prosper. Republicans had seen that from the start of Reconstruction. Because the section's problems crossed state lines, their solutions called for broad interstate programs. Without federal funding, Republicans knew, the state railroad aid programs could not fully succeed. The Reconstruction coalition had not only hoped for congressional largess, but had promised to get it, once readmission was completed. Yet these campaign promises proved hollow. Divided by the same economic rivalries and dissensions that had tainted state programs, confronting a Congress dominated by men already disenchanted with subsidy policies, the South's delegations waged an unsuccessful struggle for sectional renewal, with dire consequences for the aid program and the Republican party.

To rehabilitate their states, Southerners sought congressional backing for almost every imaginable project. Promoters hoped for land grants for projected railroads and renewal of privileges already given to existing lines but forfeited during wartime. Businessmen wanted a subsidy for a transcontinental line across Texas to the Pacific and financial backing for branches to major cities in the cotton South. State governments had pledged enough money to create a railroad network throughout the South, but they could not afford to build the lines and still finance the other improvements essential to a thriving economy: river and harbor dredging, levees, cheap homesteads, and even inland waterways. The federal government must take up the reponsibility, or the South and its railroad system would languish.[1]

Southerners were asking for nothing new. Long ago, they had demanded their fair share of internal improvements funds. What *had* happened was that Southern opposition *on principle* to federal subsidies had faded. Instead of battling other states' applications for support, the cotton states favored others' requests in return for consideration of their own.

Nor were Southern proposals much more outlandish than those which Northern representatives had obtained during the 1860s. Western railroads owed their prosperity to land grants bestowed by antebellum statutes. During the war, the United States had subsidized one transcontinental line across the Great Plains at a far higher rate than any Southern state paid for railway communications: loans of up to $48,000 a mile. In return, the government took a second mortgage. Money had always flowed liberally to improve navigation on the Great Lakes or to subsidize packet lines from New York to South American ports.[2] With war expenses no longer absorbing the public revenue, surely the taxpayers could finance a road more convenient to the Southern people than the line across Nebraska and Utah; surely Congress could tend to other sectional needs. Or were the Northerners selfish and shortsighted, after all, just as Conservatives had said?

A querulous way of putting the issue—but it is crucial to our understanding of Southern Republicanism to hear the plaintive and all too sectional tone to their appeals, for it was as characteristic as any peroration of the way they thought. True, some argued that subsidies and increased bank-note circulation would bind the sections together by proving to white Southerners that Northern Republicans cared about even former Rebels' interests, and that their motives on political issues, as on economic ones, might not be sullied with self-interest. True, too, Republicans boasted that aid would make a new kind of South in a new kind of nation, that is, a South of forge, mill, and mine, a South tied directly to "northern men, northern progress, northern ideas and capital." Undeniably, many Southern Republicans spoke as supernationalists, encouraging commercial expansion and annexation of Caribbean islands. But behind all these appeals lay the demand for sectional advantage and the implication that Northern representatives, having glutted themselves on privileges, should give their neglected brethren their proper share. Was it patriotism or sectional gain when a Port Royal editor hailed annexation of Santo Domingo or Cuba as sure to bring trade to his town, and with it the money to build a trans-Appalachian road? "Then would the Chicago connection be easily and speedily accomplished," he wrote. "Hurrah for another war, we don't care who it is with or what it is for." Was it nationalism or sectionalism that made Senator William P. Kellogg argue that a Southern transcontinental road must be built so that Mexico could become American—or was it a combination of both motivations? Certainly, there was a quiet truculence in the words of the *Alabama State Journal*: "We of the South ask but justice, and will be content with nothing less." Southerners in both parties were more than resentful, and they put the worst possible interpretation on certain Northern actions. Editors raged that only crass, corrupt motives could explain the location of the federally subsidized Central Pacific/Union Pacific; everyone knew that the Southern route was its infinite superior.[3]

Equally ungracious was the argument that the South had failed to prosper because the North meant to keep it economically subservient. All the South wanted was a fair chance to develop its agriculture and manufacturing, said the *Galveston News*. "New England is opposed to granting this change, and . . . shows it by securing special advantages for her own manufactures, by discouraging the flow of immigration and capital southward, and by so directing legislation as to prevent the South from obtaining money except at ruinous rates of interest."[4]

Conservatives could claim that they, too, cared deeply about Southern interests, but Republicans had an advantage over their foes: the Republican party ran Congress in the first years of Reconstruction, and it was more inclined to hearken to appeals from its own members. Democrats could plead, but Republicans could *demand* financial support. Then, too, many Republicans had friends in the administration. Knowing Northerners of influence was crucial to an appropriation's success. It was well known, indeed, that any shrewd Democrat passed his measures by asking a Republican to introduce them.[5]

But, alas! The Southern Republicans promised far more than they could deliver. To their constituents' dismay, the national government had little interest in the South's special needs. With a few conspicuous exceptions, Congress renounced its policy of subsidies and federal aid, and when it did give support, Southern states fared no better than any others.

Congressional neglect was not willful or malicious. Southern representatives did get much of what they sought, including a fair proportion of river and harbor improvements, a generous land grant to a Southern transcontinental line, and flood relief. Yet Southerners could not help feeling cheated. So much of what they wanted they did not obtain. The Central Pacific/Union Pacific received money; the Texas & Pacific was given only land. The nation gave nothing for building levees. By inaction on bills renewing the privileges of Southern railroads, Congress restricted the largess it had shown before the war. As of 1877, for example, the Vicksburg & Meridian had collected only half the acreage promised it, and seven other lines had either failed to acquire lands or forfeited all rights to them. Only eight roads gained or certified new acres of public domain during the Reconstruction period, usually for modest amounts. Only five got more than one acre for every four already in their grip.[6]

What had gone wrong? Southern Republicans had misread the national mood. They had underestimated the frugality of the East, overestimated their common interests with the West, and ignored the divided mind of the South. Most of all, they had failed to see that public aid had lost favor even in those states which had championed it before the war. The moral tone of Congress did not decline during the postwar period, as later historians thought. It may have improved; certainly after 1868 many contemporaries remarked on a change for the better. Challenged by public outcry and constituents' demands for retrenchment, the congressional majority proved reluctant to give any road, in any section, a subsidy or to embark on any large public works projects. In this resolve, they had the hearty support of Northern Democrats, many of whom came from states which once had welcomed subsidies and endured the corruption and bad faith that went along with aid. At every session, Democrats and New England Republicans would offer resolutions to cut government spending for public works or to ban future railroad subsidies.[7]

One man's reform is another man's parsimony. The new trend in the North baffled Southerners and enraged them. Yankees making others refrain from their own excesses struck some editors as the height of hypocrisy and self-serving impudence. Self-serving there was. Even in the frugal Congresses of the 1870s, the government used some money for internal improvements projects, and those states with members on the House Commerce Committee received a larger share of the money allocated. "I can only say that if I ever get on the committee on commerce," one Southern congressman joked, "I will report appropriations for every little river and bayou in Mississippi and nothing for Michigan and Wisconsin."[8]

Still, the North held no monopoly on self-serving inconsistency. Southerners, too, believed that federal subsidies were rife with corruption—except those granted to the South. They shared the national desire for retrenchment—except for Southern public works. The monopolist Tom Scott who helped to bribe through one transcontinental line might as well have been a different man from the statesmanlike Scott who wanted to build a road across Texas on federal largess. "There is no use talking about monopolies, land grabbers and all that," the *Charleston Daily Republican* said. "There are none in the present South Pacific bill, and if there were, the Representatives ought to have thought of opposition before, and not . . . just when the South gets ready for it."[9]

Congressional representation and Republican politics simply were not enough to assure the South preferential treatment. Nor did bills pass because of the persuasive powers and oratorical skills of Southern representatives, though all too many observers thought that these were the keys to legislative success. Legislators needed experience and an ability to join with others on a common program. They had neither, and it rendered them, as the *Florence Republican* put it, no more important "than a red ant in a meal bag."[10]

The most important division between Southern representatives was that of party. In the North, sectional and local interest dissolved party lines on economic questions. In his painstaking study of Southern congressional voting patterns, however, a modern scholar has discovered that Southerners lacked such a clear sense of sectional priorities. During the four Congresses between 1869 and 1877, more than two-thirds of all Republicans favored railroad aid. Not one put himself on record against the railway corporations. Democrats were much less friendly to railroad aid, and many of them voted against every measure that came up.[11]

The conflict of economic interests added to the disarray on Capitol Hill. Support for one comprehensive program worked hardship on another. Had the South made a concerted effort, it might have compelled congressional action for levee repairs, though the chances never were very good. Instead, legislators from states in the Mississippi valley applied their energies to that goal, while lawmakers elsewhere gave little support. The congressman with a large landless constituency might appreciate the federal homestead laws for reserving public lands for settlers, while congressmen promoting railroads found the statutes an unpardonable limitation on the South's ability to give land grants to aid construction. These clashing economic interests were aggravated by legislators who could not tell their own advantage from that of their constituents. Many of them dabbled in railroad companies: Senators Hiram Revels, Blanche K. Bruce, and James L. Alcorn of Mississippi; Thomas W. Osborne of Florida; Powell Clayton and S. W. Dorsey of Arkansas; John J. Patterson of South Carolina; Matt Ransom and Augustus Merrimon of North Carolina; J. W. Flanagan of Texas.[12] Not all of them put their own gain first, but with so many lawmakers with their own financial investments to be served, the actual needs of the South might well become lost.

The crosscurrents of Southern desires did not always show up in congressional voting. Most bills lacking widespread sectional support did not get beyond the committees to which they were referred. Without unified and specifically focused lobbying, no legislation could win a place on the calendar ahead of all the rest. Many of the measures that might have done the most good had the least support among Southerners. Republicans needed to make their supporters economically independent. Ten congressmen supported homestead bills, but Congress took no action until 1876—and then it repealed the Southern Homestead Act, which had given freedmen a slight opportunity to become landowners at bargain rates. As long as Southern states were burdened with public debts, they could not issue new bonds at par; this problem was a major weakness to state railroad aid laws. But a bill to have the federal government assume the state debts did not even get Southern backing. Too many Southerners simply wanted too many things for different reasons to unite on a common, coherent, comprehensive program of action. The least controversial measures were also the most conservative and the least innovative. That was why during these years Southern congressmen could sponsor 248 railroad bills.[13]

In view of the divisions among Southerners, the campaign to get a federal subsidy for a Southern transcontinental road assumes special importance. The Texas & Pacific bill of 1871 was not just the South's most significant victory in the Forty-first Congress and proof of what Southerners could do when they worked together. It also revealed the limitations under which any legislation passed and the tensions among congressmen from the former slave states.

A second road to the Pacific might have served national interests, but Southerners expressed more concern with how it affected their own. They felt that transcontinental line their due, particularly since Congress was prepared to give the North a second road across the country. The project must benefit the South above all. It should be a road through the cotton states, carrying Southern goods and ending at a Southern port. Thus the representatives became furious when it was proposed that the line have a 4'8" gauge, just as Northern roads did. The five-foot gauge that Southerners used must be maintained. Anything else would give Northern connections the advantage, by forcing Southern through lines to break bulk at the junction in northeastern Texas.[14]

The Southern Pacific Railroad achieved widespread popularity because it promised advantages to all. The need for a transcontinental line was felt most keenly in Arkansas, Texas, and Louisiana, where almost every railroad scheme hoped to prosper from the Pacific connection, but in other Southern states faith in the railroad's potential for local interests also helped shape public policy. Alabamians were sure that the closest route from the Pacific to the Northeast lay across the mineral region of their state and up to Chattanooga. Georgians insisted that the California trade would find its true outlet to the sea at Savannah, though the editor of the *Beaufort Republican* had no doubt that Port Royal could be the only natural terminus. Merchants in Charleston, Charlotte, Mobile, Jacksonville, Norfolk, Washington, and New York perhaps had theories of their own.[15]

A national road was supported by men with purely local interests, but this turned the debate over specific legislation into a brawl for special treatment. That the road would cross northern Texas might please Dallas businessmen, but it angered promoters in San Antonio and Galveston, hundreds of miles south of the projected line. When Alabama state senators considered a memorial favoring the Southern Pacific route, they added the admonition that the road should not begin at Norfolk, Virginia. They preferred Brunswick, Georgia, as a terminus. Northerners behind Tom Scott wanted the road to connect with lines running across Arkansas to St. Louis and from there to the railway network controlled by the Pennsylvania Railroad Company. New Orleans and Mobile saw no reason why they should not shunt the Western trade southeast to the Gulf. In Louisiana itself, different areas cherished conflicting ambitions.[16] For representatives on the Pacific Railroad committees, the pressure to give preference to their constituents was irresistible.

These ambitions erupted in the political debate from the moment the aid bill appeared. Senator Willard Warner of Alabama did nothing extraordinary in 1869 when he offered an amendment to the Memphis, El Paso & Pacific Railroad bill that would have forced the company to build a branch line to Shreveport within two years. No member from the Deep South would have wanted St. Louis to become the terminus, and certainly every Alabamian knew that Shreveport was more suited to his own state's needs. A man from Arkansas might feel differently, and Senator Benjamin F. Rice certainly did. He tried to amend similar legislation to give himself a charter to build a link between the main line and the Cairo & Fulton, in which he had a financial as well as political interest. Often localism proved its own cure. Senator Powell Clayton had railroad interests to care for in southwestern Arkansas. He managed to block the Rice amendment. The Memphis, El Paso & Pacific charter ran afoul of Senator Kellogg of Louisiana because it would have deprived his state of special benefits. Seriously ill, he struggled through a snowstorm to the Pacific Railroad Committee hearings to rouse other members against the project and succeeded in burying it.[17]

Nor was it ever disinterred. The Memphis, El Paso & Pacific, for all its resources, never built more than 6 miles of track beyond that laid down by its antebellum predecessors. The state of Texas had given a land grant of 10,210 acres to the mile, a total area slightly larger than New Jersey. Under General John Fremont, the company issued $10 million in bonds, sold more than half to French investors through fraud, and issued glowing reports of progress. These reports continued until July 1870, when the company failed and was placed in the receivership of John A. C. Gray, a Fremont cohort. Later, under peculiar circumstances, the receiver sold the line to a rival project covering the same route and operated by Tom Scott, vice-president of the Pennsylvania Railroad. Both Fremont and Gray were officers of this competing road, and it was evident that Scott had bought out the ruined company's rights after an agreement was made to "take care of the interests of Fremont, Gray, and their friends," as the *New York Sun* later charged.[18]

Even as the Memphis, El Paso & Pacific fell into receivership, Fremont and Scott had their friends press for federal aid. The House bill favoring Fremont's line gave lawmakers some incentive by making some of them incorporators and, it was charged, endowing others with gifts of stock. The Senate bill offered by Kellogg soon after had an entirely different set of incorporators. In June 1870, the upper chamber consolidated the two lists, thus satisfying the Memphis, El Paso & Pacific. Its bill vanished in the House. Scott's project gained popularity, more than it may have deserved on Capitol Hill. Bribery had grown so common, the *New York Sun* declared, that "the air of Congress was thick with . . . bonds, falling like snowflakes and dissolving like dew." It insisted that eighty congressmen had been offered bribes. Kellogg had money invested in the project, said the *Sun*; so did Congressman John Ray and Louisiana Chief Justice John Ludeling. Leading upstate Republicans, they hoped to connect the road with their own North Louisiana & Texas.[19]

In fact, the railroad bill as it left the Senate committee in May had far more persuasive incentives for Southern support than the alleged bribery. It gave Scott's transcontinental line, retitled the Texas Pacific, twenty sections of land per mile in the territories and ten sections per mile in Texas. As amended, the bill authorized three branch lines from Marshall, including John Ray's concern, and one connecting line from San Diego. By the time the Senate passed the measure in June 1870, the branches had increased to five and the land grant swollen to twenty-six million acres.[20] Though there were connections enough to placate every important Southern interest, some senators complained at the bill's parsimony and would have been happier with eight or ten branches rather than five.

Such generosity overwhelmed Northern congressmen, who blocked the measure in the House. There the Pacific Railroad Committee struck the branch lines from the bill and in doing so cut the land grant in half. The House amended the bill further to promise that the transcontinental line would get no financial subsidy in the future. Southern representatives accepted the changes quietly; their Senate allies did not. A conference committee met and decided that at least some branches should receive support. But which ones? That was the question. "I think I never went through a fight where so much watchfulness and persistence were required," one Louisiana congressman wrote, "and certainly I never expect again to be compelled to contend against so many powerful and adverse interests or so many men combined to execute malicious designs." Just obtaining a subsidy for any road to New Orleans took stamina, and the New Orleans, Mobile & Texas was left out so that the "Backbone" route running northwest from the capital could receive preference. Arkansas senators protested that the final bill had served them ill. Equally distressed, Congressman Morey of Louisiana begged for restoration of the original land grant to the North Louisiana & Texas. The bill passed into law on the last day of the session, but the dissatisfaction of so many Southerners and the limited scope of the subsidy made certain that the company would be back asking for additional aid. It was no less certain that Southern politicians would favor new federal support.[21]

Scott did return to Washington to ask new favors. An 1872 statute changed the company name to the Texas & Pacific. Unable to negotiate company bonds in Europe after the Panic of 1873, Scott needed a federal appropriation. He knew he could rely on Southerners for support. Having received less than it thought it merited in 1871, the South was ready to apply for supplementary grants. Legislatures passed resolutions endorsing Scott's project and requesting congressmen to vote for a subsidy. Prominent former Confederates joined Republicans in promoting the cause. Chambers of commerce and boards of trade in New Orleans, Atlanta, Augusta, Richmond, and Vicksburg went on record in favor of a subsidy. All the beneficiary lines sprang into action, and projects without hope of completion became advocates of aid to the great road that might revive their own prospects. Once more every town put its own interests foremost. Let it be declared "a sine qua non," Judge J. W. Clapp urged a convention called to honor Scott's road, "that Memphis shall have her branch." The delegates did better than that: they asked Congress to aid lines connecting the transcontinental road with Memphis, Vicksburg, and New Orleans.[22]

Such schemes were economically impossible and politically preposterous. By 1874, there was not the slightest chance of Congress enacting such a broad subsidy. By the time Scott's bill came out of committee in February 1877, Democrats controlled the House and had put themselves on record against any form of grant. The pulse of reform had quickened with the Panic and revelations of political corruption. Scandals had discredited all railroad aid. Consequently, Southerners, too, felt disquiet about railroad promoters. "We want no more such jobs!" exclaimed the *Alabama State Journal* of one contracting firm. "We are unwilling to have any more Credit Mobiliers, whether for the benefit of Northern or Southern 'enterprisers.' We are opposed to another cent of the people's money being given away for the aggregation of the wealth of any private company. . . . The principle is essentially a wrong one."[23]

The principle is essentially a wrong one: so Southerners had learned from the states' railroad aid policies as well as from the travails of national lines. Gradually, Southerners were adopting the Northern Democrats' point of view. During the final session of the Forty-third Congress, William Holman of Indiana introduced a resolution declaring it the sense of the House that Congress should give no further subsidies in money or lands to corporations. Texas & Pacific supporters knew that this resolution was aimed at them and, Scott wrote a North Carolinian, "especially at the southern interest." By one vote the House failed to muster the two-thirds needed to suspend the rules and put the resolution up for passage, but the sense of the chamber was clear.[24]

How well Holman's resolution reflected the will of the House became more obvious in early 1875, when the chamber voted on a bill aiding the Texas & Pacific. Under Scott's new measure, the government would guarantee the interest on the line's forty-year 5-percent bonds. In return, Scott would give federal authorities a first mortgage on the Texas & Pacific, surrender its claim to eighteen million acres of public land, and transfer to the national government at least one out of every seven construction bonds issued. Compared with Southern public aid laws and with the federal largess to the first transcontinental line, Scott's proposition seemed cautious. However, it was not cautious enough for the House. By 127 to 118, the members refused even to suspend the rules to hear the Railroad Committee's report on the measure. Had the South voted as a unit, the vote to suspend would have gone the other way.[25] But Southern disunity was not the cause of Scott's failure; most Southerners did support a suspension of the rules. With the Northeast and Midwest so strongly opposed, the measure had too many enemies to have reached a final vote before the end of the session. Not even fifty branches, each serving a different Southern constituency, could have overcome that state of things.

With the opening of the Forty-fourth Congress, the subsidy policy lost what little remaining strength it had. For the first time since 1859, Democrats controlled the House. Furthermore, their program did not encompass aid to the Texas & Pacific. On December 15, 1875, Holman's resolutions passed the House, 223 to 34. More than two-thirds of the opponents came from the Southern and border states, though more than half the Southern representatives supported the resolution. If Republicans split 6 to 5 in support, Democrats voted almost 2 to 1 for a ban on future government subsidies. They probably reflected the ambiguity of their constituents' thought: they wanted railroads but wanted tax relief more.[26]

The vote on December 15, 1875, was the final repudiation of the Republican promise. Party leaders had insisted that they should be kept in office because they could attract government funding and the Democrats could not. Instead, what had become clear was that it made little difference which party controlled Congress in the early 1870s and that both were utterly powerless to extract subsidies from Northern representatives by 1875. With the convening of the Forty-fourth Congress, indeed, Democrats could make the Republican argument their own: Would it not be best to have Southern representatives from the same party as that controlling the House?

Republicans had made federal aid a symbol of the good intentions of the North toward the South. The failure to obtain that aid could be seen to prove the reverse: the callousness and malice of Northern politicians. If, as Southerners claimed, the Middle Atlantic and New England states pursued their own interests so single-mindedly in economic legislation, it seemed logical that the same selfish motivation explained their political efforts to protect black civil rights and to suppress white terrorism. Economic legislation did not persuade Conservatives of the good faith of those instituting Military Reconstruction. It only increased their suspicion of insidious Northern purposes.

The failures of Congress did as much harm to the Southern Republicans' economic program as to the party's political plans. Without federal appropriations, the states had to divert funds to the levees. Consequently, they never had enough money to do the task properly. They only increased their bonded debts and drove down the price of securities. Without congressional aid for river improvements, the farmers needed to rely all the more on railroad construction for transport. National monetary policies prevented the South from gaining the banking facilities and large money supply vital to an expanding and self-reliant economy. This failure helped bring the downfall of the railroads and the depression of the mid-1870s. In many ways, Southerners had trusted Congress to do the work that they could not do because they had put so much of their own revenue into railroad promotion. Their trust was misplaced.

There were other sources of Northern money in which Southerners trusted, as well, though their trust was tinged with suspicion and fear. Federal funds were not the only Northern resource that could build Southern roads. Private parties were ready, and some were eager, to help finance railroads across the South. Among them were Northern businessmen, such as Tom Scott, who had the resources to make a Southern transcontinental line possible. But they would do so only on their terms, and only to benefit Northern interests. The road from Capitol Hill led directly to Wall Street; and that proved to be a mixed blessing not only for the Republicans but for the Southerners dreaming of a section reborn.

CHAPTER 11

Friends in Deed on Wall Street?
The Enemy Without

We want no *Tom Scotts, Jim Fisks* or *Vanderbilts* in this State to
govern us.

An angry Florida legislator, 1872

BELIEVING as they did in a New South that would remain master
of its own destiny, Republicans were forced to confront a terrible
dilemma. Outside financiers alone had the capital to work the South's
salvation, and they could not anticipate a quick return. How, then,
could they be induced to invest without demanding control as well?
How could those who rescued the section's economy be kept from
reducing the states to economic colonies?

That an infusion of Northern capital would benefit the South,
Republicans did not doubt. The outsiders had better standards,
said the *New Orleans Republican*. In the Northeast, "none but good
roads are tolerated." Northerners also had more energy than anyone else. Most important, these intruders had money, and Republicans had great respect for the power of the purse.[1] For more
limited goals than Radicals had set, Conservatives extended the
same welcome to all with money for railroad construction.

The welcome was evident in what the laws did not say as well as
in what they did. No statutes demanded that the incorporators all
be state residents; in at least one case, such a restriction was dropped
from a charter. The boards of directors were open to anyone. Laws
allowed connections with any other road in or out of the state. As
for public aid, much of it went to roads which had the best chance
of acquiring non-Southern support, such as trunk lines. Capital
investors were protected with guarantees of limited liability as well.

If a second invasion from the Union states was what Southerners
wanted, they were not disappointed. Sometimes the intruders were
carpetbaggers who came south to mingle railroads and Republicanism. For Milton Littlefield of New York, railroad subsidies in
North Carolina and Florida made possible a series of building contracts, gambling forays, and mergers. When Connecticut failed to

satisfy Hannibal I. Kimball's ambitions, he went south and became president of four Georgia roads that received state aid.[2] Such men had little capital of their own and fewer ethics about obtaining it, but most of them did not fit the stereotype of plundering outlanders victimizing the roads for a quick fortune. Except for the carpetbaggers in Louisiana and the Carolinas, they had long-range ambitions; after all, a completed line would bring a better return than pilfering. With little cash to spare for their plans, however, they used every imaginable method to get more and still keep control of their projects. They juggled ledgers, played the market, and siphoned funds to help finish projects in more immediate need of the money.

Men in the boardrooms of large Northern cities had greater influence and made a larger contribution to railroad construction. Banks bought bonds issued to aid the lines and sold securities to investors in London, Amsterdam, Frankfurt, and Bridgeport. Financiers also bought into the roads themselves, though none did it in a bigger way than Thomas A. Scott of the Pennsylvania Railroad. With capital in one transcontinental line and thoughts of a second, he envisioned a network that joined his holdings in the Middle Atlantic states with roads to Atlanta, Chattanooga, New Orleans, and the Pacific coast. Though a skein of trunk lines controlling the cotton as well as the corn trade would benefit Scott and Philadelphia merchants, Southerners would find such a system to their advantage as well. Though a vast, well-coordinated series of roads might pay in the long run, it would certainly entail costs and substantial loss for the first few years of operation. No company was better able to absorb the expense than the Pennsylvania Railroad with its many established thoroughfares. Its gross earnings in 1871 were $22 million, and it had nearly as many freight cars as all the companies in ten Southern states combined.[3]

Under the corporate title of the Southern Railway Security Company, Pennsylvania Railroad officials and their allies moved on Richmond. Consequently, with a lot of argument and a bit of bribing, they had the state-owned stock in two Virginia roads put up for sale. Scott bought both on easy terms. With connections to the North Carolina roads at Petersburg, the acquisitions opened the way into the Republican South. Within two years of formation, the Southern Railway Security Company had direct lines from Washington to Atlanta, Atlanta to Chattanooga, and Chattanooga to Memphis and into eastern Tennessee. At Memphis, a road to Texas was projected, with Scott on the board of directors. Across Texas and toward the Pacific stretched Scott's greatest project, his Texas Pacific Railroad, with enough branches on the eastern end to satisfy every major city west of the Mississippi. By 1873, the Southern Railway Security Company was operating thirteen lines and 2,131 miles of track, with three separate trunk lines from Virginia to Georgia and west to the Mississippi River. There was hardly a Southern state in which Scott did not have railroad interests. There was not a trunk line in the South that did not depend on Scott's empire for connections.[4]

New York and Chicago interests used the Illinois Central to counter "the Railroad King's" ambitions and channel trade from the trans-Appalachian South to the Great Lakes. In 1868, H. S. McComb had taken a lease on the Mississippi Central and hoped to clear the way to the Gulf by seizing the New Orleans, Jackson & Great Northern. Carpetbagger laws and court decisions gave him the right to buy the public stock of the road and assured his control of a route from New Orleans into Tennessee. Frugal as McComb was, he could not make the combination prosper and turned to the Illinois Central for aid. The Central's officials supported an $8 million bond issue to extend McComb's roads to the Ohio River, and between 1872 and 1876, they bought enough securities in the two lines to make a bid for control. By 1877, the consolidated line was theirs.[5]

Northerners were not the only outsiders with a desire to increase their Southern connections. Because it sought links to the West, the Central of Georgia acquired roads into Alabama and toward Florida. Its rival, the Georgia Railroad and Banking Company, carried stock in ten other lines, including the Mobile & Montgomery. The Port Royal Railroad was completed only after becoming the instrument of Augusta businessmen.[6]

That was precisely the problem. Once financiers took an interest in Southern railway construction, it was almost impossible to keep them from demanding power as well. How far out-of-state influence stretched depended largely on how much aid the company needed, and this depended on how much of the road had been built before the war and how much was left to be built. In states where major lines had been completed or at least begun by 1861, the outsiders' ambitions met a stronger resistance from local elites than in those states where communications had remained rudimentary. State ownership of railroads also retarded outside penetration. East of the Appalachians, Georgia and the Carolinas administered some roads and their residents controlled others. West of the mountains the situation was different. Vital routes had not been constructed, and in the most important cases, out-of-state capital filled the need. Northeastern financiers also bought into trunk lines already built.[7]

There was nothing unique in the South's plight. Indeed, its roads seem to have withstood outsiders' influence better than those elsewhere in the country. Bostonians dominated most Nebraska roads; New Yorkers controlled nearly all Illinois roads longer than 130 miles. The Pennsylvania and Vanderbilt interests in fact preferred the West to the South as a field of investment, and Boston capitalists had hardly any interest in the South at all. Wherever there was a profit to be made from development, the major financial centers ran the show. Thus Bostonians put their capital into Nebraska roads and left Maine and New Hampshire enterprises to fend for themselves.[8]

It must also be noted that Northern investment was quite selective. Most Southern companies had no Northern directors in the early 1870s, and of the remainder, few had a majority of Northerners. Of forty-five major roads, one historian counted only seven with Northern presidents; of over four hundred directors, he found eighty-one Northerners. Had he examined all the directors on *every* Southern road, the proportion of outsiders would have been even smaller, for Northeastern financiers preferred to invest in major arteries of commerce. The few lines they did run were mostly trunk lines, and this gave them an effect far beyond the areas the roads traversed, for they connected with so many lesser railways. Hardly a railroad in Alabama could do without the Alabama & Chattanooga or the South & North, for example: they tapped the cotton belt and mineral region and opened the northern and central counties to exploitation. Bostonians administered one, Louisville interests the other.[9]

Southerners could not do without the large capitalists, yet they could not help feeling misgivings. It was not simply the arrogance with which interlopers treated local customs that irritated them. The political allegiance of the Northerners unsettled white Conservatives. Some of the leading magnates—Henry Clews, Kimball, Littlefield, Jay Cooke—flaunted their Republican allegiance. Scott's friends provided Republican senators in Louisiana and Alabama with campaign funds.[10] Such partisanship could not have increased Conservatives' enthusiasm for paying off the state aid bonds given to such men.

More distressing still than the origins or ideals of the Northern man was his remoteness. It was not just the outsider as individual that offended Southern sensibilities but the outsider as a corporation, and in this the Louisville & Nashville was as much an alien force as the Pennsylvania Railroad.

Republicans did not oppose the corporate structure itself, but accepted it as a means of developing the section's resources. Nor did they see consolidation of different roads as necessarily a bad thing. Republicans knew it could mean cheaper freights, greater coordination, and lowered operating costs. Should two lines be run as one, they might carry more traffic and anticipate larger revenues. Large enterprises could better withstand times of economic hardship.

What Republicans feared was that such a power for good could also be a power for ill. They tempered their admiration of large enterprises with suspicion. When given a chance to do good or evil, a legislator warned, "large, all-absorbing companies generally exert their influence in an evil direction." They wrecked weaker rivals by operating at a loss. Leading railroad men had reputations for purchasing everything in the North that stood in their way, that is, from rival concerns to United States senators. Native-born promoters might have been every bit as venal, but they had less cash with which to gain their ends, and, therefore, less power. "The great curse of Florida had been dishonest corporations, rings, and cliques," said one black legislator, and he resented more skillful outside competition. "We want no *Tom Scotts, Jim Fisks* or *Vanderbilts* in this State to govern us, by means of which they would influence legislation tending to advance personal interests."[11]

The critics had cause for distress, for the most significant cases of corruption had out-of-state capitalists and consolidation schemes mixed in them somewhere. When most Alabamians thought of bribery, they remembered the Stanton brothers using Boston manners and Boston money to gain special loans. South Carolinians did not forget that it was Pennsylvanians like "Honest John" Patterson who brought the legislators to a finer sense of the interests of the Blue Ridge Railroad. In Louisiana, it was Charles Morgan of New York; in Florida and North Carolina, Littlefield. All of them were outsiders with vast ambitions.

A more valid source of concern was the remoteness of the corporation's authority. Run by Greenville merchants and planters, a line would support Greenville. As part of a network stretching from Richmond to Atlanta, its Northern owners would be more interested in making the consolidated line pay and in assuring inexpensive through shipments of goods. They might lower the rates for long hauls and make it up on short hauls, to the detriment of the towns at which the projects originated. This defeated the purpose for which the original promoters had pledged their lands and savings. Again, a community-based railroad might plow back its earnings into improvements of maintenance and operations. A consolidated enterprise might work for the stockholders and bondholders and turn the net profits into dividends and reductions on the principal of the bonded debt. For community sponsors of the road as it had first been planned, such changes were no less than betrayal. To stop such policies from being implemented, local leaders would call protest rallies, institute lawsuits, and try to block mergers.[12] In this last endeavor they had little success, but their efforts could cause enough delay and cost to cripple the consolidated road and increase the chances of eventual bankruptcy.

Consolidation was almost an obsession among Southern railroad executives, as it was among Northerners, and a dangerous fascination at that. Just as a hundred cities wanted to be the New York of the South, so a hundred promoters hoped to become the section's Tom Scott. Executives of the Louisville & Nashville dreamed of an empire through the cotton states, while George W. Swepson sensed possibilities in a combination encompassing Florida and Virginia.[13] Vast projects took cunning and audacity, and of these characteristics, Southern financiers had more than enough. But imperial visions also took plenty of money and luck, both of which the South had in very short supply. A merger took money—to buy out roads, buy off enemies, and buy up legislators. Northerners could bring about consolidation by pooling resources, but Southern lines had few resources to pool and a doubtful economic future. Yet consolidation meant wider markets for the railroads to exploit. Consequently, that gave it an urgency for the weakest roads. The money must be found, and if proceeds were not sufficient, speculation must supply the balance.

For the communities immediately served, the obsession with consolidation was doubly harmful. On the one hand, corporations would use funds otherwise available for improving the track or reducing the bonded debt to buy up other concerns. On the other hand, they could weaken the corporation by losing the money on ventures with no immediate chance for profit.

North Carolina's manipulators showed how the vision of consolidation could expand the effects of the disaster it had encouraged. With large banks in both the Carolinas, George W. Swepson still could not find the resources to finance his railroad plans. He therefore tried to get the necessary capital through bond manipulation. With other railroad presidents' support, he plotted to corner the market in state bonds given to the lines. The conspiracy nearly succeeded. Then, on September 29, 1869, while the Swepson combination was still glutting itself with securities, another set of conspirators touched off a panic by trying to corner the market in gold. In the chaos that followed, stocks of every kind tumbled, including Southern securities. Within a week North Carolina bonds were going begging at 30. One conspirator later claimed that the group lost between $300,000 and $400,000, but the real figure must have been far higher. Swepson resigned and fled the state a few steps ahead of the public prosecutor. The "Black Friday" fiasco had ruined lines he controlled in two states instead of solving their problems.[14]

Swepson's ruin made clear one of the terrible risks of large railroad combinations. Supporters of a New South hoped to end the periodic depressions from which the section suffered by establishing a broad range of industries. For this task, the railroad was essential. Yet, in their construction, the lines did not end all risk of depression. Rather, they widened its potential impact. The need for capital made the South dependent on a few commercial centers for its prosperity, for the railroads needed constant financial backing. What would happen if a firm in New York lost money in speculations outside the South, or tried to unload its Southern securities? A Northern panic would hurt every major railroad in the former Confederacy. Unwise financial practices by the leading Northern capitalists could have a tremendous effect. At the same time, the railroads proved burdensome to the best financiers of the nation, and that burden would become insupportable as the Southern governments withdrew their backing for the subsidy bonds they had placed on the markets. If a national figure could damage the Southern economy, a few Southern politicians or a few crop failures could do terrible harm to a businessman of national importance, such as Henry Clews.

This danger Southern critics of the growing corporate power did not recognize, but they did not need additional reasons to fear the loss of community control in railroad development. Out of their fear, the Republican railroad policy became something different from what it might have been. Balanced against incentives to outside capital were barriers against outside control and sporadic attacks on the corporate influence.

A case in point was provided by Charles Morgan, whose steam-ship and railroad enterprises had given him an enviable position in Louisiana's economy. As one of the major stockholders in the New Orleans, Opelousas & Great Western, he forced foreclosure on its mortgage. When the public stock was sold at auction, Morgan paid slightly more than $2 million for it, to the city and state's loss.[15] The road complemented his packet boats, which, as one legislator put it, allowed him to hold "in his grip the great highway to . . . Texas; not a barrel of flour, nor a fatted beef can reach you . . . without first bowing to the dictions [*sic*] of this financial autocrat."[16] This power spurred resentment among those who felt themselves Morgan's prey, and they looked for some way to break his grip by an independent line west from New Orleans.

For this purpose the New Orleans, Mobile & Chattanooga seemed ideal, for Northern capitalists and politicians held positions in it, and Alabama's government had given it financial support. In 1869, Louisiana lawmakers endowed the road with $12,500 a mile in bonds. A year later, they considered a bill giving it $3 million more. Morgan met the challenge: he asked for a charter to build a road of his own to Texas. The state need pay nothing, and if Morgan could not fulfill his promises in three years he would forfeit $500,000 to the state. It was an attractive offer, or would have been, had it not been made by "that great moneyed monopolist which has come here from the East, and now holds the rivers and the sea in the hollow of his hand," as one representative called him. One might accuse the Chattanooga road of using shady tactics to block Morgan's charter and enrich itself, but no one could call it a "monopoly." Legislators gave the Chattanooga's methods little scrutiny. Whenever the press defended Morgan, however, state senators discerned in it the hand and gold of Morgan. "Mr. President," a New Orleans Democrat cried, "they have endeavored to strangle this bill in the Senate just as the serpents undertook to strangle Hercules, while he was in his cradle. . . ." There had been an effort, he added, "to resist, by all legitimate and by illegitimate means, if necessary, the mere introduction of the bill. . . . We found that . . . threats of the most dire character were being held over the heads of Senators." This, said the orator, must be Morgan's work. Audacious it was, since he alone was to blame for the economic decline of New Orleans. The magnate could promise to post security, but his affluence made this guarantee worthless. To forfeit the proposed charter would cost him one twenty-fourth of his anticipated profits on the Opelousas road, said one senator. To fulfill the terms of his contract with the state would cost him millions and would rob his steamship lines of business. Such a shrewd businessman could not want a charter to build a road to Texas; he must want it to keep anyone else from building one. Raising the battle cry of "competition," the Chattanooga advocates gave their project its aid, while Morgan failed to obtain so much as a charter.[17]

Other promoters met the same reception that Morgan had, as opponents used such catchwords as "monopoly," "outsider," and "speculative concern" to degrade them. In Texas, for example, Governor Edmund Davis vetoed a bill chartering the Texas & Mexico Railroad and branded it the tool of alien speculators. The incorporators included natives, but, Davis noted, these men either had no money or had been cited without their knowledge or consent. Knowing that the Central Railroad of Georgia supported a project was enough to cool a South Carolinian's ardor for the scheme, while chauvinistic Alabama editors turned the Louisville & Nashville into a whipping boy for the state's problems.[18]

When Southerners spoke of wanting no more Tom Scotts, therefore, they did not mean Northerners as much as outside corporations. They were most afraid of losing control of their own destiny. In a way, the railroad aid laws provided the best safeguards against dictation by the moguls on Wall Street and Chestnut Street. Republican policies encouraged Northerners to involve themselves by setting up guarantees on their investment, but at the same time discouraged them by setting up procedures which made state residents the main influence on and last resort for the railroad promoters. Without Northern money, the railroads could not have been built, but the governments weakened the lines' dependence on Northern aid by putting state revenues into the major roads. Not all the company's first-mortgage bonds would reach the market. Lines aided would be able to exchange many of them for state bonds and sell those instead. The large investor might be able to pressure a corporation through control of its securities, but would find it harder to exert pressure on the company by forcing the state treasurer to come to terms.

By taking the first-mortgage bonds, the states forced the railroads to offer a prior lien and a prior allegiance to the state. Admittedly, the government and not private investors would protect local interests. Officials sitting in Montgomery might not feel the same sympathy for a north Alabama road that a merchant in Elyton might. Still, they would be more responsive to local demands than a consolidated concern would. Politicans showed unstinting interest in local conditions when their constituents put pressure on them. Should the line default, the state interests would still control it. Should the road be in danger of failure, the officers by experience and instinct would be more inclined to turn to the state authorities for further aid. With new grants-in-aid, further sureties might be given for the public interest. If the road neglected to do what its charter and promotional literature bound it to do, the directors could trust the legislature to be less harsh a taskmaster than would Northern and Southern intruders, who could and did use such a crisis to strengthen their grip on the directory.

There was only one weakness in this scenario: What if the states should refuse to shoulder their financial responsibilities when the corporations failed? Then the private bondholders would demand that the state surrender its lien, and that the investors indemnify themselves by taking total control of the line. Having marketed its bonds in the North and abroad, the Southern states would have increased outside influence on Southern lines and would have fettered the South to the major financial centers with negotiable bonds.

It was a risk, but one that Southerners had to take. Without substantial Northern support, without the aid of corporations intent on creating empires for themselves in the South, the railroads simply could not have been built. The Southerners did not have the resources, and only by putting themselves deeply in debt by bond issues could they build all the lines they wanted.

The risk was also one that Southerners did not admit could happen. The roads could not fail. The state would not have any responsibilities to shoulder, and if it did the earnings of whatever road it took over would indemnify it. This was the most tragic misjudgment in the railroad aid program. The fact was that the railroads from the start were underplanned, underfunded, oversold, and overwhelmed. In their elusive struggle for an economy independent of outside domination, Southerners made possible outside intervention on a greater scale than ever before.

CHAPTER 12

Railroad Ties and Bonds: Construction, Credit, and the "Consumptive Purse"

Have had to fight the whole market, as they seem to know
things about our affairs which should not be known.
                                        H. H. Kimpton,
                            South Carolina financial agent

IN the boom years before the Panic of 1873, the Gospel of Prosperity seemed to be transforming the Southern economy. Railroad
construction increased sharply, and Southerners of all political persuasions had faith that present progress would continue in the
future. Yet railroad promoters found these expectations dashed.
For every railroad built, a dozen were planned and not begun. For
every company that completed its main line and prospered, perhaps
twenty stopped construction and went into receivership before they
could reach their termini. Whoever profited from railroad aid, the
companies themselves did not seem to do well by it. Years later,
Southerners would blame Radical corruption and promoter peculation for the policy's failures. They would insist that public funds
had been misapplied and would try to show whose pockets had
been lined. This explanation fits many railroads, especially those
in states east of the Appalachians. Even there, however, the interpretation is inadequate. The real reasons for the failure of the
Radical program were far more banal: the directors lacked the
funds to carry out their intentions and the states lacked the financial
prestige to back lines effectively. The fate of the subsidy policy and
the Republican party was not sealed in the legislative halls or the
backcountry, but on the securities exchanges of New York and
London. Furthermore, the failure was not as much due to evil
designs by the money changers as to the blind optimism of Southern
businessmen and legislators.

Railroad construction was an expensive business. Lines projected through swamps needed money for fill, those through mountains demanded large sums to put down a gentle grade. Through most of the postwar South, entrepreneurs guessed that a substantial road could be built and equipped with rolling stock for about $25,000 a mile, and most roads came within $10,000 of so low a sum. Frugal management, level ground, and plenty of stone and timber available for construction might allow contractors to do the work for as little as $22,000 a mile; less ideal conditions made it easy for them to spend $35,000. Most of this money went for grading the route and preparing it for iron rails. S. C. Millett of the Port Royal Railroad estimated that making the ground fit for a roadbed took more than two-thirds of the $28,500 a mile he raised for his company.[1]

After the road had been completed, the company's debt per mile continued to increase. The company frequently produced insufficient revenue to fund maintenance, add to rolling stock, and still pay bond interest. Promoters were forced to issue new securities or renegotiate old ones, usually to the company's disadvantage. As a result of pressing needs and wartime damages, the Selma, Rome & Dalton, which laid a track before the war for $20,000 a mile, owed $55,000 a mile by 1872; the Alabama & Chattanooga, which could perhaps have been built for $25,000 a mile, actually cost $35,595, and by 1873 owed $44,383 per mile.[2]

Costly though construction of a projected road might be, most promoters were sure that they had resources ample for the task. Directors had to have unfaltering faith in their project to have involved themselves so deeply in its affairs, but they also had good reason for optimism. Usually, the company had local support and a chance of a land grant. Public authorities were always ready to alter the laws and open the state's coffers. But entrepreneurs made several assumptions. First, they made the lowest possible estimate of construction costs and the shortest possible estimate of the time required for completion. They were confident they could obtain as much labor and material as they wanted whenever it was required and at the price set in the initial cost estimates. Second, promoters expected that the state, county, and local assistance would be extensive enough to protect the company from the whims of Northern bankers and international securities markets. Third, directors trusted that they could sell company first-mortgage bonds at or near face value.[3] All three assumptions were open to question. Each could make the difference between a corporation's solvency and bankruptcy, and many roads suffered from all three misconceptions.

From the first, construction took more time and money than the companies had planned. The contracting firm delegated to do the actual work did not always have the same commitment to frugality and good work that the directors had. Some contractors were bare-faced rascals. When H. I. Kimball built the Cartersville & Van Wert, he did 14 miles in broad gauge and then, to save money, did eight more in narrow. Other contractors did shoddy work, used cheap materials, and then pocketed the profits. On the Western & Atlantic, an iron gang foreman testified that his superiors had used rubble to ballast the track and laid so few crossties that the rails bent when the first train passed over them. On the Wilmington, Charlotte & Rutherford, the contractor received three dollars a cubic yard for rock excavation, though for similar work the Richmond & Atlanta paid a third as much; it was easy to overcharge the W.C. & R. when its treasurer and superintendent owned four-ninths of the building contract. Boston businessman Warren Fisher stole more brazenly. Obtaining control of the board of the Little Rock & Fort Smith, he induced his handpicked directors to give him five times as much as his contract stipulated. In return for nearly $12 million in securities, he apparently spent $642,769 for actual work on the road.[4]

Though most contractors tried to fulfill their duties faithfully, they found schedules impossible to meet. Delays of every kind slowed them. When Southern planters harvested large cotton crops, every available freedman went to work in the fields rather than along the tracks. A company could import Northern and foreign laborers, but often the immigrants would accept free transportation south and then desert at the first opportunity. Delays in iron rail shipments forced employers to keep hundreds of paid employees idle. When the company shipped materials to construction sites by river, progress became dependent on the rains required to make most streams navigable. The Iron Mountain Railroad bought locomotives and cars and sent them by steamboat up to Jacksonport, Arkansas. Before the ship could reach its destination, it hit a snag and sank up to the hurricane deck. Consequently, the company had to wait to retrieve its goods until a dry spell lowered the river level. Completing any part of a route, the directors would open it for business and use the proceeds to finance construction on the rest of the line. At times, however, the road would carry so much commercial traffic that no cars would be available to bear supplies to the workers along the line. Sometimes laborers went on strike or unpaid creditors impounded construction materials.[5]

Failure of communication between directors and contractors added to the delays. The Jacksonville, Pensacola & Mobile Railroad needed supplies, but, as the general superintendent complained, a requisition to the president "ha[d] not, even in part, been responded to; and it is almost certain we shall not be able, in consequence, to place our rolling stock in a condition to meet the probable demands upon it." Another employee wrote angrily that railroad officials kept making promises they could not keep. The president kept sending wires from Europe "that 'iron is shipping by steamer' but no iron comes & the hands have all quit, work is stopped." On the other side, contractors often dragged their feet. "Ten weeks have elapsed since instructions were issued to the contractors to commence work on the tunnels," said an assistant engineer in his report on the Blue Ridge Railroad, "and little more has been done than to provide accommodations for barely an adequate force of laborers. Not a hole has been drilled, nor a cubic yard of rock or tunnel material removed. Neither can I hear of any mining tools being on the work."[6] The contract required that work be finished by September 1871, but in March the chief engineer informed the directors that he could not meet the deadline. In each case, the companies paid dearly for the delays.

Worst of all, Southern railroads were hampered by problems in raising money just when it was needed. Short on cash, some corporations offered certificates of indebtedness that workers and merchants refused to accept, and all work ceased.[7] Other companies found that the private support on which they had counted was little more than a myth.

In the first flush of railroad enthusiasm, promoters found it easy to bring together a crowd that would support railroad construction and local aid, but it was not so easy to realize the promises made. Eager as most people were to pledge others' money, and ready as they were to issue county bonds in aid, they showed less interest in spending their own resources. The idea of financing a project by assuming a tax burden that for ten or twenty years would not be much more than theoretical appealed to every community. By the time the principal fell due, citizens presumed that the railroads would have added so much to the county's individual wealth and population that the bonds might even be paid off without a tax increase. In any case, Southerners lacked ready cash. With some justice, the *Aiken Tribune* complained that the only problem with building the Spartanburg & Aiken—the country needed it badly and so many citizens clamored for it—was "the apathy of the people themselves. Each waits for some one else to move. The citizens of Edgefield county have been talking of building railroads and holding public meetings for forty years, but never went earnestly to work themselves, always waiting for some distant city or corporation to do the work."[8]

Consequently, many railroads found private subscriptions disappointingly low. Incorporated in 1866, the Mobile & Alabama Grand Trunk still had only $450,000 in paid-in capital stock seven years later: approximately $4,285.71 a mile, a sum totally inadequate for building needs and far less than the $3 million minimum capital stock that the company's charter had set as a prerequisite for construction. How much the public "subscribed" to a railroad was itself a misleading figure. Private parties often pledged a good deal more than they gave. Furthermore, the law did not require subscribers to pay every penny at the time they promised it, and sometimes it required no payment at all. States recognized the discrepancy between promise and performance when they issued charters that demanded a certain sum *paid in* before a line could incorporate. In some cases, an act of incorporation would state the sum as a percentage of the amount subscribed. When the Devall's Bluff & Auburn Railroad organized in 1872, citizens subscribed $65,000. As of December 1873, only one dollar in twenty had been paid in. A contractor could build little more than an eighth of a mile on that $3,250 and had no chance of laying the 65 miles of track that the promoters wanted.[9]

County subscriptions posed problems of their own. Most local bond issues sold badly in the North, and those from states that had once repudiated their obligations were practically worthless. The Natchez & Jackson Railroad might have had a chance of success had it been able to see the $600,000 in Adams County securities at face value. Then it might have built 25 miles of track, but no one would buy the bonds at par. In fact, for a long time no one would buy them at any price.[10]

Companies sold their own bonds more easily, but even under the best conditions they encountered problems. Northern capitalists never showed more than a moderate interest in Southern securities. For the cautious financier, Northern state bonds proved a wiser investment. For daring investors, Western railroads offered greater opportunities for a good, quick return. Most speculators preferred to put their money into roads they knew had the backing of some financier of national importance. Although a few leading financiers dabbled in Southern securities, these were exceptional men. Even the most enthusiastic and daring businessman, Tom Scott, cared more for Western than Southern investment. For additional support, the railroad companies had to look overseas. A few European banking houses took an interest in Southern enterprises, but by 1870, they, too, were growing uneasy. Some of the revelations of mismanagement from Florida, Georgia, and the Carolinas increased this distrust. When the Franco-Prussian War closed foreign money markets in 1870, it further constricted major sources of support for Southern companies.[11] At best, then, raising money took time, more time than most directors had anticipated when they drew up their construction plans.

Because they had overestimated the readiness of the bond market to absorb their issues, directors were forced to borrow from banks and to pledge their bonds as collateral. This was an expensive practice, since no financier would give the railroad as much in ready cash as it received in securities. Often the bonds were hypothecated for as little as half their face value. Unable to pay for work already done, some railroads would promise the contractors state aid securities in advance. Furthermore, to make up for the difficulties in selling these bonds on the money markets, they would allot them at less than par. By the time the state made its subsidy, much of the money that would have been available for construction was already promised for "anticipation bonds" as well as to repay promissory notes. Speculators could profit from this arrangement, but the railroad itself found that it added heavily to projected costs.[12]

Only rarely were bonds sold at face value. Because they had no better offers and needed hard currency for immediate expenses, directors might let bonds go for 80 percent of face value, and sometimes they sold securities for even less. Thus a $1,000 bond might yield $800 and cost the company $2,400 in principal and interest by the time it had matured. The companies accepted these conditions because they expected that the handsome profits the completed lines would pay would make future burdens relatively lighter than the ones they shouldered at present.

Once bond depreciation began, the problem fed upon itself. The less a railroad made on its securities in the first place, the less money it had for its tasks and the greater was its need to issue more bonds. The more securities it put on the market, the more supply outran demand, and the lower the price fell before the bonds were salable. The lower the price, the more the company was obligated for interest payments, the heavier its financial burdens, and the heavier the pressure on its directors to issue and sell additional bonds. To make matters worse, company charters limited the number of first-mortgage bonds that could be sold, and state aid laws restricted the number that the government could endorse. Once the securities were on the market, the directors could only issue second-mortgage bonds, which, because they provided a less secure lien, sold for even less.

Just putting the bonds on the market was an expensive business. The cost of printing them was considerable, and brokers took a commission for their efforts in discovering buyers. In one notorious case, the Jacksonville, Pensacola & Mobile sent its president to sell 2,800 state bonds in New York. S. W. Hopkins & Co. sold them to John Collinson of London for £138 apiece and gave the railroad £66 of it. Florida thus gave $2.8 million in bonds to the railroad, Collinson paid $1,930,000, Hopkins & Co. gave the road $600,000, and of this sum the contractors applied only $175,000 to construction and equipment.[13] Everyone except the state and the public that wanted the line seemed to have made something from the process, and since courts declared the bond issue illegal, not even the taxpayers were hurt by the diversion of funds. Nevertheless, it was an appalling way to finance railroad development. As with any venture in which the notorious Milton Littlefield was involved, the Florida transaction was an exceptional one, but in every case, a Southern railroad found that the revenue it received after its bonds had been discounted and brokers had taken their share was far less than the promoters had sought.

If the Wall Street capitalists gave the Southern lines inadequate support, it was not because they lacked the Southerners' breadth of vision, but because they saw other possibilities all too clearly. First, these investors lived in an era of shameless speculation, when operators made millions of dollars by ruining hundreds of stockholders. Men like Jim Fisk, Jay Gould, Daniel Drew, and George Swepson would have started a panic if it would have allowed them to make a "killing." They spread lies about the value of stock and printed more shares than the law allowed. Bondholders, therefore, had a right to be suspicious and ready to dump their holdings at the first hint of trouble; he who hesitated was caught short. Second, some of the railroad men actively worked to depreciate bond values. As the *Houston Union* described the strategy, "the managing men" would form rings inside the company and select outsiders as front men for their activities. Then they would circulate rumors detrimental to bond values: that the people of the state "feel outraged at the bond subsidy business, and that they denounce the whole and intend . . . to attack their validity," for example. "How much am I offered for this bond, says the broker in Wall Street? It won't sell at home for any price, but I expect a good offer here." Naturally, the security would sell for almost nothing. Then the ring would buy large amounts of bonds, publish flattering accounts of the road's prospects, deny the rumors they once had circulated, and make the bonds rise. Finally, the conspirators would sell out for a heavy profit. In this way, the directors would grow rich while the company grew poor. Perhaps it was not "always the fate of subsidized roads," as the *Union* contended, but it happened.[14]

Third, the investors had a right to think that railroad men were speculators and liars. Many of them were. The very insecurity of the Southern securities market and the realities of Southern railroads' chances made deliberate falsification and overoptimism essential to railroad financing. Each company had to exaggerate its own advantages because every rival enterprise used hyperbole, and there were more projects than there was money available to fund them. Good reasons had to be found why one project was better than another. In a worthy cause, the truth could afford embellishment. Flattering accounts, therefore, were published in Northern newspapers to drum up support: the bonds were described as better than they were, the connections of the road with metropolitan centers were stressed even though the connecting roads had not yet been built. So extravagant and frequent were the promises that some investors may have held back. Certainly, only the rash financier would have taken them all seriously.

Because the Southerners had too little money and the Northerners too little faith, railroad companies never had all the ready cash they needed. As the lines were completed and the bond interest fell due, the problem worsened. Every road needed constant attention and upkeep, but the newly built railroads required even greater maintenance expenditures than the established ones. The state aid laws had set deadlines for completion of the subsidized lines, and in their scramble to qualify for the funds they so badly needed, companies built with more emphasis on mileage than durability. Money problems also compelled contractors to use second-rate materials. As the quantity of freight and the number of passengers increased, the company had to buy additional cars and locomotives, for new roads were usually underequipped.

Most railroads also did less business than they had hoped. They could ship large cotton crops, but the South did not yet have much else to offer, and as new lines opened, they cut into the markets of existing roads. Some promoters had hoped to exploit the mineral wealth of the South, but they found this task beyond their means. Alabama roads had been planned partly as feeders to coal mines and iron mills, but financiers were slow to develop either industry. Most promoters based their faith in future prosperity on the links which their enterprises would make with other roads tapping other parts of the South. When a railroad failed to be built on schedule or ran fewer trains than the traffic allowed, other lines were hurt. To succeed, the Northeastern Railroad of South Carolina needed connections with the state's ports. Its directors had hoped that the Savannah & Charleston would provide that service, but they were disappointed. "Of the general prospects of the company," said the annual report for 1871, "we have only to remark that they are, in a great degree, dependent upon the completion of the projected roads, and . . . other improvements in our connection, . . . and not until the field of our operations can be extended by them may we expect the remunerative results which should then be realized."[15]

Laboring under these disadvantages, a luckless company found itself tangled in litigation by aggrieved creditors and contractors who wanted their money faster than they were obtaining it. Construction companies sued because they were paid in scrip. Rival companies and zealous Conservatives sought court action to annul state aid bonds and to prevent the issue of more. Injured parties, unpaid shopkeepers and laborers, as well as suspicious stockholders—all brought their grievances before the bench. Lawsuits were always a hazard, but they became more frequent and costly as the railroad fell on hard times, and as plaintiffs hastened to get their due before other creditors forced the road into receivership. Fears of bankruptcy could become self-fulfilling, as the costs of a case put a shaky enterprise into insolvency. Their confidence in the concern undermined, stockholders and bondholders might respond to litigation by dumping their holdings, and the same fears of financial collapse depreciated bond values more than ever.[16]

Had financial need been less severe, it might have promoted efficiency through consolidation. Many companies with mutual interests merged, but most railroad men did not favor such measures unless they were forced to it. Two parallel roads could not benefit from a merger unless one was prepared to surrender its trade and materials to the other. A larger road could not absorb a smaller one without making their ultimate interests one—with the consolidated business doing "through" traffic and the lesser party to the agreement becoming little more than a feeder line. Since most directors on the new lines were local men who cared more for their community's interests than for those of the South or the state, such a course seemed almost unthinkable. Consolidation might also cause a shake-up of the existing directorates, and members of the board did not welcome such a change. Mergers would give shareholders in either company a smaller percentage of the total stock, and that, too, seemed an unpleasant prospect. A merger might even compel the new company to return to the legislature for another charter, though most states gave railroads the right to consolidate with other lines serviceable to their interests.[17]

Most important, consolidation between two connecting roads could not always ease financial hardship, because both needed funds and neither had the money to fulfill its own needs, much less those of a partner. A railroad already built, well equipped, and doing a brisk trade could perhaps afford to channel some of its money into a new line still under construction. Some of the major Georgia corporations found this extension of their influence possible and profitable, as did the Louisville & Nashville, but not very many roads in the cotton South were in such good economic condition. Even the largest companies found expansion a risky, even calamitous, tactic.[18]

With so little chance of fulfilling its initial promise, the new railroad operated under the constant shadow of bankruptcy proceedings. Corporate collapse followed certain inevitable steps. First, because of economic weakness or an inability to realize on certain assets, the company would default on its bond interest payments. Lawsuits would follow, and coupon holders would call for a judgment of bankruptcy and the appointment of assignees in bankruptcy friendly to their interests. Once the litigation began, it became self-propelling. Every state had several kinds of courts, every railroad had several kinds of creditors, and the discontented parties would go through every court in the state to obtain a decision friendly to their interests. When companies built their tracks through different states and different judicial districts, confusion increased.[19] If a plea of bankruptcy failed before one judge, it could be reopened in a court a few counties away or in another commonwealth. Should the plea succeed, others were inspired to try the same appeal before another magistrate more friendly to their needs and ready to choose another receiver. It was not just possible that one court's decree would be contested in another; it was almost certain, for the interests of the state, the first-mortgage bondholders, and the holders of the second mortgage rarely coincided. Local stockholders wanted a receiver who would keep the road operating and did not care who ran the board. Contractors were prepared to let the road shut down and to have its assets divided to settle unpaid debts. The state needed a receiver who would recognize the priority of the state's investment in the company. Private bondholders wanted the receiver to show a special devotion to their interests.

Default and receivership could damage a completed railroad, and they could wreck the prospects of an unfinished one. All new sources of outside funding vanished once a company went into default. What funds the receiver had went to retire the road's debts and keep the trains running. Little was left for carrying on construction, investing in connecting roads, or adding to mileage. The receiver might issue scrip to finance repairs on the existing line, but the law prevented him from doing anything daring with the limited financial power at his command. He might not even have the money to repair more than the worst parts of the road. Certainly, he would have too little to improve its upkeep.[20] Only a fortunate receiver had the funds to increase the number of engines and freight cars, and without this increase no railroad could expand its business enough to restore solvency. Generally, receivership resulted in trains passing down the track less often, carrying less freight than before, taking more time to transport goods, and becoming more dangerous than they had been in the past. As the tracks were neglected, operating expenses rose and revenues, never very good, declined.

The future was not as bleak as it might seem from this description. When a railroad fell into bankruptcy, it did not simply vanish the way a bank or grocery might. The tracks remained and often the rolling stock as well. Once the insolvent railroad made a compromise with its creditors, new purchasers would take over the work already done and, as was often the case, connect it with a healthy railroad system. Such reorganization had a price, however. All old liens were wiped out at a fraction of their original value. Often, first-mortgage bondholders were given preferred stock so that a new bond issue could be raised to finance construction. Then stockholders, including the public ones, were either given new shares that had a face value approximating the old stock's market value or were written off and their stock voided.[21] Thus, if a railroad reorganized more than once, a mortgage bondholder could find himself a stockholder and then an outsider without any securities at all. It was a painful and time-consuming process.

Under the circumstances, railroad presidents had every reason for feeling disillusioned with their work and with the people on whom they had counted for support. "I am half a mind to resign, as Director at once," an officer in one faltering enterprise wrote a friend. "I am tired of Rail road botherations." Reformers might describe Milton Littlefield as a plunderer of the lines he ran, but Littlefield saw matters differently. "When I think of the hangers on & blackmailers, that have been sucking money blood, from myself & the interest I represent I feel like exclaiming, 'Oh! Lord How Long'!!" From the Western Railroad of North Carolina, a president wrote of the travails that his enemies had brought upon him. "In addition to trying to keep the road in running condition with a consumptive purse," he lamented, "I have been contending against these fellows, that put all these entanglements and complications upon us, not knowing how many men at home, occupying prominent railroad positions, were rendering them rapine, if not active aid, ready to pounce down on us and *buy us out*, when they thought that we were so far hampered as not to be able to extricate ourselves."[22] He did not say what was equally true: that it was the road's financial weakness that gave so many of its foes the opportunity to do it an injury.

The railroads were not the only ones with "consumptive purses." The states suffered from the same ailment. Indeed, had they not been so afflicted, the plight of the corporations would have been less severe. Corporate and state financial problems were closely linked. The railroad aid policy depended for its success on the endorsed securities' selling for close to full value, and this, in turn, depended on the governments' instilling outside financiers with confidence that the state's aegis was worth something. Had the Republican bonds been as good as their word, the railroads might have thrived. Conversely, had the railroads been able to do with less state aid and sell their endorsed bonds for more, the Reconstruction governments would have had neither such an unmanageable debt nor so foul a financial reputation. To understand why the lines did not prosper despite state aid, it is therefore necessary to examine in detail the Republicans' debt problem.

For the highest possible credit rating, the Southern states needed to keep their public debts as low as fiscal legerdemain could devise. Northern investors knew that the South's personal wealth had declined since 1860, and with it the citizens' ability to pay for government services had diminished. Reconstruction authorities would need to impose a heavier rate of taxation in 1870 just to bring in as much revenue as their counterparts had a decade before. A great increase in the states' bonded debt would be unsupportable. Repudiation might follow; that had happened in more prosperous times. The higher the debt of a Southern state, therefore, the less chance there was that the securities would be redeemed. Recognition of these facts made it imperative that the Republican officials not only show more frugality than their predecessors, but make themselves appear so parsimonious that even Conservatives would have difficulty making a case against them. Then some judicious railroad bond endorsement would fall within the states' ability. Unfortunately for the Republican party, its elected officers were not able or willing to pare expenses.

Already, when the Republicans came to power, the Southern states had heavy debts awaiting redemption. In most states, Republicans found that they had nearly empty Treasuries and no immediate source of revenue. Leading businessmen refused to make loans. The only alternative was a new bond issue.[23] With the government's legitimacy in question and politicians promising repudiation of all of its acts, investors wanted proof that the Republicans could maintain power. That proof would come only with the passage of time, and until then bonds sold at a heavy discount. From the inauguration of the Republican administrations onward, then, state debts increased sharply for reasons beyond the government's control.

The acknowledged debts were only one part of the Conservative heritage. In some states, they had made commitments that would continue to grow. By their internal improvements legislation, they had promised state funds to railroad corporations as soon as a certain mileage had been completed. Republicans felt bound to honor these commitments. Had they repudiated Conservative promises, their own would hardly have been honored once Conservatives returned to power, and the Northern and foreign bondholders would have put no faith in Southern promises. In any case, the Reconstruction governments heartily approved of railroad aid.

Earlier governments had incurred and then repudiated debts in some Southern states. To achieve financial respectability, the authorities now had to recognize these obligations. Mississippi had indebted itself heavily before the war. Until principal and interest were paid, people agreed that the state could not have sold new bonds for a fair price even if the law allowed their issue, and the law did not so allow. Fearful lest Mississippi's obligations grow larger, Republicans had forbidden the state to lend its credit to any private corporation in the future. Although they also discussed redeeming the bonds outstanding, nothing came of this, perhaps because, as the *Vicksburg Herald* remarked, any legislator fastening such a burden on the taxpayers would be lynched within a month of his vote.[24] Arkansas Republicans, however, were more interested in salvaging the state's economic reputation, and they took on a thirty-year-old debt that Democrats had created in trying to establish a state banking system. Even defenders of the Reconstruction governments condemned this assumption act as muddled in law and ethics, but the move made perfect sense to those Republicans who thought railroad aid a crucial part of the party's appeal. Until it was clear to financiers everywhere that the state would not only pay its just debts but those obligations about which there was reason for doubt, Arkansas securities could not command a good price.[25]

Florida's experience showed the risk that a state took in issuing new bonds when it had refused payment on the old ones. Before the war, the government had sold $3 million in securities and then repudiated them. When the Republicans came to power, investors hoped—and some were confident—that their claims would be recognized. In December 1870, the Council of Foreign Bondholders called a meeting of all those owning Florida securities. The gathering agreed that the state should pay 5 percent on the old bonds in cash and give its creditors five hundred acres of public land per bond. The banks which had marketed the securities should be forced to make up for their perfidy by purchasing the land warrants at five dollars an acre. English bondholders were furious that such a settlement could even be considered, surrendering as it did the investors' claim to thousands of dollars of back interest. They advised the London Stock Exchange not to countenance "such a whitewashing," but to forbid Florida "the privileges of honest borrowers." The Exchange officers agreed and notified the governor that until the old debt had been adjusted, "no bonds of the state would find a market or be suffered on the Exchange."[26] Florida did not just fail to come to terms with its old creditors; six years later, its courts disallowed most of its postwar obligations.

Finally, the Reconstruction coalition could not and would not have tried parsimony even if it had been able to do so. Republicans had not come to power as the spokesmen of a new transportation system alone. They represented a new order of things and appropriations for a multitude of projects. Had the authorities forgotten their promises to expand the public school system, blacks would have accused the government of betraying its ideals—as indeed in many states they did. In Arkansas and Louisiana, levees and rivers needed constant attention. Emancipation had made other budget increases inevitable. The antebellum legal system had left the masters to mete out justice to their slaves, but in a free society the state had to increase the number of courts and expand penal facilities drastically just to keep up with the new demands. The South had millions more citizens than it had had a decade before, and the governments had to expand services in every particular. State officeholders increased dramatically. Finally, Republicans had political expenses that a rich and more securely entrenched party would not have had. Their legislators were poorer than those elected before the war and needed larger salaries. A two-party system could not survive when one party controlled the news media. Without government support, there would have been no Republican press in the South. Voting Republican was an act of courage in many counties, and unless the rank and file there knew that the government rewarded its backers, party organization would collapse. To have eliminated every office except the most essential ones and to have given printing contracts to the lowest bidders, then, would not have been only frugality, but political lunacy. For these reasons, legislators increased their own *per diem* remuneration, endowed friendly newspapers with printing contracts, and created offices for party loyalists.[27]

Past economic and present political commitments may explain the spending policy of the party in power, but they do not excuse the lengths to which the policy was carried. Legislators in the Carolinas, Georgia, and Louisiana enriched themselves with the best of everything. They awarded printing contracts to friends and took a share of the profits, overcharged the state for mileage traveled, and found patronage for their supporters. Administrative costs rose beyond what party necessity justified, and in some states the money benefited no one but the officeholders. When one added the railroad aid appropriations to other charges, the Republicans' fiscal recklessness became staggering. Louisiana increased its obligations by nearly $8 million in four years, and Governor Robert K. Scott of South Carolina estimated that his administration had issued $9,514,000 in new securities, after all fraudulent overissues had been disallowed. By 1876, North Carolina owed more than $41 million, Alabama more than $30 million.[28] Other states had smaller commitments. In Texas, the debt rose only slightly. Florida's never reached 2 million. Mississippi had an even smaller debt. None of these states owed anything to railroads. Even at their best, however, the Reconstruction governments had greater liabilities than before the war, and all the debts were too large for taxpayers or bondholders to accept complacently.

The most confusing and misunderstood part of Southern financial responsibilities was the contingent debt, created almost entirely by the government's endorsement of first- and second-mortgage railroad bonds. In computing the state's liabilities, Democrats consistently confused these pledges with the state's bonded debt proper and thus overestimated how much the people would have to pay to rid themselves of the financial burdens incurred by the Republicans. Republicans replied that the contingent debt was a burden only in theory. The government would have to assume responsibility for the endorsed bonds only if the railroad companies defaulted, a possibility that most supporters of bond endorsement dismissed as remote. Should the lines fail to prosper sufficiently to pay interest on their securities, the commonwealth could seize and sell the offenders on terms indemnifying the taxpayers. Authorities might also run a railroad and use its profits to settle all outstanding obligations.[29]

Appealing though the argument was, it was based on assumptions. First, Republicans trusted that the railroads could prosper enough from the outset to pay construction costs, operating expenses, and the interest on their bonded debts. This belief showed remarkable overoptimism. Second, the Republicans thought that the state's prior lien would give it undisputed title to the line; when the road defaulted, the state could easily sell it. Experience proved this assumption baseless. Third, the Republicans surmised that men would always be willing to buy a company for as much as the state had invested in it; in fact, few capitalists had any interest in an uncompleted road. Such a thoroughfare would take more money to prepare for a steady trade than it would be worth. Even when the road was finished, not many buyers would be ready to pay what the government asked. In short, the contingent debt was more than an illusion. Although the state might not have to pay every penny of that debt from its own revenues, there was a good chance that it would have to pay a large part of it. The Republicans' misconception was a dangerous one. It misled many Southerners into thinking that the rapid increase in the state's contingent obligations was no cause for concern.

Indeed, the contingent debt myth contributed to the fiscal ruin of the railroads and the Reconstruction governments alike. Had the legislatures made outright grants of state bonds without any condition that the interest and principal be paid out of company funds, there would have been two results. First, fewer railroads would have had to default and go into receivership, since the state would have been responsible for payment of most of the corporate debt. Second, the governments would have had to pay immediately for their commitments to internal improvements. With large interest payments due each year, the authorities might have been more moderate and selective in promoting railroad projects. Perhaps they would have shown greater discrimination in deciding which lines were most deserving of a subsidy and in determining which were unfit because of their lack of private financial backing or absence of statewide impact. Such discretion might have helped maintain the prices of Southern securities and given them a greater value for the railroads receiving them.

Investors not only wondered whether the states could pay what they promised, but whether the Republicans would be given the chance to try. Economic and political stability were closely tied. Bondholders needed to be sure that the securities they bought one year would not be repudiated the next. As long as the party in power could not keep order, it could hardly promote the tranquility necessary for prosperity. The Republicans, however, had no more ability to control lawlessness than to control their own extravagant tendencies.

Most Reconstruction governments were unstable. Conservatives had never recognized their legitimacy and did all they could to subvert Republican administrations. They encouraged impeachment attempts against governors, though Republicans needed little encouragement. Between 1869 and 1872, one governor fled his state to avoid prosecution, another bought off his enemies, a third was convicted and removed, a fourth was suspended from office, a fifth handed out places and favors until the investigating committee dismissed all charges against him, and a sixth faced impeachment efforts on the average of once a year. In many Southern states, white terrorists flogged and murdered their political enemies and defied the courts. Other Reconstruction governments kept order by passing election laws that most white Southerners believed tyrannical and many Conservatives declared illegal. In Louisiana, fair elections had always been a rarity, but the 1872 returns were unusually inaccurate since both parties had used fraud and intimidation. So serious did Southern disorder become that the federal government was forced to intervene. It passed laws bringing the Ku Klux Klan to justice and gave recognition to Republican governments in states where each party had organized an administration of its own after counting itself a popular majority. Nevertheless, the violence did not end. Nor did the intimidation and fraud.

Where life was uncertain and the real power of the government so much in doubt, capitalists had the right to feel that their property could not be very secure. How long could such authorities continue to collect the taxes with which to pay state debts? How could railroads be safe when Northern Republicans pictured the South as a land in perpetual tumult and Conservative newspapers portrayed the governments as a mixture of chaos, cupidity, and carnival? Until 1873, Arkansas Republicans kept order better than had their counterparts, but when English investors demurred at purchasing Arkansas Central Railroad endorsed bonds, the *Little Rock Republican* expressed no surprise. The London press had reprinted lurid reports of mob violence in one county. After reading English accounts of atrocities, said the *Republican*, "we are almost disposed to wonder that anything can be done towards the negotiation of the bonds of the state of Arkansas, or any other state or railroad in the south."[30]

The terrorists worried the investor, but the Democrats alarmed him. If the bonds were to keep any value, they must be above partisan debate, and some vocal members of the party out of power refused to accord them such sacred treatment. Democrats especially disliked the public debt because it was a Republican debt, and Conservatives did all they could to persuade outsiders that a dollar given for a Radical bond was as good as thrown away. The Republicans were robbing the state into poverty, or so the philippic ran. They were corrupt and their bond issues illegal. The Reconstruction governments were illegitimate and founded on fraud. The legislators never meant to redeem the bonds they had issued. In fact, they could not do so had they wanted to: the people did not approve of their acts. The voters would feel no duty to honor the commitments that had been wrongfully forced upon them. More bonds had been issued than the law allowed, by methods in violation of the statutes' provisions. The Repubicans had sold securities for less than the legal minimum price and had misapplied the proceeds to enrich their friends. Northern brokers had taken money from the bond sales and left none for the railroads. Northern investors were all Republican sympathizers who would deserve their fate if the Southern people decided to pay nothing. There was no end to the catalogue of charges, but they could be condensed to one general statement: the bonds were a swindle and would not be paid.[31]

Republicans played the same sort of partisan game with the securities question. Democrats were portrayed as wild revolutionaries opposed to internal improvements. When a Conservative decried the railroad aid policy, Republican editors reprinted the statement as evidence of the universal sentiment of the party out of power. The charges did the opposition an injustice. A few Democrats would have repudiated the entire bonded debt of the South and revoked all grants and subsidies if they had had the chance, but the majority of the party was more circumspect in the early 1870s. A large and influential faction would have paid the whole state debt as a matter of honor. Leading Conservative businessmen would have objected to anything that would have jeopardized their own investments. Still other enemies of the Reconstruction governments fully intended to adjust the states' liabilities by invalidating only the grants corruptly given. To show that they were themselves upright and conservative statesmen, Republicans needed to stress the attitude of the extreme members of the opposition, but the tactics must have added to Northern investors' uncertainty as they watched Democrats winning elections throughout the South and concluded that the same might happen in every Republican state before the bonds had matured.[32]

At the same time, Republicans out of power adopted their enemies' charges of theft and extravagance. Governor Robert Lindsay of Alabama gave his Republican foes all the proof of irresponsibility they needed when he brought the state into virtual default. At every opportunity, the *Alabama State Journal* proclaimed that the commonwealth had lost all standing in the Northern financial centers, a self-fulfilling prophecy.[33] If the state credit had been intact before this charge was advanced, it could hardly have withstood the constant stream of invective.

Both parties wanted to preserve the South's financial honor. Democrats and Republicans alike took pride in their state and its economic potential. To each partisan, however, political considerations came first. Though editors would have insisted their real interest was in telling the truth about the state's financial condition, what they meant was that they felt it their duty to make the most unkind interpretation possible of their enemies' policies. They could no more have exalted the commonwealth's credit rating under their opponents' rule than they could have vindicated the right of thieves and traitors to hold office. At times, partisans almost welcomed financial troubles. "No greater calamity could befall the state of Florida, while under the rule of the present carpetbag, scalawag officials," said the chief Democratic organ, "than to be placed in good financial credit. . . . Our only hope is in the State's utter financial bankruptcy; and Heaven grant that it may speedily come!"[34] Politically effective as such a response might be, it did Southern bonds no good in Northern markets.

The best that can be said for Republicans is that they did not have the power to blacken the governments' reputation that the Democrats did. The Conservative press was larger, better established, and more respected among moneyed men. Its editorial writers were more vocal and included some of the more honored political figures of the South. Conservatives also had closer ties than their foes to the commercial communities south and north and a greater ability to spread one version of the facts. Democratic businessmen could meet in boards of trade and send resolutions northward. Editors might not be trusted; investors could discount much of what the press said as politically biased and financially naïve. When a businessman spoke, other capitalists listened with more respect, even though the predictions he gave were just as dire and irresponsible as those published in the party press.

Conservatives had many ways of bringing the bond issues to popular attention. They chose fact-finding committees, had boards of trade pass resolutions, called protest conventions, sent delegates to Washington, and paid agents to visit New York and London to challenge the sale of railroad and state bonds as a swindle. In Little Rock, young Democrats urged citizens to withhold taxes under the new government, and Arkansas and Louisiana protestors took laws establishing new taxes to court. The efficiency of Florida's tax equalization board led to a taxpayers' convention that blamed "the deplorable condition of the state" on "loose and reckless legislation of men formed into governing cliques . . . destructive of the principles of free American government."[35] So serious did resistance become that in November 1871 the governor issued a proclamation in which he accused prominent men of attempting to incite civil disorder. A Texas taxpayers' convention included the most notable figures of both parties, and this bipartisanship helped the cause greatly by making it appear the universal sentiment of the people.[36]

In South Carolina, the resisting groups were the most effective of all. In March 1871, the governor signed a bill permitting the state to borrow £1.2 million sterling to redeem the current public debt. With the government's obligations increasing rapidly enough already, this final act enraged the Charleston Chamber of Commerce beyond endurance. It met and resolved that the state's credit had been pledged corruptly and illegally. The sterling loan, it warned investors, would not be considered a binding obligation. The city's commercial elite vowed to resist payment on the bonds "by all legitimate means within our power," and called for a state taxpayers' convention to investigate the comptroller's accounts and to find the actual size of the public debt. In one of the largest meetings since its founding, the Charleston Board of Trade adopted the same resolutions. When the Taxpayers' Convention met, it issued a fierce address with many vague charges of corruption and malfeasance, most of which, unfortunately, were true. When the members went on to propose solutions to the state's economic plight, however, they found the task beyond their skill. Some enemies of the Reconstruction governments had hoped for repudiation of other parts of the debt or of the state's subsidies for the Blue Ridge and Greenville & Columbia Railroads, both of which were a public scandal. Partly because good Conservative men were involved in bond speculation and corporate investment, the convention took no drastic action. Indeed, when a committee chosen to consult with the executive on the size of the state debt began its labors, it decided to take the Governor's word on everything. It made a cursory examination of the South Carolina financial records, returned to the convention, and informed the delegates that the state's books were correct, pronounced the bond issues already made "of unquestionable legality and force as obligations of the State," and let the matter drop. The committee's lack of zeal in probing malfeasance allowed the governor to conceal the issue of $5 million more in conversion bonds than the law permitted, and afforded the Republican press the chance to boast that the administration had received full vindication. When the convention adjourned, the state comptroller later testified, the governor, financial agent, and attorney general had a good laugh at how they had hoodwinked their inquisitors.[37] If so, it was a costly source of amusement. The delegates' actions doomed the sterling loan. Not a single bond from it could be sold. The convention speeches and charges gained wide publicity and reappeared in congressional reports and newspaper columns for two years after; the harm delegates did to the reputation of the Republican party and the state's financial system was tremendous.

Conservatives knew more direct means of putting the bonds into disrepute. Florida Democrats sent word to the *New York Herald* that the state was about to repudiate its debt. The *Herald* published the report, but not the denial by both the treasurer and comptroller of the state. So scandalous were the *New York World*'s accusations of illegal bond issuance that the president of the Florida Railroad, a Conservative himself, wrote in defense of the governor and in denunciation of charges circulated by men who objected to all bonds illegal or otherwise. The defense did little good. In July 1870, the *World* published a telegram warning investors that the people of Florida would never consent to pay such securities as those being offered to New York investors.[38] This pronouncement made the bonds impossible to market in the United States, and the promoters had to seek foreign support.

Milton S. Littlefield and George Swepson went to England to sell their Florida bonds, but they could not escape the Conservatives. Nicholas Woodfin of North Carolina had led a legislative investigation of the two men and was angered at their misappropriation of North Carolina aid bonds to build out-of-state concerns. As soon as Woodfin reached London, he began spreading damaging reports. Potential buyers were informed that Littlefield and his cronies had no right to the bonds they were selling, that North Carolina had been cheated, that the bond sale must not take place. At first amused by the eccentric Conservative, Littlefield's brokers panicked as they saw the commercial community's reaction to the charges. "The other evening," a member of the firm wrote his client, "he dined at the writer's house, where he said Gov. Reed received $30,000 for signing the bonds and pronounced him a great fraud." Woodfin stopped spreading falsehoods once the railway promoters had promised him money for his financial schemes in North Carolina, but the scandal damaged the chances of a London bond sale. After much negotiation, the brokers sold the securities to Dutch investors at 70 cents on the dollar.[39]

Partisan politicking and financial mismanagement together were more than the markets could bear. Southern securities had sold for less than Northern ones in 1868; in the years that followed, they declined still further. Some states did well for a few years. Alabama and Arkansas bonds sold for high prices compared with those of neighboring commonwealths. Louisiana and the Carolinas did much worse from the first. Because legislators in North Carolina gave aid to railroads without raising the taxes to pay interest on the bonds lent, they ruined the state credit more swiftly than did Republicans in any other state. In 1869, the administration could not find funds to pay more than a fraction of its obligations. Extravagant government spending in South Carolina was made worse by a financial agent on the make and an overissue of bonds.

The more securities the agent made available for sale, the lower the price fell. "Have had to fight the whole market, as they seem to know things about our affairs which should not be known," he wrote the treasurer in early 1871. "It hurts us very much." Six months later, the agent found the 7 percent bonds not selling at all, and railroad aid securities had become very unpopular. "Have no January coupons on second mortgage paid at present," he confessed. "We cannot stand it." Florida laws had forbidden sale of state bonds at less than 75 cents on the dollar, but no one would pay the minimum price. To keep the government running, the Republicans gave the securities as collateral for loans worth half the bonds' face value. To borrow $100,000 for three months in 1868, Louisiana had to pay $7,000 in interest and give the moneylender an option to buy securities at 60 cents on the dollar. Later, the bonds sold for still less. Georgia bonds sold for 88 cents on the dollar, Texas securities for 89 cents, Alabama's slightly below par. In contrast, Northern bonds stood at more than their face value. California "sevens" were valued at 112, New York "sixes" at 107½.[40]

A bad credit rating was self-perpetuating. As long as a state could not raise enough money to satisfy its needs, it had to pay obligations in scrip that lost value as it became more common. Most governments allowed citizens to pay their taxes in scrip at par, and this policy cut into the tax revenues. When authorities received warrants worth half their face value in full payment of legal obligations, they found themselves without the ready money to sustain the government. This deficiency forced the legislature to raise more revenue through a new bond issue. As these securities went on the market, investors lost what confidence they had in the state's ultimate ability to redeem its pledges and refused to take the bonds without an even larger discount than before.

Financiers' distrust added to the state's economic woes, assured an even larger issue of scrip to pay operating expenses, and increased the political disorder by persuading more Conservatives than ever that the state was in the hands of thieves and imbeciles. Under such conditions, scrip went for 70 cents on the dollar in Mississippi, where the government had contracted a small debt. Arkansas warrants sold for 18 cents on the dollar by the end of Reconstruction, and Louisiana's governor, who was paid $3,500 in scrip, complained that he received only $1,000 a year in actual money. South Carolina's chief executive estimated that if all taxes had been paid on time and in real currency, the state could have issued $2.5 million less in securities than it had dumped on the market.[41]

Without adequate credit, Southern states became utterly unfit to support railroad companies. South Carolina's conditions were the most pitiful. As the *Charleston News* reported, "The financial officers of the government linger in New York, while a swarm of hungry creditors clamor at the gates of the capitol; the October interest . . . remains unpaid, and by reason of this . . . the Columbia banks decline to have any further dealings in the securities of the State. This is a gloomy picture, but it is not overdrawn." When bonds sold for less than half their par value, the state could not think that its endorsement would add prestige to a company's securities. One promoter even hinted that his company might do better without the governor's signature on its bonds than with it, though his remarks may have been hyperbole.[42] The simple fact was that railroad aid helped bring a decline in the state's credit rating, and the decline added to the difficulty that corporations had in negotiating the state aid bonds they had received.

For many bondholders, the Southern debacle was bewildering and horrifying. Certainly, it must have lessened their interest in further investment in public or private bonds in the former Confederate states. One need only read the correspondence of Governor W. W. Holden to discover how extensive was the effect of North Carolina's economic woes. From New Rochelle, Edward Whaites begged for news of the chances of his obtaining "resource or relief from my lamentable fate" as purchaser of $5,000 in state-endorsed Chatham Railroad bonds and 5,000 interest coupons on old state securities. "They are my only resource," he wrote. "Is there no remedy whereby I can find a faint hope of relief[?]" A Connecticut pastor had bought special tax bonds in good faith, but by 1869 he felt uneasy. "Is there any *good reason* for their *present low figure?*" he wondered, apparently unaware that they were in legal doubt. A Hartford man was alarmed when his investment lost value. When he damned the politicians responsible, he spoke for thousands of disillusioned bondholders across the North. "What can be expected but the grass to grow in the streets of your towns and cities, and your state to become only the abode of snakes, toads, crocodiles and skunks?"[43]

The wreckage of Southern credit had political implications as well. It undermined Republicans' confidence in their leaders and confirmed the dark predictions of Conservatives. When the South Carolina securities fell to 33 cents on the dollar, the *Beaufort Re-*

publican proclaimed the commonwealth on the way to "bankruptcy and ruin. It looks as if SCOTT and his radical sattelites were endeavoring to make money out of the bonds," it commented.[44] From a Conservative organ, the charges would have been commonplace, but they appeared in a dedicated Republican paper. When even loyal party men wondered whether a fall in bond prices was part of a swindle, not even the rise in bond values could inspire faith in the state's credit, and not even the most heroic exertions by authorities could persuade moderate men of the government's good intentions.

The State's failure and the frustration of Southerners' railroad ambitions also encouraged a search for scapegoats. Many Southerners realized that when a railroad stopped work, the circumstances were beyond its own control. Some of them welcomed reorganization of the line on any terms, as long as tracklaying went on. Others lapsed into faultfinding. The railroad program would have succeeded, they argued—if it had not been for those Northern bankers—those embezzling directors and speculators—those thieving politicians. When a company failed to keep its initial promise, it was so easy to assume that affairs had been mismanaged, and so difficult to admit that too little money had been raised from the day the corporation had opened its subscription books.[45] How much easier to blame Radicals or adventurers or Shylocks, than to blame themselves!

It was, in fact, on the Southerners themselves that the real blame should have rested. Cautious financiers thought no railroad sound unless at least half its capital came from the communities through which it ran as well as from stock sales. Experienced Wall Street bankers knew that no railroad could carry the weight of too many first-mortgage bonds. Yet Southerners did not and could not give the companies the private backing that was needed from the start, and this forced a reliance on bond sales for as much as nine-tenths of the railroad construction costs. Local men serving as directors did not think clearly about the chances of their projects breaking even. Local editors did not consider the possibility that attacks on state credit would hurt the projects they favored. Taxpayers saw no immediate need to create sinking funds to remove their communities' future debt for railroads. Furthermore, many towns simply could not afford to sustain a railroad. No one would admit these facts. Not one editor ascribed the failure of a railroad to the lack of potential wealth in the surrounding area. Not one observer concluded from a project's collapse that the land through which it ran lacked the trade to maintain rail connections.

Community shortsightedness was doubly unfortunate. First, it allowed Southerners to blame the wrong people for their own failures. It made the political situation more bitter and added to the problems of the Reconstruction governments. Second, without a confession of community failure, Southerners would not learn from their misfortunes. They might not try the same state aid system to bring about railroad development, but in other ways they would expect more from the companies than the companies could deliver. By misunderstanding the problems of railroad aid, Southerners would repeat the mistakes of the past.

PART FIVE

There Is No Salvation: The Fall of the Railroads

CHAPTER 13

The Alabama & Chattanooga Catastrophe

What sensible people want to be the owners of a railroad
that constantly brings them in debt and hurts their credit?
Alabama State Journal, 1872

So complex and varied was the Southern experience with railroad
construction that any general survey runs a risk of obscuring the
aid policy as contemporaries saw it. Examples taken from across
the South may make general themes clear without providing an
understanding of how the Gospel of Prosperity worked in any one
place. However, the profound political and economic impact of the
subsidy policy may be clarified by studying the misadventures of
one state and one railroad during the years when supportive legislation tangled their fates.

For this purpose, Alabama's support for the Alabama & Chattanooga Railroad provides an excellent case study. Both in form
and effect, the state's aid program resembled that of other Southern
states. The road itself was vital to Alabama and had significance
for connecting lines across the cotton South. As a major beneficiary
of state aid, it excited more discussion than any other road. It could
have become the Republicans' strongest argument for the efficacy
of government subsidies. Its promoters meant to keep their promise—at a price. Even legislators who were bribed to pass the aid
bills considered themselves bought for a worthy cause. Yet the best
intentions did not prevent the most ruinous consequences. Before
it passed out of government control, the Alabama & Chattanooga
had brought political ruin to everyone involved and economic ruin
to the state which had made construction possible. The state, in
turn, had given the company such curious "support" that the railway was ruined as well.

As first envisioned, the Alabama & Chattanooga was to be a
crucial link in the Southern transcontinental line from San Diego
to New York. Connecting with the Vicksburg & Meridian at Meridian, Mississippi, the road would run northeast through the central Alabama uplands, pass through the northwest corner of Geor-

gia, and end at the rail center in Chattanooga, Tennessee. Though of national significance, the line could not rely on outside backers, for of the 295 miles projected, 245 would be in Alabama. Before the war, local businessmen had begun work here and there along the projected route; in the central western counties, they incorporated the Northeast & Southwest, and in the northeast, promoters started building the Wills Valley Railroad. Neither concern obtained enough money to do very much, though the state offered loans and the federal government provided land grants. Then the war halted construction. Afterward, no one in Alabama had the funds to resume work. By 1868, the Northeast & Southwest owed the state over $300,000 for a loan contracted in 1860, and the Conservative governor R. M. Patton, decided to put the company up for public sale. It was a hard step for Patton, who was deeply interested in the road's success, but the law gave him no choice.[1]

However, with the inauguration of the Republican administration of Governor William Smith, the situation changed. First, the Republican legislature suspended the former governor's order for sale of the road. Second, Patton himself found that some outsiders might be willing to advance the necessary funds for construction. D. L. Dalton, the new executive's private secretary, saw Patton in the company of four Boston capitalists who promised to build the Wills Valley road. "They will go to work in a short time and complete the road to Gadsden," Dalton wrote. "Of that there is no doubt. I know them well. They have an ability to accomplish whatever they undertake. For twenty-five years they have been building Rail Roads: and have done more than any other firm in that line, in the United States."[2]

These financial wizards included John C. Stanton and Daniel N. Stanton, and if the brothers were not as well known as Dalton suggested, they would become far more notorious than any other promoter west of the Appalachians. They had vast ambitions but not very much money of their own to invest. What they did have was a talent for making friends. Not only Northern financiers like Henry Clews gave them money, but legislators readily pledged their support for the Stantons' plans. In fact, critics claimed that the brothers had bought the 1868 legislature beyond all chance of effective counter-bribery. Certainly when Governor Smith needed help he could rely on the Stanton brothers. Seeking the resources to pay the interest on Alabama's debt, he went to Chattanooga to talk with the two promoters and subsequently wrote his secretary that they would lend him $100,000. "I think it would be better to do that than to sell bonds," he added. Later, a witness testified that J. C. Stanton had promised the East Alabama & Cincinnati Railroad funds for construction and had actually arranged for Clews & Co. to give $80,000. The governor, three state senators, and two members of the lower house sat on the benefiting line's board of directors. The president of the East Alabama & Cincinnati allegedly claimed that Stanton "was obliged to let them have money to build their road."[3] Bribery may have helped the Stantons win influential allies, but they could have succeeded without doing very much illicitly. Alabamians had cherished ambitions for such a trunk line for many years. It was one of the most obvious objects of state support. Tokens of friendship only made a probable subsidy inevitable.

In a generous mood, the legislators did all they could to oblige the Stantons. They let the Wills Valley merge with the Northeast & Southwest under a new title, the Alabama & Chattanooga. The government endowed this corporation with all the franchises that had been granted to either of its predecessors. State law allowed the enterprise to apply for the usual $16,000 a mile in state endorsements of first-mortgage bonds, and special provisions also applied the privilege to the road's construction outside the state. The 1868 acts were not one-sided. As in all Alabama railroad aid laws, the government forbade any sale of endorsed bonds for less than 90 cents on the dollar and took a prior lien on the entire road in return for its endorsement, but no one concerned himself very much with the consequences of such conditions. Then, in March 1870, the General Assembly made a special loan of $2 million in state bonds to further the work.[4]

No one had objected to the $16,000-a-mile law, but the $2 million bill was different. It was an outright loan of state securities, not simply an endorsement of company bonds. Conservatives had never liked the Stantons, whose Republican sympathies and Northern origins had made them suspect from the first, and now the critics branded the bill a Republican steal accomplished by fraud and bribery.

Corruption there was. One black legislator admitted taking $50. Another was said to have demanded $500 for his vote. As chairman of the House Internal Improvements Committee, John Hardy was reported to have taken a large bribe to push the bill through. He had referred the measure to his committee with instructions that it be reported to the floor within fifteen minutes, and rumor declared him the recipient of $150,000, much of which was meant to buy other legislators but remained in his pockets when he went home at adjournment. These charges Hardy denied. J. C. Stanton had been an active lobbyist for the bill. In his rooms at the Exchange Hotel he organized the measure's supporters, and it is probable that he had other railroad companies working with him, since they, too, wanted benefits. Promoters of the rival South & North line insisted that the Boston businessman had his way on the legislative floor "as if he owned every member body and soul," though they admitted doing some bribery themselves and obtained a generous increase in their own subsidy.[5] The Alabama & Chattanooga could not have bribed as extensively as its enemies claimed, for the vote on the special aid measure was surprisingly close. Almost all of the Stantons' backers consistently supported railroad aid. Many would not have needed the additional inducement of a bribe to make them vote for a subsidy.

The 1870 aid bill was not a party measure, despite Conservative accusations. Many "of our able, firm and zealous Republicans" opposed it, said the *Alabama State Journal*. Partisans even disrupted a rally in favor of the bill with furious denunciations. As the opposition crystallized, it used the offices of the *Journal*, the Republican state organ, as its headquarters. There, the editor later recalled seeing "such true and honest Republicans as Frederick Bromberg, G. T. McAfee, Henderson of Wilcox, and others; and ... such Democrats as J. J. Parker, J. P. Hubbard of Pike, and others." Just before the final vote, leading Republicans published an appeal against the bill in the *Alabama State Journal*. Against them and for the Stantons' proposal stood such respected Democrats as former Chief Justice A. J. Walker and Colonel A. N. Worthy, the only Conservative in the Senate. Had the Democrats been able to unite against the bill, it might very well have been defeated.[6]

Finally, the charges of fraudulent passage were groundless. The bill was not rushed through before the public could organize against it, and the General Assembly showed more circumspection than it had in 1868. As finally passed, the bill differed greatly from the grandiose project conceived three months before. In its original form, the "Omnibus bill," as it was known, gave the Alabama & Chattanooga $3 million in state bonds for equal amounts of first- and second-mortgage securities. Any other company finishing 20 miles of track by March 1871 would be eligible for $20,000 a mile in state aid, and would continue to receive aid, provided it completed 30 miles a year thereafter. Dubbed the "Railroad Gift Enterprise bill" by disgruntled Republicans, it met serious opposition.

Most of its sections were defeated, until only the Stanton grant remained. Even that provision seemed too expensive for the House, which trimmed $1 million off the endowment. Reformers also inserted sections forcing the company to finish building and equipping its line by June 1871, and demanding "undoubted personal security" from the Alabama & Chattanooga before it could apply for any bonds.[7] The law, however it operated in practice, on paper was a cautious measure, well conceived.

Giving more aid to the Alabama & Chattanooga simply did not look like a "steal" because the company seemed to be doing so well with what it had obtained already. Between September 1868 and November 1870, the road made excellent progress. Traveling along the line early in 1869, Governor Smith reported that workers were laying high-grade iron, well above the minimum requirements imposed on all companies given state aid. At that point, 43 miles were in running order, another 156 had been graded and made ready for track, and masons had begun bridges and culverts. J. C. Stanton later complained that he could never find as much labor as he needed to build as quickly as he wished, even though he raised the pay *per diem* from $1.25 to $1.75. Frustrated in his efforts by the high demand for field hands, he hired fifteen hundred Irish and Germans from the North, provided them with tents, tools, and everything else they could want, and then stood by helplessly as they ran off at the first opportunity. At last, he began to hire Chinese workers from the Central Pacific Railroad because they were more dependable—though he still offered all white and black Southerners $1.75 a day for their services. With so much progress and so many jobs provided, the Alabama & Chattanooga became a symbol of the virtues of railroad aid. If the Stantons practiced robbery, commented the *Memphis Appeal*, "we are 'almost crazy' . . . to be 'robbed.' "[8]

Certainly, the directors feared nothing for the future. They could hardly imagine financial worries ahead. At the start of 1869, the company had spent $5,875,000 and expected that no more than $5,975,000 would be needed to complete the road. To balance off this expense, the Stantons expected approximately $4.8 million in first-mortgage bonds given Alabama's backing. The road also meant to issue $2.7 million in second-mortgage bonds. Under a federal land grant, the Alabama & Chattanooga owned 480,000 acres, much of the land rich in coal and iron, but the company anticipated getting four times as much land before finishing construction. The directors were confident that their acreage could add $3,801,600 to corporation coffers. The first annual report did not discuss the possibility that the bonds would sell under par or not be marketable at all. Nor did the company treasurer foresee the possibility that some of the lands could not be sold for two dollars an acre. Rather, the directors looked forward to an easy construction and a quick return on the freight carried. Perhaps this confidence explains J. C. Stanton's willingness to use company funds to aid the East Alabama & Cincinnati, or to buy a lease on a portion of the Selma & Meridian's track and to supply the latter company with the engines and men required to carry freight along this part of the route.[9]

Indeed, the railroad directors lacked all sense of discretion. With glorious visions before them and confidence in generous state aid, they channeled funds into interests of only peripheral importance to the Alabama & Chattanooga. It was later charged that the Stanton brothers used company funds to build a hotel in Chattanooga.[10] One of them bought land valued at $10,000 an acre and sold it to the company for $25,000 an acre. In May 1869, the directors gave themselves shares of stock worth $450,000 at par. These shares the directors as individuals then sold back to themselves as a corporate body for 10 cents on the dollar. The Stantons diverted another $200,000 of bonds to buy stock in the Vicksburg & Meridian. More corporate funds went for investments in the Roane Iron Company and in a projected coal mine. Perhaps by leading the way in developing mineral resources, the railroad would encourage further investments in the same areas; industrial growth along the line would make the railway a more profitable enterprise. But all of these projects were supported with funds raised by selling the endorsed first-mortgage bonds which Alabama law required be expended only on construction of the railroad line. Certainly, the company broke the letter of the law. Was the spirit violated? That depends on whether the law was meant to free funds earmarked for construction and to make them available for other purposes— such as feathering the directors' nests—or to help out companies so needy that public aid would be essential just to cover basic construction and equipment costs. The United States Supreme Court seemed to take the former view.[11] At best the company showed poor judgment of its priorities and made itself politically vulnerable when it needed bipartisan support to survive.

Had the Republicans remained in power for four years, the aid program might have had a chance of proving itself. Despite its recklessness, the Alabama & Chattanooga might have been able to protect its advantages. Unfortunately, the 1870 elections charged the railroad program with political significance. For two years, Democrats had sensed moral decay in the capital, and they blamed it on Republicans. By 1870, Conservatives were protesting a mounting debt which showed no visible return. Searching for an issue to supplement the white supremacy theme, they hit on the charges of fiscal irresponsibility and government corruption. They did not focus their antipathy on railroad aid in general; after all, too many of their leaders had supported or profited from it, and had been committed to public aid since the 1850s, when political brawling on the issue had set Democrat against Democrat. When possible, Conservative orators restricted their attacks to the bribe-takers and to the efforts of the Alabama & Chattanooga "railroad adventurers from abroad" to corrupt the political process.[12] No responsible leader declared all railroad aid unconstitutional, though some of them suggested the illegality of the $2 million loan. Democratic gubernatorial candidate Robert B. Lindsay branded the original act organizing the Alabama & Chattanooga a piece of unconstitutional legislation. Rival railroads, notably the South & North, had leading Democrats for friends. Thus, in a way, the election became a struggle over which corporate interest would have the more important role in Alabama politics. Lindsay himself had gone to the capitol to lobby against the special aid bill, and the Alabama & Chattanooga repaid him on Election Day by voting 925 nonresidents against him at one poll—or so Lindsay claimed.[13] For their sake, they should have voted more.* The Democrats carried the governorship and the House and won almost every county through which the railroad passed.

* Lindsay's statistics are suspect. First, in only three counties along the line did Republicans win as many as 925 votes altogether. In Sumter, there were 1,438 Republicans—but two years before, there had been 2,516, and in 1872 there would be 2,449. Greene cast 1,790 votes for Republicanism, but in 1868 there were 2,927 Republicans and in 1872, 2,508. Thus it is clear that there Stanton could not have had a perceptible effect, unless, perhaps, Democratic intimidation had so reduced the normal vote that only one in every three Republicans dared go to the polls. Jefferson County is more of a problem. The *Tribune Almanac* lists 1,131 Republicans voting for governor and only 420 two years before. Would such an increase be likely? Perhaps not, and yet Democratic votes increased from 538 in 1868 to 1,014 in 1870. In 1872, 1,024 Republicans voted there, and in 1874, a year of severe Democratic intimidation, over 800. Jefferson County was growing quickly. It was there that Birmingham was located. This growth could well explain the increased Republican vote.

Second, such a blatant fraud would have been difficult to conceal from a Democratic legislature. Yet once in power Democrats made no investigation and no attempt to unseat the representatives from the suspicious county. Surely one of the 925 would have been ready to turn state's evidence. None did.

This was no time for the company to be in political trouble. With 225 miles of track completed and with 41 miles in the middle partly done, the Alabama & Chattanooga had bought enough iron to meet its future needs. It had a small floating debt and had sold no more than $4 million of the $6 million in state and endorsed first-mortgage bonds to which it could be entitled. As it completed the rest of the line, it could expect $565,000 more in endorsed bonds, while it needed only $180,000 in cash to meet the January interest on its present bonded debt.[14] Paltry though the need was and great though these resources seemed, the directors could not raise the required amount. They needed what funds they had to complete the track before the June deadline. European wars had tightened the money markets and restricted the availability of loans. Political turmoil in Alabama made matters worse. Investors refused to risk money in railroads whose bonds Democrats had spent a year denouncing as fraudulent and hinting might be repudiated. Certainly, no one would risk buying railroad bonds at par or even close to par, and yet Alabama law forbade the sale of bonds for less than 90 cents on the dollar. Though the railroad might have been remiss in obeying the statutes before, it could not afford to be so now, with Democrats in power eager to challenge the validity of the state's contingent debt. The company could have borrowed the necessary funds, but financiers put such harsh conditions on the Alabama & Chattanooga that its directors could not accept the loan; to have done so, they pleaded, would have forced them to divert money from construction and prevented meeting the state's deadline for completion of the line. That, in turn, would have led to forfeiture of any right to state aid. If the government could offer moneylenders some additional guarantees of the railroad's stability, there might be a chance of a loan on more generous conditions. The company appealed to Lindsay for a promise of four months' extension on the time set for paying interest on the state bonds in its possession. The new governor did not even send the directors a reply. With no other alternative open, the Alabama & Chattanooga defaulted on its interest payment in late December 1870.[15]

Once the default occurred, there was little Lindsay could do about the situation. Under the law, he had a right to seize the road and run it until the company had paid its interest, but the right was an empty one until the road had been completed. Before that, the line would be worth little. The governor had no legal power to complete the line, and the State Treasury could not have afforded the project even if he had. To place the road up for public sale would never recoup Alabama's losses and would only "have been gratifying to the speculating, watchful and anxious cormorants, who are hovering over the prey."[16]

The state had a responsibility to pay the interest on the endorsed bonds if the railroad defaulted, of course, but Lindsay was not sure how much interest was outstanding because he was not sure how many bonds had been sold. Slipshod accounting practices had made the obligation of the state vague at best. The state had given $2 million in its own bonds to the Alabama & Chattanooga and endorsed at least $4 million first-mortgage securities, but which of the company's securities had been endorsed was unclear. Lindsay claimed that his predecessor had kept no record of bonds. Except in the most technical sense, this charge was true. The state had a record of bonds endorsed and the certificates of the officers of the roads benefiting, but the record was incomplete and, therefore, worthless. In December 1870, Smith had stated that he had endorsed 250 miles of the Alabama & Chattanooga for $4 million. Before Lindsay had been in office long, however, he discovered that the Stantons had another $1.3 million in bonds bearing the governor's signature. If the road was to be 295 miles long when completed, the most it could have received would have been $4.75 million. Smith himself later claimed that he had been misled and suggested that some of the endorsements be disallowed. Lindsay could not even be sure when the securities had been issued, though he hinted that Smith might have signed some of them after leaving office. It took months for the governor to determine how large the overissue had been, and he declared that he could not redeem any interest coupon handed in to the treasurer until an audit had been made.* There was another problem; nothing on the company bonds specified whether it was from a second-mortgage bond—for which payment the state was not responsible—or from a first-mortgage bond—for which it was.[17]

With so many complications, the governor found his task both

---

* Lindsay claimed that Smith had kept no record, which was false. Smith was concerned about the weakness of his records and tried to find further information on what bonds they possessed. His own statements show that he did inspect the Alabama & Chattanooga personally several times, that he urged reform of the aid laws, and made specific warnings to the legislature about the executive's lack of power to look into abuses of the aid law.

Nor did Lindsay himself keep very good records. As a special committee later reported, it found more than $20,000 in uncanceled Alabama & Chattanooga bond coupons in a mucilage box in the governor's office. Whether the interest had been paid on them the records did not show.

bewildering and politically distasteful. He was not sure of his legal right to pay off the bonds' interest, and he lacked the political audacity to take responsibility for payment on his own. Therefore, he informed the legislature that he would not act until it passed a law giving him express authority to do so.[18] Lindsay's caution may have been politically wise, but beyond doubt it was economically foolish because delay in paying the interest undermined the credit of both the railroad and the state.

By January 1871, other Southern states were calling their railroad bonds into question, and Conservatives elsewhere were talking of repudiation. The governor's assurances to New York financiers that the interest would be paid once the legislature met did not allay suspicion that the same danger existed in Alabama, and as he continued to balk at disbursing funds that the state had obligated itself to pay, the suspicion grew stronger.* Lindsay's message to the legislature on the subject denounced Republican officials and repeated his campaign innuendos about the illegality of some or all of the state's railroad endorsements. That was not reassuring to the financiers, and they needed reassurance badly. Consequently, the state's credit began to suffer, as businessmen became increasingly reluctant to touch the state's securities.[19]

The bondholders were afraid that Lindsay would leave the issue of payment to the legislature, and they were right to be afraid. The men entrusted with sustaining the state's credit were hardly con-

---

* Why did Lindsay behave with such severity to the Alabama & Chattanooga? There are several explanations; the Democratic party was tied closely to the South & North, a rival trunk line that hoped to be the first to tap the mineral belt of Alabama. This was to the advantage of Louisville and Nashville, rather than to that of Chattanooga and the Northeast. Democrats were closely tied to Southern financiers interested in dominating state commerce, and they had no love for the Northern-based promoters and bankers that held the A & C: the Stantons, Russell Sage, Henry Clews, and others. On the other hand, Lindsay had been raised in the bitter political atmosphere of antebellum Alabama, when Lindsay's brother-in-law, then-Governor John Winston, had fought a battle against state aid that had ended in the Democratic party's conversion to his point of view only after factional and sectional quarrels in the state organization had cut short Winston's political career. Lindsay was Winston's right-hand man in the legislature, and shared in a crusade that the governor portrayed as a fight for the common man against the interests. In addition, neither he nor the Winstons had much love for the interlopers in charge of the A & C. The Wills Valley Railroad, which the Stantons had swallowed into their enterprise, had been run by William O. Winston, another in-law.

Perhaps Lindsay was a true Jacksonian. Certainly, he later insisted that he believed that the Stantons' threat to have the line default was a ploy to squeeze new advantages out of the state. From his January 24, 1871, message, one might infer that Lindsay thought the directors were bluffing and meant to call their bluff. Unfortunately, the company was in very real distress.

stituted for such a delicate task. The Democrats controlling the House had no love for the Alabama & Chattanooga. Some of them wanted to declare the endorsements for that line illegal because they were convinced that bribery had been used. Others wanted to repudiate every security issued since 1868 on the grounds that the Radical government responsible was illegal from its inception. Still others feared such a course: it would do terrible damage to other railroads given aid, none more so than the South & North, the other great trunk line preparing to tap the mineral belt of Alabama. That road was having difficulties of its own already, and too sweeping an attack on the general aid law would force it into the hands of outside capitalists.[20] Many of them thought that the interest should be paid and responsibility for the endorsements accepted, but hoped for an investigation that would show just how corrupt Republican authorities had been. In the Senate, a Republican majority was torn between its wish to uphold the state's credit and its wish to discredit the Democrats. This last desire it could fulfill easily by passing resolutions defending Alabama's fiscal integrity in such terms that a majority of Democrats would be forced to kill the proposals or accept the railroad bonds as legitimate.

As soon as the governor had submitted his message, the Senate passed a resolution declaring that Lindsay did not need new legislation to pay the interest and that he should do his duty at once. House Democrats tabled the resolution and chose a committee headed by Taul Bradford to investigate the Alabama & Chattanooga. Since the committee had an overwhelming majority of Confederate brigadiers who had turned Democratic, it saw no reason to deal gently with former Governor Smith or the Stantons. In February 1871, it made a scathing report of executive incompetence. The lawmakers had intended that the $2 million loan be given in installments as work on the road proceeded. Smith had handed the money to the Stantons all at once. In return, he had received a bond of personal security which he gave to the state treasurer, who carried it about in his pocket for months. The committee could not find out how many illegal bonds Smith had endorsed, but guessed that the number was large; it could not find many specific examples of bribery in the passage of the special aid bill, but estimated that corruption was widespread; and it warned that the state had contingent debts likely to bring about financial ruin, though it did not know how much the liabilities were. Delighted as the Democrats were with the document, they were unwilling to probe further. When a resolution was offered to widen the scope of inquiry to include actions by all the railroads in the state, even Democratic ones, and to have the investigation continue past the end of the session, the majority rushed to table it and did so with most of the Republicans protesting their opponents' flagging zeal.[21]

Having fastened what guilt it could on Radical politicians, the House turned to the more important and difficult task of deciding whether to pay the interest on outstanding bonds. Three members of the Bradford committee wanted the legislature to deny the lawfulness of the acts creating the Alabama & Chattanooga and giving it special aid. Until courts ruled to the contrary, all state aid to the road was to be considered null and void. The House tabled this proposal by 59 to 33, with half the Democrats and every Republican member opposing outright repudiation. Another resolution would have paid the interest on the $2 million loan and on up to $4 million of the endorsed bonds, but no more. That measure was also tabled. It, too, would have compromised the state's credit. At the other extreme, Republicans favored payment of interest on as many bonds as existed, with no questions asked. Unlike the earlier Senate resolution, this measure would have given the governor explicit power to make temporary loans and issue bonds to raise whatever money was needed. Democrats defeated the proposal and postponed a Senate joint resolution renouncing repudiation in any form.[22] It was up to the men in the middle to find an acceptable compromise.

In the political center were two Democrats from the Bradford committee, William Oates and John A. Steele. Neither man could accept wholesale repudiation of the subsidy bonds, but each was troubled by what the investigation had uncovered. Each submitted resolutions which disallowed securities purchased illegally, but required the governor to pay the interest on all endorsed bonds sold in a legal manner. Because Steele's proposal cast less legal stigma on the aid laws and how they had been enforced, Republicans rallied behind it, and the House passed it 76 to 12. The Senate assented without debate, and on February 25, the measure became a law. When a technical oversight forced both houses to reenact the resolutions a few days later, they did so without discussion.[23] Politically, it had been a splendid session. The Republicans had shown themselves more concerned about the state credit than their opponents; the Democrats had shown that they could be responsible and statesmanlike, while their foes were fools or knaves. The only real losers in the struggle were the Lindsay administration and the Alabama & Chattanooga Railroad.

By the time the legislature had given the governor authority to protect the credit of the commonwealth two months had passed, and Northern doubts about the good faith of the state had increased. They increased even more in March when Lindsay went to New York to talk with bankers about Alabama bond issues. On the way, he gave interviews exposing the incompetence of Governor Smith and the cunning of the Stantons. He elaborated on the question of the bond overissue and boasted that he had refused payment on it. He withdrew the state's account with Henry Clews & Co., loyal Republicans, and transferred it to Duncan, Sherman & Co., good, reliable Democrats. Everywhere he hinted that more fraud in the securities issues remained to be uncovered and that the state's subsidy acts might be unconstitutional.[24]

What exactly Lindsay was trying to do was never clear, and he himself may not have been sure. However, he may have hoped to make political capital and defend himself from charges of having become the tool of the Stantons. Whatever the governor's motivation, the directors became alarmed that he would seize the road as soon as they finished building it and that he might wreck it out of spite or stupidity. In the spring of 1871, the director hired John T. Morgan, Confederate brigadier and future Conservative senator, as counsel and sent him to the governor to ascertain the executive's plans. The interview was not very satisfactory. Morgan reported that Lindsay promised to make J. C. Stanton receiver if the company fell into the state's hands. Lindsay denied that he had ever considered such an idea, and when the suggestion was made to him, he had leaped from his sickbed and shouted, "No, by God, never!" Stanton maintained that the governor had offered him the receivership on condition that the state be able to buy the road and the right to retire all state and endorsed bonds for $500,000—an offer which Stanton rejected.[25]

The directors' fears and the governor's bluster made the railroad an easy prey for cormorants. Beguiled by a locomotive builder from Jersey City and a close friend of Lindsay, Nathaniel McKay, the Stanton brothers were led to believe that the governor could be induced to leave the line in private hands, if the company president "would make it an object to him" to do so. D. N. Stanton's personal visits to the chief executive reinforced his suspicion that the offer came from Lindsay himself. In the end, the directors agreed to give the extortioners $100,000 in second-mortgage bonds, $200,000 in stock, and $15,000 in cash in return for verbal assurances and vague documents signed by Lindsay. The bargain was sealed, according to one reporter, "over sundry bottles of Piper Heidsick with considerable chuckling and mutual admiration, all at the expense of the good people of Alabama."[26]

Whether Lindsay received anything is unclear. Stanton later maintained that the extortion "was not and could not have been consummated by McKay without some knowledge and agency therein by the Governor." Democrats replied that McKay had done everything on his own and had not even discussed the subject with Lindsay until June—a claim which telegrams and witnesses contradicted. Still, the governor never mentioned money outright. Nor did McKay's correspondence with him ever sound particularly suspicious. Lindsay may not even have intended to make the guarantees that McKay kept insisting had been obtained verbally. Even so, since the payments were in installments, McKay must have believed that Lindsay would support his scheme; also, the securities received would be worthless unless the line remained in private hands. At best the railroad had been robbed, and the governor had shown himself a cat's-paw. At worst the scandal had shown that the governor was a man who betrayed the people who bought him. When the railroad found itself unable to pay its June interest, Lindsay seized the line.[27]

A crisis in the Alabama & Chattanooga's affairs had been building all spring. The whole road had been opened in time to meet the spring deadline; nevertheless, the directors knew that it could not make running expenses without better equipment, and that by opening the road they made it more attractive to others who wanted to take the management out of the Stantons' hands. While the company was making arrangements to augment its rolling stock, Federal District Judge Richard Busteed of central Alabama struck a damaging blow to the corporation's credibility. Early in June, he ruled the company an involuntary bankrupt and appointed two custodians for the property. Before the end of the month, Federal Circuit Judge Woods of Alabama overturned Busteed's decision, but as one of Stanton's apologists remarked, "No one can estimate the enormous amount of injury . . . caused to the company."[28] The directors went ahead with their attempts to put the road in first-class condition but found payment of the July bond interest impossible and moneylenders even more distrustful than before. It was then that the governor seized the road and made his personal secretary, John H. Gindrat, receiver. After two defaults, he had little choice, but his timing was unfortunate. With so little equipment on the line and so much money needed to keep a road so hastily built in good condition, the state's new possession seemed likely to cost far more than its operations could return.

To Northern investors, Lindsay's action showed him a man of little acumen. "What strikes us most forcibly at the outset," said one correspondent, "is the extreme verdancy of the State of Alabama. That she should expect these new roads building entirely by State aid should meet their interest on the bonds advanced them, shows an ignorance quite surprising." No railroad could expect to do so, and by his refusal to extend aid until the road began to turn a profit. Lindsay had made the subsidy policy "a mere trap, a splendid lure for railroad men to invest a great deal of money . . . the whole to be gobbled up by 'State aid' itself, to the ruin of a multitude,"[29] From a financial point of view, the writer was quite correct. Not many railroads under construction could pay their way immediately, and they needed financial support from the state all the more in their hard times. From the towns along the Alabama & Chattanooga to the money markets of Wall Street, seizure had a sobering effect on every investor, though perhaps for a different reason: neither the legislature nor the people had imagined that the state's investment in the road would be in jeopardy or that the company could fail to profit its backers. However economically sophisticated the correspondent may have been, he was politically naïve. Several million dollars added to the state debt was more than a trifle, and Alabamians might be excused for feeling that if state aid had been a mere trap and a splendid lure, it was the railroad men, not the taxpayers who had put out the money, who had done the specious promising and "gobbling." The public had been assured that any time the railroad defaulted, the state had a legal and moral right to take over the line. Lindsay was simply exercising a right that applicants for aid had supported heartily.

To the citizen who assumed that the first-mortgage lien would protect the state's investment in the road, the proceedings that followed must have been a terrible shock. Alabama's seizure did not end litigation and cost; it only increased them. From that moment on, the Alabama & Chattanooga became the object of the most complex litigation. The proceedings were bewildering and not very interesting in themselves, but they had a larger significance. They showed how flawed the statutory protections in the state aid program had been, not just in Alabama, but in every commonwealth that had advanced money to corporations in return for a prior lien.

From the first, the government had difficulty making its claim to the entire line paramount. Although more than four-fifths of the road was in Alabama, and although the Radicals had made endorsements for every mile of track laid, three other states could claim jurisdiction. Georgia had also tendered some support, and the road had been incorporated in Mississippi and Tennessee. Without the right to run it from end to end, Alabama officials knew that the line could not turn a profit, since it relied so much on its connections at Chattanooga and Meridian. Both the United States Circuit Court for Mississippi and the Tennessee Chancery Court made Gindrat their receiver, but Georgia appointed General W. T. Wofford, and an Alabama chancery court selected Charles Walsh of Mobile for receiver. Walsh's appointment did no harm, but Georgia's obstruction along some 20 miles of the road did. The contesting states made different schedules for running the trains and could come to no agreement on other matters.[30]

Private stockholders tried to challenge the state's right to hold the Alabama & Chattanooga in receivership. They wanted it declared a bankrupt by the federal courts and put into the hands of assignees of bankruptcy friendly to their own interests. William F. Drake of New York filed suit in the United States Circuit Court for Alabama to have the judge appoint a receiver and repudiate the state's endorsement of the securities used to build the northern half of the road. W.A.C. Jones, another creditor, filed an application in federal district court to have the corporation judged a bankrupt, and the court agreed. When the federal circuit court handed down its decision against Drake, however, it also overturned the district court's adjudication on technicalities. At once, another creditor filed suit. In Tennessee's federal district court, Hopkins & Co. and Benjamin F. Emmerson had instituted similar proceedings, but the Alabama & Chattanooga quite understandably had no objection to that suit or Drake's. Each was a close ally of the Stantons and was represented by Judge Samuel F. Rice of Alabama, the corporation's lawyer.[31] The plaintiff's motives were clear: to take company control out of government hands or else, if the assets were to be redistributed, to give stockholders, particularly those on the board of directors, prior claim over bondholders of the state.

One can pardon the Stantons' eagerness to regain control of the line, for under state authority, it was being turned from a second- into a fourth-class enterprise. Testifying before a senate fact-finding committee, J. C. Stanton described the railroad when it was seized as "in first-class condition for a new road," with the exception of about 15 miles which he meant to replace. When the authorities took over the Alabama & Chattanooga, there had been an abundance of rolling stock, first-class machine shops and machinery, and plenty of raw materials with which to construct new cars—or so its superintendent claimed. The company "was doing a fine business for a new road," said Stanton, and it could have earned $2 million in its first year of operation, while costing as little as half that much in upkeep. Six months after the seizure, a professional engineer went down the road he had helped to build and found nothing but wreckage. The roadbed badly needed repair, but the large amount of iron required for track replacement had vanished. In one place, "the track . . . is out of sight in the mud; the ditches are filled with dirt and water to such a height that the steps of the coaches drag through it as they pass along." At another spot, a landslide had blocked the way and forced travelers to disembark and take a train standing beyond the impediment. Where flatcars and engines could be found, they were in deplorable condition, but not many of them were visible in any state. Most handcars had disappeared, and so had most tools. Since the government had taken possession, an expert estimated that rolling stock had depreciated by 50 percent.[32]

Under such circumstances, service could not be anything but abominable, and the revenue gathered by the state far less than its expenses. Commission merchants complained of shipments that went halfway down the line and then were kept waiting three months before cars could be found to carry freight. With their wages eight months in arrears, laborers struck and sabotaged the rolling stock. In some places, they tore up the rails and vowed that the trains should not run until their demands were satisfied. The governor had to send his personal emissary, General James Clanton, to appease them, but six months later they still had not received full payment.[33]

As receiver for the state, Gindrat spent most of his time in litigation and could pay little attention to the actual management of the road. He and Wofford could not come to any agreement about whom the road should employ; Wofford kept firing railway officials and choosing replacements without Gindrat's consent. Gindrat did not deny that the road was in dreadful condition, but he blamed it on "the dissentions [*sic*] caused by conflicting and contradictory orders, the vile emissaries employed to produce disaffections and embarrassments, along the line, the great publicity given to false charges, and maladministration and corruption; the investigation

of committees, and the suit before the United States court at Mobile."
He argued that he could not make the necessary repairs: he had
no money with which to buy materials or hire laborers. In 1873, a
special commissioner found Gindrat himself a source of trouble.
Had he given the road the attention it deserved, the investigator
argued, most of the losses the state suffered would have been avoided.
Because it was generally understood that the road lacked an "efficient, active, responsible chief, . . . demoralization and general
disorder and recklessness prevailed to an alarming extent," a demoralization which cost Alabama about $100,000. Irresponsible
parties ran the line within Alabama; "large sums of money were
collected from freights and passengers of which no proper returns
were ever made, and the rolling stock, track and other property
of the road was greatly damaged." With consummate delicacy, Gindrat's superintendent was described as having so managed the accounts that a close examination of the books would show "that in
equity and good conscience, he would be indebted to the State in
a large sum."[34]

If the Lindsay administration did not serve the road well, there
was evidence that the line served a few members of the administration far better. According to one hostile source, "Hungry politicians who had not tasted pap since the memorable days of secession brightened up and stood gazing upon the scene, the happiest
creatures that earth ever contained. From all parts of the State,
hungry jackdaws flocked to the State House, begging to get a grab
at this huge dish of fat meat, the Alabama and Chattanooga railroad." Former Democratic Governor John Winston was given a
railroad post, Democratic Party Chairman Clanton was made a
counsel for the state in its fight to keep control of the company.
While in Tennessee obtaining a delay in the Hopkins suit until the
federal district court for Alabama's middle district had ruled on
the Jones case, Clanton got into a street brawl with another prominent Democrat and was killed; his death not only added to the
costs of his state's case, but removed one of the strongest opponents
of the bankruptcy proceedings then in progress. Others profited
from the company's misfortune as well: the receivers appointed by
Judges Woods and Busteed, and the lawyers the appointees retained
to protect their interests.[35]

By the time the legislature came back into session late in 1871,
Lindsay's policies had made him hateful to members of both parties.
Some Democrats were furious that he had paid the interest on
bonds they considered fraudulent; others joined Republicans in

blaming Lindsay for the state's declining status in financial centers. Conservatives grew still angrier when the government failed to pay the interest on the aid bonds at the end of the year.[36] Under the circumstances, it is not surprising that the legislature reconvened in a terrible temper.

From the moment they reassembled, the only thing on which the Republican Senate and Democratic House could agree was their desire to denigrate Lindsay and each other. A Senate investigation showed the financial harm done by seizure; a House investigation traduced the governor, the Republicans, and the railroads equally. Where the House's statements were not deceptive, they were petty and blatantly partisan. J. C. Stanton had been in the capital and made clear his desire that the investigators call him as a witness, but "his shameless career in Alabama had convinced them that he was unworthy of belief," said the final report, "and, therefore, they declined to summon him." Members described Gindrat's subordinates as "running riot in the absence of all system, control and accountability"; they blamed the Lindsay administration for wrecking the line, claimed that the governor had endorsed bonds illegally, and suggested that he had connived with the Stantons to turn the road over to them after the state's seizure in return for a substantial fee—a charge that the governor indignantly denied. However accurate its allegations, the House committee report was a damaging indictment of the public aid policy. It showed the companies' negligence in obeying the construction requirements placed on them, and the authorities' lack of interest in bringing any company to an accounting. On the basis of dozens of technical infractions, the bonds of every railroad were open to challenge.[37] The Stantons were by no means the only offenders, but their failure had inspired the enemies of the subsidy policy to make the investigation that would establish the preliminary grounds for repudiation of the entire program.

This legislature would not make any such retreat, but it was as parsimonious as its predecessor had been generous. Lindsay wanted the House to reimburse the lawyers he had hired but was rebuffed 27 to 55. When a motion to pay for Clanton's services came up, a Democratic chamber passed it only after adding a proviso that the vote did not concede any state obligation to pay for litigation involving the Alabama & Chattanooga. The Senate even hinted that the impeachment of the governor might be in order. Lindsay wanted express authority to pay the January installment of interest on the endorsed bonds, and the Republican Senate gave it. The House

did not assent as readily. Instead, representatives offered resolutions opposing further interest payments, declaring the governor's
July payment unauthorized by law, and charging the chief executive
with plotting to use state revenues illegally to pay interest on the
endorsed bonds. This last motion failed 17 to 44, but it was made
by Taul Bradford himself. Defenders of the state's credit finally
passed a statute legalizing a bond issue to rescue Alabama finances,
but one provision specifically forbade use of the proceeds realized
from the sale for the Alabama & Chattanooga's benefit. Finally, the
legislature gave the governor the right to buy the railroad, should
he consider the purchase necessary to protect the state's lien.[38]

It was necessary. In November 1871, District Court Judge Busteed had ruled the line bankrupt a second time. On January 25,
1872, Judge Woods had overturned this decision, but had also
reversed his own ruling of the summer before. At that time, he
had declared that federal law specifically gave the district judge no
right to rule the railroad bankrupt or to uphold his own decision
as a chancery judge. Now Woods decided that the law clearly implied those powers and that Busteed himself had the right to decide
whether his own decision made in a different capacity the year
before was valid.* Busteed had great faith in his own judgments.
He proclaimed the Alabama & Chattanooga bankrupt again and
ordered its sale, subject to the state's lien. Governor Lindsay welcomed the order. Perhaps he felt that only a sale would disentangle
the financial complications in which the state and railroad were
involved, that only by buying the road would Alabama possess the
clear title it needed to effect a sale to private parties on fair terms.[39]

On April 22, 1872, the Alabama & Chattanooga was sold to the
state for $312,000, a sum which was $1,000 more than the Stantons'
representatives offered. Even before the line had been sold, Rice
and William Haralson, appearing for the Stantons and other cred-

---

* In 1871, Judge Woods declared that Busteed's court was only a district court,
not a circuit court, which had appellate powers, despite a federal law enlarging
Busteed's jurisdiction. The law specifically denied it appellate powers, said Woods.
"It can scarcely be claimed that the judge of the middle district . . . would have
jurisdiction to review and reverse his own decree made as a bankrupt judge. The
reasons are obvious." A year later, Woods took the opposite opinion with equally
strong faith. Clearly, Busteed had all the powers of a circuit judge, he declared.
Therefore a circuit judge such as Woods had no power to interfere or take an
appeal from such a court. It was argued that a district judge should not have
jurisdiction to review and reverse his own decree made as bankrupt judge. Woods
responded, "The whole argument is a fallacy. It assumes that a judge will not revise
his own decision impartially. Such an argument ought not to be sustained," Woods
may have been wrong often, but he was never in doubt.

itors of the company, promised that they would contest the sale. They took their case to Judge Woods, who upheld Busteed's right to order a public sale, and to Judge Busteed, who, after further arguments, signed the order confirming the sale on certain conditions.[40]

The state could not meet those conditions. It could not reach a settlement with Georgia regarding conflicting liens or raise the purchase money by the time set in the terms of sale. Lindsay was to give the court $150,000 within an hour of making his bid. Given special extensions until June 10, he still could not raise the money.[41]

By June 1872, even former friends of the road admitted that state involvement had been mistaken and occasionally fraudulent. In earlier years, the *Alabama State Journal* had asserted that the endorsed bonds would never cost the state a penny as long as the law allowed the government to seize and sell the road. Now it berated the state's purchase of the Alabama & Chattanooga as the height of lunacy. Ownership meant litigation, lawyers' fees, negligence, and heavy repair expenses. "What sensible people want to be the owners of a railroad that constantly brings them in debt and hurts their credit?" the *Journal* asked. Equally desperate, Lindsay would have sold the road at a loss to the commonwealth if that had been possible, but proposed arrangements fell through.[42]

The former directors, too, were growing frantic as they watched the road deteriorate under state control. J. C. Stanton hurried to New York to negotiate some arrangement with bankers that might take the company out of Lindsay's hands. When his efforts failed, he went to Galveston to talk with Supreme Court Justice Joseph P. Bradley. As a federal judge for the Southern district, Bradley took jurisdiction over the line and ordered all litigants into his court for a hearing. Stanton wanted a receiver appointed in the interest of first-mortgage bondholders, and the state was in no legal position to make an effective argument for its right to title through purchase. Nor did it want to try.[43]

On September 25, 1872, Judge Bradley recognized the state's legal right to the Alabama & Chattanooga, but replaced the state's receivers with Rice and Haralson, the Stanton attorneys. He based this action on two facts. First, the state had defaulted on payment of the bond interest again in June 1872, and had not met the terms of sale. Second, the Lindsay administration was doing the line serious harm. The state could regain the road by paying back interest on the endorsed bonds. If it failed to do so, the $100,000 of purchase money and $300,000 already paid for bond interest would be considered a complete loss. Once in full possession of the line, the government could sell its property, but not lease or otherwise dispose of it. The new receivers were permitted to issue certificates of indebtedness to raise the funds for repairs on the track and were given complete authority, which they quickly abused.[44]

The Democrats' fumbling helped cost them the 1872 elections. Lindsay himself was such a liability that he could not even obtain renomination. The Republicans had a winning issue in Democratic mismanagement of the Alabama & Chattanooga, and they exploited it enthusiastically. Conservatives had described the Republican administration as a collection of fools and knaves, but the Republicans reminded voters that the combination had somehow given the state greater prosperity than the respectable men replacing it. Orators pointed to the falling price of state securities on Northern money markets and the dilapidated condition of the great trunk line. When Republicans defended the principle of public aid, the incumbents could not point to the scandals in their administration without tainting members of their own party; a Democratic House committee had produced the damning proof. It seemed clear: Republican aid programs had brought prosperity, Democratic interference had insured want. It was not the only issue in 1872, but it was important enough to help explain the increased Republican turnout and the party's improvement on its 1870 showing. David P. Lewis won the governorship, and his supporters gained some seats in the House.[45]

Unfortunately for the Republicans, a change in leadership did not bring a change in the basic problem. Lewis inherited a railroad in disrepair, a heavy state debt, and increasing obligations. Like his predecessor, he tried to sell the road and thought he had found a purchaser, G. T. Ingram of the New Orleans & Northeastern Railroad Company. The line would operate in New Orleans' interest rather than Mobile's, but as the *Alabama State Journal* put it, either taxpayers must operate the road to please "our only seaport or . . . make a sale at once that saves the people from further loss." In five months, the state had lost another $331,000 on the Alabama & Chattanooga, and there was no chance of receipts matching costs for months to come. The deal failed when the governor learned that the financiers Ingram had claimed were behind him had no intention of carrying out the contract.[46]

By late 1873, the desire of men in both parties to free the state from its railroad burdens had reached the level of panic. According to the *Chattanooga Times*, the Mobile & Ohio was considering taking control at a loss to the state of $4 million. Nothing came of the plan, but that Alabama seriously considered it showed how desperate the state had become. When legislators met in late 1873, they made clear their eagerness to sacrifice much to end the government's connection with the ramshackle concern. A Senate bill appointing commissioners to liquidate claims against the state arising out of its involvement with the Alabama & Chattanooga prohibited either the auditor or the governor from paying money for any security connected with railroad aid, even bonds issued with the seal and guaranty of full redemption by the Alabama Treasury. It further prohibited the commissioners from doing anything that might tend to validate any "alleged" endorsement of railroad bonds.[47]

On and on the Alabama & Chattanooga catastrophe went. Each year the courts were forced to hear new pleas and accusations. Under Bradley's order, Rice and Haralson were to borrow $1.2 million for repairs. The certificates they issued in return would become a lien prior even to that of the first-mortgage bonds. These certificates were not supposed to be sold for less than 90 cents on the dollar, but they were. The two receivers also borrowed money at a higher interest rate than the law allowed. They also gave former President D. N. Stanton $40,000 in certificates to pay his claim for services rendered as a trustee for bondholders, an act which gave him priority when the company accounts were settled. The courts arranged two different sales of the line, but no one could meet the purchase conditions. In 1877, the road was finally sold to J. C. Stanton, subject to all liens. The new owner quickly transferred his bid to John Swann, representing a syndicate of London bankers that was organizing the Alabama Great Southern Railroad Company. Even after the bankers took possession, litigation continued.[48]

By 1877, the state was freed both of Republican rule and the railroad and complications, though in neither case did it sever its ties gracefully. In the 1874 elections, the Democrats, combining the race issue with charges of financial disaster, for which the subsidy policy was largely responsible, swept back into power and prepared to "adjust" the debt left by their predecessors. The State Debt Commission of 1875–1876 abandoned all hope of Alabama's recovering its losses. Just to be freed from further expense, it surrendered every state claim to the road to first-mortgage bondholders and paid back interest as well as an additional $1 million. The $2 million loan was repudiated entirely, but some compensation was given in land grants to the bondholders. Not until the legislature ratified the arrangement was the commonwealth free.

It took another nine years for authorities to bring the Stantons to court for damages. Even then, the state lost its case for lack of proof that the Stantons actually had been guilty of fraud and that diversion of endorsed bonds to expenses not directly related to railroad construction had been the cause of the road's bankruptcy.[49]

Nor should all the blame have been placed on the Stantons. All parties and groups were to blame for the line's failure and all had suffered for it. In August 1872, the *Alabama State Journal* had published a damning catalogue of the terrible consequences of Democratic rule. Alabama's Treasury was empty, its "credit . . . gone. She is tabooed in the money market. Her interest is unpaid, and for the first time in her proud history of more than half a century, she is practically, if not literally, under protest." Railroad men could not sell their bonds either. Many projects had stopped and some would be forced into bankruptcy unless the state's credit revived. Alabama was ruined, and it was the Democrats' fault, said the *Journal*.[50] In fact, the real cause of the crisis in finance was the Alabama & Chattanooga Railroad scandal. State credit might have remained high had legislators not lent it to the corporation, and had the company not defaulted and the state then followed suit. Lindsay had made financiers doubt the value of Alabama securities, but no more than his predecessor had by endorsing more bonds than the law allowed and then confessing it.

Everything the railroad aid business touched it tainted. Politics became rotten with charges of corruption and with jockeying for partisan advantage. Commercial life continued to be inconvenienced by bad service and high costs. Bondholders lost both confidence and money. Worst of all, the Alabama & Chattanooga scandal destroyed the credibility of the subsidy program. No one noticed that the road had been built and in good time, or that other corporations had made a profit from their connections with this necessary trunk line. No one outside of Birmingham noticed that the railway made possible the exploitation of mineral resources in the northern counties. It would be years before Southerners realized that the line made possible the creation and growth of the state's first and greatest industrial city. What the public did see in 1874 was that it would be paying far more than it had expected for a commercial highway that had been guaranteed to pay for itself. The problems forced a reassessment of the subsidy policy and spurred the desire of many politicians to free the state from involvement with private enterprises. That was, perhaps, the worst consequence among many that the unfortunate Stantons, Lindsays, Smiths, and Gindrats had brought about.

CHAPTER 14

"They Have Thus Prostituted . . .":
Republicanism Riven

Utterly without shame, devoid of any ability, save cunning,
destitute of personal or political principle, they have thus
prostituted the noblest political organization of any age.
Beaufort Republican
on other Republicans, 1872

THE two-party system could have a ruinous effect on railroad aid—
Alabama had shown that—but the reverse was just as true: railroad
aid wrought real damage to the Southern party system in the long
run. Possibly the Gospel of Prosperity kept some white voters from
concentrating on the race issue. Republican newspapers certainly
used the railroad issue as if they believed it appealed to otherwise
conservative Southerners. Yet if the subsidy program did help keep
whites from uniting against the Reconstruction governments, it also
helped sow dissension in the Republican ranks as it was applied.
Factionalism did not stem from the railroad aid policy alone, but
invariably the railway lines were drawn into political quarrels, and
support for them became one more liability that the faction holding
power had to bear. Sometimes Radicals used the aid policy as an
illustration of their own leaders' inadequacies or as a symbol of the
legislature's unjust sense of priorities. At other times, the subsidy
issue split governor from legislature. In every state, however, intraparty bickering on the question undermined the implementation
of railroad aid, and sapped the internal strength of the Reconstruction coalition. Republicans found that their most dangerous
enemies were in their own ranks, and for this discovery they had
railroad aid policies in part to thank.

Party unity was the first rule in nineteenth-century politics. The
independent vote rarely made any difference, and partisan sympathies ran deep. The Civil War added to the ferocity of political
combat. To call a foe a Democrat was often the same as labeling
him a traitor. To call one's enemy a Republican was to brand him

a defiler of constitutional liberty and perhaps a miscegenationist as well. This animosity at times led to a general willingness to dodge sensitive issues and unite against a common foe. At the same time, the strong convictions that the war instilled encouraged an ideological quarrelsomeness. Rather than waver on a cardinal principle, many men would create dissident organizations, form independent slates, or even join in coalition with their longtime enemies. Under such conditions, the war gave added impetus to party disintegration and formation of political parties as organizers tried to maintain ideological purity and form a majority against the opposition on any terms they could arrange.

Conditions peculiar to the South intensified these characteristics. Party unity was not just desirable; that is, for Southern Republicans, it was crucial to political survival. A defeat would give power to opponents determined to use the legal machinery to nullify the black vote in white counties and coax native whites from Republican ranks. In much of the South, the political conflict was not so much a canvass as a war, and many lives were lost. Republicans had to keep their ranks unbroken and retain power at all cost.

The situation made it more difficult to keep the party unified. From the first, Democratic pressure threatened the fragile biracial coalition by threatening to deprive it of the few whites it had. Thousands of whites found their beliefs difficult to defend against local prejudice and would have welcomed the excuse to return to the party of their friends and relatives. Pragmatic Republican leaders willingly gave up many principles to keep the scalawag vote, but this willingness only irritated other coalition members, who felt that the leaders were slighting the needs of the black rank and file. Idealists objected to the pragmatic approach as the first step to a betrayal of the organization, and Democrats encouraged all such rebellions.

Republicans were particularly susceptible to disaffection because they expected so much from their party: honest, liberal, economic government *and* expanded social services, free schools *and* no distinctions of class or color; equal taxation with special privileges for none *and* encouragement of private enterprise. Each of these promises contradicted another in some way—and each had a symbolic importance. Together, they were expected to make society new. "In fact a political meliennium [*sic*] was looked for," admitted the *Beaufort Republican*.[1] The promise had been partially kept, but for a party so idealized, moderate success did not seem enough, especially when it did not bring with it political revitalization and moral regeneration. In addition, the party's tenuous hold on power made it particularly necessary to keep its integrity unstained. On Republican failure the nation's judgment of the whole experiment with Negro suffrage would be based. Such a pressing situation made it almost a duty of a good Republican to denounce the male-factors around him and to show that the party contained men of real moral sensitivity as well as the venal few.

In so charged an atmosphere as the South's, reasonable discourse gave way to billingsgate, and compromise between factions was stressed less than the need to purge traitors and thieves. Republicans outdid Democrats in defaming their own leaders. Political disagreements degenerated into fights over personalities. Alabama Republicans, for example, were charged by the party organ with having chosen men "without character, without residence, without talent, without principle, without everything, save a restless ambition to . . . rob and plunder the people."[2]

Railroad aid was neither the only nor the most important quarrel to rend the party. Some battles concerned ideals, while others were sordid scrambles for spoils. Ambition produced not only factionalism but anarchy and lingering political damage. In such disputes the railroads played only a modest role. Had there been no subsidy issue, Republicans everywhere, no doubt, would have found other causes for disagreement.

Still, the subsidy policy had a way of aggravating political tensions. "Honest John" Patterson had purely political reasons for saving the governor of South Carolina from impeachment, but Patterson was a known railroad promoter and used his friends in the business to persuade the legislature to drop all charges.[3] When North Carolina and Georgia legislators wanted to drive out an official, they brought up charges that the offender had abused his powers under the railroad aid laws. Mississippi Democrats needed grounds to impeach Governor Adelbert Ames and needed to look no further than his railroad aid policy. A dogged opponent of members of his party who gave public resources to the corporations, Ames did all he could to prevent the aid laws of 1873 from going into effect. In 1874, he instituted an injunction to stop delivery of $350,000 in university funds to the Vicksburg & Nashville. Republican Chancellor Peyton, appointed during the State Senate's recess, dissolved the injunction. Though the chancellor had been in office for nearly a year, the governor refused to send his name to the Senate for confirmation and vowed that the offensive ruling should never appear on the Mississippi law books. It was even charged that Ames tried to work through the chancellor's father, state Chief Justice Peyton, to encourage a reversal, though this both Ames and the elder Peyton denied. Democrats made Ames's use of his executive authority into an article of impeachment, though it is true that they could have trumped up another article just as easily.[4]

In one state, the issue actually set off a brief civil war. Arkansas Governor Elisha Baxter did much to offend the Republicans who had elected him through a creative counting of votes cast in the 1872 election. To obtain Conservative cooperation and maintain his office, Baxter began to dismantle the political machinery that gave Republicans their strength. He signed an act allowing the people to amend the state constitution to restore the franchise to former Confederate officers, appointed Conservatives to office, and helped shift control of the legislature into Conservative hands. All of these betrayals angered the party leadership, but the break did not occur over these issues. It came over Baxter's challenge of the railroad investments and public aid programs of Republican leaders such as Senators Powell Clayton and S. W. Dorsey. Having made a reputation for himself in 1873 as a foe of supplementary railroad aid bills, the governor was not content to hold the line. On March 16, 1874, he declared the general aid law itself unconstitutional. Though he declared new issues illegal, his words assured that bonds already issued would be declared invalid in the future. Less than a month after Baxter's pronouncement, the regular Republican leadership, deeply committed to the railroads thus jeopardized, threw its support to Joseph Brooks, the man bested in the 1872 election. The chief justice declared him legally elected, and Brooks took the executive office by bayonet law. For a month the two self-proclaimed governors massed their forces and sent them skirmishing. Disgusted by a struggle that he had oversimplified into a scuffle for railroad aid spoils, the President intervened on Baxter's side. That fall, the Republican party was not only defeated but obliterated by an election that Conservatives had rigged to assure their own permanent ascendancy.[5]

It was natural that railroads should enter intraparty quarrels over spoils, for railroads and subsidies were a form of spoils. Governors used the lines to buy themselves friends in the legislature. In Arkansas, for example, Governor Powell Clayton built himself a political machine partly by his disbursal of aid to certain deserving lines. In 1871, Clayton hoped to move on to the Senate, but would not accept the promotion until he had found a loyal successor. To do so, he had to force the lieutenant governor from office. Making common cause, the Democrats and the disaffected "Brindletail" Republicans brought resolutions of impeachment against Clayton. They accused him of taking bribes for aiding the Memphis & Little Rock and the Little Rock & Fort Smith, and of illegally giving the Mississippi, Ouachita & Red River state bonds. To make the charges stick, the House chose only Democratic managers, who began to compile the evidence necessary to convince a Republican Senate. Then, suddenly, railroad men began to call on legislators, especially committee members, with arguments in Clayton's favor. As president of the Mississippi, Ouachita & Red River, Judge Thomas Bowen offered one Brindletail a job as station agent and promised to pay him a salary even before the job fell vacant. State Senator E. A. White was reputed to have received $25,000 in railroad stock for his support for Clayton. The committee chairman had already been informed that the railroad of which he was president had qualified for $1.5 million in state aid; now, other company directors worried that the award might be retracted. On March 4, the chairman reported that he could find no grounds for impeachment, that state records did not sustain the accusations, and that the evidence Brindletails had promised had not been made available. The House dropped all charges. Defeated, the lieutenant governor agreed to take another post. The secretary of state was ready to make way for him in return for $30,000 in railroad bonds. Then the legislature sent Clayton to the Senate.[6] No one could prove that the governor had orchestrated this lobbying, though foes tried. Railroad executives either liked the governor or would have preferred to see him leave the state. They would not have needed undue executive pressure to work on his behalf. Probably the charges could not have been substantiated: historians have praised Clayton for his discretion in awarding aid only to worthy companies for work accomplished. The affair, however, showed that railroad policies intertwined with factional disputes.

Railroad aid aggravated party feuds also because many internal divisions were sectional, and railroads given aid were necessarily of greater interest to communities benefited than to towns neglected. In South Carolina, efforts to exchange the state's prior lien for a second mortgage on the Blue Ridge and Greenville & Columbia lines brought a legislative explosion. Charleston Republicans declared the issue no more than a quarrel between honest men and thieves, but since both sides contained vicious as well as virtuous spokesmen, the argument was not entirely persuasive.

B. F. Whittemore, who sold cadetships, and Timothy Hurley, who sold his legislative influence, joined in voting against the measure. Not that their arguments lacked merit—far from it: they insisted that bribery was being used to back the bill and that little or no work would be done on either road, and in both claims they were quite correct. The Speaker of the House himself managed to stop a filibuster by pocketing a bribe from the friends of cloture, and in 1872 the Greenville & Columbia, under foreclosure and proceedings of bankruptcy, was sold to another line. But more pertinent, perhaps, was the fact that the Greenville & Columbia was an upstate concern and did not benefit low-country representatives at all; yet the entire state had paid for the project's support.[7] Supporters of Governor Edmund Davis in Texas tried to cast their battle against subsidies in the same moralistic terms, but here, too, the fight had sectional ramifications.

Still, Republican dissidents were not merely cynical when they used the railroad issue to best their opponents. The subsidy policy exacerbated party tensions because it was a source of concern. Even self-interested men could sincerely object to aid for other parts of the state and inveigh against their own leaders' treachery. Often, conscience very conveniently works in perfect harmony with personal advantage. Few in number the opponents of grafting might be, Speaker Ira Evans of Texas conceded, but "we were strong in the consciousness that we were fighting the battles of the People." The sense of wrongdoing went deep in Republican ranks. One gathering of Texas radicals called on their elected representatives favoring railroad aid to resign "and give place to some one who ha[d] a more pious regard for that position of the Lord's Prayer which says, 'Lead us not in temptation, but deliver us from evil.' "[8] The friends of railroads could talk just as righteously. They were no less sincerely convinced that their rivals were leading the party to perdition.

This was so because the issues seemed so simple. Opponents feared that the cost of the program would bring the state to insolvency, and, as has already been noted, they had good cause. Financial ruin would cast shame on the Reconstruction coalition. Democrats were not the only Southerners who thought that the Reconstruction governments were spending too much and for too little return. Republican legislators voiced their dread "of the impending horrors of bankruptcy, that . . . will come upon our state like a fearful simoon, blasting with its hot breath all the promising future that lays before it."[9] Each dollar of railroad aid, too, was one dollar less that the General Assembly could spend for militias, levee improvements, or retiring the public debt.

Railroads were also among the clearest symbols of that close working arrangement that conservative Republicans seemed to have with the Democratic opposition. In both Florida and Texas, the governors' enemies united in attacking them and in pressing for certain subsidies. There was real ideological disagreement in Texas. Senator J. W. Flanagan championed railroad aid of every kind. In the constitutional convention, his supporters had joined Conservatives to defeat motions outlawing special charters and privileges for select corporations. According to Flanagan, the body "had but few old fogies in it; the delegates were generally of vigorous and progressive minds—railroad men." To such Republicans, "progressive" thinking meant little more than support for railroad aid. For public schools, civil rights, and an effective state police to protect the black voters, the Flanagan faction in the legislature showed scant enthusiasm. One senator caught the mood of the moderate-Conservative coalition perfectly when he offered this toast, "The militia bill without amendments and two grand trunk Railroads." Indeed, major railroad lines joined the lobbying effort to block the militia bill. They were accused of offering bribes to prevent existence of a quorum and may well have tried to keep Governor Davis from vetoing subsidies by holding up his entire program. Alabama radicals freely charged that the Alabama & Chattanooga Railroad had joined forces with moderate Republicans in 1870 to keep a black off the state ticket, and one black leader declared that he had been paid $10,000 for that purpose.[10] To men like Flanagan or Warmoth, railroads were a sign of that broadening of the party's base that was necessary if a biracial party were to survive in a predominantly white South. To their enemies, railroads were a sign of how expediency could erase that most elementary precepts of Republican doctrine.

Finally, railroads were the most obvious example of the corruption that was eroding public trust in the Reconstruction coalition. If there were a place for disgruntled reformers to draw the line of battle inside the Republican party, railroad aid seemed the obvious choice. When the Blue Ridge Railroad came to the South Carolina legislature to ask that the state replace its bond guarantee with $1.8 million in certificates of indebtedness, to be issued at once, reformers were scandalized. They did not like the three-mill tax that the bill provided; and they knew perfectly well that the scrip would not be redeemed. Described as a bill "to relieve the State . . . of all liability of its guaranty of the bonds of the Blue Ridge Railroad," the measure could better have been dubbed "a bill to relieve the Blue Ridge of any responsibility to the State," since the government lost its lien. "*Modest* highwaymen!" D. T. Corbin protested. "Why do you not demand four millions? why not ten or twenty? . . . Mr. President, the arch fiend himself has concocted the plan." Corbin's outrage was fully justified, as became clear when the bill passed and the governor returned it with his objections. The Blue Ridge officers used persuasion and railroad funds in equal measure to convince legislators to override the governor. The General Assembly proved open to both.[11]

So flagrant was the corruption in Florida in 1869 that even Governor Harrison Reed became distressed. Lobbyists working for Milton Littlefield's Jacksonville, Pensacola & Mobile road descended on the capital to obtain a grant for their road across the state. They found the lieutenants of Governor Reed's foe, Senator Thomas W. Osborne, indispensable to success. Informed that the legislature was being bought, Reed sought and received the lobbyists' promise (it was quickly broken) that no more money would be used in that way. According to one state senator, indeed, Littlefield contributed $22,000 to a fund to help overthrow the chief executive. Six months later, when the railroad needed an increased subsidy, Littlefield was forced to pay Osborne again—this time by signing a forged letter incriminating Reed.[12] None of the attempts to convict Reed of corruption succeeded, though in each case it obtained party support in the legislature from those most concerned with the corruption of the Republican party.

It is difficult to gauge how much factional differences over railroad aid undermined the Republican coalition in the South. Certainly, the effect was different in each state. Yet everywhere, railroad aid became a cause for debate and a major reason for Republican disunity. In South Carolina, the two bills consolidating the Greenville & Columbia with the Blue Ridge line and relieving the Blue Ridge of its obligation to the state crystallized Radical indignation against the low moral tone of their leaders, stirred the reformers to fight the Scott administration, and led to a bolt from the party in 1872. "Radical plundering" became a *cause célèbre* and later Conservatives used the two bills as some of their strongest charges in an indictment of the entire Reconstruction government. In Florida, most of the fighting stemmed from the clashing ambitions of Reed and Osborne, but it found a vent in the railroad aid issue. Corrupt administration of the subsidy program was the source for the impeachment charges that Republicans in coalition with the Democratic minority leveled at Reed in 1870 and 1872. The effects were not the mere internal unpleasantness that showed itself in South Carolina. In Florida, factional turmoil led to legislative chaos and the disaffection in the Republican party that helped throw the legislature into Democratic hands. More seriously still, the railroad issue helped define the dispute between the governor and the legislature in Texas. There, the party was degraded and demoralized. Furthermore, many of the foremost Republicans left the organization before 1872. The party never got a second lease on power. Worst of all was the Arkansas experience, where intemperate rhetoric gave way to violent action.

Most states had experiences closer to those of South Carolina and Florida Republicans. Railroad aid was one aggravation among many, not big enough to tear the party apart, but big enough to demoralize it. Yet the poisonous effect that railroad aid had on political morale as the program lost its popularity cannot be discounted. The bitterness was intense. South Carolina members were so disgusted by the Consolidation bill that they tried every means to prevent its passage. Opponents even fled the House to prevent a quorum. So hot did tempers grow that one enemy of the measure had to be restrained from striking the chairman of the House Railroad Committee. Fistfights broke out. Texas Senator Flanagan was so displeased by one of the governor's vetoes of a railroad aid bill that he was reported to have "almost floundered himself out of the Republican party." He also tried openly to read the governor and his radical friends out of the organization. His cohorts deprived the *Austin State Journal* of printing contracts for having objected to one major subsidy, and then went on to depose the Speaker of the House for his resistance to this and other Republican measures.[13]

Words could be as painful as deeds. Republicans who were disgusted by subsidies spoke with brutal candor. The *San Antonio Express* called for a thorough purge in which rank and file would "use the scalpel without fear or favor." When Democrats called for a new legislative election for the fall of 1871, many Republicans, including the Speaker of the House, joined their appeal.[14] So bitter had internal dissension become on railroads and other matters by 1873 that Republicans lost the capacity to recognize their common interests against the Democrats. Some sat home on Election Day rather than see the ruling faction triumph. Others actually made coalition with Conservatives to drive out their onetime allies, and coalition always led to party destruction and a paralysis of political will. It was not just a failure to protect themselves against Democratic terrorism that undid Republicans in so much of the South before 1876. It was the failure of nerve and of purpose that railroad aid, among other issues, had brought about. A party without a clear sense of mission could not wage a successful fight.

This factionalism cost the Republican party dearly in credibility, for Radical virtue had been one of the sources of its strength. In 1868, Republicans had proclaimed their mission with messianic fervor. By 1872, their repeated summoning of the South to peace, purity, and prosperity had lost its initial force. Now the rank and file were informed that their leaders had betrayed them. If Republican polemics could be believed, their own governors had sold out Louisiana and Tennessee, while Republican senators had betrayed Arkansas, Texas, and Alabama. Authors of the Republican constitutions of 1868 had helped unmake the Republican regimes. In two separate elections, leading Republicans had declared the South Carolina party beyond salvation and had bolted to run tickets of their own. "Utterly without shame, devoid of any ability, save cunning, destitute of personal or political principle, they have thus prostituted the noblest political organization of any age," said the *Beaufort Republican* of party leaders.[15]

The editor hit painfully close to the mark. Some leading Republicans had shown themselves to be fools, among them Governor William Smith of Alabama. Those not fools all too often branded themselves knaves in railroad matters. Everyone knew that a handful of United States senators had bought their seats with money that railroads supplied. More honest men had shown themselves ineffectual against railroads' abuses or unable to restrain their more predatory colleagues.

To every charge against them, the incumbents replied by heaping equal blame on dissident Republicans, and with good reason; but if each group of partisans spoke the truth of the other, what had become of the moral regeneration that the Reconstruction coalition had promised? After 1872, the best that Republicans could say was that in their innocence they had shown themselves no judges of men and poor judges of measures, but that they would do better in the future. Nevertheless, that was not a very persuasive argument. A party unable to distinguish between moralists and mountebanks in 1868 would be no more selective in whom it allowed into its ranks in 1872, when it needed every vote it could get. Railroad aid alone had not destroyed the Republicans' credibility, which had never been very great among white Southerners anyway.

However, it always played some role. Because of it, Republicans lost not only reputation, unity, morale, but finally office.

With their destruction, they damaged the railroad policy beyond repair. By using the aid program to blacken the names of their foes inside the party, disaffected Republicans undermined the public reputation of railroad aid. Over and over they insisted that the aid program was being mismanaged, that the schemes were sheer robbery, that the party leaders profited from these speculative enterprises. Democrats could do a great deal of damage among their own members, and certainly among the class of Republican who put his trust in what a Democratic newspaper would say. But for those Republicans who trusted their own party organs, the picture was nearly as black. Conservatives could make more plausible their case against the aid program and official corruption by citing Republican attacks on Republican policies.

Doubtless, members of each faction felt their grievances sincerely. Yet one truth is inescapable; in making their case against other party members, they believed what they wanted to believe, and they wanted to believe that the most important traits of their opponents were dishonesty and greed. As a result, Republicans blackened the most honest administration of railroad aid.

In Arkansas, for example, the Brindletails made a very damning indictment of the aid that Governor Clayton administered. According to the governor's enemies, railroad aid had not built a mile of track in Arkansas. The Cairo & Fulton should have built 300 miles for its money, but, said the *Arkansas Gazette*, only 38 had been built by 1871. The Memphis & Little Rock should have finished 120 miles to qualify for its $2.25 million in state aid, but had only built 95. Without a mile in operation, the Arkansas Central had received $300,000 and the Little Rock & Helena $400,000. Only half as much had been built on the Little Rock & Helena as the government had paid for, and only a sixth as much on the Little Rock, Pine Bluff & New Orleans. In all, state aid had built 257 miles by 1871 at a cost of $12 million to taxpayers. As Clayton's enemies explained it, the governor, "owing to over-anxiety to complete the roads, or for some other cause," had ignored explicit statutory requirements and given too much too soon. That "some other cause," as Brindletails saw it, was utterly sordid. James L. Hodges claimed that he had sought aid for one company and paid the Governor $300,000 to see it done. Other critics noted the connections between leading regular Republicans and railroad positions and suggested that the governor aided both his friends and railroads that could do him political services.[16]

Most of the charges were half-truths or buncombe. As Dorsey of the Arkansas Central wrote in reply to the *Gazette*'s attack, the Memphis & Little Rock had completed its track, but only when all grading and laying of ties had been done. Thus, while the Little Rock & Fort Smith had 82 miles of track completed, it also had 70 miles more ready for iron; it had rails enough for another 140 miles. In all, Conservatives had underestimated mileage fit for aid by nearly half. The $12 million statistic was another illusion, for only $3.45 million in bonds had been issued by 1871. The rest of the securities *might* be issued if and when the railroads that the commissioners ruled *qualified* for aid did more grading. The Conservatives had mistakenly treated the declaration of a railroad's right to receive aid and the aid it had been given as if they were the same, which they were not. Even if they had been, the total amount of aid authorized never exceeded $9,900,000. Of that amount, only $5,350,000 was ever issued. The Brindletail and Conservative estimates on individual lines had no relation to reality. They claimed that the Little Rock, Pine Bluff & New Orleans had received $2.4 million, but the commissioners authorized only $1.8 million and issued only $1.2 million of that. In their feature of $1.6 million given to the Mississippi, Ouachita & Red River, Conservatives made a $1 million overestimate. Clayton kept the railroads relatively honest. He demanded every affidavit required by law, enforced the conditions set for the grants, and awarded only for miles built. His successors were just as vigilant as he. With some justice, Clayton boasted that on taking office he had found only 45 miles of "dilapidated railroad in the State," but that state aid had built 315 miles of track. Before Democrats made the state aid statute ineffective in 1874, the policy had built 445 miles, 63 percent of all track built in Arkansas during Reconstruction. Railroad presidents agreed with Clayton's claims that without state aid, none of the construction could have taken place, except on one road that had declined a subsidy from the state government and accepted aid from the federal authorities.[17]

Brindletails had no more basis for their charges of executive venality. To claims that the governor had signed bonds only on promise of a tithe of the proceeds from their sale, the Cairo & Fulton president published an angry denial. Hodges' charges had no substantiation either.[18] Where money was involved, Clayton was incorruptible. Like other Radical bosses, he was always a partisan, often an opportunist, but never a thief. Possibly Clayton dangled the promise of aid over other politicians' heads to win their loyalty, but he gave aid to no line that did not deserve it.

None of these facts stopped the abuse of railroad aid in Arkansas. It was not the truth that killed the subsidy policy in the state, but the fabrications that Conservatives and Brindletails made and tended to believe. In other states, the charges against railroad aid—often more accurate than in Arkansas—made Republicans' stand in favor of aid an embarrassment. The Blue Ridge Railroad was able to pass its scrip bill in 1872, but in doing so it so discredited aid policies among South Carolina Republicans that this steal proved to be the railroads' last.

In 1872, the railroad aid policy was imperiled all across the South. The failures of the construction program had damaged the policy's credibility; the financial weakness of Southern governments had marred the subsidy laws' designs as much as corruption and self-interest had injured their reputation. Worst of all, perhaps, was the wreckage that the party divisions had made of the aid policy. It had become the *cause célèbre* that the "outs" among Democrats and dissident Republicans used to drive the "ins" from office. The manipulation of the aid issue to serve political ends was only natural. From the first, railroad aid had been a political panacea as well as an economic one. Aid could not have been separated from politics, had its sponsors wanted to do so. But the quarreling was no less disastrous for being natural. Railroad corporations could endure corruption, and they could overcome special interests and localism. Because their success was based on legislative support, the companies, however could not withstand factionalism.

The final irony was that the economic crisis for the roads had come just as a political crisis was developing; for, by 1872, the railroads had come as far as they could on the aid given. They had to go back to the legislatures for new concessions—legislatures which, because of the growing political controversy, examined each proposal with an unwelcome scrutiny.

The corporations had not run out of friends—not yet. They had run out of funds, however; and in the political climate of the Southern legislatures, they had run out of something far more important. They had run out of time.

CHAPTER 15

"A War Now Begins between These Roads and the People," 1873

These leeches have clung to us until we were well-nigh exhausted.

A Little Rock businessman

By 1873, the South's initial optimism about its commercial future had subsided. Taxpayers, promoters, farmers, merchants, Conservatives, Republicans—all agreed that something had gone wrong with the Gospel of Prosperity. Railroads had been built, but they had not brought the promised affluence. Cotton brought a good price, but the planters had not regained their antebellum influence. The government had taken an active role in the Southern economy, but in doing so had compromised its own integrity and wrought only indifferent results. Construction and commercial expansion had brought neither the social stability that Radicals had promised nor the political hegemony they had promised each other. Party factionalism and financial incompetence abounded. They fed on one another. Poor planning and parochial interests marred the railroad vision, and this, too, affected political events. Months before the Panic of 1873, the authors of the railroad aid policy had begun to recant, reform, and repeal.

On the surface, Southern interest in railroad aid did not seem to have diminished by 1873. Many communities still clamored for subsidies. Proponents still petitioned the governor to extend financial support to their projects. Enemies of railroad aid continued to profess their devotion to the principle of commercial development. "I am for railroads here, there, and everywhere," said one legislator, and he added that he was sure the chief executive felt the same way. Only then did he echo the chief executive's appeal for retrenchment.[1] As late as 1873, companies seeking special treatment received all they wanted in many states. Their success is less important, however, than the circumstances under which aid was given. Supplicants did not want aid so much as relief. Nor did they carry their point as easily as in the past. The opposition had become more formidable, so much so that, indeed, 1873 marked the last time that the corporations could raid the Treasury. There would not be another General Assembly as generous for another generation.

No longer did railroad aid command statewide legislative support. Local jealousies and ambitions had sharpened; consequently, it was hard to form a coalition sufficient to pass subsidy measures. At the same time, Southerners were growing critical even of bills working to their own local advantage. As the major paper from Montgomery, the *Alabama State Journal* had community interests at heart. A special aid bill offered in 1873 would have helped that city as much as any other, but the editor would not mute his protests that the measure was a fraud. Much as railroad expansion would enrich San Antonio and Houston, the Republican press in both cities waged relentless war on state subsidies. Admitting that one bill would enrich his constituents, a New Orleans legislator explained, "I have a higher duty to perform. I am here to serve the best interests of those that sent me here," interests better served by defeating costly railroad schemes.[2]

The coalition also had lost its most influential members. Without the strong support of the commercial community, the subsidy policy would not have passed. Gradually, however, businessmen began to voice concern at what one commercial publication called "a hemorrhage of debt." When the Arkansas Central Railroad sought a $100,000 subscription from Little Rock, the local chamber of commerce met to denounce the request as "the height of impudence." Everything the railroad touched it impoverished, one businessman cried. "These leeches have clung to us until we were well-nigh exhausted." Resolutions were even offered to close all business establishments on Election Day so that commercial men could hold a vigil at the polls "to see that our wishes are carried out." Such an assault defeated the subsidy. In the November referendum, it was voted down 331 to 698.[3]

Railroad aid also required the tacit support of the governor in most states, but increasingly the Republicans elected chief executives who were suspicious of privileged corporations and committed to retrenchment. All gave lip service to railroad expansion, but none proposed programs to further construction. Abandoning his predecessors' policy, Adelbert Ames of Mississippi typified the new breed. He called for economies and insisted that the railroads pay their tax obligations. In a special message to the General Assembly, he urged repeal of acts bestowing tax-exemption on the Grenada,

Houston & Eastern and surrendering education-fund lands and government trust funds to the Vicksburg & Nashville. When the legislature paid him no heed, Ames repeated the warning and went to court to block payment of aid. Informed that his lieutenant governor was using the executive's powers to sign aid bills, Ames canceled a vacation and rushed home to thwart such plans. Circumstances differed, but in every state the governor took the same basic stand—even in Louisiana.[4]

Governors, businessmen, localists, idealists: these four sets of converts to the opposition made it harder to create a winning coalition for aid bills and easier to organize a lobby against any measure pledging the public funds. Promoters still had a vision and ideology with which to tempt the people, but so did their critics.

First, opponents of aid increasingly played on Southerners' suspicions of outsiders. As they described many aid bills, one state would pay and another commonwealth benefit. Foes of one Alabama railroad bill insisted that it had been created by Georgians interested in the Savannah & Memphis as well as Kentuckians connected with the Louisville & Nashville. Nor were the people of Alabama to blame that their money had enriched aliens. Everyone knew that many legislative endorsements had passed at the behest and by the bribery of New York stock jobbers, said the *Livingston Journal*, and Alabama taxpayers "were powerless to resist." The charge was largely fustian, for legislators and local interests had never been powerless to stop outside predators. They had taken part in the pillage and made little murmur until, as one editor put it cynically, they had plucked the goose and softened their own pillows. But the charge was sound politics. Relieving natives of blame for the railroads' wrongdoing made it possible to repudiate Southern favors to corporations without seeming inconsistent or guilty of bad faith.[5]

In the second line of attack, foes of railroad aid suggested that public financing was no longer necessary and perhaps never had been. They charged that the privileges given the lines had led to overfed executives running underfunded projects. "Gentlemen may talk of the poverty of railroads," said one of the leading expounders of the Gospel of Prosperity, "but I have seen very little of it. They could pay the most exorbitant salaries for their officials, and good wages to all their employees." Apparently, critics could not imagine that money appropriated had gone for construction or been lost in bond transactions, as most of it had. They were convinced that all the funds had been funneled into a few pockets and could be brought forth and applied to new construction, if the states remained adamant against new appropriations. Never had politicians used the word "monopoly" so commonly or loosely in describing railroad interests. Never had they inveighed so heartily against giving "rich corporations the substance of the people, and calling it internal improvement."[6]

Again, the charges distorted the truth. The railroads were not rich; their inability to pay much more than operating costs showed that. In fact, almost no railroad outside Georgia declared a dividend in 1872. Most Southern roads had not declared one since their founding. In a time when shopkeepers and laborers could not get reimbursement for their services, the charge of opulence showed an audacious disregard for the facts. Indeed, outside of North Carolina, no legislature sought an investigation of any railroad's books to account for the disposition of funds.[7]

If anything, railroads' weaknesses came from their unanticipated poverty and insufficient trade. They had been handicapped by competition in an underdeveloped South—precisely the reverse of the condition which monopoly might have afforded them. A little more monopolistic price-fixing might have saved a few roads from bankruptcy. But how could a monopoly be obtained? That was the puzzle. Visionaries who tried to consolidate many lines under one head found the task beyond their power or else beyond their resources. In extending themselves for this purpose, they did not tighten their grip on Southern farmers. Rather, they brought themselves down.[8] Had monopoly existed, the best cure for it would have been the very policy that foes of government aid would have objected to most: public subsidies to river transport, turnpike construction, new lines that could cut into the traffic of the old, and programs establishing government-owned railroads.

The opponents' third and most powerful line of attack emphasized the comparative poverty of the South. By 1873, leaders of both parties were promising retrenchment. If anything must be cut back, surely it should be those programs that brought the least return. For many Southerners, this meant the railroad aid policy. Certainly, the governments could not afford to continue support with the same liberal hand they had shown in years when state bonds sold for a good price and taxes had been relatively light.

Had the railroad aid program failed? Yes, said critics. They not only charged the companies with misappropriation of funds, but argued that the funds legitimately spent had done no good. After all, most of the roads receiving aid in Georgia, Alabama, Arkansas,

Florida, and South Carolina had fallen into default or receivership by July 1873. Other roads had used up state money and then submitted to Northern financiers, who bought the lines and worked them for their own advantage. Railroad men could promise prosperity and self-supporting lines, but the broken promises of the past rose to haunt them now. The Mobile & Grand Trunk Railroad had been heralded as a certain asset, said one Democrat: sure to pay all expenses, even its bond interest, on completion. "Now all was reversed. It was stuck in the mud or run into a river, and it would never be worth anything unless . . . Alabama came to its relief and lifted it up by a new draft of the people's money."9

A few individuals even began to question the assumption that railroad construction enhanced the economy of the counties most directly affected. It was a good omen for public policy and a bad one for railroad promoters when State Senator R. W. Cobb of Shelby rose to challenge the claim that railroads had enhanced Alabama property values. Before the Alabama & Chattanooga crossed eight counties in 1869, they had had a $10,789,796 assessed value; three years later, they had an assessed value of only $10,610,011, though the counties, known for their coal and iron deposits, should have prospered from rail connections. The South & North crossed seven counties, the assessed value of which had also fallen. Cobb found eight counties without railroads, too, the assessed value of which had increased by a bit over 15 percent.10 Of course, Cobb chose his figures with care. Many men had made money from railway development. Certainly no county with a line would have asked that it be removed. In a less extreme form, however, the lawmaker made a point worth considering. If the railroad brought prosperity to an area, it did not assure a dramatic increase in values or trade. Lacking other advantages, thus, many towns aspiring to become new Atlantas and Birminghams would never be more than depots and junctions.

Railroad companies could not deny that the aid programs had failed. Their very actions made clear that money *had* been spent in vain. Not only did the corporations pose as impenitent and impecunious wards of the state, but in 1872 and 1873 they returned to the capital with demands for additional financial support. Their needs had not changed; their arguments had. In 1868, they had vowed that the money they received would be ample to complete the lines and bring general prosperity. Four years later, they argued that the aid given over the past few years had been too little. When critics declared the companies in sound financial conditions and unworthy of renewed support, lobbyists replied that the corporations were in far worse straits than people imagined. Railroad aid had not made them prosper at all. Arkansas lines were so deeply in debt that a new bond issue would not "sell for enough to pay for the printing." If true, then all that enemies of aid had said had official verification; supporters of aid had recanted all their original promises. Of what value, then, was the corporate insistence now that one last grant "assures the completion of these unfinished roads"?[11]

With both impudence and imprudence, the railroads went further. In 1868, the states had received promises. Now they heard threats. Officials were informed that all safeguards on the original public investment were a sham. Without new appropriations, all state expense would go for nothing; that is, the roads would not be built. The people might still pay taxes on endorsed bonds, but without visible return for their outlay. The state, therefore, must assume new responsibilities with no better protections than before, and it must do so because it had no choice. This was no application for public generosity. It was a demand for tribute on the terms set by the companies, a demand strengthened by the threat that any other course would work economic and political disaster. In 1868, a strong and generous state had given aid to pitifully weak enterprises. Three years later, it was the state that needed pity and fair treatment, but the railroads did not choose to give in. With rare exceptions, they wanted all they had been promised. Exploiting the state's financial weakness, they drove hard bargains and tried to purchase state properties at a sacrifice to the taxpayer. Citizens might well ask where the process of aid would stop. If the state gave additional support, what would keep the railroads from returning in another year to demand more aid and from brandishing the same threats of bankruptcy? To many Southerners, no time seemed better than the present for governments to accept their losses and refuse new responsibilities.

Railroads did not see their appeals in such terms, of course. Promoters claimed that they had the states' best interests at heart. Only by succeeding in their work could the railroads protect the South from a heavier real debt, a higher tax rate, and bond repudiation. But critics could ask, if the people stood on the brink of "the damning gulf of repudiation," as one editor predicted,[12] who had brought them there? If the state's excellent railroad system failed to materialize, who was most to blame, and, even under the best circumstances, what chance remained that the system would be completed?

It was precisely the wrong time for the companies to seek new support, but seek it they did. They won a series of Pyrrhic victories, adding to the public outcry and augmenting the coalition against railroad aid. Railroads in Alabama provided the most remarkable examples of shortsightedness. There, the state aid program had been so corrupt and mismanaged that bond repudiation seemed a very real prospect. Yet neither the politicians nor the promoters had learned their lesson.

Under the 1868 statute, the government had endorsed $16,000 a mile in company first-mortgage bonds. Four years later, the railroads tried to exchange these depreciated securities at one-fourth their face value for state bonds, which had a better sale value. After days of quarreling, opponents managed to exclude five major lines from benefits and then to table the entire question. In 1873, the Republicans returned to power and the railroad supplicants to Montgomery. Though the House Internal Improvements Committee did safeguard Alabama's interests, the bill was still extraordinarily generous. Any company "which is now or may hereafter become entitled" to endorsements could surrender its claim for further state guarantees and would receive $4,000 a mile in state bonds. When three-fourths of all endorsed bonds had been returned, the state would relinquish its lien on the road. Like advantages were promised to any road that built 20 miles of track by November 1874, with its own resources. For the first five years, the companies could pay one-half of 1 percent of their gross earnings into a sinking fund to redeem the state debt. Thereafter, they would pay 5 percent in state bonds at par value. The state auditor could raise the assessment whenever he considered it insufficient to liquidate the bonds given under the aid law.[13]

On its face, the bill seemed innocent enough, but foes in both parties spotted another "steal" by the promoters. By surrendering the state's lien while the companies still held $4,000 in endorsed bonds, the government did not cancel its own obligation to pay interest and principal on those securities when the road defaulted. It simply deprived itself of the right to seize and sell the roads and make up for its losses. Critics did not deny that the state would lose nearly $3 million on its initial investment by sale, but insisted that the amount was trivial compared with the losses that the present bill would assure. Financially, the bill seemed a queer boon to the railroads. If they could not afford to pay their way at present, how could they pay an additional twentieth of gross earnings into a sinking fund, without bringing default or bankruptcy—against which the state would have no protection? Worse, a few roads that had forfeited all prior claims to state aid were now made eligible.[14] For the government to exchange bonds about which there could be no questioning for ones of dubious legal validity seemed the most outrageous cheat of all.

Unable to kill the bill, the bipartisan coalition strove to water it down. The legislature agreed to exempt three companies from the law, though it spared the South & North. Democrats could not bar new lines from the bill's provisions, for as one legislator remarked, 15 votes rode on that part of the measure. In the end, only the South & North availed itself of the law. No other enterprise could raise the cash to build 20 miles of track the following year. Nor did Northern bondholders choose to surrender three endorsed bonds for every state bond they gained, especially since Alabama seemed likely to devalue its securities as other states were doing.[15] The law's real effect was not economic, but political. It gave the enemies of railroad aid a new *cause célèbre*.

During the same session, Alabama railroads made other requests that were equally galling. George Opdyke, a New York capitalist, wanted the state to sell him the Mobile & Eufaula Railroad at a loss. Though critics protested that at a public sale the line would bring enough to pay every penny Alabama had lost in liabilities and costs, they were defeated. The Mobile & Ohio sought banking privileges and the right to issue scrip as legal tender. Legislative support was insufficient to pass the bill over the governor's veto. Even less judiciously, the Birmingham, Chickasaw & Tuskaloosa sought a ten-year tax-exemption. In 1868, the bill might have passed easily. Now, even leading Republicans were outraged. Railroads had ruined the state, said one party member, and now they wanted to escape payment of the debt they had created. Let there be no coddling for "the cause of all our woe, while there was no relief for the people," another representative shouted. The bill failed.[16]

Alabama was an extreme but not an isolated case. In Mississippi, railroads asked for and received far more than they should have. The New Orleans, Jackson & Great Northern applied for a bill merging it with the Mississippi Central, to create one trunk line from the Ohio valley to the Gulf of Mexico. It asked only for all the rights "in perpetuity" that either of the two old companies had enjoyed, including a tax-exemption originally granted for twenty years and meant as a spur to construction. Senator A. T. Morgan damned the bill as more insidious than a permanent tax-dodge. By depriving Mississippi of its preferred-creditor status, the carpet-bagger warned, the measure would make it difficult to collect money that both roads owed to the public school fund. Its backers knew precisely what they were doing: when an amendment declared the consolidated enterprise liable for all obligations contracted by either road, it was tabled by 18 to 10. Other senators called attention to the bill's provisions allowing the consolidated road to charge whatever freight rate it pleased, elect a majority of nonresidents to the directory, and write bylaws to suit itself. These changes portended a road worked for the benefit of outsiders and against local merchants. In effect, said critics, Mississippi would sire "a powerful and pernicious railroad monopoly," able to swallow or starve out every other line within the borders of the state. Alas, then, for the private citizen's rights! The bill passed, but over loud protest.[17] Other railroads received tax-exemption in all but name. Flouting the state constitution, the government loaned the Vicksburg, Pensacola & Ship Island up to $10,000 a mile.[18]

This loan was all the more distressing in view of the truculence of companies already indebted to the Chickasaw School fund. What they owed the state they expressed no desire to repay. Under an 1871 statute, the roads could honor their debts in depreciated state warrants at par, and the state would surrender all claim to four years' worth of back interest. Several shrewd promoters bought up the debts of the New Orleans, Jackson & Great Northern, entered into contracts with the governor, and paid him in state warrants issued to the Ripley Railroad under the subsidy act of 1871—warrants that legislative investigation showed to be of doubtful constitutionality and procured through the possible bribery of the attorney general. A House investigating committee chastised the chief executive for his readiness to take a pittance for company debts, but at least he had received something. The presidents of the Mississippi Central, Mobile & Ohio, and Mississippi & Tennessee made a public appeal to be released from payment entirely. The first two roads had paid their interest in Confederate currency in wartime at far under par, an arrangement that a Conservative constitutional convention, a Republican state supreme court, and legislatures controlled by both parties had denounced as wrong in equity as well as law. The companies remained adamant. They stalled on payment, denied the authorities' right to collect, and forced court appeals. In 1874, seven roads, including the New Orleans, Jackson & Great Northern and the Mississippi Central, compounded the offense by refusing to pay the taxes assessed against them. Such obstinacy, as the governor had warned one railroad president, did nothing to soothe an enraged public.[19]

In other states, there were variations on the pattern in Mississippi and Alabama, though the basic outlines remained the same: the corporations brought themselves into the public eye in an unfavorable way. Florida's attorney general issued a report undermining the largest grant that Republicans had put through. Under the law aiding the Jacksonville, Pensacola & Mobile, he announced, the company was duty-bound to pay Florida's interest on state bonds it had received. The government, in turn, would pay that interest to the bondholders. The money would come out of a sinking fund taken from the road's net earnings. As it turned out, the line had no net earnings. The bonds had been misapplied and sold at preposterous discounts. The government did not have to pay its own funds for interest on the subsidy bond; this was so only because the company had used the bonds' principal to fill that need, instead of using the money for construction.[20]

In Arkansas, friends of the railroads attempted a retreat from the subsidy policies of the past that turned into a political disaster. "Minstrel" Republican Chief Justice J. J. McClure and his corporate allies pressed for a bill relieving the companies of all obligation to pay interest and principal on state aid bonds received. Arkansas would take full responsibility for the $5 million issued, but would not have to give the $6 million more to which state commissioners had declared them entitled. In return for assuming this debt and enacting a three-mill tax to redeem it, the government would receive some $5 million in paid-in corporate stock. It was a good thing for the companies, certainly, but since the government had no real protection from loss on the money it had already given, and since the act would cancel over half of the commonwealth's contingent debt, it was also a good thing for the taxpayers.

That, at least, was what the "Minstrels" argued. But Governor Elisha Baxter, until now one of that faction, and many of his allies in both parties saw the proposal less charitably. "This bill is an infamous, unmitigated steal," one representative cried. "The men who support it write 'thief' upon their foreheads, and 'perjury' on their hearts. When the time shall come that I . . . shall band myself with infamy by voting for such a measure, may the children who have sprung from my loins disown me; may the mother in whose bosom I have found solace drive me from her presence." To add a tax to an overtaxed people's burdens would be political suicide, another shouted. "A war now begins between these roads and the people. Let it come. See who first dies." So fierce a struggle did the Baxter faction wage that not even bribery could sway enough legislators to the corporate viewpoint, though Senator Dorsey of the Arkansas Central did apply $200,000 to sweeten the lawmakers' tempers. Leading Minstrels even tried to buy the governor. Memphis & Little Rock officer Samuel Tate claimed that he would pay Baxter $25,000 for his support and sent a state senator to make the offer. It was refused. To save the bill, supporters amended it to drop the three-mill tax and to give the state preferred stock in the companies. The House passed the bill, the Senate returned it with amendments. Then, for two weeks a coalition of Baxter Republicans and Democrats stalled action. On the final day of the session, McClure forces tried to bring the bill to a vote and failed. The legislature adjourned in pandemonium.[21]

So badly had Louisiana been cheated that its representatives became suspicious of the most innocuous legislation. The Louisiana Central wanted a charter to lay track between New Orleans and Shreveport. Its incorporators asked for no financial backing and promised to start work within sixty days of the bill's passage. Two years before, the bill would have passed without debate, but times had changed. Foes suspected the new company of being the New Orleans, Mobile & Texas under another name and saw the charter as a ruse to save the latter's right to state aid. A tiny minority introduced resolutions to investigate or harass the directors. Day after day, dissidents used roll calls and motions to adjourn in an effort to kill the bill. One day they locked themselves in the Speaker's room and defied the sergeant at arms' attempts to summon them for a quorum call. In the end, both houses passed the bill by wide margins, but not before the minority had so enraged the chairman of the Senate Railroad Committee that he tried to resign.[22]

However high the cost, the railroads had won a series of victories, but these were the last they would win for many years. Even as they made gains in some states, the firms lost ground in others. The retreat from railroad aid had begun before 1873. In 1872, the Louisiana legislature released the state partially or completely from liability to two subsidized roads, the New Orleans, Baton Rouge & Vicksburg and the North Louisiana & Texas. More railroads would be chartered, but never again would the commonwealth subscribe stock or endorse any line's securities. The South Carolina lawmakers had quickly repented their act allowing the Blue Ridge Railroad a $1.8 million issue of state scrip. With the state supreme court behind him, the state auditor instituted a suit to keep the scrip out of circulation. A $10,000 bribe could not change either his or the governor's opinion; even venality has limits. By the time a Republican chief justice had ruled the scrip illegal in April 1873, state officers were no longer collecting taxes to pay any part of the public debt, and the General Assembly had repealed the tax provisions in the 1872 Revenue Bond Scrip Act.[23]

Florida's retreat was still more pronounced. Without dissent, the 1872 legislature passed a resolution declaring the Jacksonville, Pensacola & Mobile guilty of vast frauds and commanding the governor to issue it no more securities until the courts had ruled on the original subsidy law's constitutionality. In 1873, under pressure from Governor O. H. Hart, the legislature repealed all measures providing for railroad aid or bond endorsement. Administrative and judicial agencies furthered the flight. Abandoning a custom begun before the war, Internal Improvements fund trustees ruled that any federal swamplands given to railroads must serve the function for which they had been intended: the railroads must drain and settle them to qualify for any grants. A federal court blocked a grant under even such restrictive conditions. In the *Vose* decision, it ruled that the Internal Improvements fund already owed one claimant more public land than remained in the state's possession and ordered the fund trustees to reclaim lands already granted. The plaintiff's claims only thus could be satisfied.[24]

Elsewhere the reaction against railroad aid turned into a complete rout. North Carolina had supported construction more generously than any other Southern state, but the public enthusiasm quickly died as original promises were broken and as the state debt increased by tens of millions of dollars in a year. In one case, a county had voted for a stock subscription by a 700-vote margin. The promoters' promises were dazzling: construction without cost to taxpayers, even local affluence great enough to do away with the poll tax. Then, after the referendum, everything changed including the route of the track. The line's length nearly doubled, and with it the cost. Instead of buying horses and mules from local residents, the contractors went to Kentucky to make their purchases, "& at June Term of our county court they levied a tax of 2 dollars on the poll & 40 cts on Real Estate," an excited resident wrote the governor. They had informed the voters that a $100,000 bond issue would suffice, but with bonds sold at 61 cents on the dollar, the promoters had found themselves short of cash and vowed to sell county bonds every month until they made a full $100,000, even if it meant issuing three times that much in securities. Had there been a second referendum six months after the first, said one citizen, two-thirds of the subscription's backers would have voted differently. Friendly though Governor W. W. Holden had been to leading railroad men, by 1869 he had begun to doubt the wisdom of the subsidy policy. He helped block construction of state-owned lines and withheld $8 million in special tax bonds when there were grounds to challenge their constitutionality. As early as 1868, a few Republicans had called for an investigation and put the capital "in a blaze on the subject." If accusations proved correct, one visitor warned, "the Republican party is 'gone up'—particularly the 'Carpet Bag' portion of it."[25] A legislative majority managed to stave off any effective investigation that year, but the subject would not die.

During 1869 the issue grew more serious, as more and more Republicans broke with their leaders over the corruption around them. When the General Assembly reconvened that autumn, it chose two new investigating committees, neither of which was allowed to do much. By the time the two chambers had discharged the inquisitors, however, the need for scrutiny had already passed. Without inspection, the General Assembly had decided to abandon the program it had enacted little more than a year before. Politicians were panicking, wrote Daniel R. Goodloe. Because railroad promoter Milton Littlefield was in such bad standing, the legislature meant to abolish the office of state printer, from which he received some of his revenue. "The trouble is that everybody wants to get into the new movement." Holden and United States Senator John Pool both had afflictions of penitence, while party colleagues spoke of a thorough purge and reorganization of Republicans. State Senator George Welker offered a bill recalling all unsold securities. The act, which sailed through both houses, also repudiated any bond sale after the date of the bill's introduction. It even forced the companies to return the money realized from bond sales but not yet spent.[26]

Most legislators thought this law too lenient. Led by Senators John W. Graham and J. B. Cook, they backed a measure repealing all subsidy laws passed since the first meeting of the General Assembly in 1868. It was all but outright repudiation of the bonds already issued and sold—bonds made possible by the same lawmakers' work a year before. Inconsistent policy was political consistency itself. As before, legislators only wanted to do the popular thing. With an election approaching, they saw that the promise of low taxes would outweigh the assurance of eventual railroad development. The Senate passed the Graham-Cook bill by 32 to 3, and the House did so by 56 to 30. With that act the state did not rid itself of its obligation for bonds issued, but it did relieve itself of any right to a voice in corporate decisions on the lines it had aided with securities and stock subscriptions. Private stockholders took a liberal interpretation of the statute and concluded that they were the sole managers of the roads. They began a long and successful fight to deprive the public directors of any influence in corporate decisions.[27]

Abandonment of the railroads thus often meant that the state would surrender anything to escape responsibility. In some cases, the abnegation of any role was astonishing. The Western Railroad of North Carolina, for example, had only $142,600 in private stock. The state had subscribed $2.6 million, and the Cook act annulled only $1 million by recalling the special tax bonds financing the subscription. With public shares still outnumbering private ones by eleven to one, it would not have seemed that the government's control should have been jeopardized, but on certain technical grounds it was. Private stockholders drew up a bill restoring their original control over company affairs, and a Democratic legislature passed it overwhelmingly.[28] It was the culminating giveaway in North Carolina, but this time the Republicans had nothing to do with it.

Georgia Republicans went through the same experience of hubris and remorse. By August 1870, many Republicans were beginning to question the wisdom of state ownership of the Western & Atlantic Railroad and wondering whether a private enterprise could leave Georgia with greater profit than political hacks could assure. Too much has been written about the corruption involved in the leasing of that road to require discussion of it here. More important, however, is the tone assumed by advocates of the bill surrendering the right of management to leading Conservative politicians and businessmen. The road, in fact, had been mismanaged under the Republicans and had been a political tool for all parties. Its rates might please northern Georgians, said one legislator from a southern county. "Hundreds of them ride on it free of cost." They sold lumber, firewood, and their services to the company at prime rates. The rest of the state sustained the road with taxes. Because of partisan management, no one on the line tried to keep down costs. Managers could neither prevent corruption nor obstructions in the line's operations. Furthermore, they could not run the cars on time or bring freight as quickly as could private railroads. "Individuals and corporations can take it and make it profitable," said one Republican, "but no state government can do it, in my judgment, for what belongs to the State belongs to everybody, and everybody seems to think they have a right to finger the pie. . . . Rather than see a continuation of such demoralization and corruption I would . . . take a yard broom and at one stroke brush it out of existence."[29]

Unable to obtain a special appropriation for its repair, friends of the Western & Atlantic looked for some other means of keeping it running. Leading railroad men wanted the state to sell what Chief Justice Joseph Brown had called "this great connecting link—this key to the mountains—which unlocks the great West, and connects it with the Atlantic." For just that reason Brown, himself deeply committed to railroad enterprises, thought that Georgia should keep hold of it. When proponents of sale offered their bill in October 1870, therefore, backers of the Western & Atlantic called for a lease. They passed a bill written by the chief justice himself, promising the state legal title and a modest profit, and any businessman willing to devote himself to the line the chance to reap large gains. The governor could lease the road to as many lessees as he saw fit, but a majority must be Georgia residents of five years' standing. They must give an $8 million bond jointly, and $5 million of it must come from within the state. The governor could set any terms he chose, but no lower rent than $25,000 a month.[30] In one piece of legislation, Georgians of both parties had demonstrated their dread of outsider control and their loss of faith in the promises of public railroad policy.

That a lame-duck governor two months later used the law to enrich one syndicate of railroad men at the expense of another and gave the line to private parties at the minimum price in no way detracts from the intentions or possibilities of the original law. Indeed, perhaps the terms of sale show that the governor, too, recognized the folly of further state ownership and chose to take whatever fee he could obtain. If the General Assembly meant to protect the road for Georgia interests, Rufus Bullock's award had additional merit. The lessees included representatives of the two major railway systems emanating from Augusta and Macon, as well as the political leadership of both parties.[31]

North Carolina and Georgia not only led the way in showing Southern Republicans how to renounce state aid, but also showed why such a renunciation would be necessary. Repentance came too late for either administration. In 1870, Conservatives carried both legislatures overwhelmingly, though Klan violence and intimidation as well as outrage over public extravagance certainly explained the returns. If Republicans had hoped to translate their friendship for railroad expansion into political support, they had failed. If Bullock awarded the lease to create a coalition of moderate Republicans and Democrats sympathetic to civil rights and economic change, as has been suggested, he, too, failed. Supporters of the Western & Atlantic lease found their transaction in such disrepute that they had to spend all their energies to save the lease and none to save the governor. To escape indictment, Bullock fled the state. A Democratic investigating committee excoriated the Republicans and the methods by which Brown, Benjamin Hill, and their cohorts had obtained the lease, but their recommendation that the agreement be revoked was rejected by a Democratic legislature. In both Georgia and North Carolina, the Redeemers dismantled the political machinery connected to the railroads, partially repudiated the public debt, and talked about even more serious disavowals of railroad aid bonds in the future.[32]

If the Republican friends of railroad aid were to salvage any part of their program, therefore, they would have to make concessions. The companies would have to be called to account for the money spent and be given nothing more. Nor was this the only shift. Before 1873, the companies had been allowed to charge what they liked for freight, and trunk lines tended to favor through traffic over local. Now the governments took a deeper interest in such discrimination. Several passed laws specifically correcting it.[33]

Southern dissatisfaction could not be gauged just by what was done that year, but by what was threatened. By midsummer, even Republicans were calling for liquidation of the railroad aid policy and new constitutional barriers to bond endorsement. Men in both parties advised that the Southern debts be scaled. Debt adjustment had an ugly sound. It meant impairment of the public credit and evoked memories of antebellum repudiation. Yet that was what leading Republicans were proposing when they denied the state's duty to pay off the bonds that corrupt promoters had fobbed off on foreign accomplices. Democrats had no such qualms about using the word "repudiation." They had never believed in the Reconstruction governments' legitimacy, and now a growing number of Conservatives declared that they never would recognize the obligations contracted over the past five years. In some cases, they had the state's fundamental law on their side. The railroads' disregard of the conditions placed on their grants and the legislators' contempt for the restrictions placed on their power to give aid raised doubts about the value of subsidy bonds. In other places, Democrats did not worry much about constitutional niceties. They urged repudiation because they found the appeal popular.[34] Among landowners taxed beyond endurance, any scheme to remove a large part of the state debt was popular, however rationalized.

The growing distrust of railroad ventures and the increasing desire for repudiation had dire effects on railroad development. In April 1873, Pickens county commissioners refused to levy a local tax to redeem the coupons on their subscription to the Selma, Marion & Memphis. No one thought the subscription illegal or dishonestly obtained. Rather, the officials contended that since there was no likelihood of the project's completion in the near future, the county did not think itself honor-bound to pay its share. Sometimes a rumor was all that was needed to stop construction. The president of the Vicksburg & Nashville had made arrangements to buy 20 miles of iron with Mississippi's aid. "But before any iron had been shipped," he wrote, "Mr. Lowe, the manager of the Chattanooga mill, was informed that certain patriotic (?) gentlemen in Mississippi proposed to enjoin our State officers and prevent the delivery of the Agricultural Land Scrip Fund to our road. This fund constitutes the most available, and by far the larger portion of the aid given us by the legislature." Lowe went to Mississippi to learn the truth and found such an injunction only "talked of." That was enough. He declined to deliver the iron. As a result, the Vicksburg & Nashville ceased construction.[35]

Doubt and fear: even more than resentment or repentance, these terms characterized Southern attitudes toward railroad aid. By July 1873, the consensus for a subsidy policy had vanished, but in its place was an ambivalence. Men still invoked the railroad as the symbol of progress, still foretold excellent times for the South, and yet they spoke with more hope than conviction. It was this renewed doubt that the companies could keep their promises and fear that the state had gone too far—not the conviction that railroad aid had been wrong and should be repudiated—that pushed Reconstruction legislatures to reconsider their generosity. Nor did the Democrats cause this partial retreat, though they drove the men in power toward abandonment of Republican programs. The process was gradual, halting, inconsistent.

With the Panic of 1873, the pace would quicken, and the resentment of the railroads grow more bitter. The depression that followed would obliterate the Gospel of Prosperity and with it the chance for Republicans to form a biracial party in the South; but it should not obscure the crucial fact. Even before the Panic made railroad aid useless as an instrument of policy, the Republicans had taken the first steps to stultify their own laws.

CHAPTER 16

"Men are Giting Desperate . . .": The Panic, Collapse, and Survival of the Gospel of Prosperity, 1873–1880

You have ruined me, you fool, me and the Louisville &
Nashville Railroad Company. The railroad will not pay for
the grease that is used on its car wheels! Where are those coal
mines and those iron mines you talked so much about and
write so much about? Where are they? I look, but I see
nothing!

Albert Fink

IN 1873, lawmakers, had treated the railroad issue with a proper
ambivalence. Never had construction proceeded more rapidly—in
spots. Contractors laid more track than in any previous year: 1,137
miles in eight former Confederate states, five hundred in Texas
alone. In three states the companies broke all records for construction. But in Alabama, Virginia, and the Carolinas, building slack-
ened, while in Louisiana, Florida, and Mississippi, not one mile of
track was set down.*

Small wonder that by late summer Southern optimism about

* The figures differ on railroad construction in the South during 1873. Poor's
Manual of Railroads, 1877–1878, provides the numbers used, but the New York
Railway Monitor for December 31, 1873, had a different set of statistics. It claims
that only 847 miles were built in the Confederate states and Kentucky together. By
its statistics, Texas built only 219.7 miles during 1873 and Mississippi added 37
miles to its track. I cannot help being sceptical of its calculations. In the *Monitor* for
January 15, 1873, the editors calculated that Texas already had 1,301 miles in
operation; in its later figures the magazine put the mileage at year's end at 1,330
and declared that at the start of 1873 it had had only 1,110 miles built. North
Carolina, by year-end statistics, would seem to have fallen from 1,316 miles of track
in 1872 to 1,280 miles in 1873—yet 17 miles were built! Louisiana did not add a
single mile to its railroads during the year—yet the number fell from 568 to 560.
Alabama built 11 miles, the *Monitor* claimed, bringing its total to 1,869, or a net loss
of 20 miles since disclosure of the preceding year's statistic. All of this does not
prove the *Railway Monitor* particularly unreliable. It was respectable and conservative; so was Poor's *Manual*. It does, however, suggest the problems with gathering
even the most elementary statistics from an age when businessmen had to rely on
railroad companies' own estimates of their wealth and progress.

railroad development had given way to uncertainty and suspicion. The railroads did not seem to be prospering. Nor were most of the communities through which they ran. To keep their line running, stockholders of the Selma & Gulf met in late June to discuss the sale of their enterprise to outsiders. So close was the Selma, Marion & Memphis to bankruptcy that the *New York World* predicted that Governor David Lewis of Alabama would seize it to protect the state's investment. This rumor the governor denied. On the contrary, he wrote the company president, state officials had "the utmost confidence" in the road's success. Since bankruptcy proceedings against the line had just been dismissed and the road had paid no interest on its endorsed bonds since March 1872, Lewis's optimism was inexplicable. Arkansas citizens had a more understandable response to the failures of the Little Rock & Fort Smith, which one group implied had been arranged to extort a "bonus" from taxpayers.[1] Along with their financial strength, the companies had lost their reputations. Since the railroad boom was founded largely on faith in the promoters, this was a serious loss.

The Southern economy was no more secure than its railroad projects. "A year ago times were hard," said the *Fayetteville Democrat*, "—this year they are harder. A year ago business was dull—this year there is scarcely any business. A year ago there was a little capital and enterprise seeking investment in Arkansas—this year none." Land could be sold in 1872, the editor went on, but no one wanted to buy it now. Others glimpsed a fundamental weakness in the Southern economy: the overproduction of cotton and the failure of farmers to diversify their economy. If anything, the *Little Rock Republican* remarked, the former Confederate states were more devoted to cash crops than before the war. Then, at least every slave had had a "truck patch" with vegetables for consumption or sale. Some bondsmen owned brood sows and chickens. Modest though these cultivations were, they had a large effect that the sharecropping system diminished. Because he could add to his income through cotton planting, the tenant devoted every acre to that end. He bought his food and clothing at local stores, which, in turn, imported supplies from the North and West.[2]

Southerners could have kept their money home, had they erected cotton mills and other factories, but industrial construction had barely begun. Southerners could not diversify their economy without an abundant money supply and extensive loans. They had neither in 1873. "Very little money has been spent on permanent improvements," said one newspaper, "at least in the valley of the

Mississippi, and there has not been even an average outlay for tools, farming implements, machinery, livestock, etc. The money has gone, and already planters complain that they have nothing left to buy provisions and breadstuffs for their hands."³ With so little money of its own and so little chance of enticing Northern capital, the South had fundamental weaknesses that railroad construction had not altered. By 1873, those weaknesses were jeopardizing the section's prosperity.

The South's most fundamental economic weakness was one that the rest of the country shared, a dependence on outside capital. Because of the South's poverty, the reliance was more pronounced there than in New England and the Northeast, though it was a difference of degree and not of substance. One New York commercial publication estimated that one-third of all the money invested in American railways came from overseas. Capitalists guessed that 8,500 miles of track would be built in 1873 at a cost of $240 million; the $80 million that Europeans were expected to provide would have a significant effect on national construction.⁴

The foreign influence on American finance was all the stronger because Northerners shared the Southern faith in railroad construction. Westerners, too, spent more money than they had to lay more track than they needed. Most railroad mileage may have been well built, Wall Street observers agreed, but as one railroad journal warned, "some of it has been very bad work. At least the financial part is bad, whatever we may say about the engineering." It was a commonplace among financiers that a "safe" road would not cost much more than $30,000 a mile, and that half of its financing should come from stock subscription. These rules had been ignored. Instead, promoters relied on bond sales to meet their expenses. As a result, city bankers had more effect on construction than the people along the projected lines, and outsiders played a larger role than cautious financial practice would have permitted. Where governments could apply less tax revenue to county and state bond issues, and the people lacked the commerce needed to keep all their roads operating at a clear profit, the financial weaknesses and dependence on outsiders was all the more marked.* Yet

* Of some 33,000 miles built in the nation between 1865 and 1873, more than 80 percent was done in the West or South. The Northeast built 1,438 miles, the Middle States (including Maryland and West Virginia) laid 4,527, but the South added 5,414 miles to its mileage. From the *Railway Monitor's* financial statistics, it would seem that nearly every Southern state was below the average national ratio of railroad miles to property value. In the United States as a whole, there was one mile of railroad for every $205,907 in property values, but in Alabama it was one

no one asked what would happen if Wall Street bankers and London magnates went broke or closed their books to new investments.[5]

By the end of 1872, the question was no longer academic. Europeans had lost their taste for American investments. Prominent German bankers predicted that loans overseas, already less than expected, would not grow significantly in the new year. If progress were to continue, domestic bankers would need to make up for the loss, but this course was fraught with risk. Respected houses were already overloaded with bad securities. In their readiness to lend, firms had lowered their own reserves and were unprepared to meet sudden demands.[6] A flurry on the market would force an overextended company to suspend payment. Suspension did not always mean bankruptcy, but the one condition usually led to the other. No suspended business could keep its depositors' confidence on reopening, except under extraordinary circumstances.

An alternative suggested by the *Railway Monitor* was no better. Its editors advised the railroads themselves to make up for the decline in European investment by spending their net earnings on new construction. According to the *Monitor*'s calculations, the average line made 5 percent on its aggregate cost per year, or $175 million net earnings nationwide. Surely the companies could divert $80 million of this to develop additional roads.[7] In this hope the *Monitor* was quite mistaken. Much of the $175 million was unavailable for new construction because companies needed it for bond redemption. Many lines turning a large profit ran through states where new roads were neither needed nor desired. Companies in the states most in need of construction were least likely to do much more than cover operating expenses. By 1873, therefore, the North needed new capital as badly as did the South, and had an equally poor chance of getting it.

Indeed, almost every problem plaguing Southern railroad construction had its equivalent elsewhere in the nation. The same petty localism and anger with rate discrimination that embittered upland

---

to $84,601, in Arkansas it was one to $13,217, in Florida one to $69,552.

These figures were significant. They showed how ill equipped the Southern property holders were to sustain large railroad enterprises. Vernon, *ARM*, concluded that to support railroads in Kansas to the extent that Massachusetts did its own, citizens of Kansas would have to pay $61 per capita, or nearly five times the amount that citizens of Massachusetts paid. This was so because Kansas had fewer people and less commerce to keep the railroads running. No system that called for more than $20 per capita per year could be considered firmly established, Vernon added. Yet most Southern states were closer to Kansas than to Massachusetts in their condition.

farmers in Alabama also characterized Western farmers and merchants. From Wisconsin to Massachusetts, politicians inveighed against monopolies. Where local aid was legal, taxpayers sought constitutional restrictions against it. The same mingling of political office and private stock ownership that troubled Southerners had begun to disturb Northern voters. All of these political complications had economic effects. As railroads forfeited public confidence, their financial reputations suffered damage.[8]

The railroad boom had not come to an end in the North, but long before September 1873, shrewd investors could detect warning signs. All that spring and summer, major lines in the West defaulted on their interest payments or failed outright. Southern conditions made the national economy all the more unstable. Southern speculations, for example, had nearly ruined a few Northern financiers. One of the biggest was Henry Clews. From the first he had been among the most enthusiastic backers of Southern securities. It was he who had induced the stock exchanges in Berlin, Frankfurt, and London to carry Georgia bonds. In 1872, European bankers had procured $770,000 in that state's securities, and when the government did not pay the interest that winter, Clews bolstered the bonds' reputation by paying it himself. When Brunswick & Albany endorsed bonds were issued, the New Yorker had convinced German investors that they could make no better purchase. At his behest, they had taken up a million dollars worth at 104, while Clews' firm sold another hundred thousand dollars worth for 97½. Then Georgia repudiated its Brunswick & Albany bonds and a large part of its debt. Enraged, the committee heading the Frankfurt Stock Exchange excluded every Georgia bond issue from its market until the bondholders' claims had been met.[9] If Georgia's word could not be trusted, could that of Clews? From this blow the financier could not recover. The same may very well be true of the reputation of every other important financier who dabbled in Southern securities and put his name behind them. The investments that Collis Huntington and Thomas Scott made in Southern lines depleted them of funds that could have been reserved for special emergencies. Worse, their connection with faltering concerns reflected on their judgment and honesty.

So notorious was the history of Southern railroads that their ill fame may have had national consequences. The horror stories of peculation and mismanagement by economic carpetbaggers had not gone unnoticed in the North. If anything, the tales gained more credence and a wider circulation than they deserved. Southerners tempered their distress with a keen desire for railroad construction and the conviction that the lines would overcome their predators. Nevertheless, the Northern public shared no such hopes. For all it knew, the Alabama & Chattanooga was ruined beyond salvage, and the Southern people were in insurmountable debt. Conservatives continued to report north that state bonds had been fraudulently sold, would be repudiated, and that with repudiation the entire basis of railroad construction would vanish.[10] No wonder Northern investors grew shy! It took no leap of imagination to wonder whether the same slipshod practice that disgraced the South might exist in enterprises nearer home.

With foreign investment sharply decreased and public confidence lost, the financiers could not prevent a panic. It was swift to come. The national money supply always tightened near harvest time, but in September 1873, it was unusually so. Though Jay Cooke was the nation's foremost banker, he could not save himself. Having committed most of the banking house's ready cash to the Northern Pacific and having borrowed to the limit of his ability, Cooke was living dangerously. By September, his partner confessed later, any untoward circumstance shaking their confidence "might touch the spark to the magazine and blow us all sky-high." When the New York Warehouse and Security Company suspended payments on September 8, it struck that spark. Other respected firms with railroad investments closed their doors. The crisis spread as houses called in their loans. Then, on September 17, Jay Cooke & Co. suspended. As the official announcement of the failure was read on the Stock Exchange, there was "a monstrous yell" that "seemed to literally shake the building in which all these mad brokers were for the moment confined."[11]

The panic was on. In the ensuing pandemonium, stocks of every kind tumbled. More than four hundred thousand shares were sold that day. As the fear spread, other firms closed their doors. On September 19, twenty-five New York financial houses failed in four hours. To stave off a further fall, Exchange officers closed the boards shortly after noon. By easing the money supply, the federal government gave a little relief to the financial crisis, but Wall Street did not recover. Nor did the nation's economy.[12]

Cooke's failure was the worst of the lot for two reasons. First, the very size of his company meant that its fall brought loss to thousands of investors throughout the country. Many had entrusted their modest savings to his Northern Pacific because they could not imagine its failure. Financiers, too, had been ruined by their faith in Cooke. Where he went, lesser businessmen were likely to follow. His loss meant theirs. Second, Cooke's house had a prestige that no other firm possessed. If Cooke could suspend payments, what business was safe? If his projects could not prosper, what venture could? Investors in other companies must have asked these questions. In their doubt, they withdrew the support they had for railroads and brought on the fate they dreaded, financial insolvency. It was no coincidence that so many banks clearly tied to the railroads were among those that fell. Even the Union Trust, with its connections to Commodore Vanderbilt, could not survive its reputation as a supporter of several unprofitable roads.

Bankers tried to see the Panic as a fit of financial hysteria, but their wish was father to the thought. Perhaps the Panic occurred not because the public had lost its faculty of reflection, but because it had regained it. No financier would have liked to consider that possibility, for it would have been an admission that the whole railroad boom had been founded on ignornace and error. But Cooke's failure was not just a fluke. It was something inevitable, as long as financiers habitually overextended themselves and looked to a swift profit from a road that usually paid only in the long run. There was nothing irrational in discerning that a railroad bond would not pay off quickly, unless the area through which the line ran filled up quickly with people, and unless construction was done at the lowest possible cost. It was no distortion of reality to see the chance, even the probability, of a new road's failure when the company relied on first-mortgage bonds, watered stock, and blind faith. The Panic was not so much a sign of creditors losing their reason as a sign that they had spotted a clear and present danger that promoters had concealed from them earlier.

That was why this Panic was unlike that of 1869. Then, Wall Street had regained its poise after a few days of agitation. The country had been unaffected. This time, the upheaval continued long after the Panic ended. By the end of 1873, 4,183 businesses with a total capitalization of $228,499,000 had closed their doors.[13] Railroads continued to suspend interest payments. Money supplies continued to tighten. Factories closed. That winter the unemployed took to the streets in New York and had to be dispersed by the police. Railway construction did not end, but it became more difficult to carry on anywhere, and impossible to further where the return was least certain. Certainly, foreign bankers had lost their taste for development in areas where meager private support and limited industrial production made railroad construction a gamble.

"In the human organism, growth, to be safe, requires intermission and rest," the *Railway Monitor* preached, "that the gristle may harden into bone. Something like this is true of the social organism."[14] Indeed it was, but the appeal for a pause could not have pleased Southerners, many of whom had placed their hopes for prosperity on roads now farther from completion than they had been a year before.

Clews, Cooke, and Huntington had enmeshed institutions across the South in their operations, not the least victims of which were the freedmen's savings banks. When the Cookes fell, the freedmen's banks had to suspend payment as well. Other Cooke affiliates in the South collapsed too. Branches of other New York houses suspended payments, while banks across the South tried to save themselves by calling in their loans and cutting back on credit. This crisis could not have come at a worse time for the cotton trade. "The lack of Money to pay for Cotton has caused our Cotton business to fall down suddenly to almost nominal," R. H. Hardaway wrote from Savannah. The *Alabama State Journal* reported one sale of fifty bales at less than 15 cents a pound, "which was the top of the market. What will become of our planters, who have mortgaged lands, crops, mules, and everything, and now will not receive enough to pay the expense of raising a moderately good crop, much less so small a crop as they have made this year?" Farmers were reported to be taking their cotton to small towns outside of Alabama's capital and selling it for any price it could bring. Other businesses felt the Panic badly. So tight was the money supply in Pensacola that the mills began to discharge hands because there was no currency for wages. By the end of November, Jacksonville reported all but two factories closed.[15]

In some towns, Southerners found palliatives to revive credit. Neither city scrip nor loan certificates could bring the South the permanent legal tender it needed so badly. Only an act of Congress could have done that, but President Grant vetoed such an act when it passed in April 1874. The Panic deepened into a full industrial depression in the South. By 1875, unemployment in New Orleans threatened some five thousand families with starvation. The city could not afford to give them all relief, though it sent two thousand men, women, and children into the rural parishes to work on the plantations. Factories closed everywhere, and foundries worked on half-time. Dwellings fell vacant or were put up for sheriff's sale. Credit facilities continued to close their doors. A bank might have title to dozens of plantations, but these assets were as bad as liabilities in a time when land values were decreasing. Because credit was so tight, agriculture languished. Planters sought the customary spring advances and were rebuffed. Agricultural laborers' wages were cut sharply. Those tenants who labored for a share of the final crop found that their work brought them far less than in years past. Cotton hands, despairing of improvement or a decent wage, left Alabama for the Mississippi bottomlands and Texas; there, they found conditions no better. Because farmers had had to cut back on supplies ordered from the towns, grocers and suppliers found themselves overstocked and underpaid.[16]

The catastrophe cut deep into railroad revenues. In prosperous times, Albert Fink of the Louisville & Nashville had been persuaded that his company would profit hugely from control of the South & North Alabama. The Panic made him realize the truth. Meeting the South & North's engineer on the street, Fink shouted, "You have ruined me, you fool, me, and the Louisville & Nashville Railroad Company. The railroad will not pay for the grease that is used on its car wheels! Where are those coal mines and those iron mines you talked so much about and write so much about? Where are they? I look, but I see nothing!"[17]

Certainly, no promoter could look northward for rescue now. "I am appalled and see nothing but ruin ahead," one employee wrote the president of a Georgia line. "Fly as rapidly from New York as Lot did from Sodom, things look equally as bad." That was how matters stayed. Southern railroads had done poorly in good times and dismally in bad. Within a month of Cooke's fall, sixteen roads with over two thousand miles of track were in default. A year later, the number had risen by ten and by 1876, another 29. One historian has estimated that 43 precent of all Southern mileage had gone into receivers' hands by 1876. In Virginia, Florida, Alabama, Arkansas, and Kentucky, half or more of the lines defaulted. Even these figures understate the debacle, since many roads on one list of failures were reorganized and did not appear the following year. In all, twenty-five major lines passed into receivership in the 1870s, affecting 6,056 miles of track. Many others were able to survive from day to day on expedients. "This Company has had to this writing an awful time," R. H. Hardaway wrote of the Atlantic & Gulf. "So far, we have kept our heads above water, but we have not reached land yet and dont [*sic*] know if we shall: Times are gloomy and squally and begin to look worse daily"[18]

Times were especially "squally" for the larger beneficiaries of Republican railroad aid. No roads had been more essential to the

Alabama improvements program than the Alabama & Chattanooga, the Mobile & Montgomery, the South & North, and the Selma, Rome & Dalton. All defaulted except the third. South Carolina had hoped for Western connections through the Port Royal line and the Greenville & Columbia. Both roads defaulted. Even the conservatively run South Carolina could not pay its bond interest. Elsewhere the same misfortunes prevailed. The Western North Carolina, the Brunswick & Albany, the Little Rock & Fort Smith, the Cairo & Fulton, the Macon & Brunswick, the Mobile & Ohio, and the Jacksonville, Pensacola & Mobile—all had shared in government largess, but all failed. Other lines had received the promise of state aid. Then, with the Panic, they found that they lacked the means to build and had to let their grants lapse.[19] Clearly, railroad subsidies had spurred construction, but had not made hardy corporations.

Even the largest railroad concerns could not sustain their Southern investments. No enterprise was better equipped for construction of trunk lines than Thomas Scott's Pennsylvania Railroad. Lucrative subsidiary lines through the Middle Atlantic states gave his company the funds to make up moderate losses in the South, but the losses proved more than moderate. By 1873, the Southern Railway Securities Company, with thirteen roads between Memphis, Baltimore, and Atlanta, was foundering. Late in the year, the company's directors met in emergency session to seek remedies and replace its president. A Pennsylvania Railroad stockholders' investigating committee called on Scott to abandon his Southern ventures. The holding company began to reconsider its purchases. It gave up its lease on the Memphis & Charleston, then began to liquidate other holdings. By 1876, the Southern Railway Securities Company had cut its capital stock in half. To escape the burden of the roads, it willingly sold stock in subsidiary lines at a loss of nearly $3 million.[20]

Other vast concerns found that Southern roads had worked the same hardship on them. H. S. McComb had managed the New Orleans, Jackson & Great Northern and the Mississippi Central as a trunk line from the Gulf to the Ohio River, but he could not make a sufficient profit to pay the bonded debt and still make improvements. The Illinois Central offered help, but with the Panic, the consolidated road's gross earnings fell to less than that of either of the two former roads. With a debt of $21,391,000, the trunk line could hardly pay the interest due; it fell months behind on workers' wages. By May 1875, merchants had begun to refuse

McComb's employees any more credit. At last, in 1876, the Illinois Central forced foreclosure and receivership.[21]

The most obvious of the many reasons for Southern railroads' failure was their inability to make enough to pay off a bonded debt that had been too big to begin with. Most Southern railroads had three dollars or more in bonded debt for every two dollars in capital stock, whereas in the rest of the United States the ratio was more nearly even. This meant that Southerners' interest payments weighed more heavily than those in the rest of the country. The roads could not make enough revenue to outweigh this special burden. Usually their operating expenses were heavy, sometimes requiring two-thirds or more of gross receipts. Unlike Northern lines, which could afford to pay dividends out of net earnings, Southern firms almost never could declare a dividend. Roads with net earnings no greater than 5 percent of their total funded debt could hardly pay the bond interest due, which varied between 6 percent and 12 percent. To make up for their deficits, they might take out special loans and add to their obligations, but the depression in the North and abroad made such loans nearly impossible to arrange.[22] Many roads had been jerry-built. Others were badly run. The more it cost the company to construct and operate a line, the greater the possibility that the enterprise would go into receivership.

In the general debacle, Southern-controlled roads did better than those in outsiders' hands. One historian examining eighteen roads that escaped receivership in the 1870s found that only ten of their 174 directors were Northerners; the twenty-five major lines that did fail had 71 Northerners among their 252 directors. Five major lines paid dividends regularly up to 1873. Not one Northerner sat on their boards. Did outsiders, then, lack Southern efficiency in railroad operations? Perhaps they lacked the expertise in dealing with local conditions affecting railroad construction that natives had. But there are better explanations. Roads with Southern management tended to have been established before the war, and they relied less heavily on outside capital. With a larger ratio of capital stock to bonded debt, these companies did not need to pay as much in net earnings for interest. Also, Northern control meant Northern dependence. When a New York sponsor failed, he could bring down the road with which he was involved. When Brown, Lancaster & Co. of Baltimore failed, for example, its suspension ended construction on the Savannah & Memphis. Even with three major Southern companies guaranteeing the Savannah & Memphis against default, European investors would not take its bonds at any price.[23]

Not all the efficiency in the world nor the soundness of the enterprise could make up for the tightness of capital north of the Mason-Dixon line.

Indeed, though Southern construction proved unprofitable for the Scotts and McCombs, Northern penetration actually accelerated. When lines went into receivership, outsiders held the first-mortgage bonds and used their holdings to force bankruptcy or reorganization. Either result was in their interest. At public sales of the roads, Northerners might have money to buy; Southerners did not. Of the twenty-five major defaulting lines in the South, only six remained in natives' hands by 1879. By 1883, outsiders ran them all. Roads already lost to local control before the Panic remained lost. Memphis, Louisville, and Nashville businessmen extended their activities into the Republican South. The Richmond & Danville bought or built lines to Atlanta, while Henry B. Plant established a network throughout the Southeast. Sam Tate's interests spread from Texas to North Carolina and south to Alabama, while the Georgia Central augmented its influence in neighboring commonwealths.[24]

For this result supporters of railroad aid had been indirectly responsible. Their subsidies may have delayed outsiders' efforts to obtain absolute control of the Southern railway system, but as Republicans dismantled their programs and sought to free the states from debt, they opened the section to Northern entrepreneurs more than ever. On the other hand, Radicals' retreat made it all the more difficult for Southern directors to obtain credit from Southern sources. Northerners had money to offer when the worst of the depression had passed, but they drove particularly hard terms. The annulment of state aid securities furthered the process of corporate collapse and reorganization.

Reorganization usually canceled much or all of the local stockholders' interest. Then the bondholders would get preferred shares and a voice in company affairs in exchange for their old securities; new bonds could be issued to whomever was prepared to buy. At the same time, Southern governments wanted to escape their contingent debts at any cost. Therefore, they surrendered their liens in return for a release from past commitments, sold off state holdings, and annulled the subsidy bonds. In doing so, they gave up their influence in railroad management and increased the importance of the private bondholders, most of whom were outsiders. More than before, the railroads were run to serve the interests of cities outside of the cotton South, even at the expense of the communities which had first put money into them.

The depression, then, did not alter patterns of railway construction and control as much as it strengthened certain trends already visible. The postwar Southern economy had always been weak; it now grew weaker. The railroads had been at the mercy of Northern money markets and ambitious businessmen from the start. Hard times made outsider support all the more crucial. Prosperous companies had always favored consolidation and expansion of influence. Now poverty and receiverships made their ambitions easier to realize. New companies and those relying on public financing had never had an easy time remaining solvent. Now they found the pressure to cease construction, default on bond interest, and sell out to other companies almost irresistible.

In Southern politics, too, the depression simply gave a new impetus to movements already well underway—but they were movements which boded ill for the internal improvements policy and the Republican party. Railroad aid lost its meaning; suddenly it became clear to most Southerners that with or without state support, the roads could not be built. Now the tax revolt became irresistible. Costly government became politically impossible, and railroads lost much of the support they still kept. Out of this change in emphasis the Republicans reshaped their vision of the Gospel of Prosperity one last time.

A year before the Panic, Southern taxpayers were complaining that their burden was too great. Republican leaders argued that taxes were not as heavy as they seemed; that property assessments did not match real values; that payment in depreciated auditors' warrants and scrip at par value made the cost to the taxpayers less than it appeared on the books, that an efficient and active government needed a large revenue, that, if anything, the governments had underfunded important programs, that landowners' real objections lay in their increased share of the taxes and not in the tax rate itself, and finally, that a higher tax rate would help redistribute property. They were quite correct, but Conservatives were just as correct when they charged that rates had never been higher, that assessments in many states approached real values or even exceeded them, that depreciated warrants often were hard to find, and, most of all, that the taxes were more than an impoverished section could afford to pay. Critics did not need to use their own sources to back these contentions. Republican governors corroborated the charge that Southerners were paying too much. Besides a state tax, citizens paid their taxes to the county, sometimes to the city, and usually to the school fund; there might be a poll tax as well. A Southerner paying thirty to fifty dollars before the war could find himself paying $700 ten years after. Even in 1872, a prosperous year with a lower tax assessment than before or after, 2,900 acres were sold at public auction in Orangeburg County.[25]

The Panic and depression added to Southern dissatisfaction. Property values often fell sharply, but taxes and assessments did not. Agricultural receipts declined and with them the ability to pay what was due on the lands. Increasingly the states were forced to seize and sell private estates large and small. Not one acre had been forfeited for taxes in Anderson county, South Carolina in 1873, and only two acres in 1874, but by December of the following year, the sheriff's sale was doing a thriving business. In one South Carolina county in May 1874, nearly four thousand acres went up for public bidding. In another, nearly fourteen thousand acres were sold, and in a third, almost twenty thousand. In one week, over two thousand pieces of Charleston real estate fell to the government for nonpayment of taxes. By January 1875, Mississippi held 4.5 million acres forfeited for the same reason, and the state board of levee districts held another 1.5 million. This added up to one acre in every five in the commonwealth.[26]

Well might officeholders feel concern. By late 1873, the tax issue had become the hottest topic in the South. Tax resistance mounted in Mississippi, Louisiana, and South Carolina. In South Carolina, property holders called a taxpayer's convention to publicize their grievances. State tax unions translated complaints into political action. Taxpayers also met in convention in Mississippi in 1874 to decry the cost of Republican administration to the people.[27]

Historians have treated the conventions as a Conservative ploy, and this view cannot be wholly discounted. The enemies of Reconstruction did hope to ride popular discontent into office. Yet the men heading the movement had every right to feel concern about the tax rates, and they did their best to make the movement apolitical. Congressman George C. McKee, Republican, described the Mississippi manifesto as the ablest paper he had seen in that state for years. He urged the legislature to heed the protectors' pleas. "The evil is too enormous." In South Carolina, important Republicans served in the convention and went to deliver its petition to Congress. J. G. Thompson, editor of the *Port Royal Commercial and Beaufort Republican*, addressed the delegates. He was a Radical, he told them, and proud of it. It was for this reason that he wished the tax revolt well and hoped that it would attract widespread Negro support. "That movement which does not seek aid from the honest part of the Republican leaders and the votes of colored and white members of that party, will assuredly fail." Other Republicans echoed Thompson's appeal even when they remained aloof from the movement itself. Congressman Robert B. Elliott praised the convention for "seeking to do the work which it was the duty of the Republican party to have accomplished." Blacks must lead the reformers, he said, to prove to the North that they were fit for the suffrage.[28]

In their zeal, Radicals could be just as implacable foes of government expense as the most conservative businessman. No Conservative could have spoken more fiercely, nor gone beyond the Republican county convention's pledge to remedy "by every means in our power" the present evil of taxation. The convention demanded biennial legislative sessions, abolition of certain court systems, and even repeal of the registration law which protected Republican voters. Republicans sincerely meant their appeal for austerity. More than the rich property holder, the poor man of either race needed tax relief. It was he whom the Reconstruction coalition claimed to represent. Every dollar that the employer or landowner paid the government was just one less that he could give his workers in wages and one more he would extract from his tenants in rent and prices for supplies advanced. So poor were most Republicans that even a small tax was beyond their means. Every dollar should have been sacred to party leaders, said the *Columbia Union-Herald*. "It is part of the life and labor of the poor Republicans; it is part of their bread and meat." At worst, the taxes forced small landowners to turn tenant, as sheriffs' sales claimed their property. Thus it was not surprising that party members should announce, "We will by no means consent to argue the question of the reduction of taxes with salaried office-holders, who have no right to be heard in defense of wrongs in which they alone are benefitted."[29]

This bipartisan tax revolt meant death for railroad legislation. Rash the legislator who would propose a subsidy for any line or to ask an addition to the current public debt. A longtime friend of railroad aid, the Republican paper in Vicksburg changed its views as the local tax rate rose. The editor announced of two projects that neither the city nor county should grant another dollar in subsidy or loan. Even without this new burden, local taxpayers were irate enough to sweep the current administration from office and

use armed force to take control of the legal system.[30] Southerners
were also ready to repudiate their debts, if they could not cut
expenses any other way. By 1874, respected businessmen had found
theoretical backing for their refusal to pay legal obligations. Since
the property of the citizen had moral rights paramount to those
of the corporate creditor, said one New Orleans committee, the
state had the right to disregard its pledges, however constitutional
the law under which the aid had been given. Such a doctrine—that
if the people were reluctant to pay their railroad debts, that reluctance gave them the right to repudiate—was revolutionary. It was
also popular.[31] Such rationalizations were hardly necessary, for
irregularity in the way the aid laws had been written, enforced, and
passed made the repudiators' job easy. Nor would the Southerners
have stooped to rationalizations had the railroad aid policy been
all that it had been promised. Whatever the reasoning behind it,
the pressure to repudiate public debts grew stronger with the
depression and the default of so many railway corporations.

The Reconstruction governments could not withstand public
pressure. None of them actually repudiated their debts, but they
"scaled" them, and that was the same thing to a lesser degree. In
Louisiana, Governor Kellogg appointed a committee of citizens to
scrutinize the public debt. It reported that a constitutional amendment limiting the debt to $25 million had made every act appro-
priating money since December 1870 null and void. Another $13
million in contingent liabilities created before that date was invalid
because the railroads receiving such aid had not met the statutory
conditions imposed upon them. The committee advised the state
to annul its $2.5 million bond issue for a stock subscription to the
New Orleans, Mobile & Texas as well. By these steps, a debt estimated at $53 million could be trimmed to as little as $12 million.
A pliant General Assembly passed a funding act consolidating and
reducing Louisiana's debt. Holders of valid securities could trade
them for new consolidated bonds at 60 cents on the dollar. The
measure had the support of the New Orleans Chamber of Commerce and the antagonism of Northern railroad investors, who
protested that the act endangered their holdings in New Orleans,
Mobile & Texas state aid bonds. So it did: that was one of the act's
purposes. To make their aims clearer, the legislators later passed
a bill forbidding the board of liquidation to fund any of the $14
million in "questionable and doubtful obligations of the State" until
the state supreme court had ruled them legal. The offensive issues
included nine different contingent liabilities for railroad compa-

nies. In 1876, a Republican high court validated most of the bonds promised to enterprises other than railroads, but declared the $2.5 million stock subscription illegal. Both parties supported the debt adjustment. "All are repudiators," said one resident. ". . . The negroes especially are in favor of the repudiation of all State debts."[32] Many citizens clamored for still more "adjusting."

South Carolina officials made a similar retreat. So reluctant were Republican authorities to pay the bonded debt that Morton, Bliss & Co. of New York finally took the state comptroller to court. It won a decision forcing the General Assembly into special session to pass a new tax for bond redemption. But South Carolinians would not stand new burdens, and the lawmakers knew it. "Are we to pay a thirty mill tax this fall?" the *Beaufort Republican* asked. "If so, there will be an emigration in the spring." The special session stripped the comptroller of his power to collect taxes and made the court's writ of mandamus unenforceable. With state bonds selling for 15 cents on the dollar, the legislature passed a law consolidating all old liabilities and issuing new securities in their place. Republicans voided nearly $6 million in "conversion bonds" and forbade enactment of any tax to pay interest or principal on any bonds except the ones created under its most recent act. It allowed bondholders to exchange their old securities for new ones at the rate of two for one.[33] With "frugality" the watchword of the party, there was no place for new railroad subsidies, and none reached a third reading in either house.

Florida's retreat from railroad aid also turned into a rout. The 1874 legislature did away with special legislation by passing a general incorporation bill. Another measure compelled railroad companies to make annual tax returns on their property's total value. There had only been one railroad subsidy issue negotiated, the $4 million given to the Jacksonville, Pensacola & Mobile in exchange for the same amount in company securities. In 1876, a Republican state supreme court ruled the bond issue unconstitutional. "This *swapping*," it commented acidly, ". . . is certainly a new idea begotten by those who believe . . . that it only requires a sufficient number of legislative votes to do anything." The judges freed the state from all obligation to pay and transferred the state's lien to Dutch bondholders. Three years later, the United States Supreme Court upheld the decision. Since the railroad had been bought from the state with a bad check, the government retained its prior lien on the road and was given the right to sell it at auction. In 1882, it did so.[34]

At the same time, Republicans in all three states made sure that future governments would never make the same mistakes. Florida legislators offered constitutional amendments establishing the state's right to tax corporate property and forbidding the use of public credit for any individual or corporation's benefit. South Carolina's General Assembly ratified an amendment which made endorsements and loans of credit conditional on a referendum in which two-thirds of all qualified voters supported such aid. In effect, this made a subsidy impossible. Louisiana legislators proposed constitutional amendments to reduce the state debt to $15 million, scale the bonds, and limit tax rates to 12½ mills. All of these proposals were ratified in 1874.[35]

Thus, in Florida, Louisiana, Arkansas, Alabama, Mississippi and the Carolinas, Republicans either wrote restrictions on aid into the Reconstruction constitutions and went on to tighten them, or else retreated from their subsidy policy and made aid more difficult in the future. Texas Republicans outdid Democrats in their defense of the public credit. By 1874, the railroad issue no longer made any difference; that is, neither party wanted to be responsible for the expense. Both wanted to demonstrate their fiscal austerity

Between this new frugality and the tightening of money markets, railroads found construction difficult to continue. Statistics show the close link between mileage built and the support that Northern financiers and Southern governments could give. In 1873, Arkansas laid 250 miles of track. Early in 1874, Governor Baxter put the aid bonds' constitutionality into question. Not one mile was put down in 1874, only 40 in 1875, 27 in 1876, none in 1877. Alabama began its retreat from railroad aid two years before the Panic. Railroad construction had peaked in 1871, just as Conservatives began their attacks on existing legislation. In 1872, new mileage decreased by more than half. In 1874, only 60 miles were built. That winter, further repealing of aid laws began. A Democratic debt commission and constitutional convention finished the "adjustment" in 1875. Only 18 miles were built that year, none in 1876, and only 1 in 1877. Texas expanded its constitutional powers to aid construction in 1872, and the next legislative session gave liberal land grants. Five hundred miles of track were laid in 1873. Fiscal conservatism followed, and with it cutbacks in construction: 72 miles in 1874, and 35 in the year after. Georgia repudiated only gradually. The year before Democrats began the process, railroad construction was at its height. In 1872, it fell to 52 miles, and in 1873 contractors set down no more than one hundred. The 1874 legislature repealed most of the aid laws benefiting several dozen railroads. Over the next two years, promoters laid 4 miles of track. Louisiana gave no aid after 1871, and building came to a halt. Between 1873 and 1877, South Carolina added only 33 miles to its network. Thus railroad aid had been dropped from the litany of the Gospel of Prosperity.[36]

Indeed, one should not have expected it to survive in any terms. The Republicans had stultified themselves by pronouncing their own internal improvements policies a failure. They had cut back on the South's public debts and in some states had tried to reduce taxation. No longer could they fund sweeping programs of any kind to foster commerce and industrial growth. Their own statements confessed how little they had achieved. No Conservative could have bettered Governor Kellogg's announcement that Louisiana could no longer afford to give levees even the scant attention they had hitherto received, that the bayous and streams had become clogged with drift, that financial weakness kept the state from opening public schools to thousands of children, that in one parish alone sixty-five plantations had gone to the block for nonpayment of taxes over the past year.[37]

Yet the Gospel of Prosperity lived. Its rhetorical flourish still rang through Republican doctrine. Considering the hard times afflicting the South in 1874, one is baffled on encountering a Louisiana lawmaker's peroration:

When this measure passes, the banks of the river will be whitened with cotton, the levees sweetened with sugar, printing presses will multiply, and school houses be established in every ward in our country parishes; then will the pure gospel of peace and good will to men be preached in every church and practiced in every family, and then will Louisiana become what she ought to be—the garden spot of America! then shall we stand together, shoulder to shoulder, and exclaim, Happy, happy, proud Louisiana! thine is the higher law, and thine the consecrated home of liberty!

The talk was buncombe, of course, but more interesting than its silliness is how many of the old elements of the Gospel of Prosperity were present. The hope of unimaginable prosperity and social progress from passage of an economic measure—the belief that only through affluence did the South find peace and order—that only through production and profit did the black man's rights remain secure: these lived on.[38] What had changed was the means by which this millennium could be realized. The legislator did not defend railroad aid, but a funding act, which would cut government expenses, repudiate portions of the public debt, limit the taxing power, and eliminate the subsidy program. Here was a different concept of prosperity: that the government serving the economy best was one that taxed and interfered the least. No less than railroad aid had been, retrenchment was made *the* panacea for all the South's ills.

For railroad aid the new gospel had no place at all. As one of the defenders of fiscal austerity, the *New Orleans Republican* suddenly discovered that it had never favored the New Orleans, Mobile & Texas subsidy. "We have always regarded it as the most impudent system of swindle ever perpetrated," said the editor, "and trust it will receive no encouragement here or elsewhere." Instead, Republican platforms lauded party members for cutting state budgets. The South Carolina convention pronounced against "local and special legislation . . . whenever private interests can be protected under general laws." Like other Republicans central committees, it promised further tax relief to the agricultural interest, biennial legislative sessions, item vetoes, and scrutiny of departmental expenditures. South Carolina delegates even went on record against their own agricultural lien law and in favor of convict-leasing.[39] Now Republicans put the taxpayer before the promoter and the agricultural interest before the commercial or industrial interest.

Having fettered state spending, Republicans called for federal support more loudly than ever. Louisiana's funding bill made extensive repairs on the levees impossible. Yet, said the administration organ downstate, everyone knew that the commonwealth's prosperity depended on holding back the river. The general government must act. Other Southerners called for national river and harbor legislation, reciprocal trade pacts with South America, government-run packet lines to Caribbean ports, and even annexation of tropical isles as a cure for financial sluggishness. Never had Republicans lobbied more diligently for the Texas & Pacific Railway project or for expansion of the nation's money supply. Their pleas were useless.[40]

Republicans could change their arguments, but it was too late to change the mood of the white South. Their failure to bring prosperity made their version of the Gospel of Prosperity politically suspect. Certainly, it had not reconciled white property owners to government by a party that permitted Negro officeholding and depended on black suffrage. By mid-1874, there was widespread despair about the chances of restoring Southern prosperity. "The old men are helpless, crying, 'what can we do?' " a New Yorker wrote. "The young men are violent, rude and uneducated. Everybody feels that this is the era of disaster and despair."[41]

Impoverished by circumstances beyond his control, a reputable man could do very disreputable things. One venerable gentleman wrote Louisiana's governor that Radical debt adjustments had ruined him and robbed him of honor in the eyes of Northern creditors. Someone's "clothing will have to stand such a blackpot washing and no white scouring, that none ever have received the like in this country," he warned. "Men are giting desperate, and you Sir! must not be surprised if some of the Banditti who have and are yet Plundering & Blackmailing the People out of every copper they have left will be forced to run the Intian Geuntled [*sic*] before long. . . ." Even as the governor read the letter, white Southerners were preparing such an "Intian Geuntled" for their foes. Dr. Thomas Cottman saw the situation most clearly. A moderate Conservative, he expressed concern at the militance of young whites in Louisiana. Almost all of them lacked employment. "They attribute this state of things to the general ruin produced by carpetbag rule," he explained. "They are ready for any emergency. The present pall over business has not existed for more than six months and yet their despair is driving the young men of the South to extremes which may end very disastrously for reconstruction."[42]

Cottman was not talking about a tax revolt, but a war of the races. He saw that the economic debacle to which the Republicans and the railroad policy had contributed was responsible for the impending conflict. Moreover, he expected the outbreak soon. "I think the crisis will occur about September next, he said. "It is sure to come, in my opinion, as that the sun will rise."

The doctor's prognosis was correct to the last detail. Between 1873 and 1876, the Reconstruction coalition was broken beyond repair by a coalition of taxpayers and terrorists, the danger of which became starkly clear in September 1874 when the Louisiana White Leagues, paramilitary Conservative groups dedicated to white supremacy and retrenchment, overthrew the Kellogg government. The federal government reinstated the ousted officials. However, it could not revive the party's fortunes, and allowed other, slightly less overt uprisings to succeed rather than commit troops to Southern administrations.

Ostensibly, the change in Southern politics had little to do with the railroad issue. Plan though the Republicans might for a New

South, it seemed that the Old South, the society of planters and prejudices, had beaten them. Yet, in another sense, the failure of the Gospel of Prosperity had everything to do with the Redeemers' triumph. The failure of the aid policy, the financial damage it did to the Southern governments, the feelings of neglect it had engendered among the blacks, and the Conservatives' acceptance of the basic tenets of the Gospel—all forced issues of retrenchment and race to take the place of those which Republicans had exploited. By its own weaknesses, made worse by the Gospel of Prosperity, the Republican party made repeal of its program possible. The Reconstruction coalition collapsed inwardly when it could no longer use the economic issue; when it became what it had professed to be from the start, that is, the party of human rights and Union sympathies, it became far more vulnerable. Then it perished ignobly.

Republicans contributed directly to the renascence of the race issue in 1873–1874. Instead of dodging the question, the party in power championed human rights as never before. It pressed for state and federal civil rights laws, strengthened existing statutes, and applauded its judges for rulings in favor of equality in public accommodations. Party leaders did so for many reasons that this study cannot discuss in depth; perhaps they saw the 1872 election returns as a sign that advances could be safely made; they claimed and may have believed that the race issue had faded from Southern politics. Probably they were afraid of losing the black vote. Evidence abounded that freedmen were becoming disenchanted with their leaders, many of whom, as one black remarked, did nothing to protect voting rights while they bargained with "railroad monopolists." Indeed, railroads epitomized the injustices done to freedmen. Most companies practiced blatant discrimination in accommodations. White lawmakers had refused to link financial support of the lines to racial justice, and the injustice festered in Republican ranks. Fusion movements had failed in 1870 and 1872, but how could the Republican leadership wave the specter of slave owner domination and hold blacks in line, if the party catered to businessmen and planters while slighting Negro rights? Whatever their reasons, Republicans seriously miscalculated. The debates over civil rights bills brought into plain view racial differences and resentments inside the party.[43]

Democrats responded more furiously still, the more so because their attempts to break Republicans' hold on the black vote seemed so unsuccessful. Moderate Conservatives had muted the race issue and only added to white voters' apathy. Nor did moderate councils hold any longer. Although Democrats might grudgingly accept universal suffrage, they balked at steps toward social equality. Suddenly there seemed to be a clear and present danger to the white South, just as the property-holding Southerner was wondering what all his acquiescence in the Republican subsidy policy had given him.

Economic and race issues merged. Inevitably, a discussion of hard times became a discussion of politics; Republican railroad aid had helped assure that; Republican promises that their policies would enrich the South had made prosperity a political issue. Naturally, a conversation on politics turned into a discourse on the "damned nigger" and his misgovernment. To meet this new disaffection, Conservatives shifted their strategy. Where it made good political sense, they would talk in favor of a biracial coalition against the Radicals; but white supremacists would set the tone on the state level. Moderates were brought to heel—for the white-liner revolution was aimed as much at bringing Conservative party leaders around as it was to topple Republican officials. One Democratic candidate for the Alabama legislature had accepted black testimony as mayor of Mobile. Consequently, his constituents forced him to do public penance for it. Newspapers that opposed the white line were disciplined.

Familiar though the racial rhetoric sounded, white supremacist dogma had changed since 1868, and not just in its reluctant acknowledgment of the freedmen's right to vote. Instead, Conservatives could use the experience of the past six years to make an economic argument against Negro rule. As white-liners saw it, blacks had proven their unfitness to govern by their mismanagement of the Southern economy. Republicanism had hurt not just the white man, but the black; if the freedmen knew their true interests, white-liners insisted, they, too, would vote Conservative. Leading Conservatives agreed with scalawags that public schools should be built, that immigration, industry, and, above all, railroads should be encouraged. But Republicans had not furthered these ends and could not. Conservative rule would bring about the Negro's economic improvement, White Leaguers argued. "White men of Louisiana!" the *Shreveport Times* exhorted readers. "Look around you and behold the ruin of the State; look at its deserted fields, its decaying sugar and gin houses; look at your thousands of fellow-citizens on the verge of famine; think of your immense State debt, and nothing to show for it."[44] Change a word here and there, and the indictment might have done any Republican proud in 1867.

The combination of race and economics into one issue made excellent political sense because it allowed nuance. In white counties, editors could show that economic hardship had proven blacks unfit to govern and the enemies of the white race. In black counties, Conservatives could emphasize the poverty all around them, and make the issue more one of a failure of leadership, a failure which men of either race should avenge. In addition, orators found that crowds responded as enthusiastically to the issue of hard times and high taxes as to white supremacist doctrine. The issue was all the more powerful because the South retained much of its faith in railroads as a means of insuring industrial and agricultural development. Conservatives insisted that by removing Republicans, Southerners might revive outside capitalists' faith in sectional prospects. Thus investment in Southern railroads would begin anew. Conservatives might not support state aid, but some favored local subscription and wanted foreign capital in order to rebuild the South and add to its industry.

This is not to say that the Democratic party was a unit on economic questions any more than on racial matters. Conservatives differed over railroad aid, bond redemption, and the need for industrial growth. But the double campaign made a resolution of such differences unnecessary. White Leaguers could favor repudiation, but would make race their main issue to keep party unity. Grangers could inveigh against the railroad freebooters, but damn the Negro-scalawag governments that had given corporations so much. Conservative businessmen would deprecate white-liner tactics, but ignore excesses and find unity in the promise of economic regeneration.[45]

The double issue and the two-sided campaign made every businessman an enthusiastic Democrat. They had many reasons for their commitment. For one thing, many commercial men, for all their verbal moderation, were fervent white supremacists who would have been glad to see the Negro removed from politics. Some of them joined the White Leagues and took high positions. Unfortunately, commercial men detesting the extremists' tactics had to go along. They dared not defy thousands of irate whites. An unwise merchant would find that his deprecation of violence or even recognition of its existence would cut into his trade. Small farmers would boycott him, country merchants would refuse to do business with his agents.

Not even the railroad companies that the Republicans had aided could withstand the white-liners. J. C. Stanton's Alabama & Chattanooga had benefited more from railroad aid than almost any other line in the South. According to the *Tuscaloosa Times*, however, it gave the Republicans scant help in the 1874 election. Instead, Stanton was understood to favor the Conservative party. Conservative railroad men went further. The *Alabama State Journal* claimed that every line was arrayed against the Republicans, "and with a bitterness that exceeded, if possible, any other class." A Florida railroad passed out numbered ballots to its employees, so that it could tell which had voted Conservative once the votes were counted. Such acts were pure common sense. Once the government changed hands, railroad bonds would come into question. A contribution at the right moment to the proper political organization might protect against repudiation. This fear may explain why the Alabama Conservatives had one of the largest campaign funds in the state's political history: Northern investors in Southern securities supplied much of it.[46]

The Conservatives had no need to frighten businessmen, for most of the latter had learned to hate Republican rule, and the retreat from railroad aid made enemies wherever the aid bonds had been sold and depended on the states' guarantee. Bondholders were furious at Republicans for having scaled Southern public debts. They protested angrily that the governments could afford to pay the entire debt, and pointed out that if they took less than face value for their securities, one "adjustment" might lead to another scaling-down.[47]

For such perfidy, the angry creditors were quite prepared to drive Republicans from power. Emissaries were sent south to spread the word that as long as Republicans ruled, local projects could expect no support. A more sinister note was struck by a leading Louisiana Democrat, who privately confided that the state funding bill would bring to the Conservative cause "all the influences of the Northern & foreign holders of State bonds." He added, "Already they have subscribed $1^{00} for every $100 of bonds to carry the bill through and then to help us overthrow Kellogg. They believe that if the State can be freed from Radical domination the bill will be repealed, the State credit rise, and their bonds well advanced in the markets & then finally paid." Perhaps much of that money went to buy the guns with which the Republican government was overturned, but there were better ways to aid Conservatives. In every disreputable act, the commercial element gave the White Leaguers a respectable front. When rebels took to the New Orleans boulevards, the Cotton Exchange closed its doors "as a mark of sympathy with the movement to establish the legitimate government of Louisiana."[48] Such a respectable vanguard for the Conservatives had a powerful effect on Northern opinion. After all, who could doubt the best and most responsible members of society? Yet such solidarity of the elite would not have been possible without the hard times, heavy public debts, and increased taxes that characterized the South after the Panic; all of these could be traced in one way or another to the Republican railroad aid policy as well as the failure of the railroads' economic promise to the South.

Without economic support, the Republicans were seriously hampered. They could not finance their campaigns. If a party chairman was vulnerable, how much more so were regulars with less authority; small farmers needing loans to market their cotton crops, for example! The economically powerful coupled their claims of sympathy for the blacks with threats of what would happen should Democratic overtures meet with an unfavorable response. Cost what it might in lives or livelihoods, whites made clear that they would win the South. Violence was needless when nocturnal drills and rattling sabers and cocking rifles at Republican gatherings were enough to show that whites would not allow their plans to be thwarted. Assassination and the burning of black churches proved effective means of undermining Republican morale, but economic sanctions may have been more important.[49]

Against the Democratic onslaught, Republicans were powerless. Beleaguered Republicans invoked the Gospel of Prosperity, but with economic ruin all about them, they argued at a disadvantage. The *Houston Union* could have been speaking for any state in the cotton South when it complained, "When we point to the railroads somebody is going to build, they will point to the schoolless children and depreciated bonds. When they ask, where are those great lines of road that were to be built, we will point to the last heavy rains that raised all the creeks and hindered construction, and be laughed at for our smartness." With justice, incumbents could say that the South's well-being depended largely on factors beyond its borders and outside of its control. Their contention came too late for Southern voters to accept it. In 1867, after all, Republicans had tried to show that the sector's economic plight was due not to Northern conditions, but to Conservative mismanagement at home. Republicans had contended that a change in government would bring about a change in economic conditions as well. In 1870, they had proclaimed that government policies had been responsible for the

South's renewed prosperity. If good times were all their doing, hard times must be all their fault.[50]

Republicans deserved to bear the responsibility for hard times. True, for example, New Orleans suffered commercial embarrassment because other cities had taken the Crescent City's river trade. Yet Reconstruction governments could have built lines tapping the Texas and Arkansas trade. Money had been raised, but the roads had not been laid down. The Northerners had not bought Southern bonds at par, especially railroad aid bonds, but state governments had done little beyond deploring the situation. Republicans could protest that they had reformed, but the defense only admitted past transgressions.[51] It could be argued that corruption had nothing to do with hard times, but in fact corruption in its broadest sense went to the heart of Republicans' failures in economic legislation. Had lawmakers seen beyond their personal and community interests more often, the railroad aid policies might have proven more successful. Had there been less blackmail, stock-watering, and misappropriation of funds, perhaps Northern purchasers would have paid a higher price for Southern securities, and Southern debts might have remained both politically and financially manageable. Certainly, the businessmen building the railroads were negligent, but the Republican governments that aided them had a duty to examine the work being done to make sure that the taxpayers' money was being well spent.

Republicans' failures were clear to party members themselves. Never before had they inveighed against one another so bitterly. In no campaign did the rank and file give its wholehearted support to the nominees. Local conventions were broken up by quarreling. The appearance of the governor at one such gathering was enough to cause fistfights, curses, and attempts to knock him down. Nor could the governments quell the White Leaguers. More interested in economics than in ending terrorism, administrations had disbanded their militia or made them ineffective. With the organization of the White Leagues, counter measures were no longer possible. The federal government did as little as it could. Like most Northerners, the President was convinced that Southern Republicans included more rascals than honest men—and railroad corruption had helped bring him to that conviction.[53]

Coupled with Southern Republicans' impotence and federal restraint, the Conservative campaign proved unbeatable. Between 1874 and 1876, the Republicans lost control of every state government. The Reconstruction coalition claimed that its foes had won through fraud and force alone, but the election returns and Republicans' private admissions suggest a more complex explanation. Intimidation and ballot-box stuffing worked in some counties, but not in others. Indeed, Republicans increased their votes in many places and did well at the state level. Democrats simply did much better. That was where the two-issue campaign had made a difference: among undecided and apathetic whites who had not voted in past elections.[53]

The Reconstruction coalition was broken. It had invited its own defeat. Even without the terror and intimidation, Republicans could not have held Alabama, Arkansas, North Carolina, Georgia, Florida, or Texas in 1874—not after the Panic and party factionalism had done their work. Even in Mississippi and Louisiana, the final result would have been doubtful.

A second conclusion is inescapable. Judged by the gap between their promises in 1867 and their performance over the seven years that followed, the Republican leaders deserved to lose power. For the liberal historian this conclusion is a bitter one, at first unthinkably ruthless. Surely the blacks who died violently did not deserve to die. Nor did those who lost their rights deserve to be cast out of the political process. Nor did the Republicans' foes deserve to win. They had proven themselves no more scrupulous than their rivals in financial matters and far less fastidious in using lawless tactics to get their way. Yet Republicans had done so much so badly and delivered so little of what they had promised in railroad construction that here at least they had invited rebuke. With many conspicuous exceptions, Republicans had ruled badly, and they admitted it. They had elected incompetents and mountebanks, corruptionists and self-serving mediocrities. They had failed to bring the promised peace, prosperity, and order, though it must be added that theirs was virtually an impossible task. In railroad legislation, as in so much else, the legislators had lost all sense of purpose in local struggles for advantage—though again, their delicate political position made it necessary for them to strengthen themselves by giving their own constituents as much as they could. When citizens required protection, it was not given. When blacks needed land, little was done to provide it. Republicans could not even invest themselves with a look of legitimacy. Conservatives were partly responsible, but only partly. The charge is a terrible one to make: Reconstruction had succeeded in its creation, but had failed in its execution. The renewal of the color line did nothing but make the failure more visible.

And the Gospel of Prosperity? Certainly, its time should have passed, for the original meaning had been lost and the railroads had lost much of their government support; but nineteenth-century American history lacks the symmetry of nineteenth-century fiction. Just as the vanquished Republicans continued to campaign, and the politicians continued to tighten the legal restrictions on their own power to give aid, so, too, the railroads kept much of their following. With the ascendancy of the Conservative Redeemers of the South, the commercial and industrial interests found new friends, almost as benign as the old ones. The Gospel of Prosperity had been transformed, not killed. As the memory of the Reconstruction years receded, the doctrine of a New South reappeared in another form.

Many of the Redeemers neither wanted the Old South nor believed that it could be restored. Some men identified with commerce had risen to the highest posts in the Conservative organization. Such men spoke of a section reborn, in which the political issues and planter economy of the antebellum years would be modified. The New South's doctrine had more articulate spokesmen than did the reactionary, or Bourbon, point of view, and many planters and farmers adapted New South rhetoric and goals to their purposes.

Nonetheless, the agricultural interests challenged and often defeated the aspirations of commercial men. Many Southerners saw the railroads and industrialists as betrayers of all that the section had represented. If the New South had Henry Grady, the precious values of the antebellum past had Robert Toombs and M. W. Gary as their champions. They in turn, had powerful followings. Divisions among Redeemers and Bourbons became most apparent when the railroad aid issue arose. In a general way, Southerners of all factions favored railroad development. Even so, they could not countenance the programs that Republicans had enacted. Such subsidies were hateful because Radicals had been responsible for them—an oversimplification which Democratic leaders never tired of making in public and contradicting in private—and because the beneficiaries had failed to keep their promises.[54]

A true friend of the New South would fear repudiation of the subsidy bonds, lest the states' credit ratings be destroyed, in some cases for the second time in thirty years. Many leading Redeemers did voice such fears. They included some of the most respected Democratic champions: Joseph Brown and Colonel John Screven of Georgia, U. M. Rose and Senator Augustus Garland of Arkansas, and the editors of the *Montgomery Advertiser* in Alabama. But the supporters of fiscal responsibility could not control the voters. In every commonwealth, public obligations were "adjusted," scaled down, or invalidated entirely. Chief Justice David Walker of Arkansas pronounced the railroad aid securities unconstitutional in 1877. Lest this decision prove insufficient, Arkansas voters amended the constitution to forbid their lawmakers to pay principal or interest on the aid bonds. Georgia's 1877 constitution did the same. North Carolina disavowed all bonds issued by Radicals and offered to pay off railroad aid bonds dating before 1868 at one-fourth their original value. Alabama scaled its debts and bought out bondholders to the Alabama & Chattanooga for one-ninth of what they claimed from the state. Elsewhere Republicans had left little of their railroad aid program to undo and had already "adjusted" their state debts. Conservatives made minor alterations and negotiated new consolidated bonds at lower interest.[55] Florida and Mississippi had no railroad debt to adjust, while Texas Democrats continued their land grant policy until 1882.

Conservatives resolved further never to make their predecessors' mistakes. They wrote provisions into the state constitutions forbidding the loan of state credit to private enterprises: Florida and Alabama in 1875, North Carolina and Texas in 1876, Georgia in 1877, and Louisiana in 1879. Four constitutions forbade the government to become a stockholder in any private enterprise, and six deprived localities of the same privilege. Other measures made it harder for the legislature to levy new taxes or borrow money for any purpose.[56]

The public's enthusiasm for giving money in aid had vanished, but its faith in railroads lingered on. The fascination with other forms of aid—tax advantages, public lands, liberal charters—persisted into the 1880s. With such support, the railroads revived and flourished, though mostly with large infusions of Northern money and greater Northern corporate control than at any time during Reconstruction. Nashville and Louisville businessmen dominated the routes to the Gulf, while Georgia and Virginia financiers bought roads throughout the Southeast. Large companies grew by swallowing smaller ones. By 1890, a dozen large companies held over half of the South's railway mileage.[57]

The postwar Conservatives *did* give financial aid, but cautiously, without direct cost to taxpayers. Furthermore, they inherited many of the problems that had dogged the Republican governments: politicians owning stock in the lines for which they legislated, localism, outsiders' investment and control of Southern corporations, and company corruption of public officials. When the Populist movement challenged the hegemony of the ruling Redeemers and New South businessmen in the 1890s, the railroads' depredations would become an important part of the insurgents' indictment of the government in power. Indeed, the Gospel of Prosperity itself did more to tear the Redeemers apart than it did to bring them together. Just as much as the Republicans, the new leaders disagreed about bond redemption, immigration, public education, as well as who should benefit the most from the postwar South's political economy.

Just as the Gospel of Prosperity had outlived its founders, it outlived their successors. But then, it was adaptable to every purpose and political belief, adaptable at times beyond recognition. The Southern political climate—and its economic character—as the Reconstruction experiment had shown, was not. That, at the heart, was the tragedy of the postwar South.

CODA

"And Was Jerusalem Builded Here?"

And did the Countenance divine
Shine forth upon our clouded hills?
And was Jerusalem builded here
Among these dark Satanic Mills?
William Blake

As Republican witness before the congressional investigation committee, Samuel F. Rice grew restive. Instead of asking about Ku Klux Klan outrages, Democratic representatives had demanded the facts about scalawag economic policies. By showing the Radicals' corruption they hoped to mitigate the night riders' offenses. The government had been extravagant and unresponsive to popular need; that was why desperate natives had adopted lawless means. Conservative witnesses had made just such a case, but Rice would not defame the government he had helped create. Pressed by accusatory questions, he burst out that the state owed more to Republicans than it could ever repay. "Before the republicans had power in Alabama," he exclaimed, "we had nothing like a system of railroads." Taking office, Republicans confronted a hostile white population and an empty Treasury. "All they had to go on was the credit of the State. ... Yet ... the republicans have caused an unprecedented amount of railroad to be constructed. The railroad system which has been inaugurated is one of the most perfect and complete in any State in the Union." A road now tapped the mineral country in the uplands and connected the cotton belt with Chattanooga. Within the year, Rice predicted, another trunk line would be finished. It would open up rich coal lands and bring trade from the Ohio River valley to Montgomery. Alabama had made an excellent bargain, exchanging the risk of an increased state debt for a vast increase in state wealth and in the potential for industrial growth in the future.[1]

Naturally, Rice made the kindest interpretation of a distasteful issue. The trunk line from Chattanooga and others like it had cost the South more than money. They had compromised its honor. The South had railroads at the end of Reconstruction, but no system. Corruption, extortion, local rivalries, grudges, partisan and sectional prejudices, and unfounded optimism—all had shaped the laws. Clumsiness, extravagance, mismanagement, and rivalries had weakened what plans the Republicans had made. States had striven for advantages over their neighbors, rather than for a New South. Too many lines had vied for too little traffic. Too many Southerners hoped for too much prosperity too soon. Inexperience and self-interest had undone the Gospel of Prosperity and with it the Republican party. Politically and economically, the railroads had not provided the solution Republicans had sought. Nor had Republicans provided the salvation that Southerners demanded. A New South had not yet reached maturity.

Yet when all these criticisms have been made of the railroad aid program, Rice's claims remain unshaken. Without public aid, the South would have had to rely on Northern capital more than ever for sectional development. All the more quickly, the South would have been transformed into the economic colony of Philadelphia, New York, Chicago, and St. Louis. Communities dreaming of the chance to become the Atlantas of the future would have been deprived of that chance. The companies may not have prospered during the 1870s, but that was beside the point. The roads into the mineral country and between Southern communities had to be built. Until they were, the South could not develop its manufactures, lure immigration, open its mines, or give its struggling farmers an outlet on world markets. Until the basic routes had been built, Southern communities could not construct the branch lines that would permit industrial expansion. It was not on the ledgers of a failing corporation that the profit and loss of railroad aid was to be found, but in the prosperity and industrial growth that the South would experience over the next two generations. It was not in the shame that citizens felt at the corruption around them that we should seek the spiritual meaning of the Gospel of Prosperity. It is in the reviving pride and confidence that Southerners felt in their section's future.

Politically, the Republicans had failed in their attempt to remake the South, but an effort is no less worthy for being in vain. They had hoped to make the race issue secondary to the economic one in the white voter's mind. They had no choice. Concentration on the race or wartime loyalty question would have doomed the Reconstruction coalition to minority status from the start. The strategy failed. Perhaps it could never have succeeded—or perhaps it might have changed the course of Southern politics. For one brief moment, the Republicans shattered political patterns and opened up possibilities for men of all races and economic conditions. The moment passed, but the reconstructed states would not be the same again. The South was transformed, though not in the way Republicans would have liked. The Henry Gradys and Joseph Browns adapted the Gospel of Prosperity to fit their own ends. They could tempt the South with dreams of development; they could not persuade all poor whites that white supremacy mattered more than economic improvement for all. More than they admitted, perhaps more than they imagined, the spokesmen of the New South were the progeny of Republican doctrines. So, in a different sense, were the insurgent Southerners who, in the 1890s, rose to challenge the power of the Bourbons, bankers, and businessmen who had defined the limits of the New South. The Republican strategy, thus, had not only been worth the effort: it was the only kind that made sense in the postwar South. Rice had given the best defense of Republicanism possible. It was just as an Opelika editor had said: "There is statesmanship in a Railroad, and a statesman is the builder."[2]

APPENDIX

Could the Democrats Have Done Better?

THIS study of railroad aid raises an issue both irresistible and beyond satisfactory resolution: Could the railroad aid issue have been handled better, had there been no Radical Reconstruction? Would the Conservatives or Democrats have shown more judgment and restraint in planning for the South's economic future?

Like all contrafactual history, my conjectures are exercises of imagination and not prescience. Still, there is more than whimsy to this speculation. The Conservatives *did* control the Southern governments in Virginia and Kentucky, and as a minority party in the Republican states, they left a record affording unmistakable indications. Here, then, are my guesses:

1. Conservative ascendancy would have done little to clean up the governing process in railroad matters. The variety of influences on railroad aid were too broad, the temptation of the corporations to settle their conflicts through bribery too strong. The Conservative lawmakers proved themselves open to bribery, often of the most shameless kind. Changing legislators would not assure an end to corruption. The applicants for aid and the circumstances surrounding the awarding of aid would themselves have had to be altered. The same respected businessmen would have descended on the Southern legislatures and battled one another for favored treatment. It was the process of special aid and the limitations on the state's resources that made railroad legislation a scramble for advantage.

Nor did Conservatives oppose the mingling of public offices with private railroad positions. Long after Reconstruction, they filled both roles simultaneously and saw no conflict of interest in doing so. Democrats had never abjured the use of railroads for political ends. The Georgian and North Carolinian companies had been tools of the presiding administrations before the Radicals came to power. There is no reason to think that Conservatives would have altered their ways.

2. Railroad aid would certainly not have come to an end. Conservatives may have objected to subsidies, though in North Carolina, Alabama, South Carolina, Georgia, Florida, Louisiana, Arkansas, and Tennessee they had begun the process and put the laws giving public money to the lines on the books. In some of these states, Conservatives were adding to the subsidy program when the Republicans came to power. Even where the Democrats did abandon the subsidy program—and there is no reason to imagine that they would have abandoned it entirely—their votes in Radical legislatures and in states as far apart as Virginia and Texas suggest that they would have turned to some other kind of aid to achieve their ends. These might have been more extensive land grants, greater bestowals of privileges, more exclusive rights—the very policies followed after Conservatives had restored their hegemony in the 1880s. Surely the process of selling state stock in private corporations would have gone on. Democrats favored this method of aiding corporations, and in Virginia they gave stock away for a pittance.

Railroad aid might have been better administered under general subsidy laws than Radicals had administered it. The Democrats did represent the taxpayers and would have tried to protect them from loss. But Republicans failed to protect the public interest not because they were callous, but because they were inattentive and trusted too much the companies' good intentions. So did the Democrats. If they had given subsidies, the same end might have resulted, with a similar loss to the state.

3. If the Democrats had *not* given new subsidies, the South would not have had as great a railroad expansion as Republicans assured. Land grants were not enough to build a line. Experience with the Texas & Pacific had shown that. Special privileges meant nothing without the support of Wall Street bankers and brokers ready to buy the company bonds. A cautious, clean, and virtuous Southern government would have put such firm restrictions on aid that construction would have been virtually impossible, except on condition of total Northern control over the Southern railway system. There was simply not the private capital in the South to support railway expansion.

4. Democratic rule would not have made the railroads prosper. There were factors neither party could do much about: the Franco-Prussian War, which closed foreign money markets at a critical time, the 1873 Wall Street Panic, which dried up railroad financing

throughout the South, and the general economic condition of the South, which could not yet sustain an extensive railroad system.

Democrats could have made the bonds they gave to railroads sell for more than could Republicans; after all, it was in large part the Democratic threat to repudiate the Reconstruction governments' bonds that had depreciated their value on Northern markets. Yet they probably could not have brought their bonds up to par; Virginia could not, and none of the Southern states before the Republicans took charge had been able to extinguish their public debts or obtain a good credit rating for their securities. Furthermore, without a *massive* infusion of capital, the roads could not have been built. Such a massive infusion entailed public bond issues that would have destroyed the Southern states' credit.

5. An apocalyptic result might have followed: the economy not yet recovered and railroads unbuilt, the South saddled with a tremendous debt, and the people, furious at Democratic mismanagement and at the lack of facilities, overwhelmed by the state debt and the national economic depression—all would have contributed to a political upheaval. The voters might have risen to turn out the Conservatives, made common cause with the Republicans of the North, and brought in a new coalition based on economic issues. Such a situation occurred in Virginia, when William Mahone and his Readjusters drove out the defenders of the state debt. Fusion movements did well in other Southern states during the 1880s.

Spared the squalid experience of Radical Reconstruction, a disgruntled South might have given Republicans their chance. It is a possibility.

But only a faint possibility. Had the Republicans assumed command, they would have had to abandon all interest in blacks. In Virginia they had had no record of misrule with which to contend, and in 1873 they stood on the perfect platform: Conservative corruption and fiscal mismanagement, predatory monopoly, and the need to attract federal aid and industrial capital. The Republican candidate was more like a Conservative than a Radical in his ideas. Yet the Republicans were trounced by the incumbent party and the white-liners. The Readjuster coalition a few years later survived only briefly. Then the race issue smashed its power. From the mid-1880s to the early part of the twentieth century, Virginia remained safely Conservative. Other states, where the larger black population made the fear of social equality more real to many whites, would not have been any more fertile soil for Republican-dominated coalitions. Attempts in Kentucky and Tennessee in the 1870s and 1880s as well as North Carolina in the late 1890s showed that.

Democratic rule, thus, would have meant fewer railroads but no less corruption, and no fewer economic problems than Republicans encountered. It would not have assured the ultimate triumph of Republicanism and the institution of a two-party system. The Gospel of Prosperity *was* the best and only chance of the Republican party and of the South—and it was a frail one at that.

ABBREVIATIONS

ASDAH	Alabama State Department of Archives and History
ASJ	*Montgomery Alabama State Journal*
Ala.	Alabama
Ark.	Arkansas
ARM	*American Railroad Manual*
CG	*Congressional Globe*
CR	*Congressional Record*
Const. Conv.	Constitutional Convention
Fla.	Florida
Ga.	Georgia
Hse. *Jnl.*	*Journal* of the House of Representatives
Jnl.	*Journal*
LC	Library of Congress
LSU	Louisiana State University
La.	Louisiana
Miss.	Mississippi
N.C.	North Carolina
NCDAH	North Carolina Department of Archives and History
S.C.	South Carolina
SHC	Southern Historical Collection, University of North Carolina at Chapel Hill
Sen. *Jnl.*	*Journal* of the State
Tex.	Texas
UGa	University of Georgia, Athens
Va.	Virginia

NOTES

Chapter 1. "Our Poor Distressed Country"

1. Trowbridge, *The South*, pp. 113, 144–147, 553–556; Andrews, *The South Since the War*, pp. 1, 30–31, 338–339.

2. Trowbridge, *The South*, p. 451; Harris, *Presidential Reconstruction*, p. 23; *Merchant's Magazine*, November 1866, vol. 55, pp. 361–364; *U.S. House Reports*, 39th Congress, 2nd session, no. 34, pp. 16, 796, 863, 912, 983 (hereafter referred to as "Affairs of Southern Railroads"); *Charleston Mercury*, December 7, 1866; Fleming, *Alabama*, p. 260; Shofner, *Nor Is It Over Yet*, p. 111.

3. Coulter, *Reconstruction*, p. 13.

4. Fleming, *Alabama*, pp. 277–285; Trowbridge, *The South*, pp. 455, 462, 563; Harris, *Presidential Reconstruction*, p. 29.

5. Andrews, *The South Since the War*, p. 340.

6. Harris, *Presidential Reconstruction*, pp. 197–198; "Affairs of Southern Railroads," p. 870.

7. *Merchant's Magazine*, February 1867, vol. 56, p. 126.

8. See Trowbridge, *The South*, p. 426.

9. *Little Rock Arkansas Gazette*, August 11, 27, 1867; *New York Herald*, July 27, August 17, 1867.

10. *West Baton Rouge Sugar Planter*, March 30, 1867.

11. *Little Rock Arkansas Gazette*, August 8, 17, 27, 1867; *West Baton Rouge Sugar Planter*, May 5, 1866; *New Orleans Picayune*, May 11, 1867.

12. *West Baton Rouge Sugar Planter*, September 15, 1866.

13. Poor, *Manual*, 1868–1869, p. 184; see "Affairs of Southern Railroads," pp. 890–891, 900–902, 911, 962–964, 995.

14. Simkins and Woody, *South Carolina*, pp. 193–194, 196, 201; Thompson, *Reconstruction in Georgia*, p. 96; Fleming, *Alabama*, p. 589; Reed, *Texas Railroads*, pp. 148–149.

15. *Augusta Weekly Chronicle and Sentinel*, July 27, 1870; Shofner, *Nor Is It Over Yet*, p. 109; Goodrich, *Government Promotion*, pp. 150–151, 158–159; Poor, *Manual*, 1874, pp. 794, 801, 811, 814.

16. Reed, *Texas Railroads*, p. 148; Harris, *Presidential Reconstruction*, pp. 215–216, 291; Taylor, *Louisiana Reconstructed*, pp. 86–87; Blake, *William Mahone*, pp. 76–84.

17. Ga. Sen. *Jnl.*, 1866, pp. 483–489, 528, 541, 559; Taylor, *Louisiana*

Reconstructed, p. 87; *Jackson Pilot*, February 25, 26, 1871; *Charleston Mercury*, December 6, 1866.

18. Harris, *Presidential Reconstruction*, p. 190; *Iberville Weekly South*, January 25, 1868; *Charleston Mercury*, November 20, 1866; *Merchant's Magazine*, January 1868, vol. 58, pp. 31–35; Moore, *Juhl*, p. 181.

19. *Washington Chronicle*, quoted in *Charleston Courier*, January 10, 1868.

20. *U.S. House Reports*, 42nd Congress, 2nd session, no. 22, vol. 1, pp. 102–103, 105–107, 109–111, 115–117, 125–127, 160–162, 169–170, 179–180, 183–184, 189–190, 213–215 (hereafter referred to as "Condition of Affairs"); Hamilton, ed., *Worth*, vol. 1, p. 512.

21. *West Baton Rouge Sugar Planter*, April, May, 1867; C. J. Barrow to Anna Barrow, September 1, 1867, Barrow Papers, LSU; Moore, *Juhl*, pp. 148, 160.

22. David Schenck Diary, September 1, 1866, SHC.

23. U.S. Bureau of the Census, *Compendium of the Ninth Census*, p. 20.

24. *New Orleans Republican*, August 18, 1868; see also Carrier, "Texas," pp. 167, 177.

25. Foner, *Free Soil, Free Labor, Free Men*, pp. 11–72.

26. Va. Const. Conv. *Debates*, pp. 170–171.

27. *Little Rock Republican*, October 28, 1867; *Augusta National Republican*, April 5, 1868; *New Orleans Republican*, November 1, 1867; *Vicksburg Republican*, April 7, May 12, 1868; *ASJ*, September 15, 1870.

28. *National Anti-Slavery Standard*, October 19, 1867; *Vicksburg Republican*, April 28, 1868; Va. Const. Conv. *Debates*, p. 294.

29. *Little Rock Republican*, July 11, 1868.

30. Speech of Thomas Settle, probably April 1867, Settle Papers, SHC; *Vicksburg Times*, May 23, 1873; *New York Herald*, July 27, 1867; *Little Rock Republican*, November 4, 1867; *Vicksburg Republican*, May 12, 1868; *Charleston Daily Republican*, March 23, 1870; *Carrollton Republican Standard*, July 21, 1869.

31. *ASJ*, May 17, 1873; *Charleston Daily Republican*, March 17, 23, 25, 1870; *New Orleans Republican*, September 26, 1867; *Augusta National Republican*, April 5, 1868; *Flake's Galveston Bulletin*, December 19, 1867; *Little Rock Republican*, June 24, July 15, September 14, 1867; January 30, 1868.

32. *Little Rock Republican*, May 15, September 11, 1868; *Atlanta Daily New Era*, February 29, March 11, 1868; *New Orleans Republican*, October 20, December 5, 1867; Va. Const. Conv. *Debates*, p. 164.

33. *Atlanta Daily New Era*, November 4, 1870.

34. *Little Rock Republican*, June 27, July 11, 1868; *Flake's Galveston Bulletin*, October 6, 1867.

35. *Little Rock Republican*, May 15, 1868; January 22, 1873; see also *San Antonio Express*, July 14, 1871.

36. *Flake's Galveston Bulletin*, January 26, 1868; *New Orleans Republican*, April 10, October 20, November 3, 15, December 7, 17, 1867; *Little Rock Republican*, November 20, 1867; February 5, 1868.

37. *Little Rock Republican*, September 16, 1867; June 15, 1868; see also Joseph E. Brown to William D. Kelley, July 9, 1867, Brown Papers, UGa; New Orleans *Tribune*, September 22, 1866.

38. *New Orleans Republican*, December 28, 1867.

39. *Little Rock Republican*, January 17, 1868; *Flake's Galveston Bulletin*, October 2, 1867; *New Orleans Republican*, July 28, 1867.

40. *Little Rock Arkansas Gazette*, May 17, 22, 31, 1867.

41. *Tribune Almanac* for 1868, pp. 62–65.

42. La. Const. Conv. *Jnl.*, p. 109; D. H. Bingham to Thaddeus Stevens, October 23, 1867, Stevens Papers, LC; Carrier, "Texas," pp. 195, 212, 262–278.

43. La. Const. Conv. *Jnl.*, p. 110; Ark. Const. Conv. *Debates*, pp. 160–161, 229; Ala. Const. Conv. *Jnl.*, pp. 181–182.

44. Daniels, *Prince of Carpetbaggers*, p. 145; Olsen, *Tourgee*, pp. 110–111; D. H. Bingham to Thaddeus Stevens, October 23, 1867, Stevens Papers, LC; Ga. Const. Conv. *Jnl.*, p. 580; Ala. Const. Conv. *Jnl.*, pp. 46–47, 199–200, 213.

45. S.C. Const. Conv. *Debates*, pp. 116–120, 128–131, 192–193, 376–390, 410–413, 421–428, 438–439, 507–509, 596; *Atlanta Daily New Era*, February 2, 1868; *Augusta National Republican*, March 6, 1868; *Little Rock Republican*, February 12, 14, 1868; Scroggs, "Carpetbagger Influence," pp. 160–163; *Constitution of Alabama*, 1868, Article 14; Fla. Const. Conv. *Jnl.*, p. 10; Ark. Const. Conv. *Debates*, p. 232; Ga. Const. Conv. *Jnl.*, pp. 240–241; N.C. Const. Conv. *Jnl.*, pp. 278–279; La. Const. Conv. *Jnl.*, p. 108; Holt, "Emergence of Negro Political Leadership," pp. 214–216, 226–227.

46. Fla. Const. Conv. *Jnl.*, p. 129; La. Const. Conv. *Jnl.*, pp. 75, 212; Va. Const. Conv. *Debates*, pp. 197, 199; Ga. Const. Conv. *Jnl.*, pp. 438, 488; *Atlanta Daily New Era*, January 29, March 7, 1868; *Augusta National Republican*, March 3, 1868; Ala. Const. Conv. *Jnl.*, pp. 30, 86–87, 104.

47. N.C. Const. Conv. *Jnl.*, pp. 326–327, 360–367, 393–399, 466, 470–471, 476–477.

48. Reed, *Texas Railroads*, p. 148; *New Orleans Tribune*, December 12, 1867; *Little Rock Republican*, February 19, 1868; *Raleigh Standard*, March 9, 1868; *Constitution of Alabama*, 1868, Article 4; Ark. Const. Conv. *Debates*, pp. 248, 390; Ala. Const. Conv. *Jnl.*, pp. 127–128, 137–138; La. Const. Conv. *Jnl.*, pp. 199, 268–270; N.C. Const. Conv. *Jnl.*, pp. 308, 310–311, 354–355; Miss. Const. Conv. *Jnl.*, p. 59; S.C. Const. Conv. *Debates*, pp. 498, 629–633; Ga. Const. Conv. *Jnl.*, pp. 340–344.

49. S.C. Const. Conv. *Debates*, pp. 362–364; La. Const. Conv. *Jnl.*, p. 186; N.C. Const. Conv. *Jnl.*, pp. 304–305.

50. *Constitution of Alabama*, 1868, Articles 12, 13; *Constitution of Texas*, 1869, Articles 10, 11, 12.

51. *New York World*, January 2, 1868; *Atlanta Daily New Era*, March 11, 13, 29, 31, 1868; *Augusta National Republican*, March 26, April 16, 17, 19, 23, 1868; *Little Rock Republican*, January 11, February 28, 1868.

52. *Little Rock Arkansas Campaign Gazette*, February 28, 1868; see also *Bossier Banner*, March 28, 1868.

53. *Iberville Weekly South*, March 28, August 8, 1868; Jonathan Worth to S. S. Jackson, April 9, 11, May 4, 1868, in Hamilton, *Worth*, vol. 2, pp. 1184, 1185, 1192–1193; R. Wolcott to Elihu Washburne, December 4, 1868, Washburne Papers, LC.

54. George Ely to Elihu Washburne, February 9, 1868; D. Richards to Washburne, February 11, April 20, 21, May 6, 1868, Washburne Papers, LC; M. D. Brainard to Benjamin Butler, March 23, 1868, Butler Papers, LC.

55. *Little Rock Republican*, February 20, March 9, 1868; *Atlanta Daily New Era*, September 18, 1868.

56. Arthur McAllyn to Washburne, July 13, 1868, Washburne Papers, LC; M. D. Brainard to Butler, March 23, 1868, Butler Papers, LC; Carrier, "Texas," pp. 393–395, 399; McGee, "North Carolina Conservatives," pp. 260–262; *Little Rock Republican*, May 7, 1868.

57. Milton Saffold to Thaddeus Stevens, March 2, 1868, Stevens Papers, LC; George E. Spencer to Washburne, May 23, 1868; D. Richards to Washburne, May 18, 1868; C. W. Buckley to Washburne, May 1, 1868, Washburne Papers, LC; *Flake's Galveston Bulletin*, August 14, 1868.

58. See, for example, *Acts of Alabama*, 1868, pp. 26, 27, 41, 45, 55–57; *Acts of Florida*, 1868, pp. 18–27, 127–131, 137–140, 146–149; *Charleston Courier*, August 27, 28, September 2, 1868.

59. *Laws of Florida*, 1868, pp. 133–135, 141–143; *Little Rock Republican*, October 26, 1868; *Acts of Alabama*, 1868, pp. 40–41, 43–44; *Acts of Arkansas*, 1868, pp. 302–310.

60. *Little Rock Republican*, June 6, August 10, September 7, 18, October 9, 12, November 3, 11, 14, December 2, 12, 1868; C. L. Hicny to W. W. Holden, August 20, 1868, Holden Papers, NCDAH.

61. *Little Rock Republican*, November 20, 1868; Ark. Const. Conv. *Debates*, p. 681.

Chapter 2. *The Necessities of State Aid*

1. *Atlanta Daily New Era*, September 22, November 4, 1870; *Jackson Pilot*, June 10, 1871; *Little Rock Republican*, June 30, 1873; *Beaufort Republican*, November 16, 1871; March 6, 1873.

2. Clayton, *Aftermath of the Civil War*, p. 42.

3. *Little Rock Republican*, April 9, 1868; *Atlanta Daily New Era*, November 4, 1870; *North Carolina Legislative Documents*, 1869–1870, no. 2, p. 29.

4. *Vicksburg Times and Republican*, February 7, 1873; King, *The Great South*, p. 280; *Jackson Pilot*, June 3, 8, 1871; *San Antonio Express*, May 19, 20, 24, June 2, 4, 9, 28, 1871; *Little Rock Republican*, June 2, 1871; August 9, 1872.

5. *Atlanta Daily New Era*, August 31, October 27, 1870.

6. *ASJ*, March 29, 1869; November 12, 1871; March 21, 1873; *Atlanta Daily New Era*, November 4, 1870; *Jacksonville Florida Tri-Weekly Union*, March 8, 1873.

7. Poor, *Manual*, 1877–1878, p. lx.

8. Goodrich, *Government Promotion*, pp. 152–161.

9. La. Sen. *Debates*, 1870, p. 632; *ASJ*, October 15, 1870.

10. Goodrich, *Government Promotion*, pp. 151–152, 156, 158.

11. *ASJ*, March 11, 1870; *Atlanta Daily New Era*, November 4, 1870; *San Antonio Express*, April 6, 1871.

12. *Carrollton Republican Standard*, July 28, 1869; *San Antonio Express*, June 23, 1871.

13. *Jackson Pilot*, May 31, June 3, 8, 1871.

14. Ibid., May 11, 1871.

15. *Acts of Arkansas*, 1868, pp. 290–311; *Laws of North Carolina*, 1869, pp. 51–53, 103–111; *Laws of Louisiana*, 1868, p. 179; *Acts of Alabama*, 1868, pp. 560–561; *Laws of Georgia*, 1869, p. 154; *Acts of South Carolina*, 1874, pp. 676–677; *Laws of Mississippi*, 1873, pp. 599–603; *San Antonio Express*, May 21, 1871; *Charleston Daily Republican*, January 27, 1870.

16. *Acts of Georgia*, 1869, pp. 156–157; *Acts of South Carolina*, 1873, pp. 443–445; *Acts of Arkansas*, 1868, pp. 302–305, 307, 310; *Acts of Alabama*, 1869–1870, pp. 87–89.

17. *Acts of Arkansas*, 1868, p. 310; Fleming, *Alabama*, pp. 604–605; *Laws of North Carolina*, 1869–1870, pp. 103–111, 122–124; *Acts of South Carolina*, 1871, p. 572; 1873, pp. 411–413; *Acts of Georgia*, 1868–1869, p. 156; *Laws of Mississippi*, 1873, pp. 521–542, 555, 598–599, 604–605; *Acts of Louisiana*, 1868, p. 179; *Acts of Alabama*, Special session, 1868, pp. 214–216; 1868–1869, pp. 395–397, 439–440, 442, 443, 479; 1869–1870, pp. 29–30, 39–40, 42, 228–229, 309.

18. *ASJ*, January 8, May 17, 20, December 2, 1869; *Little Rock Republican*, March 16, August 8, 1872; Odom, "Louisiana Railroads," pp. 197, 201; Fleming, *Alabama*, pp. 604–605.

19. *Vicksburg Times and Republican*, February 5, 1873.

20. Odom, "Louisiana Railroads," pp. 197, 201; Reed, *Texas Railroads*, p. 151; Fleming, *Alabama*, p. 591; *Acts of Louisiana*, 1870, pp. 55–63; 1871, pp. 211–213.

21. *Jackson Pilot*, May 31, 1871; *ASJ*, October 4, 1870; *Acts of Florida*, 1869, pp. 29–38; *Acts of Arkansas*, 1868, pp. 148–153; *Acts of Alabama*, 1868, pp. 17–19, 198–203; 1869–1870, pp. 89–92, 149–157; Stover, *Railroads of the South*, pp. 60–98; Ala. Hse. *Jnl.*, 1869–1870, pp. 17–19; *Acts of Georgia*, 1868–1869, pp. 154–155; D. L. Dalton to Messrs. Porter King, L. L. Perkins, and B. F. Saffold, June 1, 1869, Governor Smith Papers, ASDAH.

22. *Acts of Alabama*, 1869–1870, pp. 175–179, 374, 376–377; 1870–1871, pp. 61–62.

23. *Acts of Georgia*, 1868, pp. 141–143; 1869, pp. 56–57, 65–66; *ASJ*, March 30, 1873; *Laws of Mississippi*, 1873, pp. 517, 557–559, 573, 576–579, 588; *Laws of North Carolina*, 1869–1870, pp. 51–53.

24. *San Antonio Express*, August 7, 1870; April 21, 30, 1871; *Jackson Pilot*, May 6, 1871; *Little Rock Republican*, May 3, 6, 1873.

25. Goodrich, *Government-Promotion*, p. 426; Stover, *Railroads of the South*, p. 78; *Charleston Daily Republican*, February 24, March 3, 4, 8, 1871; *Little Rock Republican*, April 1, 5, 21, May 1, 1873.

26. *Acts of Alabama*, 1869–1870, pp. 290–291; *Laws of Mississippi*, 1873, pp. 567–573; *Acts of Georgia*, 1869, pp. 58–59; *Laws of North Carolina*, 1868, p. 29.

27. Odom, "Louisiana Railroads," pp. 184–194; Stover, *Railroads of the South*, pp. 72–78, 84–86, 110–112; Thompson, *Reconstruction in Georgia*, pp. 245–255; Pike, *Prostrate State*, pp. 173–174; Davis, *Florida*, pp. 657–659.

Chapter 3. An Imaginative Reinterpretation of the Law

1. Jay, "Forrest as a Railroad Builder," pp. 20–22.

2. I do not mean to claim that no laws were tightened. In some cases, the legislature made the statutes clearer and more restrictive. Nor am I speaking of the period after 1872, when disenchantment set in. As a general rule, however, the years of the railroad mania were a time of maladministration and misconstrued law.

3. *Atlanta Daily New Era*, October 27, 1870; *Constitution of Alabama*, 1868, Articles 4, 12; *Dallas Herald*, March 5, 1870; *Constitution of Texas*, 1869, Articles 10, 12.

4. *Jackson Pilot*, May 31, 1871; *Vicksburg Times*, October 22, 1873; Ala. Sen. *Jnl.* 1871–1872, pp. 482–483, 532–533; 1872–1873, pp. 306–307; Miss. Hse. *Jnl.*, 1874, p. 17; Ala. Hse. *Jnl.*, 1871–1872, pp. 456, 458, 564, 568; 1872–1873, p. 552.

5. Ala. Sen. *Jnl.*, 1871–1872, pp. 474–475.

6. Ga. Hse. *Jnl.*, 1868–1869, pp. 727–728.

7. Taylor, *Louisiana Reconstructed*, pp. 203, 213–214; Price, "Railroads and Reconstruction," pp. 385–389; *Laws of North Carolina*, 1868–1869, pp. 48–51; *Calloway versus Jenkins*, North Carolina Reports, vol. 63, p. 147, 1869.

8. *Little Rock Republican*, April 21, 1873; *ASJ*, April 12, 1873; *Florida Central Railroad Co. versus Schutte*, U.S. Reports, vol. 103, pp. 118-145, 1880.

9. Thompson, "Leadership in Arkansas Reconstruction," pp. 442–443.

10. *Atlanta Daily New Era*, October 27, 1870; Miss. Sen. *Jnl.*, 1873, p. 1154; *Robert T. Chisholm versus the City of Montgomery*, U.S. Circuit Court Cases, Woods, vol. 2, pp. 584–596, 1875; *Lewis versus City of Clarendon*, U.S. Circuit Court Cases, Dillon, vol. 5, pp. 329–340, 1880.

11. Thompson, *Reconstruction in Georgia*, p. 231; Ala. Hse. *Jnl.*, 1871–1872, pp. 305–318.

12. *ASJ*, February 14, 1871.

13. Thompson, *Reconstruction in Georgia*, pp. 232, 243.

14. Ala. Hse. *Jnl.*, 1871–1872, pp. 308, 309, 316.

15. Hamilton, *Reconstruction in North Carolina*, p. 434; *ASJ*, April 12, 1871; D. L. Dalton to the secretaries of the Montgomery & Eufaula and the Alabama & Chattanooga Railroads, June 15, 1869, and acknowledgment of a letter on the subject from Soutter & Co. of New York, Governor Smith Letterbook, ASDAH.

16. *ASJ*, February 10, 1871; Ala. Hse *Jnl.*, 1871–1872, pp. 254–255; 1872–1873, p. 736; Shofner, *Nor Is It Over Yet*, p. 200.

17. D. L. Dalton to Porter King, L. L. Perkins, and B. F. Saffold, June 1, 1869, Governor Smith Letterbook, ASDAH.

18. Reed, *Texas Railroads*, p. 152; Hamilton, *Reconstruction in North Carolina*, p. 440; Pereyra, *James Lusk Alcorn*, p. 110; *Atlanta Daily New Era*, October 27, 1870; La. Sen. *Jnl.*, 1870, p. 236; Ala. Hse. *Jnl.*, 1869–1870, p. 18.

19. La. Sen. *Jnl.*, 1870, p. 237.

20. Report of Messrs. Farrand and Thom, Railroad Commissioners, November 9, 1871, in Ala. Hse. *Jnl.*, 1871–1872, p. 40.

21. Ala. Sen. *Jnl.*, 1871–1872, p. 344; Ala. Hse. *Jnl.*, 1871–1872, pp. 351–352.

22. *State of Alabama versus I. T. Burr et al.*, U.S. Reports, vol. 115, pp. 413, 429, 1885.

23. Ala. Hse. *Jnl.*, 1872–1873, p. 295.

24. *Mason Young et al. versus the Montgomery and Eufaula Railroad Company*, U.S. Circuit Court Cases, Woods, vol. 2, pp. 614–616; *Lewis versus City of Clarendon*, U.S. Circuit Court Cases, Dillon, vol. 5, pp. 329–340, 1880.

25. *Lewis versus City of Clarendon*, U.S. Circuit Court Cases, Dillon, vol. 5, pp. 329–340, 1880.

Chapter 4. "Railroad Fevers" and the Party Line at the Capitols

1. *Little Rock Republican*, March 16, 20, 1871.

2. *ASJ*, February 17, 18, 19, 21, 22, 1871; *San Antonio Express*, March 17, June 2, 1871; *Port Royal Commercial and Beaufort Republican*, February 19, March 19, 1874.

3. See sessional lists in the House and Senate journals of all the Southern states; in particular, Miss. Sen. *Jnl.*, 1870, pp. 14–16; 1872, pp. 14–16; Ala. Hse. *Jnl.*, 1869–1870, pp. 114–115; Ark. Hse. *Jnl.*, 1868–1869, pp. 97–99; 1871, pp. 56–59.

4. *Galveston Tri-Weekly News*, June 15, 1873; Tex. Sen. *Jnl.*, 1871 special session, pp. 313–314.

5. See S.C. Hse. *Jnl.*, index, 1868–1873.

6. *Charleston Courier*, March 2, 7, 1871.

7. La. Sen. *Debates*, 1870, pp. 626, 668.

8. *Atlanta Daily New Era*, August 31, September 8, 20, 22, 23, 24, October 7, 1870.

9. S.C. Hse. *Jnl.*, 1868–1869, pp. 431–434, 487; 1869, pp. 427–434; *Charleston Daily Republican*, March 7, 1871; S.C. Sen. *Jnl.*, 1868, pp. 198–199, 292–294, 306; 1869, pp. 189–190, 495, 506; 1870, pp. 464–465; 1872, pp. 227, 502–503, 526, 574. It must be stressed that in almost every vote Republicans joined the Democratic minority to oppose bills or to offer crippling amendments.

10. For example, see S.C. Hse. *Jnl.*, 1868–1869, pp. 355–357, 394–395, 420, 435; S.C. Sen. *Jnl.* 1868–1869, p. 309; 1869–1870, pp. 9–10.

11. *Charleston Daily Republican*, February 27, March 2, 7, 1871; *Charleston Courier*, September 11, 1868; S.C. Hse. *Jnl.*, 1868–1869, pp. 277–278, 450–452, 466; 1869–1870, pp. 339, 488–492; 1872–1873, pp. 100–104, 555; S.C. Sen. *Jnl.*, 1871–1872, pp. 353–354, 538–539.

12. Miss. Sen. *Jnl.*, 1870, pp. 341, 545–547; 1871, pp. 667–669; 1872, pp. 133, 184, 199, 332–335, 362–365, 454–455, 537–538; Miss. Hse. *Jnl.*, 1870, pp. 342–345, 548–549, 578–579, 607; 1871, pp. 1051–1055; 1872, pp. 481–482; 1873, pp. 1713, 1901.

13. *Jackson Pilot*, May 12, 15, 31, June 3, 1871.

14. Miss. Sen. *Jnl.*, 1871, pp. 645–646, 667–669; 1872, pp. 242–243, 332–335; Miss. Hse. *Jnl.*, 1871, pp. 1051–1055.

15. *Jackson Pilot*, March 24, May 6, 1871; Miss. Sen. *Jnl.*, 1871, pp. 599–600; 1872, pp. 105, 121, 125, 184–185, 199, 268–269, 332–335, 376–379, 416, 454–455, 494–495, 536; 1873, pp. 1154, 1323–1324, 1432, 1435–1436, 1510–1511, 1617, 1643, 1683, 1753–1754, 1774–1776; Miss. Hse. *Jnl.*, 1871, pp. 887–888; 1872, pp. 481–482; 1873; p. 1713.

16. Miss. Hse. *Jnl.*, 1875, pp. 48–49; see also *Jackson Weekly Clarion*, February 18, 1875.

17. *Wilmington Journal*, December 2, 1868, quoted in Price, "Railroads and Reconstruction in North Carolina," p. 361. Price's work is magnificent. It is thorough on railroad financing, detailed on political alignments and scrupulous in its lack of prejudice. It is virtually impossible to augment his work on North Carolina railroad aid policies, though I have tried. Shorter, but no less valuable for its size, is Allen W. Trelease's article, "Republican Reconstruction in North Carolina: A Roll-Call Analysis of the State House of Representatives, 1868–1870," in the *Journal of Southern History*, August 1976, pp. 319–342. It is excellent quantification. Some historian should do the same for every Southern legislature during the Reconstruction period. That would be quite a task, however: at least forty-six different legislative lists (twenty-three of each house), and hundreds of votes for each. Yet only some good roll call analysis which divides legislators on the basis of section and economic condition can answer questions about the course of legislative Reconstruction.

Price, "Railroads and Reconstruction," pp. 362–363; *Laws of North Carolina*, 1868–1869, pp. 46–54, 61–74, 77–104. Bills not pledging state funds usually passed unanimously.

18. Price, "Railroads and Reconstruction," pp. 282–283, 291–293, 301–

304, 312–315, 360–361, 374, 425–426, 523, 535–536; Trelease, "Republican Reconstruction in North Carolina," pp. 323, 325, 328, 329–330; N.C. Sen. *Jnl.*, 1868, pp. 189, 204–205, 233; 1868–1869, pp. 56–57, 66, 73–74, 79–80, 154, 200, 207, 520, 535–536, 580.

19. N.C. Sen. *Jnl.*, 1869–1870, pp. 10-11, 23, 26, 116, 185, 216, 223–227, 295, 297–298, 314–315, 477, 590; N.C. Hse. *Jnl.*, 1869–1870, pp. 359–360, 373.

20. Ark. Sen. *Jnl.*, 1868, pp. 206, 222, 245–247, 266; 1868–1869, pp. 541, 545, 546–548, 671; 1871, pp. 104, 240, 317, 363; Ark. Hse. *Jnl.*, 1868, pp. 436–437, 520; 1868–1869, pp. 841–842, 932–933, 936–937; 1871, pp. 622–623, 910–911, 917, 937–938, 978–979; *Little Rock Republican*, December 17, 18, 1868.

21. Ark. Sen. *Jnl.*, 1873, pp. 536–539, 567–568, 750–752, 760; *Little Rock Republican*, April 3, 4, 5, 10, 21, 22, 25, May 3, 1873; Thompson, *Arkansas and Reconstruction*, pp. 147–152; *Springfield Republican*, April 17, 24, 1874.

22. Ga. Hse. *Jnl.*, 1868, pp. 374–375, 394–395, 404–405; 1869, pp. 246–247, 493–494; Ga. Sen. *Jnl.*, 1868, pp. 312–313, 378, 423–427, 467–468; 1869, pp. 46, 96, 505–506, 516–517, 564, 629–630, 636–637, 666–667, 819.

23. *Atlanta Daily New Era*, August 28, 1870.

24. Ga. Sen. *Jnl.*, 1870, pp. 61–67, 106–107, 118–119, 131, 169–170, 210, 220–221, 265–266, 269, 436, 518–519; Ga. Hse. *Jnl.*, 1870, pp. 278–281, 288–289, 296–297, 431, 437–438, 450–451, 480–484, 486, 587–588, 726–731, 752–755, 759–763, 890–891, 1085; *Atlanta Daily New Era*, March 3, September 17, 20, 24, 25, 1868; August 25, 30, September 22, October 14, 27, 1870.

25. Ga. Hse. *Jnl.*, 1870, pp. 1008–1025; Ga. Sen. *Jnl.*, 1870, pp. 569–570; *Atlanta Daily New Era*, September 16, 1868; October 13, 1870.

26. *ASJ*, March 25, 1870; Ala. Hse. *Jnl.*, 1868, p. 274; 1869–1870, pp. 295–296, 350, 353–354, 369–370, 433–435, 460–461, 482–483, 490, 513.

27. *ASJ*, March 25, 1870.

28. *ASJ*, December 16, 23, 1869; February 22, 23, 25, 28, 1871; April 8, 9, 12, 16, 1873; Ala. Hse. *Jnl.*, 1869–1870, pp. 295–296, 353–354, 369–370; 1870–1871, pp. 339–340, 348–356, 361–365, 374–375, 394, 416–417, 418, 436–460, 465–468; Ala. Sen. *Jnl.*, 1870–1871, pp. 239, 242, 306.

29. *ASJ*, February 22, 25, 1872.

30. Fla. Hse. *Jnl.*, 1868, pp. 139, 158–159, 161; 1869, p. 89; 1869 extra session, pp. 78, 82, 90; 1872, pp. 172, 187, 286, 296; 1874, pp. 310, 314, 335; Fla. Sen. *Jnl.*, 1868, p. 85; 1869, pp. 63, 119, 156; 1869 extra session, pp. 59, 60; 1873, pp. 240, 245; 1874, p. 308.

31. *Jacksonville Florida Tri-Weekly Union*, November 5, 1872; March 20, 1873; Fla. Hse. *Jnl.*, 1869, pp. 94, 118, 160; 1869 extra session, pp. 79, 90; 1870, p. 26; 1871, pp. 146, 164, 178; Fla. Sen. *Jnl.*, 1869, p. 109.

32. Fla. Sen. *Jnl.*, 1873, p. 257; 1874, pp. 160, 198–202, 213, 223, 231,

271–272, 274–276; 1875, pp. 155–156, 169, 212, 250, 377, 397–398, 413–414; Fla. Hse. *Jnl.*, 1874, 180, 284, 290, 319; 1875, pp. 95–96, 144–145, 333, 335, 353–354, 370–379; *Jacksonville Tri-Weekly New South*, February 10, March 10, 1875.

33. La. Hse. *Jnl.*, 1870, pp. 43, 63, 72–74, 90–95, 238–243, 301, 303, 311, 324, 370; 1871, pp. 182, 204; La. Sen. *Jnl.*, 1869, pp. 116–117, 119, 174; 1870, pp. 180–183, 237; 1870 extra session, pp. 268, 303; 1872, pp. 98–99, 110, 116, 153–156, 188–189, 197, 213–214; 1871, pp. 157, 179, 218; La. Sen. *Debates*, 1870, pp. 654–657, 766, 768.

34. La. Hse. *Debates*, 1870, pp. 74–76; La. Sen. *Debates*, 1870, pp. 74–76; La. Sen. *Debates*, 1870, p. 768.

35. La. Sen. *Debates*, 1870, pp. 766–767.

36. Brockman, "Railroads, Radicals and the Militia Bill," pp. 105–122.

37. *Galveston News*, January 19, August 12, 26, 1870, *Dallas Herald*, June 10, 1871; January 11, 25, 1873; Tex. Hse. *Jnl.*, 1870, pp. 457–459, 462, 463, 516–520, 527, 632, 646–647, 703–705, 719–729, 760–761, 861, 965, 968, 995, 1004; 1871, pp. 215, 589–590, 691–693, 734, 946–947, 958–959, 1119–1125, 1128–1129, 1150, 1153, 1197, 1273, 1402, 1517, 1570, 1634, 1651–1652, 1692, 1711; 1871 extra session, pp. 91, 308, 313–317, 339, 343–345; Tex. Sen. *Jnl.*, 1870, pp. 194, 411, 435, 445, 454–455, 463, 465, 472, 518, 532, 534, 550, 562, 607, 681, 698; 1871, pp. 320–321, 469, 480, 498, 711, 1013, 1021, 1071–1076, 1085, 1120, 1131, 1145, 1148, 1211, 1222.

38. Tex. Hse. *Jnl.*, 1870, pp. 848–849, 890, 895, 991–993; 1871, pp. 518–520, 1128–1129, 1570, 1572; Tex. Sen. *Jnl.*, 1870, pp. 411, 463, 534, 549–551, 562; 1871, pp. 920–921, 1122, 1211–1222; *Galveston Tri-Weekly News*, April 19, 1871; *Dallas Herald*, April 23, 1870; *Houston Union*, June 18, August 5, 1870; *San Antonio Express*, August 3, 6, 11, 1870; April 13, 30, May 21, 31, 1871.

Chapter 5. The Enemy Within: Parochialism Run Amok

1. *Little Rock Republican*, November 22, 1871; *Dallas Herald*, February 22, 1873; *Jackson Pilot*, January 11, February 19, 1871; *New Orleans Republican*, September 25, October 4, November 6, 1870.

2. *ASJ*, November 9, 1873.

3. R. H. Hardaway to John Screven, January 5, 1871, Arnold-Screven Papers, SHC.

4. *Charleston Courier*, February 10, 1870; *Charleston Daily Republican*, February 10, 11, 14, 15, 23, 1870; E. Houstoun to J. P. Sanderson, April 15, 1869, L'Engle Papers, SHC.

5. *Jackson Pilot*, March 23, 1871; *Vicksburg Times and Republican*, March 2, 1873; *San Antonio Express*, April 27, 30, 1871; *Galveston Tri-Weekly News*, January 30, February 1, March 7, 1871.

6. *Atlanta Daily New Era*, September 22, 1870.

7. William Welker to W. W. Holden, May 11. 1869, Holden Papers, Department of Manuscripts, Duke University; *Atlanta Daily New Era*, October 27, 1870.

8. Price, "Railroads and Reconstruction," pp. 282–283, 315–320.

9. *Atlanta Daily New Era*, October 27, 1870.

10. *Charleston Daily Republican*, February 8, 1870.

11. La. Sen. *Debates*, 1870, p. 656; Price, "Railroads and Reconstruction," p. 375.

12. *Beaufort Republican*, January 16, February 6, April 17, 1873; *Charleston Daily Republican*, April 7, 1871; *Charleston Courier*, September 11, 1868.

13. *San Antonio Express*, May 22, July 2, 1870; April 4, 13, 18, 21, 25, 27, 30, May 26, 1871; *Galveston Tri-Weekly News*, April 21, May 17, 1871.

14. *Dallas Herald*, April 23, 1870; *San Antonio Express*, February 4, July 30, 1870; April 13, June 6, 11, 1871.

15. *Dallas Herald*, April 15, May 20, 1871; *San Antonio Express*, April 25, 1871.

16. *Jacksonville Florida Tri-Weekly Union*, February 25, 1873; *ASJ*, January 8, 18, 1869; January 22, February 8, March 16, 20, 23, 27, April 4, 5, July 8, 1873; Shofner, "Chimerical Scheme," p. 18; Bailey, "Alabama and West Florida Annexation," pp. 225–226.

17. *Vicksburg Times and Republican*, March 2, 1873; *ASJ*, March 23, 1873.

18. Fla. Hse. *Jnl.*, 1869, pp. 55, 57; *ASJ*, May 15, 26, 31, 1869; May 4, 1873.

19. *ASJ*, May 31, 1869.

20. Shofner, *Nor Is It Over Yet*, p. 209.

21. *Acts of Florida*, 1869 extra session, pp. 25–36, 40–42; 1870, pp. 10–13.

22. *Jacksonville Florida Tri-Weekly Union*, April 22, 1873; *ASJ*, January 30, February 4, 5, 7, 1874.

23. *Charleston Daily Republican*, December 17, 1869; *ASJ*, May 7, 8, 11, December 17, 1869; August 16, 1870; September 27, November 12, 1871; February 20, 25, 1872.

24. *Jacksonville New South*, October 7, 24, 1874.

25. *Atlanta Daily New Era*, September 25, 1868; there were sporadic exceptions to this blind localism: the *Alabama State Journal*, for example, and the *Houston Union*.

26. *Dallas Herald*, December 21, 1872; *ASJ*, May 29, 1870; January 1, 1874; *Jackson Pilot*, February 9, 1871.

Chapter 6. *Winning Friends and Influencing Legislation*

1. *Atlanta Daily New Era*, September 25, 1868; *Report of the Commission to Investigate Fraud and Corruption under Act of Assembly Session 1871–72* (Raleigh, 1872), pp. 142, 176–177, 210, 256–257, 400–401, 489–491 (hereafter referred to as *Shipp Report*).

2. "Allegations Against Senator Powell Clayton," *U.S. Senate Documents*, 42nd Congress, 3rd session, no. 512, pp. 91, 99 (hereafter referred to as "Allegations Against Senator Powell Clayton"); *San Antonio Express*, July 22, 1870; *ASJ*, February 14, 1871; *Dallas Herald*, May 7, 1870; P. Thweatt to John Screven, September 11, October 21, 1870, Arnold-Screven Papers, SHC.

3. Daniels, *Prince of Carpetbaggers*, pp. 175–176; "Allegations Against Senator Powell Clayton," pp. 352–360; *Charleston Daily Republican*, March 18, 1871.

4. Raper, "Political Career of William Woods Holden," pp. 63–64, 269; *Little Rock Republican*, April 15, 17, 1873.

5. *Charleston Daily Republican*, February 7, 1870; *Jackson Pilot*, August 22, 1871; *Charleston Daily Republican*, February 7, 1870; *Jackson Pilot*, August 22, 1871; *Charleston Courier*, February 19, 1870.

6. Price, "Railroads and Reconstruction," pp. 407–408; *Vicksburg Times*, October 14, 1873; *San Antonio Express*, June 10, 1870.

7. Price, "Railroads and Reconstruction," pp. 408–413.

8. S.C. Sen. *Jnl.*, 1868, p. 76; S.C. Hse. *Jnl.*, 1873, p. 141.

9. *San Antonio Express*, February 22, 1870; "Fraud Report," *Reports and Resolutions of South Carolina*, 1877–1878, pp. 1582–1583 (hereafter referred to as "Fraud Report").

10. "Fraud Report," p. 1583; *U.S. House Reports*, 42nd Congress, 2nd session, no. 211, p. 396.

11. G. A. Sheldon to Henry Clay Warmoth, February 6, 1870, Warmoth Papers, SHC; Wallace, *Carpet-Bag Rule in Florida*, p. 119.

12. Warmoth's successor was also under the impression that the governor had run a shakedown against railroad enterprises. See William P. Kellogg to J. J. Creswell, January 29, 1874, Kellogg Papers, LSU.

13. H. S. McComb to Warmoth, May 14, 1872, Warmoth Papers, SHC; Williamson, *After Slavery*, p. 387; W. J. Hawkins to Alexander B. Andrews, September 9, 10, 1868; W. B. Gulick to Andrews, September 13, 1868, Andrews Papers, SHC; *Charleston Courier*, September 14, 15, 1868.

14. Wallace, *Carpet-Bag Rule in Florida*, pp. 103–104; "Fraud Report," p. 1633.

15. "Fraud Report," p. 1581; Price, "Railroads and Reconstruction," pp. 413–417, 419–420.

16. *Charleston Courier*, February 25, 1871; *ASJ*, February 14, 1871.

17. La. Sen. *Debates*, 1870, pp. 721, 797, 800; *New Orleans Republican*, January 23, 1873.

18. *ASJ*, February 14, 1871; *U.S. House Reports*, 42nd Congress, 2nd session, no. 211, p. 396; "Testimony Taken Before the Joint Committee of the Senate and House to Inquire Into and Ascertain What Disposition Has Been Made of the Blue Ridge Railroad Bonds," *S.C. Legislative Documents*, 1872, p. 819.

19. "Condition of Affairs," vol. 4, p. 748; vol. 9, p. 262; *Little Rock*

Republican, August 1, 1873; *Charleston Daily Republican*, January 27, March 10, 18, 1871; Grosz, "Pinchback," p. 543.

20. "Condition of Affairs," vol. 4, p. 748; vol. 8, p. 238; Grosz, "Pinchback," p. 543; Conway, *Reconstruction of Georgia*, p. 206; *Charleston Daily Republican*, March 18, 1871; Stover, *Railroads of the South*, p. 91; "Fraud Report," pp. 1630–1631, 1634–1645; *Dallas Herald*, September 23, 1871; *U.S. House Reports*, 42nd Congress, 2nd session, no. 211, p. 443.

21. "Fraud Report," pp. 1632–1633, 1648, 1649.

22. *Vicksburg Times*, November 22, 1873.

23. *San Antonio Express*, July 22, 1870; "Condition of Affairs," vol. 4, pp. 729, 730, 736, 740; vol. 8, p. 238.

24. *Charleston Courier*, February 19, 1870; Wallace, *Carpet-Bag Rule in Florida*, pp. 103–105.

25. *U.S. House Reports*, 42nd Congress, 2nd session, no. 211, p. 332; *ASJ*, October 16, 1870; Coulter, *Reconstruction*, p. 153.

26. *New York Herald*, October 12, 1874; Evans, *Ballots and Fence Rails*, p. 162; *Charleston Daily Republican*, February 27, March 1, 3, 4, 1871; *Charleston Courier*, January 31, 1870; *Houston Daily Union*, August 14, 1870; Daniels, *Prince of Carpetbaggers*, p. 239; D. Richards to Elihu Washburne, January 6, 1869, Washburne Papers, LC.

27. *New York Herald*, April 10, May 31, 1875; *Galveston News*, January 19, 1870.

28. "Condition of Affairs," vol. 4, p. 500; *U.S. House Reports*, 43rd Congress, 3rd session, no. 261, p. 973; *New York Herald*, October 19, 1874.

29. Bradley, *Triumph of Militant Republicanism*, pp. 330, 335, 338; Elliott, *Nevada*, pp. 159–161; Knapp, *New Jersey Politics*, pp. 159–160; *New York Commercial and Financial Chronicle*, March 20, 1869; *New York World*, November 22, 1867.

30. [New York] *Nation*, January 11, 1872.

31. *Vicksburg Times*, October 10, 14, 1873; *Jackson Pilot*, February 7, 1871.

32. *ASJ*, October 1, 1870; "Condition of Affairs," vol. 8, p. 232.

33. *Vicksburg Times*, October 14, 31, 1873; January 13, March 19, April 5, 12, 1874; see also Joseph E. Brown to the political editor of the *Sun*, October 11, 1871, Brown Papers, UGa.

34. Ala. Hse. *Jnl.*, 1872–1873, pp. 583, 707; Conway, *Reconstruction of Georgia*, p. 205; Daniels, *Prince of Carpetbaggers*, pp. 224–227.

35. *Charleston Daily Republican*, January 13, 1870.

36. Ibid., January 14, March 19, 1870.

Chapter 7. "Let the Representatives . . . Have a Hand in It"

1. *New York Herald*, May 11, 1871.

2. La. Hse. *Debates*, 1869, p. 122.

3. *Acts of South Carolina*, 1871, pp. 597–598; 1872, pp. 118, 176, 269–272; 1873, pp. 434–435; 1874, pp. 595, 694–697; *Laws of North Carolina*,

1869–1870, pp. 103–111, 122–124; *Acts of Louisiana*, 1873, pp. 152–156; Vernon, *ARM*, p. 293; La. Sen. *Jnl.*, 1870 extra session, p. 304; *New York Herald*, April 30, 1875; *ASJ*, March 4, May 8, November 14, 1869.

4. "Condition of Affairs," vol. 8, p. 232; Vernon, *ARM*, pp. 392, 396, 397; Lyles, *Official Railway Manual*, pp. 431, 444, 464, 469, 477; Daniels, *Prince of Carpetbaggers*, pp. 174–177, 220; Price, "Railroads and Reconstruction," p. 287; *Acts of South Carolina*, 1872, pp. 204–205; 1873, pp. 356–359.

5. *Laws of North Carolina*, 1868 special session, p. 29; La. Sen. *Jnl.*, 1870, p. 304; Ga. Sen. *Jnl.*, 1870, p. 436; Tex. Hse. *Jnl.*, 1871, pp. 589, 692–693, 870; S.C. Sen. *Jnl.*, 1872, p. 593; 1873, pp. 535, 560–561; *Acts of South Carolina*, 1872, pp. 210–211; 1874, pp. 639–640; *Laws of Mississippi*, 1871, pp. 138–155.

6. *Little Rock Republican*, May 16, September 26, November 13, 1871; October 7, 1872.

7. J. W. Berry to Tod R. Caldwell, March 27, Caldwell Papers, NCDAH; see also Marcus Ervin to W. W. Holden, October 15, 1869, Holden Papers, NCDAH.

8. *Charleston Daily Republican*, February 3, March 26, April 7, 1870; *ASJ*, May 31, 1872; petition signed by many and sent to the president of the North Carolina Railroad; J. J. Mott to Holden, July 18, 1868; J. W. Berry to Tod Caldwell, March 27, 1869; James H. Boone to Holden, August 10, 1868; Josiah B. Davis to Holden, August 13, 1868; Robert N. Hager to G. L. Harris, July 6, 1868, all in Holden Papers, NCDAH.

9. Price, "Railroads and Reconstruction," pp. 268–269; Thomas B. Long to Holden, December 1, 1868, Holden Papers, NCDAH; *Atlanta Daily New Era*, September 19, 20, 1868.

10. Thompson, *Reconstruction in Georgia*, pp. 238–242; Price, "Railroads and Reconstruction," pp. 274–277, 280.

11. O. H. Blocker to Tod Caldwell, January 6, 1871, Caldwell Papers, SHC; extract of a stockholder's meeting, May 6, 1871; Holden to W. A. Guthrie, James Bowman, and others, April 8, 1869, Holden Papers, NCDAH; *Atlanta Daily New Era*, September 13, 16, 1868.

12. *New Orleans Crescent*, January 30, 1869; E. C. Anderson diary, February 8, 1871, SHC; C. Happoldt to Caldwell, March 22, 1869, Tod Caldwell Papers, SHC; Price, "Railroads and Reconstruction," pp. 282, 301–304, 312–320, 535–536.

13. J. J. Mott to Holden, July 2, 1870; W. A. Smith to Holden, January 1, 1870; Tod Caldwell to Holden, August 17, 1869; James Sinclair to Holden, April 25, 1870, Holden Papers, NCDAH; Jonathan A. Colgrove to Caldwell, December 22, 1868, Tod Caldwell Papers, SHC; Price, "Railroads and Reconstruction," pp. 271–272; Thompson, *Reconstruction in Georgia*, p. 240; "Condition of Affairs," vol. 8, p. 183; *Columbus Daily Enquirer*, December 17, 24, 1870; *ASJ*, November 1, 1872; *Charleston Daily Republican*, January 31, 1870.

14. *Charleston Daily Republican*, March 2, 7, 1871.

15. Vernon, *ARM*, pp. 393–394, 397–400; Clayton, *Aftermath of the Civil War*, p. 238; *Little Rock Republican*, August 29, 30, 1871; March 1, 1872; *ASJ*, May 8, 1869.

16. *ASJ*, March 4, 1869; February 10, 1871; March 6, 1872; Ala. Hse. *Jnl.*, 1869–1870, pp. 7–19; 1871, pp. 23–24, 88–89; H. S. McComb to Henry Clay Warmoth, May 14, 1870, Warmoth Papers, SHC; *U.S. House Reports*, 42nd Congress, 2nd session, no. 211, p. 395; Vernon, *ARM*, p. 392; Price, "Railroads and Reconstruction," pp. 425ff.; Davis, *Florida*, p. 667.

17. Miss. Hse. *Jnl.*, 1873, pp. 1532–1539, 1544–1546, 1551–1555, 1564.

18. *Little Rock Republican*, September 26, 1871; see also *New York Herald*, April 30, 1875.

Chapter 8. Testing the Gospel of Prosperity, 1870–1871

1. *ASJ*, November 4, 1870.

2. U.S. Bureau of the Census, *Ninth Census*, 1870, vol. 3, pp. 72, 81–83; *New Orleans Crescent*, January 30, 1869; *Charleston Daily Republican*, February 15, 1870; *Beaufort Republican*, October 8, 1871.

3. *ASJ*, March 11, 1869; *San Antonio Express*, September 17, 1870; *Charleston Courier*, January 6, 1872; *Jackson Pilot*, March 28, 1871.

4. *Beaufort Republican*, May 9, 1872; February 6, 1873; *ASJ*, March 29, April 30, July 16, 1870; *Dallas Herald*, February 22, 1873; *Little Rock Republican*, May 5, July 24, 1871.

5. *New Orleans Price-Current*, November 2, 1870.

6. U.S. Bureau of the Census, *Compendium of the Tenth Census*, 1880, pp. 452, 453, 455, 458, 460, 462.

7. Ibid., pp. 14–15, 20–23, 52–55.

8. Ibid., p. 332.

9. U.S. Bureau of the Census, *Tenth Census*, 1880, vol 5, pp. 38, 49, 71.

10. Ibid., pp. 116–118, 122, 155, 174.

11. *ASJ*, September 14, 17, 1870; *Dallas Herald*, July 17, 1869; February 3, 1870; *Little Rock Republican*, February 20, 1872; Poor, *Manual*, 1877–1878, p. ix.

12. Poor, *Manual*, 1877, p. ix.

13. *San Antonio Express*, June 23, 1870; *ASJ*, July 20, 24, September 13, 1870; *Charleston Daily Republican*, February 23, 1870; see also, "Address of the State Central Committee of the Republican Party, December 8, 1870," in Mississippi Department of Archives and History Broadside Collection; *Atlanta Daily New Era*, November 12, 13, 17, December 2, 1870.

14. *Little Rock Republican*, November 20, December 18, 1871; *San Antonio Express*, June 16, 1870.

15. *New Orleans Republican*, September 12, 1870, *ASJ*, March 20, April

10, 1869; March 8, 1870; *Charleston Daily Republican*, December 21, 22, 1869; March 8, 24, 1870.

16. *New Orleans Republican*, September 24, 1870; *Atlanta Daily New Era*, November 14, 1870.

17. *Charleston Daily Republican*, April 19, 1871; *New Orleans Republican*, October 26, 1870.

18. *ASJ*, May 4, 1869; July 19, 1871; see also *Atlanta Daily New Era*, November 12, December 10, 1870.

19. *Huntsville Daily Democrat*, August 15, October 5, 1870; *New Orleans Republican*, October 23, 1870; *New Orleans Times*, February 21, 1869; *Macon Georgia Weekly Telegraph*, November 15, 22, 1870; *Columbus Daily Enquirer*, September 6, October 15, 1870.

20. *Charleston Daily Republican*, July 28, 1870; February 23, 1871; *ASJ*, July 20, September 15, 1870; *Aiken Tribune*, August 31, 1872.

21. *ASJ*, March 8, August 18, September 13, October 15, 18, November 5, 1870; October 31, 1872.

22. *Jackson Pilot*, June 3, 1871; *ASJ*, March 17, 1871.

23. *New Orleans Republican*, November 6, 1870; Poor, *Manual*, 1870–1871, p. 504.

24. All figures are from the *Tribune Almanac*, 1870, 1871, 1872, 1873.

25. *Tribune Almanac*, 1871, pp. 69–73; 1872, pp. 74, 77.

26. For intimidation, see Trelease, *White Terror*, pp. 240–242, 244–245, 270–273.

27. *Tribune Almanac*, 1871, p. 70.

28. Moneyhon, *Republicanism in Reconstruction Texas*, pp. 212–213; *Macon Georgia Weekly Telegraph*, December 24, 1870; *Tribune Almanac*, 1871, pp. 69–73.

29. *New Orleans Republican*, November 6, 1870.

Chapter 9. *"They Must Stand Aside . . .":*
The Republican Mission in Peril

1. *Little Rock Republican*, January 17, 1868.

2. *Mobile Register*, January 28, 1872.

3. La. Hse. *Debates*, 1870, pp. 221–222, 225, 276–277; Tex. Hse. *Jnl.*, 1871, p. 1528.

4. *Vicksburg Times*, May 10, 15, 24, June 3, 1873; *San Antonio Express*, March 17, 22, 1871; Fla. Hse. *Jnl.*, 1872, pp. 92, 266.

5. *N.C. Legislative Documents*, 1869–1870, no. 2, p. 30.

6. *Carrollton Republican Standard*, August 14, 1869; *Vicksburg Times*, May 10, 1873.

7. *Charleston Courier*, February 4, 1868.

8. *Little Rock Republican*, December 2, 3, 1868; *Jackson Weekly Clarion*, December 31, 1874; *Acts of Georgia*, 1870, p. 401.

9. La. Hse. *Debates*, 1870, pp. 155–156, 166, 239–240; *Little Rock Republican*, March 22, 1871; *Jackson Pilot*, April 21, 1871.

10. La. Hse. *Debates*, 1870, p. 225.

11. *Acts of Louisiana*, 1873, pp. 83–96; M. Jeff Thompson to Henry Clay Warmoth, September 6, 1870, Warmoth Papers, Duke; *Acts of Arkansas*, 1868–1869, pp. 80–84, 197–200.

12. *ASJ*, January 5, 6, 1871.

13. David Hodgin to B. S. Hedrick, January 16, 1869, Hedrick Papers, SHC.

14. *Laws of Mississippi*, 1873, p. 353.

15. *Atlanta Daily New Era*, August 26, 1870; under an earlier statute, *Acts of Georgia*, 1870, pp. 41, 61, half of the Western & Atlantic net earnings were reserved for the school fund.

16. Nunn, *Texas under the Carpetbaggers*, p. 37; *Vicksburg Times and Republican*, February 27, April 10, 1873; *ASJ*, October 1, 1870; Fla. Sen. *Jnl.*, 1873, pp. 52–65.

17. *Vicksburg Times and Republican*, February 27, 1873.

18. Ibid., February 27, 1873; Fla. Hse. *Jnl.*, 1872, pp. 14–17.

19. *Vicksburg Times*, July 15, 1873; March 29, 1874.

20. Ibid., February 27, August 3, 1873; *Jackson Pilot*, August 22, 1871; see also Ames, *Adelbert Ames*, p. 390.

21. *San Antonio Express*, August 10, 1870; Tex. Hse. *Jnl.*, 1871, pp. 1551–1559.

22. Williamson, *After Slavery*, pp. 144–148.

23. *Houston Union*, August 6, 1870; *Carrollton Republican Standard*, December 22, 1869; Shugg, *Origins of Class Struggle*, p. 262; Holt, *Black over White*, p. 298.

24. *Little Rock Republican*, August 26, 1872.

25. Shugg, *Origins of Class Struggle*, p. 261.

26. See *Beaufort Republican*, February 1872, for tax lists; for examples of relief from taxation and penalties for delinquency, see *Acts of Alabama*, 1870, p. 30; Fla. Hse. *Jnl.*, 1871, p. 151; *Acts of Arkansas*, 1869, pp. 130–131; 1871, pp. 8–9; 1873, pp. 31–32.

27. Fla. Hse. *Jnl.*, 1869, p. 131; Ala. Sen. *Jnl.*, 1872, p. 482.

28. Reed, *Texas Railroads*, pp. 164–177.

29. *ASJ*, January 4, 1871; see also Ark. Sen. *Jnl.*, 1871, pp. 276, 362–365.

30. Rogers, "Agrarianism in Alabama," pp. 21, 23–25; Holt, *Black over White*, pp. 289–298, 315–319; La. Hse. *Jnl.*, 1873, pp. 211–217; *New Orleans Republican*, March 2, 1873; Ala. Hse. *Jnl.*, 1868, pp. 210–211, 320; Ala. Sen. *Jnl.*, 1870–1871, p. 120; 1871–1872, pp. 436–437, 545.

31. Cooper, *The Conservative Regime*, p. 120; *Little Rock Republican*, March

16, 1871; *Charleston Daily Republican*, December 24, 1868; Kemp P. Battle to Attorney General Olds, August 27, 1869, Holden Papers, NCDAH.

32. *Charleston Daily Republican*, March 19, 1870; Vincent, "Negro Leadership in Louisiana," p. 124.

33. Pike, *Prostrate State*, p. 277.

34. *San Antonio Express*, November 28, 1871.

35. Richardson, *Negro in the Reconstruction of Florida*, p. 210.

Chapter 10. Friends in Need on Capitol Hill

1. *Acts of Alabama*, 1868, pp. 142–144; 1868–1869, pp. 594, 597–598, 601–602; *Acts of Arkansas*, 1868, pp. 348–349; *ASJ*, April 9, 1869; *New Orleans Price-Current*, September 13, 1871; *Galveston Tri-Weekly News*, July 30, 1869; *Vicksburg Times*, June 13, 1874; *New York Herald*, April 23, 1874; *CG*, 41st Congress, 3rd session, Appendix, p. 177.

2. *ASJ*, January 28, 1869; *CG*, 41st Congress, 3rd session, Appendix, p. 178.

3. William P. Kellogg to B. F. Flanders, April 9, 1872, Flanders Papers, LSU; *New Orleans Republican*, January 17, 1873; Hood, "Brotherly Hate," p. 126; *CG*, 41st Congress, 3rd session, Appendix, pp. 173, 178, 237; *Charleston Daily Republican*, February 15, March 6, 1871; *New Orleans Price-Current*, December 28, 1873; *Vicksburg Times and Republican*, January 29, 1873; *Jackson Pilot*, January 17, 1871; *ASJ*, January 18, 1869; *New Orleans Times*, January 28, February 2, 23, 1869.

4. *Galveston Tri-Weekly News*, July 30, 1869.

5. *ASJ*, April 23, June 24, 26, 1869.

6. See, for example, *CG*, 41st Congress, 3rd session, pp. 203–204; *ASJ*, February 11, 12, March 1, 19, April 7, 24, 1869; *Beaufort Republican*, January 30, February 6, 1873; Thompson, "Leadership in Arkansas Reconstruction," pp. 371–373; Seip, "Southern Representatives and Economic Measures," pp. 208–209, 263–265; Poor, *Manual*, 1877–1878, pp. 988–991.

7. *Springfield Republican*, July 22, 1870; *New York Herald*, March 4, 1875; Woodward, *Reunion and Reaction*, p. 61.

8. *New Orleans Crescent*, January 28, 1869; *ASJ*, January 18, February 15, 1869; *Vicksburg Times and Republican*, March 3, 1873; Seip, "Southern Representatives and Economic Measures," pp. 207–208; *CG*, 42nd Congress, 3rd session, Appendix, pp. 814–816, 2443–2452.

9. *Charleston Daily Republican*, February 24, 1871.

10. *ASJ*, February 6, 1874.

11. Hood, "Brotherly Hate," pp. 115–120, 198; Seip, "Southern Representatives and Economic Measures," pp. 104, 105, 212–215.

12. *Dallas Herald*, February 22, 1873; Coulter, *Reconstruction*, p. 272;

Charleston Daily Republican, March 31, 1870; *New York Sun*, February 13, 1875; *U.S. Sen. Jnl.*, 41st Congress, 2nd session, pp. 877–878.

13. Hood, "Brotherly Hate," pp. 143–148; *Vicksburg Times*, November 6, 1873; *Port Royal Commercial and Beaufort Republican*, December 11, 1873.

14. *Dallas Herald*, August 26, 1871; *ASJ*, September 13, 1870; *CG*, 41st Congress, 2nd session, pp. 4770, 4775, 4776, 4901–4903.

15. *Beaufort Republican*, April 17, 1873; *Charleston Daily Republican*, March 22, 1870; *New Orleans Times*, February 4, 1869.

16. Ala. Sen. *Jnl.*, 1870–1871, p. 235; G. A. Sheldon to Henry Clay Warmoth, February 7, 1870, Warmoth Papers, SHC.

17. *Little Rock Republican*, May 1, 1872; *ASJ*, March 27, April 20, 1869; *Donaldsonville Chief*, February 22, 1873; G. A. Sheldon to Warmoth, February 7, 1870, Warmoth Papers, SHC; *CG*, 41st Congress, 2nd session, pp. 4719–4722.

18. *Dallas Herald*, November 6, 13, 1869; *Jacksonville Florida Tri-Weekly Union*, March 15, 1873; Woodward, *Reunion and Reaction*, pp. 71, 158; *New York Sun*, February 13, 1875; see also Senator Jacob Howard's diatribe, a thorough description of Fremont's culpability and French gullibility, in *CG*, 41st Congress, 2nd session, pp. 4763–4766.

19. Woodward, *Reunion and Reaction*, p. 158; *New York Sun*, February 13, 1875; *Jackson Pilot*, February 23, 1871; *U.S. Sen. Jnl.*, 41st Congress, 2nd session, pp. 660, 843, 869, 876, 896–898; *CG*, 41st Congress, 2nd session, pp. 4730, 4731, 4766–4767, 4776.

20. *San Antonio Express*, May 22, 24, June 7, 24, July 3, 12, 1870; *CG*, 41st Congress, 2nd session, pp. 4638–4640, 4720–4722, 4909–4910; *CG*, 41st Congress, 3rd session, pp. 4763–4776.

21. J. R. West to Warmoth, March 2, 3, 1871; L. A. Sheldon to Warmoth, March 5, 1871, Warmoth Papers, SHC: R. P. Littlejohn to Thomas B. Pugh, March 20, 1871, W. W. Pugh Papers, LSU; *New York Herald*, March 2, 4, 1871; Seip, "Southern Representatives and Economic Measures," pp. 165–173; *CG*, 41st Congress, 3rd session, p. 1959.

22. Woodward, *Reunion and Reaction*, pp. 75–89, 97–99; Tom Scott to Matt Ransom, December 15, 1874, Ransom Papers, SHC; *Vicksburg Times and Republican*, August 24, 1874; *The Road*, September 1, 1875; February 15, June 1, 1876.

23. *ASJ*, February 11, 12, 1874.

24. Tom Scott to Ransom, December 15, 1874; see also the president of the Richmond & Danville to Ransom, February 19, 1875, Ransom Papers, SHC; Seip, "Southern Representatives and Economic Measures," pp. 259–261.

25. Seip, "Southern Representatives and Economic Measures," pp. 260–261; 43rd Congress, 2nd session, p. 1600.

26. [New York] *Nation*, December 23, 1875; Seip, "Southern Congressmen and Economic Measures," pp. 290–291.

Chapter 11. Friends in Deed on Wall Street? The Enemy Without

1. *New Orleans Republican*, October 28, 1870.
2. Ibid., October 30, 1870; La. Sen. *Debates*, 1870, p. 619; *ASJ*, April 19, 1869, Lyles, *Official Railway Manual*, 1870–1871, pp. 173, 426; Vernon, *ARM*, pp. 392, 394, 398; Thompson, *Reconstruction in Georgia*, pp. 230, 236.
3. Stover, *Railroads of the South*, pp. 99–103.
4. Ibid., pp. 105–119; Pearson, *Readjuster Movement*, p. 28; Vernon, *ARM*, pp. 319, 328–329, 341.
5. Stover, "Southern Ambitions of the Illinois Central Railroad," pp. 499–510.
6. Somers, *Southern States Since the War*, pp. 81–82, 87; Thompson, *Reconstruction in Georgia*, pp. 311–313.
7. Vernon, *ARM*, pp. 401–407.
8. Ibid., pp. 450–632.
9. Stover makes these estimates in "Northern Financial Interests in Southern Railroads," p. 210. The numbers do have room for error: for one thing, the residence listed in railroad manuals for directors is not necessarily their real address, and it is that listing on which their classification as Southerners or outsiders is based. See also Vernon, *ARM*, pp. 334, 345, 375, 381, 384, 387, 388, 391, 398, 405, 407, 696.
10. Hirshson, *Grenville M. Dodge*, pp. 182–188; Thompson, *Reconstruction in Georgia*, p. 232; Davis, *Florida*, p. 656.
11. *ASJ*, August 5, 1873; *New York World*, February 8, 1868; Elliott, *Nevada*, pp. 159–160; Stover, *Railroads of the South*, p. 102; Wallace, *Carpet-Bag Rule in Florida*, pp. 156–157; *Huntsville Daily Democrat*, January 14, 1872.
12. *Charleston Courier*, February 19, 1870; *ASJ*, August 16, 1870; June 8, July 25, 1873; January 1, 1874; *Dallas Herald*, March 1, 1873; *Little Rock Republican*, September 13, 15, 1871; *Jackson Pilot*, April 25, 1871.
13. Price, "Railroads and Reconstruction," pp. 404–406.
14. Ibid., pp. 423–426; Davis, *Florida*, pp. 659–663.
15. Baughman, *Charles Morgan*, pp. 149–156.
16. La. Hse. *Debates*, 1870, p. 69.
17. Ibid., pp. 68–69, 154; La. Sen. *Debates*, 1870, pp. 617, 618, 622, 624; *Carrollton Republican Standard*, January 29, 1869, quoting the *New Orleans Republican* of January 25.
18. *Jacksonville New South*, February 20, March 10, 1875; Tex. Sen. *Jnl.*, 1870, p. 699; Fla. Hse. *Jnl.*, 1869, p. 95.

Chapter 12. Railroad Ties and Bonds: Construction, Credit, and the "Consumptive Purse"

1. *Beaufort Republican*, August 28, 1873.
2. Vernon, *ARM*, pp. 370, 373, 381.

3. *Charleston Daily Republican*, February 23, 1870; *Jackson Pilot*, June 30, August 1, 1871.

4. Conway, *Reconstruction of Georgia*, pp. 205–206; Price, "Railroads and Reconstruction," pp. 446, 535–536; Thompson, "Leadership in Arkansas Reconstruction," pp. 416–428; *Little Rock Republican*, August 28, 1871.

5. Thompson, "Leadership in Arkansas Reconstruction," pp. 375–376, 380; *Jackson Pilot*, July 8, 1871; *Little Rock Republican*, January 16, 1873; *Charleston Daily Republican*, April 6, 1870; Miss. Hse. *Jnl.*, 1873, p. 1548; E. M. Cheney to J. P. Sanderson, August 29, 1870, L'Engle Papers, SHC.

6. General superintendent of the Jacksonville, Pensacola & Mobile Railroad to Sanderson, August 1, 1870; Cheney to Sanderson, August 29, 1870, L'Engle Papers, SHC; *Charleston Daily Republican*, February 23, March 19, 1870.

7. Cheney to Sanderson, August 29, 1870, L'Engle Papers, SHC.

8. *Aiken Tribune*, November 9, 1872.

9. Vernon, *ARM*, p. 395; Thompson, "Leadership in Arkansas Reconstruction," pp. 431–432; *Laws of Mississippi*, 1871, p. 156; 1873, p. 605; New York *Railway Monitor*, October 15, 1873.

10. *Jackson Pilot*, June 17, September 8, 1871; some of the bonds were sold, however. See Vernon, *ARM*, p. 388.

11. Price, "Railroads and Reconstruction," p. 538; *N.C. Legislative Documents*, 1869–1870, no. 33, p. 16. Another reason for slack interest in Southern securities was the railroad boom worldwide. Greenberg, *Financiers and Railroads*, pp. 41–43.

12. E. M. L'Engle to J. P. Sanderson, August 24, 1870, L'Engle Papers, SHC; Thompson, "Leadership in Arkansas Reconstruction," p. 432; *Charleston Daily Republican*, January 24, 1871.

13. *Jacksonville Florida Tri-Weekly Union*, February 20, 1873; Daniels, *Prince of Carpetbaggers*, p. 264.

14. *Houston Union*, August 3, 1870.

15. *Charleston Daily Republican*, April 6, 1871.

16. E. M. L'Engle to Sanderson, August 19, 23, September 11, 1870; E. Houstoun to Sanderson, September 7, 1870; M. D. Papy to L'Engle, August 30, 1872, January 8, 27, 1873; F. B. Papy to L'Engle, January 2, 13, 17, 1873; Milton S. Littlefield to L'Engle, January 2, February 1, 1873; E. Houstoun to L'Engle, September 7, 1870; Henry Jackson to L'Engle, December 13, 1871; John A. Henderson to L'Engle, July 15, 1872; Peeler and Rainey to L'Engle, July 19, 20, 1872; R. B. Hilton to L'Engle, January 3, 1873; H. E. Young to L'Engle, January 9, 1873; W. B. Woods to L'Engle, January 23, 1873; A. Huling to Milton S. Littlefield, April 15, 1871; Jackson, Lawter and Basinger to Littlefield, December 1, 11, 1871, L'Engle Papers, SHC; *Charleston Daily Republican*, April 6, 1870.

17. *Little Rock Republican*, February 26, 1872.

18. Thompson, "Leadership in Arkansas Reconstruction," pp. 392–397; Klein, *Louisville and Nashville Railroad* pp. 119–122; Vernon, *ARM*, pp. 359–368; *Beaufort Republican*, August 7, 1873.

19. S. W. Hopkins & Co. to M. S. Littlefield, August 30, 1870; E. Houstoun to Littlefield, June 17, 1871; E. Houstoun to L'Engle, May 27, 1872; Henry R. Jackson to L'Engle, December 22, 1871; M. D. Papy to L'Engle, May 24, 28, June 2, 1872; F. B. Papy to L'Engle, May 31, 1872, L'Engle Papers, SHC.

20. M. D. Papy to L'Engle, June 13, 1872; Peeler and Rainey to L'Engle, July 15, 1872, L'Engle Papers, SHC.

21. New York *Railway Monitor*, October 15, November 15, 1873.

22. M. D. Papy to L'Engle, May 28, 1872, L'Engle Papers, SHC; M. S. Littlefield to Ransom & Merrimon, May 16, 1874, Ransom Papers, SHC; L. C. Jones to D. F. Caldwell, November 29, 1871, D. F. Caldwell Papers, SHC.

23. Price, "Railroads and Reconstruction," pp. 370–371; Taylor, *Louisiana Reconstructed*, pp. 178–179, 202–203.

24. *Jackson Pilot*, February 8, 24, April 26, May 25, September 26, 1871; *Vicksburg Herald*, April 5, 1873.

25. Thompson, "Leadership in Arkansas Reconstruction," pp. 312–332; *Little Rock Republican*, October 15, 1872.

26. McGrane, *Foreign Bondholders*, pp. 298–302.

27. *Jackson Pilot*, August 26, 1871; *Jackson Weekly Clarion*, December 31, 1874; *Charleston Daily Republican*, April 26, 1871; *Port Royal Commercial*, January 8, 22, 29, 1874; *Jacksonville New South*, October 14, 1874.

28. *ASJ*, February 24, 1874; *Port Royal Commercial*, January 29, March 26, 1874; *Jackson Pilot*, August 30, 1871; *Beaufort Republican*, June 5, 19, 1873; "Condition of Affairs," vol. 1, p. 330; vol. 3, pp. 370–371; Poor, *Manual*, 1872–1873, pp. 666–683; 1874–1875, pp. 793–819; Going, *Bourbon Democracy in Alabama*, pp. 63–70.

29. *Little Rock Republican*, March 9, 1872; *Jacksonville Florida Tri-Weekly Union*, February 20, 1873.

30. *Little Rock Republican*, March 9, 1872.

31. *Jackson Pilot*, April 1, 1871; *Columbus Daily Enquirer*, September 6, 1870; *Macon Georgia Weekly Telegraph*, November 15, 22, December 13, 20, 1870; McGrane, *Foreign Bondholders*, pp. 347–349; *ASJ*, January 14, September 5, 26, 1873.

32. *Jackson Pilot*, April 1, 1871; *New York Herald*, May 13, 1871; *Houston Union*, July 26, 1870.

33. *ASJ*, May 20, 1873.

34. Wallace, *Carpet-Bag Rule in Florida*, p. 148.

35. *Iberville Weekly South*, September 19, 1868; *Little Rock Republican*, February 21, 27, 1872; Davis, *Florida*, p. 676.

36. Nunn, *Texas under the Carpetbaggers*, pp. 93–97.

37. *Charleston Daily Republican*, March 31, April 1, 7, 1871; *Columbia Daily Union*, May 15, 1871; Simkins and Woody, *South Carolina*, pp. 157–160.

38. Shofner, *Nor Is It Over Yet*, pp. 200, 247.

39. Daniels, *Prince of Carpetbaggers*, pp. 259–264; S. W. Hopkins & Co. to M. S. Littlefield, August 30, September 1, 2, 6, 7, 8, 10, 1870, L'Engle Papers, SHC.

40. *New York Commercial and Financial Chronicle*, July 10, 17, 24, 31, August 7, 14, 21, 28, 1869; September 24, 1870; Shofner, *Nor Is It Over Yet*, p. 201; Taylor, *Louisiana Reconstructed*, p. 204; H. H. Kimpton to Niles G. Parker, quoted in "Fraud Report," pp. 1586–1587.

41. *New York Herald*, April 9, 1875; *Jackson Pilot*, August 30, 1871; Taylor, *Louisiana Reconstructed*, p. 200; *Beaufort Republican*, November 30, 1871.

42. *Beaufort Republican*, November 16, 1871; *Aiken Tribune*, November 30, 1872; *Houston Union*, August 3, 1870.

43. Edward P. Whaites to W. W. Holden, n.d.; Seymour N. Case to Holden, November 20, 1869; F. B. Bunn to Holden, January 1, 1870, Holden Papers, NCDAH.

44. *Beaufort Republican*, November 16, 1871.

45. *San Antonio Express*, May 15, 1873.

Chapter 13. The Alabama & Chattanooga Catastrophe

1. *Acts of Alabama*, 1868, p. 5; Armes, *Coal and Iron in Alabama*, pp. 104–121; Thornton, *Politics and Power in a Slave Society*, p. 291.

2. D. L. Dalton to Alfred Balle, August 22, 1868, Governor Smith Letterbook, ASDAH.

3. William H. Smith to D. L. Dalton, quoted by Dalton, in a letter to Lehman, Durr & Co., March 8, 1869, Governor Smith Letterbook, ASDAH; Armes, *Coal and Iron*, p. 243: "Condition of Affairs," vol. 8, p. 361.

4. Ala. Hse. *Jnl.*, 1868–1869, p. 274; *Acts of Alabama*, 1868, pp. 198–203, 207–208, 345–348, 354–356; 1869–1870, pp. 89–92.

5. *ASJ*, November 1, 1870; August 9, 1871; "Condition of Affairs," vol. 8, p. 232; vol 10, pp. 1411, 1424, 1467, 1468; Ala. Hse. *Jnl.*, 1869–1870, pp. 295–296, 369–370; see also Armes, *Coal and Iron*, p. 216, which all but concedes that John T. Milner bribed through additional aid for the South & North during the same session.

6. "Condition of Affairs," vol. 8, p. 199; vol. 9, p. 520; vol. 10, p. 1418; *ASJ*, December 23, 30, 1869.

7. *ASJ*, December 16, 23, 30, 1869; March 8, 1870; Ala. Hse. *Jnl.*, 1869–1870, pp. 296, 353–354, 369–370, 433–435; "Condition of Affairs," vol. 8, p. 195.

8. *ASJ*, March 15, April 10, May 4, 1869; July 13, December 22, 1870.

9. *First Annual Report to the Directors of the Alabama & Chattanooga Railroad, January 1869*; *ASJ*, July 8, 1870; *State of Alabama versus I. T. Burr et al.*, U. S. Reports, vol. 115, pp. 413–429, 1885.

10. "Condition of Affairs," vol. 8, p. 196; DuBose, *Alabama's Tragic Decade*, p. 322; Armes, *Coal and Iron*, p. 243.

11. *State of Alabama versus I. T. Burr et al.*, U.S. Reports, vol. 155, pp. 413–429, 1885; Armes, *Coal and Iron*, pp. 218–220.

12. *ASJ*, September 16, 17, November 1, 1870; March 22, 1871; *Huntsville Daily Democrat*, October 11, 19, 1870.

13. "Condition of Affairs," vol. 8, p. 183.

14. *ASJ*, March 16, 1871.

15. Ibid., January 26, February 1, March 16, 1871; see also a letter from D. N. Stanton in *ASJ*, August 22, 1871.

16. Ala. Sen. *Jnl.*, 1870–1871, pp. 80–82.

17. "Condition of Affairs," vol. 8, pp. 183, 193, 195, 197, 198; *ASJ*, February 10, April 12, 1871; Ala. Sen. *Jnl.*, 1870–1871, pp. 78–79; Ala. Hse. *Jnl.*, 1869–1870, pp. 17–18; D. L. Dalton to the secretary of the Montgomery & Eufaula Railroad, June 15, 1869, Governor Smith Letterbook.

18. Ala. Sen. *Jnl.*, 1870–1871, pp. 80–82.

19. *ASJ*, January 28, February 1, 12, 1871.

20. *ASJ*, February 10, March 17, 1871; John A. Watson to Robert McKee, February 21, 1871, McKee Papers, ASDAH; *Mobile Register*, March 11, 1871; *Selma Southern Argus*, March 1, 1872; *Huntsville Daily Democrat*, January 7, 9, 1871.

21. *ASJ*, January 21, February 4, 10, 11, 14, 1871; Ala. Hse. *Jnl.*, 1870–1871, pp. 124–125.

22. *ASJ*, February 21, 22, 23, 28, 1871; Ala. Hse *Jnl.*, 1870–1871, pp. 348–352.

23. *ASJ*, February 12, 19, 22, 23, 24, 25, 28, March 1, 1871.

24. *ASJ*, April 12, 13, 15, 1871.

25. DuBose, *Alabama's Tragic Decade*, pp. 184–186.

26. *Louisville Commercial*, August 18, 1871; *New York Tribune*, August 15, 1871; *ASJ*, August 22, 1871.

27. Ala. Hse. *Jnl.*, 1871–1872, pp. 14–15.

28. *Jackson Pilot*, May 24, 1871; *ASJ*, June 29, 1871; *Alabama & Chattanooga Railroad Company versus Jones*, National Bankruptcy Register Reports, vol. 5, pp. 98–111, 1873.

29. *ASJ*, August 25, 1871.

30. Ala. Hse. *Jnl.*, 1872–1873, pp. 373–374; Ala. Sen. *Jnl.*, 1871–1872, p. 16; *Blake versus Alabama & Chattanooga Railroad Company*, National Bankruptcy Register Reports, vol. 6, pp. 331–338, 1872.

31. Ala. Sen. *Jnl.*, 1871–1872, pp. 10–18, 314–328; *ASJ*, September 28, 30, November 24, 1871; March 5, 13, 14, 26, 1872; *Blake versus Alabama & Chattanooga Railroad Company*, National Bankruptcy Register Reports, vol. 6, pp. 331–338, 1872; *In Re Alabama & Chattanooga Railroad Company, an Alleged Bankrupt*, U.S. Circuit Court Reports, Blatchford, vol. 9, pp. 399–400, 1872; *Alabama & Chattanooga Railroad Company versus Jones*, National Bankruptcy Register Reports, vol. 7, pp. 145–174, 1873.

32. Ala. Sen. *Jnl.*, 1871–1872, pp. 355, 397.

33. Ibid., pp. 362–365, 397–398; *ASJ*, August 25, September 17, 1871; July 13, 1872.

34. Ala. Sen. *Jnl.*, pp. 367, 373, 391–394; Ala. Hse. *Jnl.*, 1873–1874, pp. 88–96.

35. *ASJ*, September 10, 1871; May 31, 1872; Ala. Sen.*Jnl.*, 1871–1872, pp. 264–265.

36. *ASJ*, December 5, 20, 1871.

37. Ala. Sen.*Jnl.*, 1871–1872, pp. 162–163; Ala. Hse.*Jnl.*, 1871–1872, p. 127.

38. Ala. Sen. *Jnl.*, 1871–1872, pp. 112–120, 158, 170–171, 220, 263, 264; Ala. Hse.*Jnl.*, 1871–1872, pp. 44, 87, 112, 132–133, 167, 170, 191, 341, 465–466, 501; *ASJ*, February 4, 1872.

39. *Alabama & Chattanooga Railroad Company versus Jones*, National Bankruptcy Register Reports, vol. 5, pp. 98–111, 1873; *Alabama & Chattanooga Railroad Company versus Jones*, National Bankruptcy Register Reports, vol. 7, pp. 145–174, 1873; *ASJ*, February 24, March 6, 14, 17, 24, 26, 1872.

40. *ASJ*, April 24, 25, May 30, 31, June 4, 5, 1872.

41. *ASJ*, June 4, 5, 9, 16, 28, 1872.

42. Ibid., April 24, 1872.

43. *ASJ*, June 5, 1872.

44. Ibid., September 25, 1872.

45. Going, *Bourbon Democracy in Alabama*, p. 67; see also Rufus K. Boyd to Robert McKee, May 2, 1872, McKee Papers, ASDAH; *Montgomery Advertiser*, May 1, November 17, 1872.

46. Ala. Hse. *Jnl.*, 1872–1873, pp. 132–145, 698, 703, 710–713, 717–719, 765–766; Ala. Sen.*Jnl.*, 1872–1873, pp. 154, 578; *ASJ*, February 12, 13, March 26, April 1, 2, 3, 4, 8, 9, 12, May 18, 20, 24, 1873.

47. Ala. Sen.*Jnl.*, 1873–1874, pp. 173–176, 197–200; *ASJ*, October 16, November 12, December 11, 1873; January 22, 1874.

48. *John C. Stanton et al., trustees, versus Alabama & Chattanooga Railroad Company*, U.S. Circuit Court Reports, Woods, vol. 2, pp. 506–509; *John C. Stanton et al. versus Alabama & Chattanooga Railroad Company*, Federal Reports, vol. 31, pp. 585–586, 1887; *T. H. Davenport versus Receivers of Alabama & Chattanooga Railroad Company*, U.S. Circuit Court Reports, Woods, vol. 2, pp. 519–523, 1875; *Stanton and Others versus Alabama & Chattanooga Railroad Company*, Federal Reports, vol. 31, pp. 523–531, 1887; Poor, *Manual*, 1878, pp. 520–521.

49. Going, *Bourbon Democracy in Alabama*, pp. 69–74; *State of Alabama versus I. T. Burr et al.*, U.S. Reports, vol. 115, pp. 413–429, 1885.

50. *ASJ*, August 20, 1872.

Chapter *14*. "They Have Thus Prostituted . . .": Republicanism Riven

1. *Beaufort Republican*, May 23, 1872.

2. *ASJ*, September 2, November 5, 6, 8, 1871.

3. Lamson, *Glorious Failure*, pp. 142–144.

4. Garner, *Reconstruction in Mississippi*, pp. 302, 394–395.

5. *Little Rock Republican*, August 8, 26, 28, September 30, 1873; *Springfield Republican*, April 17, 24, 1874; *U.S. House Reports*, 43rd Congress, 2nd session, pp. 103, 245.

6. "Allegations against Senator Powell Clayton," pp. 91, 99, 102, 146, 150, 189–191, 249, 351–362; Driggs, "Issues of the Powell Clayton Regime," pp. 70–71.

7. *Charleston Daily Republican*, February 25, 27, 28, March 1, 1871; *Charleston Courier*, February 25, 27, 28, 1871.

8. *San Antonio Express*, August 13, 16, 19, 20, September 10, 1870; August 20, 1871.

9. *Dallas Herald*, April 29, 1871.

10. Brockman "Railroads, Radicals and the Militia Bill," pp. 113–120; *Houston Daily Union*, July 27, August 10, 1870; *San Antonio Express*, August 5, 1870.

11. Simkins and Woody, *South Carolina*, pp. 217–221.

12. Wallace, *Carpet-Bag Rule in Florida*, pp. 102, 119.

13. *Charleston Courier*, February 25, 28, 1871; *Houston Union*, August 7, 9, 1870; Moneyhon, *Republicanism in Reconstruction Texas*, pp. 137–138, 142–143; *San Antonio Express*, July 26, 1870; *Galveston Tri-Weekly News*, April 24, 1871. For a similar reading-out of party members, see Warmoth, *War, Politics and Reconstruction*, p. 91.

14. *San Antonio Express*, November 28, December 7, 1871.

15. *Beaufort Republican*, May 23, 1872.

16. *Little Rock Arkansas Gazette*, August 27, 1871; "Allegations Against Senator Powell Clayton," pp. 162–166.

17. Clayton, *Aftermath of the Civil War*, pp. 238–240; Thompson, *Arkansas and Reconstruction*, pp. 232–233.

18. *Little Rock Republican*, February 22, 1872.

Chapter 15. "A War Now Begins between These Roads and the People," 1873

1. *New Orleans Republican*, January 22, 1873.

2. *ASJ*, March 26, April 12, 15, 1873; *San Antonio Express*, June 10, July 31, 1870; *Houston Daily Union*, July 26, August 10, 1870; *New Orleans Republican*, January 22, 1873.

3. *New Orleans Price-Current*, quoted in Odom, "Louisiana Railroads," p. 218; *Little Rock Republican*, November 6, 8, 1871.

4. Harris, *Day of the Carpetbagger*, pp. 630–631; Garner, *Reconstruction in Mississippi*, pp. 296–297, 302, 394–395; Miss. Sen. *Jnl.*, 1874, p. 178; *Donaldsonville Chief*, January 25, 1873; *ASJ*, July 29, 1873; Lonn, *Recon-*

struction in Louisiana, pp. 226–227, 248–249; Simkins and Woody, *South Carolina*, pp. 475–479.

5. *ASJ*, February 21, 1871; April 12, May 16, October 3, 7, 1873; see also the handbill of New Orleans & Carrollton Railroad Company, December 29, 1875, In Beauregard Papers, LSU.

6. *ASJ*, April 9, 12, 1873.

7. Stover, *Railroads of the South*, p. 134.

8. Woolfolk, *The Cotton Regency*, pp. 144–146.

9. Vernon, *ARM*, p. xlviii; *ASJ*, April 12, 1873.

10. *ASJ*, April 16, 1873.

11. *Little Rock Republican*, April 21, 1873.

12. Ibid., April 5, 21, 1873.

13. Ala. Hse. *Jnl*, 1871–1872, pp. 517–518, 535–536, 549; *ASJ*, April 12, 1873.

14. *ASJ*, April 12, 15, 16, 17, 20, 1873.

15. Ala. Hse. *Jnl.*, 1872–1873, pp. 726, 745–752, 828–830; *ASJ*, April 8, 12, 13, 15, 16, 19, 20, 1873.

16. *ASJ*, March 15, 18, 19, 22, 26, 28, April 5, 6, 9, November 21, December 7, 9, 12, 1873; January 1, 23, 1874.

17. Miss. Sen. *Jnl.*, 1873, pp. 1694–1696, 1753–1754, 1765, 1774–1780.

18. Ibid., pp. 1510–1511, 1617, 1645; Miss. Hse. *Jnl.*, 1873, pp. 1713, 1900–1903, 2012–2017.

19. *Vicksburg Times*, June 25, July 29, August 8, November 4, 1873; February 18, March 25, 27, 1874; Miss. Sen. *Jnl.*, 1873, pp. 1262–1268.

20. *Jacksonville Florida Tri-Weekly Union*, February 20, 1873.

21. *Little Rock Republican*, April 3, 4, 5, 10, 11, 21, May 1, 21, July 8, 1873; Thompson, *Arkansas and Reconstruction*, p. 122; *U.S. House Reports*, 43rd Congress, 1st session, no. 771, pp. 246, 249, 250.

22. *Acts of Louisiana*, 1874, pp. 25–36; *New Orleans Republican*, January 22, 23, 24, 29, 30, 31, February 11, 1873.

23. *Acts of Louisiana*, 1872, pp. 13–14, 29–31; Odom, "Louisiana Railroads," pp. 217–219; *Beaufort Republican*, May 8, June 5, 19, 1873; Simkins and Woody, *South Carolina*, pp. 181–182, 219–221.

24. Shofner, *Nor Is It Over Yet*, pp. 217–218, 249–252, 291–292; Fla. Sen. *Jnl.*, 1873, pp. 52–66, 177–178.

25. W. Gibbins to W. W. Holden, December 19, 1868; W. M. Coleman to Holden, March 2, 1869, Holden Papers, NCDAH; J. B. Keogh to Thomas Settle, December 3, 1868, Settle Papers, SHC.

26. Price, "Railroads and Reconstruction," pp. 366–367, 466–472, 560–562; Daniels, *Prince of Carpetbaggers*, pp. 222–227; Daniel Goodloe to B. S. Hedrick, February 6, 1870, Hedrick Papers, SHC.

27. Price, "Railroads and Reconstruction," pp. 516–520, 563–568; N.C. Sen. *Jnl.*, 1869–1870, pp. 361–366, 533–539.

28. Price, "Railroads and Reconstruction," pp. 577–578.

29. *Atlanta Daily New Era*, March 10, 1869; September 22, 29, October 13, 1870; Thompson, *Reconstruction in Georgia*, pp. 242–243.

30. *Atlanta Daily New Era*, March 10, 1869; October 13, 1870; Thompson, *Reconstruction in Georgia*, pp. 219–220, 225–226, 245–246.

31. Parks, *Joseph E. Brown*, pp. 451–453; Joseph Brown to A. J. White, December 19, 1870; Alexander Stephens to Brown, December 10, 15, 28, 1870; Linton Stephens to Brown, January 26, 1871; Brown to the political editor of the *Sun*, October 11, 1871; Georgia General Assembly, *Joint Committee to Investigate the Western and Atlantic Railroad*, pp. 118–155.

32. Thompson, *Reconstruction in Georgia*, pp. 246–254; Nathans, *Losing the Peace*, pp. 208–211, 216–218; G. W. Morrill to Simon Cameron, November 16, 1871, Cameron Papers, LC; Price, "Railroads and Reconstruction," pp. 472–475.

33. *Jackson Pilot*, February 12, 1871; *Acts of Arkansas*, 1873, pp. 169, 435; Odom, "Louisiana Railroads," p. 197.

34. *ASJ*, April 18, 20, July 29, August 2, September 7, October 3, 17, December 12, 1873; January 23, 1874; *Port Royal Commercial*, October 30, 1873; *Jacksonville Florida Tri-Weekly Union*, February 20, 1873; Miss. Sen. *Jnl.*, 1874, pp. 178–179; Thompson, "Leadership in Arkansas Reconstruction," pp. 443–444.

35. *ASJ*, July 25, 1873; *Vicksburg Times*, August 3, 1873.

Chapter 16. *"Men are Giting Desperate . . .": The Panic, Collapse, and Survival of the Gospel of Prosperity, 1873–1880*

1. *ASJ*, July 3, 25, August 1, 14, 1873; *Little Rock Republican*, June 24, September 25, 1873; Poor, *Manual*, 1877–1878, p. ix; New York *Railway Monitor*, December 31, 1873.

2. *Little Rock Republican*, June 24, September 25, 1873; Coulter, *Reconstruction*, p. 189.

3. *Little Rock Republican*, June 24, 1873.

4. New York *Railway Monitor*, March 15, October 15, 1873; for differing estimates, see Greenberg, *Financiers and Railroads*, p. 43.

5. New York *Railway Monitor*, January 15, October 15, November 15, 1873; [New York] *Nation*, August 15, 1872; *New York Commercial and Financial Chronicle*, November 15, 1873; Vernon, *ARM*, pp. xlvi–li.

6. New York *Railway Monitor*, February 15, October 15, 1873; *Philadelphia Public Ledger*, August 30, 1873.

7. New York *Railway Monitor*, March 15, 1873.

8. Miller, *Railroads and the Granger Laws*, pp. 66–102; Vernon, *ARM*, pp. xlviii–lviii.

9. Vernon, *ARM*, pp. xlviii–li; *New York Herald*, October 28, 1874; McGrane, *Foreign Bondholders*, pp. 307–310; Davis, *Florida*, pp. 655–656; Conway, *Reconstruction of Georgia*, p. 213.

10. Chicago *Railroad Gazette*, vol 4, 1872, p. 87; see also *ASJ*, September 7, 1873; Vernon, *ARM*, p. liii.

11. H. C. Fahnestock to W. E. Chandler, October 7, 1873; Jay Cooke to Chandler, October 6, 1873, Chandler Papers, LC; *New York Herald*, September 18, 19, 1873; Oberholtzer, *Jay Cooke*, pp. 420–424.

12. *New York Herald*, September 19, 20, 23, 1873.

13. Ibid., September 19, 20, 22, 23, 1873.

14. New York *Railway Monitor*, January 15, November 15, 1873; *New York Herald*, October 28, 1874; [New York] *Nation*, August 5, 1875; *ASJ*, February 17, 1874.

15. Osthaus, *Freedman, Philanthropy and Fraud*, pp. 150–199; Simkins and Woody, *South Carolina*, pp. 271–272; *ASJ*, September 25, 28, October 1, 1873; Shofner, *Nor Is It Over Yet*, p. 273.

16. *New Orleans Republican*, September 5, 6, 1874; Coulter, *Reconstruction*, p. 194; *ASJ*, January 15, 1874; McKenzie, "Reconstruction in the Alabama Iron Industry," pp. 186–188; *New York Herald*, October 10, 1874; May 24; 1875; King, *The Great South*, p. 96.

17. Armes, *Coal and Iron*, p. 252.

18. R. H. Hardaway to John Screven, October 15, 28, 1873, Arnold-Screven Papers, SHC; *ASJ*, October 10, 1873; Stover, *Railroads of the South*, pp. 122–124; New York *Commercial and Financial Chronicle*, September 20, November 15, 1873.

19. New York *Commercial and Financial Chronicle*, November 15, 1873; Vernon, *ARM*, pp. xlviii-l; Stover, *Railroads of the South*, p. 130; Simkins and Woody, *South Carolina*, pp. 194–195, 199, 221–222; Shofner, *Nor Is It Over Yet*, pp. 248–249, 254; Thompson, *Reconstruction in Georgia*, pp. 299–301.

20. *Report of the Investigating Committee of the Pennsylvania Railroad Company*, pp. 75–77; Stover, *Railroads of the South*, pp. 119–120; [New York] *The Road*, December 15, 1876.

21. Stover, *Railroads of the South*, pp. 165–172; Corliss, *Main Line to Mid-America*, pp. 202–204.

22. Stover, *Railroads of the South*, pp. 123–124, 131–134; Poor, *Manual*, 1873–1874, pp. xxx–xlv.

23. *ASJ*, September 27, 1873.

24. Stover, *Railroads of the South*, pp. 134–135; Bond, *Negro Education in Alabama*, p. 54.

25. Taylor, *Louisiana Reconstructed*, pp. 205–208; *St. Joseph North Louisiana Journal*, March 23, July 6, 1872; Sansing, "Scalawag in Mississippi Reconstruction," pp. 82–83; *New York Herald*, May 24, 29, 1875; *Aiken Tribune*, May 25, 1872; Davis, *Florida*, pp. 675–677.

26. Simkins and Woody, *South Carolina*, p. 180; Williamson, *After Slavery*, pp. 151–152, 154; Miss. Hse. *Jnl.*, 1875, pp. 11, 40–41.

27. Taylor, *Louisiana Reconstructed*, p. 207; Williamson, *After Slavery*, p. 158; Garner, *Reconstruction in Mississippi*, p. 297.

28. Harris, *Day of the Carpetbagger*, pp. 625–630; *Port Royal Commercial*, February 26, April 2, 9, 1874; Lamson, *The Glorious Failure*, pp. 184–185.

29. *Vicksburg Times*, August 24, 1874; *New York Herald*, June 5, 1874; *Port Royal Commercial*, April 2, 1874.

30. *Vicksburg Times*, August 24, 1874; Nordhoff, *Cotton States*, p. 82.

31. Odom, "Louisiana Railroads," pp. 224–225.

32. *New Orleans Republican*, January 6, 7, 16, 20, 21, 22, 24, 30, February 3, 7, 10, 22, March 22, 1874; McGrane, *Foreign Bondholders*, pp. 318–321; William Pitt Kellogg to J. J. Creswell, January 29, 1874, Kellogg Papers, LSU; *New York Herald*, June 5, 1874.

33. Simkins and Woody, *South Carolina*, pp. 166–168; *Port Royal Commercial*, October 23, 30, November 6, 13, 20, December 25, 1873; January 1, February 5, 1874; *Beaufort Republican*, September 4, 11, 1873.

34. Shofner, *Nor Is It Over Yet*, pp. 250, 292; McGrane, *Foreign Bondholders*, p. 303; Wallace, *Carpet-Bag Rule in Florida*, pp. 237–239, 326–327.

35. U.S. Bureau of the Census, *Tenth Census*, 1880, vol. 8, pp. 650–672.

36. Poor, *Manual*, 1880, p. v.

37. *New Orleans Republican*, February 6, 1874; *Donaldsonville Chief*, January 25, 1873; *New York Herald*, September 30, 1874.

38. *New Orleans Republican*, January 20, 30, 1874.

39. *Vicksburg Times*, August 24, 1874; *New Orleans Republican*, September 10, 1874; Reynolds, *Reconstruction in South Carolina*, pp. 277–278, 369–370.

40. Reynolds, *Reconstruction in South Carolina*, pp. 369–370; *New Orleans Republican*, January 14, 17, 30, 31, 1873; March 18, June 17, 1874; *Port Royal Commercial*, November 20, 27, 1873.

41. *ASJ*, January 14, 23, 27, 30, 1874; *New York Herald*, September 16, 1874.

42. F. Baum to William P. Kellogg, July 13, 1874, Kellogg Papers, LSU; *New York Herald*, June 5, 1874.

43. Shofner, *Nor Is It Over Yet*, p. 291; *ASJ*, September 23, 1870; February 25, March 1, 5, 7, 13, 14, 19, 20, 26, July 9, September 6, 1873; *Vicksburg Times*, May 27, 1873; *Charleston Daily Republican*, December 9, 13, 1869; Schweninger, "Black Citizenship and the Republican Party," pp. 90–92.

44. *Aiken Tribune*, November 12, 1872; *New York Herald*, May 18, August 12, 25, 28, September 3, 4, 11, 16, 26, October 19, 30, 1874; *Charleston Daily News and Courier*, August 12, 14, 17, 26, September 4, 5, 6, 7, 8, 9, 15, 19, 22, 23, 1876; *Shreveport Times*, July 10, 21, August 13, 1874; *Galveston Tri-Weekly News*, October 31, November 17, 1873; *Natchitoches People's Vindicator*, June 27, July 18, August 29, 1874; Harris, *Day of the Carpetbagger*, pp. 674–675.

45. Going, *Bourbon Democracy in Alabama*, pp. 13–14; Cooper, *Conservative Regime*, pp. 45–48.

46. *New Orleans Republican*, January 7, 1873; *ASJ*, November 6, 14, 1874; Shofner, *Nor Is It Over Yet*, p. 309; Fleming, *Alabama*, p. 792.

47. *New York Herald*, October 16, 1874; Council of Bondholders to Ap-

pleton Oaksmith, November 10, 1873, Kellogg Papers, LSU; McGrane, *Foreign Bondholders*, pp. 318–319.

48. *Shreveport Times*, August 4, 1874; *New York Herald*, October 16, 1874; *Port Royal Commercial and Beaufort Republican*, April 2, 1874; *New Orleans Republican*, September 19, 1874; E. John Ellis to Thomas Ellis, March 23, 1874, Ellis Papers, LSU.

49. Daniel Russell to Thomas Settle, September 16, 1874, Settle Papers, SHC; *New York Herald*, June 5, August 18, September 11, October 16, 19, 1874; *Columbia Daily Union Herald*, October 7, 17, 18, 21, 23, 1876.

50. *Houston Union*, July 27, 1870; *New Orleans Republican*, September 16, 17, 24, 1874.

51. *Columbia Daily Union Herald*, October 24, 1876; *New Orleans Republican*, September 10, 15, 17, 22, 1874.

52. *New York Herald*, September 5, October 9, 16, 21, 24, 29, 1874; Paul Strobach to W. E. Chandler, May 7, 1875, Chandler Papers, LC; Williamson, *After Slavery*, pp. 400–401; E. John Ellis to Thomas Ellis, August 3, 1874, Ellis Papers, LSU.

53. *Tribune Almanac*, 1875, 1876, 1877.

54. For a full and excellent consideration of the Redeemers, see More, "Redeemers Reconsidered: Change and Continuity in the Democratic South, 1870–1900," *Journal of Southern History*, vol. 45, pp. 357–378.

Atlanta Constitution, June 26, 1877; *Raleigh Sentinel*; October 17, 21, November 10, 1874; Woodward, *Origins of the New South*, pp. 7–21; Kirwan, *Revolt of the Rednecks*, p. 9; Hair, *Bourbonism and Agrarian Protest*, pp. 24–26, 76–81.

55. *Atlanta Constitution*, September 9, 1877; *Mobile Daily Register*, October 31, November 4, 1875; *Little Rock Arkansas Gazette*, July 25, 30, August 4, 1880; Thompson, "Leadership in Arkansas Reconstruction," pp. 447–455; Price, "Railroads and Reconstruction," pp. 583–593; McGrane, *Foreign Bondholders*, pp. 307–311, 338, 340–341; Cooper, *Conservative Regime*, pp. 46–49; Reed, *Texas Railroads*, pp. 154–155; Going, *Bourbon Democracy in Alabama*, pp. 70–74.

56. U.S. Bureau of the Census, *Tenth Census*, 1880, vol. 7, pp. 650–672.

57. Poor, *Manual*, 1890, pp. ii–v; Woodward, *Origins of the New South*, pp. 120–121; *Raleigh Sentinel*, November 2, 6, 16, 17, 18, 19, 20, December 4, 5, 7, 1874; Going, *Bourbon Democracy in Alabama*, p. 110; Stover, *Railroads of the South*, pp. 195–208.

Coda. "And Was Jerusalem Builded Here?"

1. "Condition of Affairs," vol. 8, p. 519.
2. *Opelika Weekly Era and Whig*, October 8, 1870.

BIBLIOGRAPHY

MANUSCRIPTS

Southern Historical Collection, University of North Carolina, Chapel Hill
    James Lusk Alcorn Papers
    Alexander Boyd Andrews Papers
    Arnold-Screven Papers
    David Franklin Caldwell Papers
    Tod Robinson Caldwell Papers
    Governor's Correspondence, Mississippi
    Hentz Family Papers
    E. M. L'Engle Papers
    Jason Niles Diary and Scrapbook
    Papers Relating to Railroads in Mississippi
    Matt W. Ransom Papers
    Daniel Lindsay Russell Papers
    Thomas Settle Papers
    George W. Swepson Papers
    Samuel McDowell Tate Papers
    William Worrell Vass Papers
    Henry Clay Warmoth Papers
Flowers Collection, Duke University, Durham
    John E. Bryant Papers
    Joseph Fulton Boyd Papers
    Jesse Turner Papers
Archives Department, Library of Congress
    Frederick G. Bromberg Papers
    Benjamin F. Butler Papers
    William E. Chandler Papers
    James A. Garfield Papers
    John Sherman Papers
    Thaddeus Stevens Papers
    Elihu Washburne Papers
Alabama State Department of Archives and History, Montgomery
    Governor Robert B. Lindsay Papers
    Robert McKee Papers
    Governor R. M. Patton Papers

Governor William H. Smith Letterbook
Governor William H. Smith Papers
University of Georgia, Athens
    Joseph E. Brown Papers
Mississippi Department of Archives and History, Jackson
    James Lusk Alcorn Papers
    Adelbert Ames Papers
    H. C. Sharkey Papers
North Carolina Division of Archives and History, Raleigh
    Governor's Papers of Tod Robinson Caldwell
    Governor's Letterbook of William Woods Holden
    Governor's Papers of William Woods Holden
    George W. Swepson Papers
Louisiana State University Archives
    E. John Ellis Papers
    B. F. Flanders Papers
    William Pitt Kellogg Papers

FEDERAL DOCUMENTS

Congressional Globe, 1866–1873
Congressional Record, 1873–1877
U.S. Congress. *Executive Documents*. 39th Congress, 1st session, no. 4: "Report of the Comptroller of the Currency."
U.S. Congress. *Executive Documents*. 39th Congress, 1st session, no. 155: "Railroad Property."
U.S. Congress. *House Reports*. 39th Congress, 2nd session, no. 34: "Affairs of Southern Railroads."
U.S. Congress. *House Reports*. 42nd Congress, 2nd session, no. 22: "Testimony Taken by the Joint Select Committee to Inquire into the Condition of Affairs in the Late Insurrectionary States."
U.S. Congress. *House Reports*. 42nd Congress, 2nd session, no. 92: "Affairs in Louisiana."
U.S. Congress. *House Reports*. 43rd Congress, 2nd session, no. 101: "Indebtedness of Certain Southern Railroads."
U.S. Congress. *House Reports*. 43rd Congress, 2nd session, no. 261: "Condition of the South."
U.S. Congress. *House Reports*. 43rd Congress, 2nd session, no. 262: "Affairs in Alabama."
U.S. Congress. *Senate Reports*. 42nd Congress, 3rd session, no. 512: "Allegations Against Senator Powell Clayton."
U.S. Congress. *Senate Reports*. 42nd Congress, 3rd session, no. 457: "Louisiana Investigation."

UNITED STATES CENSUS

United States Bureau of the Census. *Ninth Census of the United States, 1870. Population.* Washington: Government Printing Office, 1872.

United States Bureau of the Census. *Ninth Census of the United States, 1870. Wealth and Industry.* Washington: Government Printing Office, 1872.

United States Bureau of the Census. *Tenth Census of the United States, 1880. Manufactures.* Washington: Government Printing Office, 1884.

United States Bureau of the Census. *Tenth Census of the United States, 1880. Population.* Washington: Government Printing Office, 1883.

United States Bureau of the Census. *Tenth Census of the United States, 1880. Cotton Production in the Eastern, Gulf, Atlantic and Pacific States.* Washington: Government Printing Office, 1884.

United States Bureau of the Census. *Compendium of the Tenth Census.* Washington: Government Printing Office, 1888.

CONVENTION JOURNALS

Debates and Proceedings of the Convention which Assembled at Little Rock, January 7th, 1868, Under the Provisions of the Act of Congress of March 2nd, 1867, and the Acts of March 23rd and July 19th, 1867, Supplementary Thereto, to Form a Constitution for the State of Arkansas. Little Rock: J. G. Price, Printer to the Convention, 1868.

Journal of the Constitutional Convention of the State of North Carolina, at its Session, 1868. Raleigh: Joseph W. Holden, Convention Printer, 1868.

Journal of the Proceedings in the Constitutional Convention of the State of Mississippi, 1868. Jackson: E. Stafford, Printer, 1871.

Journal of the Proceedings of the Constitutional Convention of the People of Georgia, Held in the City of Atlanta in the Months of December 1867, and January, February and March 1868: And Ordinances and Resolutions Adopted. Augusta: E. H. Pughe, Book and Job Printer, 1868.

Journal of the Proceedings of the Constitutional Convention of the State of Florida, Begun and Held at the Capitol, at Tallahassee, on Monday, January 20th, 1868. Tallahassee: Edward H. Cheney, Printer, 1868.

Journal of the Reconstruction Convention, Which Met at Austin, Texas, December 7, A.D., 1868. Second Session. Austin: Tracy, Siemering and Company, Printer, State Journal Office, 1870.

Journal of the Reconstruction Convention, Which Met at Austin, Texas, June 1, A.D., 1868. Austin: Tracy, Siemering and Company, 1870.

Official Journal of the Constitutional Convention of the State of Alabama Held in the City of Montgomery, Commencing on Tuesday, November 5th, A.D., 1867. Montgomery: Barrett and Brown, Book and Job Printers and Binders, 1868.

Official Journal of the Proceedings of the Convention, for Framing a Constitution for the State of Louisiana. New Orleans: J. B. Roudanez and Company, Printers to the Convention, 1867–1868.

Proceedings of the Constitutional Convention of South Carolina, Held at Charleston, S.C., Beginning January 14th and Ending March 17th, 1868: Including the Debates and Proceedings. 2 vols. Charleston: Denny and Perry, 1868.

The Debates and Proceedings of the Constitutional Convention of the State of

Virginia, Assembled at the City of Richmond, Tuesday, December 3, 1867; Being a Full and Complete Report of the Debates and Proceedings of the Convention, Together with the Reconstruction Acts of Congress, and Those Supplementary Thereto, the Order of the Commander of the First Military District Assemblying the Convention, and the New Constitution, Vol. 1 (no other volumes published). Richmond: Printed at the Office of the New Nation, 1868.

LEGISLATIVE JOURNALS

Alabama House *Journal*, 1868–1875
Alabama Senate *Journal*, 1868–1875
Arkansas House *Journal*, 1868–1873
Arkansas Senate *Journal*, 1868–1873
Florida House *Journal*, 1868–1875
Florida Senate *Journal*, 1868–1875
Georgia House *Journal*, 1866, 1868–1870
Georgia Senate *Journal*, 1866, 1868–1870
Louisiana House *Journal*, 1868–1876
Louisiana Senate *Journal*, 1868–1876
Louisiana House *Debates*, 1869, 1870
Louisiana Senate *Debates*, 1869, 1870
Mississippi House *Journal*, 1870–1875
Mississippi Senate *Journal*, 1870–1875
North Carolina House *Journal*, 1868–1871
North Carolina Senate *Journal*, 1868–1871
South Carolina House *Journal*, 1868–1876
South Carolina Senate *Journal*, 1868–1876
Texas House *Journal*, 1870–1873
Texas Senate *Journal*, 1870–1873

LAWS

Acts of the General Assembly of the State of Arkansas, Passed at the Session Held at the Capitol, in the City of Little Rock. Little Rock: Little Rock Publishing Co., 1868–1875.
Acts of the Session of the General Assembly of Alabama, Session of—. Montgomery, Ala.: State Printers, 1866–1876.
Acts and Resolutions Adopted by the Legislature of Florida. Tallahassee: Edward W. Cheney, 1868–1875.
Acts of the General Assembly of the State of Georgia, Passed in Atlanta, Georgia, at an Annual Session. Atlanta: Samuel Bard, 1868–1870.
Acts Passed by the General Assembly of the State of Louisiana at the— Session of the—Legislature, Begun and Held in the City of New Orleans, New Orleans: A. L. Lee, 1868–1876.

Laws of the State of Mississippi. Jackson: Public Printers, 1866–1867, 1870–1876.

Laws and Resolutions Passed by the General Assembly of the State of North Carolina. Raleigh: Published by Authority, 1866–1874.

Acts and Joint Resolutions of the State of South Carolina. Columbia: Republican Printing Co., 1868–1877.

General Laws of the Twelfth Legislature of the State of Texas. Austin: Tracy, Siemering and Co., 1870–1871.

RAILWAY MANUALS

Official Railway Manual of the Railroads of North America Compiled by James H. Lyles. New York: Russell's American Steam Printing House, 1869, 1870.

Poor, Henry V. *Manual of the Railroads of the United States. Showing their Mileage, Stocks, Bonds, Cost, Traffic, Earnings, Expenses, and Organization, with a Sketch of their Rise, Progress, Influence, Etc.* New York: H. V. and H. W. Poor, 1868–1879.

Vernon, Edward. *American Railroad Manual for the United States, and the Dominion, Containing Full Particulars of the Mileage, Capital Stock, Bonded Debt, Equipment, Earnings, Expenses, and Other Statistics of Railroads, As Now Built and in Process of Construction.* New York: n.p., 1874.

NEWSPAPERS

Outside the Republican South
    Frankfort Commonwealth
    Louisville Commercial
    New York Herald
    New York Times
    New York World
    Philadelphia Public Ledger
    Springfield Republican
North Carolina
    Raleigh Sentinel
    Raleigh Standard
    Wilmington Morning Star
South Carolina
    Aiken Tribune
    Beaufort Republican
    Charleston Courier
    Charleston Mercury
    Charleston News and Courier
    Charleston Daily Republican
    Columbia Daily Union Herald
    Port Royal Commercial

Georgia
Atlanta Constitution
Atlanta Daily New Era
Augusta National Republican
Columbus Daily Enquirer
Macon Georgia Weekly Telegraph and Journal & Messenger
Florida
Jacksonville New South
Jacksonville Florida Tri-Weekly Union
Alabama
Florence Lauderdale Times
Huntsville Daily Democrat
Mobile Register
Montgomery Advertiser
Montgomery Alabama State Journal
Opelika Weekly Era and Whig
Mississippi
Forest Register
Jackson Clarion
Jackson Pilot
Vicksburg Weekly Republican
Vicksburg Times
Vicksburg Times and Republican
Louisiana
Alexandria Caucasian
Bossier Banner
Iberville South
Natchitoches People's Vindicator
New Orleans Crescent
New Orleans Daily Picayune
New Orleans Republican
New Orleans Times
New Orleans Tribune
Shreveport Times
St. Joseph North Louisiana Journal
West Baton Rouge Sugar Planter
Arkansas
Little Rock Arkansas Gazette
Little Rock Arkansas Campaign Gazette
Little Rock Republican
Texas
Dallas Herald
Flake's Galveston Bulletin
Galveston Tri-Weekly News
Houston Union
San Antonio Express

Bibliography

PERIODICALS

Chicago *Railroad Gazette*
De Bow's Review
Merchant's Magazine and Commercial Review
New York *Nation: A Weekly Journal Devoted to Politics, Literature, Science, and Art*
New York *Commercial and Financial Chronicle*
New York *Tribune Almanac*
New York *Railway Monitor*
New York *The Road*

LETTERS AND ORIGINAL ACCOUNTS

Ames, Blanche Butler, comp. *Chronicles from the Nineteenth Century: Family Letters of Blanche Butler and Adelbert Ames.* 2 vols. Clinton, Mass.: Colonial Press, 1957.

Andrews, Sidney. *The South Since the War: As Shown by the Fourteen Weeks of Travel and Observation in Georgia and the Carolinas.* Boston: Ticknor and Fields, 1866.

Avery, I. W. *The History of the State of Georgia from 1850 to 1881, Embracing the Three Important Epochs: The Decade before the War of 1861–1865; The War; The Period of Reconstruction, with Portraits of the Leading Public Men of This Era.* New York: Brown and Darby, Publishers, 1881.

Clayton, Powell. *The Aftermath of the Civil War in Arkansas.* New York: Neale Publishing Co., 1915.

DuBose, John W. *Alabama's Tragic Decade, 1865–1874.* Birmingham: Webb, 1940.

First Annual Report to the Directors of the Alabama & Chattanooga Railroad, January 1869. Boston: n.p., 1869.

Freeman, John D. *Petition of the New Orleans, Jackson and G. N. Railroad Company to the Governor and Legislature of Mississippi.* Jackson: Clarion Book and Job Printing Co., 1870.

Great Southern Railway: A Trunk Line between the North and the Tropics, to within Ninety Miles of Havana. New York: William P. Hickock, 1878.

Hamilton, Joseph Gregoire de Roulhac, ed. *The Correspondence of Jonathan Worth.* 2 vols. Raleigh: Edwards and Broughton Printing Co., 1909.

Henry, James P. *Resources of the State of Arkansas, with a Description of Counties, Railroads, Mines, and the City of Little Rock.* 3rd. ed. Little Rock, Ark.: Prince and McClure, State Printers, 1873.

Herbert, Hilary A., ed. *Why the Solid South, or Reconstruction and Its Results.* Baltimore: R. H. Woodward and Co., 1890.

King, Edward. *The Great South.* Edited by W. Magruder Drake and Robert R. Jones. Baton Rouge: Louisiana State University Press, 1972.

Moore, John Hammond. *The 'Juhl' Letters to the Charleston Courier: A View of the South, 1865–1871.* Athens, Ga.: University of Georgia Press, 1974.

Nordhoff, Charles. *The Cotton States in the Spring and Summer of 1875.* New York: D. Appleton and Co., 1876.

Pike, James Shepherd. *The Prostrate State: South Carolina under Negro Government.* New York: Appleton, 1874.

Report of the Investigating Committee of the Pennsylvania Railroad Company, Appointed by Resolution of the Stockholders at the Annual Meeting Held March 10th, 1874. Philadelphia: n.p., 1874.

Somers, Robert. *The Southern States Since the War.* New York: Macmillan, 1871.

Trowbridge, John T. *The South: A Picture of the Desolated States and the Work of Restoration, 1865–1868.* Hartford, Conn.: L. Stebbins, 1868.

Wallace, John. *Carpet-Bag Rule in Florida, the Inside Workings of the Reconstruction of Civil Government in Florida after the Close of the Civil War.* Jacksonville, Fla.: Da Costa, 1888.

Warmoth, Henry Clay. *War, Politics and Reconstruction: Stormy Days in Louisiana.* New York: Macmillan, 1930.

SECONDARY ACCOUNTS: MONOGRAPHS AND GENERAL STUDIES

Ames, Blanche Ames. *Adelbert Ames, 1835–1933: General, Senator, Governor.* New York: Argosy-Antiquarian, 1964.

Armes, Ethel. *The Story of Coal and Iron in Alabama.* Birmingham: Chamber of Commerce, 1910.

Baughman, James P. *Charles Morgan and the Development of Southern Transportation.* Nashville: University of Tennessee Press, 1968.

Blake, Nelson M. *William Mahone of Virginia: Soldier and Political Insurgent.* Richmond: Garrett and Massie Co., 1935.

Bleser, Carol K. *The Promised Land: The History of the South Carolina Land Commission, 1869–1890.* Columbia: University of South Carolina Press, 1969.

Bond, Horace Mann. *Negro Education in Alabama: A Study in Cotton and Steel.* Washington, D.C.: n.p., 1939.

Conway, Alan. *The Reconstruction of Georgia.* Minneapolis: University of Minnesota Press, 1966.

Cooper, William J. *The Conservative Regime: South Carolina, 1877–1890.* Baltimore: Johns Hopkins University Press, 1968.

Corliss, Carlton J. *Main Line of Mid-America: The Story of the Illinois Central.* New York: Creative Age Press, 1950.

Coulter, E. Merton. *The South During Reconstruction, 1865–1877.* Baton Rouge: Louisiana State University Press, 1947.

Daniels, Jonathan. *Prince of Carpetbaggers.* Philadelphia: J. B. Lippincott, 1958.

Davis, William Watson. *Civil War and Reconstruction in Florida.* Gainesville: University of Florida Press, 1964.

Degler, Carl N. *The Other South: Southern Dissenters in the Nineteenth Century.* New York: Harper and Row, 1974.

Dozier, Howard Douglas. *A History of the Atlantic Coast Line Railroad.* Boston: Houghton Mifflin Co., 1920.

Elliott, Russell R. *A History of Nevada.* Lincoln: University of Nebraska Press, 1973.

Evans, William McKee. *Ballots and Fence Rails: Reconstruction on the Lower Cape Fear.* Chapel Hill: University of North Carolina Press, 1966.

Fleming, Walter L. *Civil War and Reconstruction in Alabama.* New York: Columbia University Press, 1905.

Foner, Eric. *Free Soil, Free Labor, Free Men: The Ideology of the Republican Party Before the Civil War.* New York: Oxford University Press, 1970.

Garner, James W. *Reconstruction in Mississippi.* Originally published in 1901. Gloucester, Mass.: Peter Smith, 1964.

Going, Allen J. *Bourbon Democracy in Alabama, 1874–1890.* University, Ala.: University of Alabama Press, 1951.

Goodrich, Carter. *Government Promotion of American Canals and Railroads, 1800–1890.* New York: Columbia University Press, 1960.

Greenberg, Dolores. *Financiers and Railroads, 1869–1889: A Study of Morton, Bliss and Company.* Newark, Del.: University of Delaware Press, 1980.

Hair, William Ivy. *Bourbonism and Agrarian Protest. Louisiana Politics, 1877–1900.* Baton Rouge: Louisiana State University Press, 1969.

Hamilton, Joseph Gregoire de Roulhac. *Reconstruction in North Carolina.* New York: Columbia University Press, 1914.

Harris, William C. *The Day of the Carpetbagger: Republican Reconstruction in Mississippi.* Baton Rouge: Louisiana State University, 1979.

Harris, William C. *Presidential Reconstruction in Mississippi.* Baton Rouge: Louisiana State University Press, 1967.

Hesseltine, William B. *Confederate Leaders in the New South.* Baton Rouge: Louisiana State University Press, 1950.

Hirshson, Stanly P. *Grenville M. Dodge: Soldier, Politician, Railroad Pioneer.* Bloomington, Ind.: University of Indiana Press, 1967.

Holt, Thomas. *Black over White: Negro Political Leadership in South Carolina during Reconstruction.* Urbana: University of Illinois Press, 1977.

Johnston, James Houston. *The Western and Atlantic Railroad of the State of Georgia.* Atlanta: The Stein Printing Co., 1931.

Kirwan, Albert D. *Revolt of the Rednecks: Mississippi Politics, 1870–1925.* Lexington: University of Kentucky Press, 1951.

Klein, Maury. *A History of the Louisville and Nashville Railroad.* New York: Macmillan, 1972.

Knapp, Charles. *New Jersey Politics during the Period of the Civil War and Reconstruction.* New York: W. F. Humphrey, 1924.

Lamson, Peggy. *The Glorious Failure: Robert Brown Elliott and the Reconstruction of South Carolina.* New York: W. W. Norton, 1973.

Lonn, Ella. *Reconstruction in Louisiana after 1868.* New York: Putnam, 1918.

McGrane, Reginald Charles. *Foreign Bondholders and American State Debts.* New York: Macmillan, 1935.

Maddex, Jack P. *The Virginia Conservatives, 1867–1879: A Study in Reconstruction Politics.* Chapel Hill: University of North Carolina Press, 1970.

Martin, William Elejius. *Internal Improvements in Alabama.* Baltimore: Johns Hopkins University Press, 1902.

Miller, George H. *Railroads and the Granger Laws.* Madison, Wis.: University of Wisconsin Press, 1971.

Moneyhon, Carl H. *Republicanism in Reconstruction Texas,* Austin: University of Texas Press, 1980.

Nathans, Elizabeth Studley. *Losing the Peace: Georgia Republicans and Reconstruction, 1865–1871.* Baton Rouge: Louisiana State University Press, 1968.

Nunn, William Curtis. *Texas under the Carpetbaggers.* Austin: University of Texas Press, 1962.

Oberholtzer, Ellis J. *Jay Cooke, Financier of the Civil War.* 2 vols. Philadephia.

Olsen, Otto H. *Carpetbagger's Crusade: The Life of Albion Winegar Tourgee.* Baltimore: Johns Hopkins University Press, 1965.

Osthaus, Carl R. *Freedmen, Philanthropy and Fraud: A History of the Freedman's Savings Bank.* Urbana: University of Illinois Press, 1976.

Parks, Joseph H. *Joseph E. Brown of Georgia.* Baton Rouge: Louisiana State University Press, 1977.

Pearson, Charles Chilton. *The Readjuster Movement in Virginia.* New Haven: Yale University Press, 1917.

Pereyra, Lillian A. *James Lusk Alcorn: Persistent Whig.* Baton Rouge: Louisiana State University Press, 1966.

Perman, Michael. *Reunion without Compromise: The South and Reconstruction, 1865–1868.* Cambridge: At the University Press, 1973.

Reed, St. Clair Griffin. *A History of Texas Railroads and of Transportation Conditions Under Spain and Mexico and the Republic and the State.* Houston: St. Clair Publishing Co., 1941.

Richardson, Joe M. *The Negro in the Reconstruction of Florida, 1865–1877.* Tallahassee: Florida State University, 1965.

Shofner, Jerrell H. *Nor Is It Over Yet: Florida in the Era of Reconstruction, 1863–1877.* Gainesville, Fla.: University of Florida Press, 1974.

Shugg, Roger W. *Origins of Class Struggle in Louisiana: A Social History of White Farmers and Laborers during Slavery and After, 1840–1875.* Baton Rouge: Louisiana State University Press, 1939.

Simkins, Francis B., and Woody, Robert H. *South Carolina during Reconstruction.* Chapel Hill: University of North Carolina Press, 1932.

Stampp, Kenneth M. *The Era of Reconstruction, 1865–1877.* New York: Knopf, 1965.

Staples, Thomas S. *Reconstruction in Arkansas, 1862–1874.* New York: Columbia University Press, 1923.

Stover, John F. *The Railroads of the South, 1865–1900.* Chapel Hill: University of North Carolina Press, 1955.

Taylor, Joe Gray. *Louisiana Reconstructed, 1863–1877.* Baton Rouge: Louisiana State University Press, 1974.

Thompson, C. Mildred. *Reconstruction in Georgia.* New York: Columbia University Press, 1915.

Thompson, George H. *Arkansas and Reconstruction: The Influence of Geography, Economics, and Personality.* Port Washington, N.Y.: Kennikat Press, 1976.

Thornton, J. Mills. *Politics and Power in a Slave Society: Alabama, 1800–1860.* Baton Rouge: Louisiana State University Press, 1978.

Wiener, Jonathan M. *Social Origins of the New South: Alabama, 1860–1885.* Baton Rouge: Louisiana State University Press, 1978.

Wiggins, Sarah Woolfolk. *The Scalawag in Alabama Politics, 1865–1881.* University, Ala.: University of Alabama Press, 1977.

Williamson, Edward C. *Florida Politics in the Gilded Age, 1877–1893.* Gainesville, Fla.: University of Florida Press, 1976.

Williamson, Joel. *After Slavery: The Negro in South Carolina during Reconstruction, 1861–1877.* Chapel Hill: University of North Carolina Press, 1965.

Woodward, C. Vann. *Origins of the New South, 1877–1913.* Baton Rouge: Louisiana State University Press, 1947.

Woodward, C. Vann. *Reunion and Reaction: The Compromise of 1877 and the End of Reconstruction.* Boston: Little, Brown, 1951.

Woolfolk, George Ruble. *The Cotton Regency: The Northern Merchants and Reconstruction, 1865–1880.* New York: Bookman Associates, 1858.

ARTICLES

Atkinson, James H. "The Brooks-Baxter Contest." *Arkansas Historical Quarterly* 4 (Summer 1945): 124–149.

Bailey, Hugh C. "Alabama and West Florida Annexation." *Florida Historical Quarterly* 35 (October 1956): 219–230.

Berthoff, Rowland T. "Southern Attitudes Towards Immigration, 1865–1914." *Journal of Southern History* 17 (August 1951): 328–360.

Bond, Horace Mann. "Social and Economic Forces in Alabama Reconstruction." *Journal of Southern History* 23 (July 1938): 290–328.

Brockman, John M. "Railroads, Radicals and the Militia Bill: A New Interpretation of the Texas Quorum-Breaking Incident of 1870." *South-Western Historical Quarterly* 83 (October 1979): 105–122.

Brown, Cecil Kenneth. "The Florida Investments of George W. Swepson." *North Carolina Historical Review* 5 (July 1928): 275–288.

Campbell, E. G. "Indebted Railroads: A Problem of Reconstruction." *Journal of Southern History* 6 (May 1940): 167-188.

Donald, David. "The Scalawag in Mississippi Reconstruction." *Journal of Southern History* 10 (November 1944): 447–460.

Driggs, Orval Truman, Jr. "The Issues of the Powell Clayton Regime, 1868–1871." *Arkansas Historical Quarterly* 8 (Spring 1949): 1–75.

Ellem, Warren A. "Who Were the Mississippi Scalawags?" *Journal of Southern History* 38 (May 1972): 217–240.

Ellis, David Maldwyn. "The Forfeiture of Railroad Land Grants, 1867–1894." *Mississippi Valley Historical Review* 33 (June 1946): 27–60.

Fenlon, Paul E. "The Florida, Atlantic and Gulf Central Railroad: The First Railroad in Jacksonville." *Florida Historical Quarterly* 32 (April 1954): 231–261.

Gonzales, John Edmond. "William Pitt Kellogg, Reconstruction Governor of Louisiana, 1873–1877." *Louisiana Historical Quarterly* 29 (April 1946): 394–495.

Goodrich, Carter. "Public Aid to Railroads in the Reconstruction South." *Political Science Quarterly* 71 (September 1956): 407–442.

Grosz, Agnes Smith. "The Political Career of Pinckney Benton Stewart Pinchback." *Louisiana Historical Quarterly* 27 (April 1944): 527–653.

Harris, Francis Byers. "Henry Clay Warmoth, Reconstruction Governor of Louisiana." *Louisiana Historical Quarterly* 30 (April 1947): 523–653.

Harris, William C. "The Creed of the Carpetbaggers: The Case of Mississippi." *Journal of Southern History* 40 (May 1974): 199–224.

Harris, William C. "A Reconstruction of the Mississippi Scalawag." *Journal of Mississippi History* 32 (February 1970): 3–42.

Jay, John C. "General N. B. Forrest as a Railroad Builder in Alabama." *Alabama Historical Quarterly*, 24 (Spring 1962): 16–31.

Loewenberg, Bert James. "Efforts of the South to Encourage Immigration, 1865–1900." *South Atlantic Quarterly* 33 (October 1934): 363–385.

McKenzie, Robert H. "Reconstruction of the Alabama Iron Industry, 1865–1880." *Alabama Review* 25 (July 1972): 178–191.

Moore, A. B. "Railroad Building in Alabama during the Reconstruction Period." *Journal of Southern History* (November 1935): 421–441.

More, James Tice. "Redeemers Reconsidered: Change and Continuity in the Democratic South, 1870–1900." *Journal of Southern History* 45 (August 1978): 357–378.

Nunn, Walter. "The Constitutional Convention of 1874." *Arkansas Historical Quarterly* 27 (Autumn 1968): 177–205.

Odom, E. Dale. "The Vicksburg, Shreveport and Texas: The Fortunes of a Scalawag Railroad." *Southwestern Social Science Quarterly* 44 (December 1963): 277–285.

Olsen, Otto H. "Reconsidering the Scalawags." *Civil War History* 12 (December 1966): 304–320.

Randolph. Bessie Carter. "Foreign Bondholders and the Repudiated Debts of the Southern States." *American Journal of International Law* 25 (January 1931): 63–82.

Schweninger, Loren. "Black Citizenship and the Republican Party in Alabama." *Alabama Review* 29 (April 1976): 83–102.

Scroggs, Jack B. "Carpetbagger Constitutional Reform in the South Atlantic States, 1867–1868." *Journal of Southern History* 27 (November 1961): 475–493.

Shofner, Jerrell M. "The Chimerical Scheme of Ceding West Florida." *Alabama Historical Quarterly* 33 (Spring 1971): 5–36.

Stover, John F. "Northern Financial Interests in Southern Railroads, 1865–1900." *Georgia Historical Quarterly* 39 (September 1955): 205–220.

Trelease, Allen W. "Republican Reconstruction in North Carolina: A Roll Call Analysis of the State House of Representatives, 1868–1870." *Journal of Southern History* 42 (August 1976): 319–344.

Trelease, Allen W. "Who Were the Scalawags?" *Journal of Southern History* 29 (November 1963): 445–468.

Williamson, Edward C. "The Alabama Election of 1874." *Alabama Review* 17 (July 1964): 210–218.

THESES

Binning, Francis Wayne. "Henry Clay Warmoth and Louisiana Reconstruction." Ph.D. dissertation, University of North Carolina, 1969.

Carrier, John Pressley. "A Political History of Texas during the Reconstruction, 1865–1874." Ph.D. dissertation, Vanderbilt University, 1971.

Holt, Thomas. "The Emergence of Negro Political Leadership in South Carolina." Ph.D. dissertation, Yale University, 1973.

Hood, J. "Brotherly Hate: A Quantitative Study of Southern Reconstruction Congressmen, 1867–1877." Ph.D. dissertation, Washington State University, 1974.

Hume, Richard L. "The 'Black and Tan' Constitutional Conventions of 1867–1869 in Ten Former Confederate States: A Study of their Membership." Ph.D. dissertation, University of Washington, 1969

Odom, Edwin Dale. "Louisiana Railroads, 1830–1880: A Study of State and Local Aid." Ph.D. dissertation, Tulane University, 1961.

Price, Charles Lewis. "Railroads and Reconstruction in North Carolina, 1865–1871." Ph.D. dissertation, University of North Carolina at Chapel Hill, 1959.

Raper, Horace Wilson. "The Political Career of William Woods Holden with Special Reference to His Provisional Governorship." M.A. thesis, University of North Carolina at Chapel Hill, 1947.

Raper, Horace Wilson. "William Woods Holden: A Political Biography." Ph.D. dissertation, University of North Carolina at Chapel Hill, 1951.

Rogers, William Warren. "Agrarianism in Alabama, 1865–1896." Ph.D. dissertation, University of North Carolina at Chapel Hill, 1959.

Sansing, David Gaffney. "The Role of the Scalawag in Mississippi Reconstruction." Ph.D. dissertation, University of Southern Mississippi, 1969.

Scroggs, Jack Benton. "Carpetbagger Influence in the Political Reconstruction of the South Atlantic States, 1865–1876." Ph.D. dissertation, University of North Carolina at Chapel Hill, 1951.

Seip, Terry Lee. "Southern Representatives and Economic Measures During Reconstruction: A Quantitative and Analytical Study." Ph.D. dissertation, Louisiana State University, 1974.

Thompson, George H. "Leadership in Arkansas Reconstruction." Ph.D. dissertation, Columbia University, 1968.

Vincent, Charles. "Negro Leadership in Louisiana." M.A. thesis, Louisiana State University, 1966.

Windham, Allie Bayne. "Methods and Mechanisms Used to Restore White Supremacy in Louisiana, 1872–1876." M.A. thesis, Louisiana State University, 1948.

INDEX

Library of Congress Cataloging in Publication Data

Summers, Mark W. (Mark Wahlgren), 1951–
Railroads, reconstruction and the gospel of prosperity.

Bibliography: p.   Includes index.
1. Railroads and state—Southern States—History—19th century.
2. Reconstruction. 3. Republican Party (U.S.)—History—19th century.
4. United States—Politics and government—1865–1877. I. Title.
HE1061.S94   1984   385'.1   83-43094
ISBN 0–691–04695–6 (alk. paper)

ORIGINS OF CONTAINMENT

Origins of Containment

A PSYCHOLOGICAL EXPLANATION

By Deborah Welch Larson

PRINCETON UNIVERSITY PRESS
PRINCETON, NEW JERSEY

Published by Princeton University Press, 41 William Street,
Princeton, New Jersey 08540
In the United Kingdom: Princeton University Press, Guildford, Surrey

Library of Congress Cataloging in Publication Data will be
found on the last printed page of this book

ISBN 0-691-07691-X

Publication of this book has been aided by a grant from the
Whitney Darrow Fund of Princeton University Press

This book has been composed in Linotron Galliard

Clothbound editions of Princeton University Press books
are printed on acid-free paper, and binding materials are
chosen for strength and durability

Printed in the United States of America by Princeton University Press
Princeton, New Jersey

To David